CENSORED

"Project Censored is one of the ▮▮▮▮ organizations that we should listen to, to be assured that our newspapers and our broadcasting outlets are practicing thorough and ethical journalism."—Walter Cronkite

"[*Censored*] should be affixed to the bulletin boards in every newsroom in America. And, perhaps read aloud to a few publishers and television executives."—Ralph Nader

"[*Censored*] offers devastating evidence of the dumbing-down of mainstream news in America.... Required reading for broadcasters, journalists and well-informed citizens."—*Los Angeles Times*

"A distant early warning system for society's problems."
—*American Journalism Review*

"One of the most significant media research projects in the country."
—I. F. Stone

"A terrific resource, especially for its directory of alternative media and organizations.... Recommended for media collections."—*Library Journal*

"Project Censored shines a spotlight on news that an informed public must have...a vital contribution to our democratic process."
—Rhoda H. Karpatkin, President, Consumer's Union

"Buy it, read it, act on it. Our future depends on the knowledge this collection of suppressed stories allows us."—*San Diego Review*

"This volume chronicles 25 news stories about events that could affect all of us, but which we most likely did not hear or read about in the popular news media."—*Bloomsbury Review*

"*Censored* serves as a reminder that there is certainly more to the news than is easily available or willingly disclosed. To those of us who work in the newsrooms, it's an inspiration, an indictment, and an admonition to look deeper, ask more questions, then search for the truth in the answers we get."—*Creative Loafings*

"This invaluable resource deserves to be more widely known."
—*Wilson Library Bulletin*

CENSORED 2006

2006

The Top 25 Censored Stories

PETER PHILLIPS & PROJECT CENSORED

INTRODUCTION BY NORMAN SOLOMON
CARTOONS BY TOM TOMORROW

SEVEN STORIES PRESS
New York / London / Melbourne / Toronto

Contents

Introduction to *Censored 1999* by Gary Webb 9

Preface 15

Acknowledgments 17

Introduction by Norman Solomon 29

CHAPTER 1   The Top 25 Stories of 2004 and 2005 by Kate Sims,
Peter Phillips, Tricia Boreta, Theodora Ruhs,
Michelle Salvail, Brooke Finley, Josh Sisco,
Marcia Simmons, Chris Cox, Kristine Snyder,
Tina Tambornini, Celeste Vogler, Joni Wallent
and the students of Project Censored 35

1   Bush Administration Moves to Eliminate
Open Government 38

2   Media Coverage Fails in Iraq: Fallujah and the Civilian
Death Toll..41

3   Another Year of Distorted Election Coverage....................48

4   Surveillance Society Quietly Moves In...............................52

5   U.S. Uses Tsunami to Military Advantage in
Southeast Asia 58

6   The Real Oil-For-Food Scam..60

7   Journalists Face Unprecendented Dangers to Life
and Livelihood 64

8 Iraqi Farmers Threatened by Bremer's Mandates 68

9 Iran's New Oil Trade System Challenges U.S. Currency 71

10 Mountaintop Removal Threatens Ecosystem and
   Economy..75

11 Mandatory Mental Screening Program Usurps Parental
   Rights...78

12 Military in Iraq Contracts Human Rights Violators 82

13 Rich Countries Fail to Live Up to Global Pledges 85

14 Corporations Win Big on Tort Reform, Justice Suffers........86

15 Conservative Plan to Override Academic Freedom
   in the Classroom 88

16 U.S. Plans for Hemispheric Integration Include Canada 91

17 U.S. Uses South American Military Bases to Expand
   Control of the Region...93

18 Little Known Stock Fraud Could Weaken
   U.S. Economy..98

19 Child Wards of the State Used in AIDS Experiments 101

20 American Indians Sue for Resources; Compensation
   Provided to Others 103

21 New Immigration Plan Favors Business Over People 106

22 Nanotechnology Features Exciting Possibility But Health
   Effects Need Scrutiny 110

23 Plight of Palestinian Child Detainees Highlights
   Global Problem 112

24 Ethiopian Indigenous Victims of Corporate and
   Government Resource Aspirations 116

25 Homeland Security Was Designed to Fail 122

CHAPTER 2 Déjà vu: Updates on Prior Censored News:
Haiti: Diplomacy By Death Squad, U.S. and Global
Wealth Inequality, Alien Tort Claims Act, Bush Censors
Scientists, Dangers of Depleted Uranium, The Federalist
Society & The Christian Legal Society, 9/11 RICO
Lawsuit, New Nuke Plants, Fox News Can Legally Lie,
Reinstating The Draft, Voter Fraud & The Sale of
Electoral Politics...137

CHAPTER 3 No Paper Trail Left Behind: The Theft of the 2004 Election
by Dennis Loo, Ph.D..185

CHAPTER 4 Unanswered Questions of 9/11 by Peter Phillips,
Ambrosia Pardue, Jessica Froiland, Brooke Finley,
Chris Kyle, Rebekah Cohen, and Bridget Thornton
with Project Censored and Guest Writer Jack Massen......203

CHAPTER 5 Junk Food News and News Abuse by Mark Thompson,
Sean Arlt, Brittny Roeland, Tricia Boreta,
and Kate Sims...237

CHAPTER 6 Corporate Media is Corporate America
by Bridget Thornton, Britt Walters, and Lori Rouse..........245

CHAPTER 7 Media Democracy in Action by: Project Censored Interns:
Sandy Brown, Joni Wallent, Kristine Snyder, Luke Judd,
Christopher Cox, Jacob Rich, Lori Rouse, Mark Thompson,
Sean Arlt, Brittny Roeland, and Britt Walters................263

CHAPTER 8 Pulling Back the Curtain: The Best of PR Watch
by Laura Miller..281

CHAPTER 9 FAIR's Fifth Annual "Fear & Favor" Report—2004
by Peter Hart and Julie Hollar 295

CHAPTER 10 Index on Censorship: Annual Report
by Rohan Jayasekera 307

CHAPTER 11 Non-embedded Reporting from Iraq by Dahr Jamail.........321

CHAPTER 12 Political Economy of Mass Media
by Ann Strahm 337

CHAPTER 13 U.S. Military and Media by Robin Andersen, Norman
Solomon, David L. Altheide, Jennifer N. Grime,
and Lisa Parks 355

CHAPTER 14 Junk Library Science by Geoff Davidian and Project
Censored Interns: Sean Arlt, Jacob Rich, Bridget Thornton,
and Michele Salvail 381

CHAPTER 15 Cowardice and Conflicts: The Lynching of Dan Rather
by Greg Palast..397

APPENDIX Censored 2006 Resource Guide 403

Index 413
About the Editor 431
How to Support Project Censored 432

CENSORED 2006 IS DEDICATED TO
GARY WEBB
1995–2004
Investigative Reporter and Author Dedicated
to Freedom of Information and the Truth

Introduction to Censored 1999

By Gary Webb

When the newspaper I worked for in Kentucky in the 1970s, *The Kentucky Post*, took the plunge and hiked its street price from 20 cents to a quarter, the executive editor, Vance Trimble, instructed our political cartoonist to design a series of full-page house ads justifying the price increase. One of those ads still hangs on my wall. It depicts an outraged tycoon, replete with vest and felt hat, brandishing a copy of our newspaper and shouting at a harried editor: "Kill that story, Mr. Editor...or else!"

Well worth a quarter, the ad argued, because we weren't some "soft, flabby, spineless" newspaper. We'd tell that fat cat to take a long walk off a short pier.

"Our readers would be shocked if any kind of threat swayed the editor," the ad declared. "If it happens, we print it. Kill a story? Never! There are no fetters on our reporters. Nor must they bow to sacred cows. On every story, the editor says: 'Get the facts. And let the fur fly!' Our reporters appreciate that. They are proud they can be square-shooters."

The newspaper for the most part held to that creed. When the executive editor was arrested for drunk driving, a photographer was dispatched to the city jail and the next day the paper carried a picture of our disheveled boss sitting forlornly in a holding cell.

The newspaper had done the same thing to many other prominent citizens, he reminded the stunned staff after his release. Why should he be treated any differently?

How quaint that all sounds 20 years later. And how distant that post-Watergate era seems. Today, we see corporate news executives boasting not of the hardness of their asses, but of the value of their assets. We witness them groveling for public forgiveness because something their reporters wrote offended powerful interests, or raised uncomfortable questions about the past. Stories that meet every traditional standard of objective journalism are retracted or renounced, not because they are false-but because they are true.

The depth of this depravity (so far) was reached the day New York attorney Floyd Abrams decided CNN/Time Warner should retract its explosive report on a covert CIA operation known as Tailwind, which was alleged to have involved the use of nerve gas against American deserters in Southeast Asia in the 1970s. I saw Abrams on a talk show afterwards arguing that the ultimate truth of the Tailwind story was irrelevant to CNN's retraction of it.

"It doesn't necessarily mean that the story isn't true," Abrams insisted. "Who knows? Someday we might find other information. And, you know, maybe someday I'll be back here again, having done another report saying that, 'You know what? It was all true.'"

Stop and savor that for a moment. Let its logic worm its way through your brain, because it is the pure, unadulterated essence of what's wrong with corporate journalism today. Could anyone honestly have dreamed that one day a major news organization would retract and apologize for a story that even it acknowledges could well be true?

For that matter, who could have envisioned the day when a veteran investigative reporter would be convicted of a felony for printing the voice mail messages of executives of a corporation that was allegedly looting, pillaging, and bribing its way through Central America? Yet, like CNN producers April Oliver and Jack Smith, *Cincinnati Enquirer* reporter Mike

Gallagher was fired, his work "renounced" as his editors ludicrously wrote in this front-page apology, and he has been uniformly reviled in the mass media as a fabricator for his devastating exposé of Chiquita Brands International. So far, however, no one has shown that his stories contain a single, solitary inaccuracy. Again, the truth seems irrelevant, a sideshow not worthy of serious discussion.

Astute readers may well wonder what the hell is going on, and the answer is this: the rules are being changed, and they are being changed in such a way as to ensure that our government and our major corporations won't be bothered by nettlesome investigative journalists in the next millennium.

When I started in the newspaper business the rules were simple: Get as close to the truth as you possibly can. There were no hard and fast requirements about levels of proof necessary to print a story—and there still aren't, contrary to all the current huffing and puffing about "journalistic standards" being abused. I worked as a reporter for nearly 20 years, wrote for dozens of different editors, and each had his or her own set of standards. Generally, if you diligently investigated the issue, used named sources, found supporting documentation, and you honestly believed it was true, you went with it. Period. That was the standard that gutsy editors used, at any rate. Some—like Ben Bradlee during Watergate, for example—occasionally went with less because instinct and common sense told them the story was right even if everything wasn't completely nailed down.

Nervous editors, on the other hand, used different standards.

"Raising the bar" was the usual trick they used to avoid printing troublesome news. The squeamish demanded an admission of wrongdoing (preferably written) or an official government report confirming up the story's charge. What that meant, of course, was that stories about serious, unacknowledged abuses never got printed and eventually the reporters learned that it was useless to turn rocks over on their own if no one would officially confirm that something hideous had slithered out. And at that point they ceased being journalists and became like ancient scribes, doing little more than faithfully reproducing the pharaohs' words in clay.

It is this latter standard that was championed by Abrams in the Tailwind case and to some extent by *San Jose Mercury News* editor Jerry Ceppos in the case of my "Dark Alliance" series in 1996. Under these new rules, it isn't enough anymore for a reporter to have on-the-record sources and supporting documentation. Now they must have something called "proof." Investigative stories must be "proven" in order to reach the public; having "insufficient evidence" is now cause for retraction and dismissal.

"Having read all your stuff, as much as I can about this...I can't see where you prove it," CNN commentator Bill Press whined to former CNN producer April Oliver. "None of your sources add up to that."

"What is the standard of proof in a black operation where everyone's supposed to deny, or information is tightly compartmentalized?" Oliver demanded.

Her question, which cuts to the heart of the debate, went unanswered. But judging from Abrams' report, "proof" apparently is a statement no one disagrees with, or something that can be demonstrated, as Ted Turner phrased it, "beyond a reasonable doubt"—the courtroom standard of proof.

Some, including Turner, say this is good for journalism, that it will keep unsubstantiated stories out of public circulation, and there's no doubt about that. But it will also have the same muffling effect on a lot of important stories that happen to be true. Such a standard would have kept Watergate out of the papers. Love Canal, the CIA's mining of Nicaragua's harbors, the El Mozote massacre in El Salvador—all would have been suppressed. Don't believe it? Consider the Iran-Contra scandal. It was only after Ronald Reagan and Edwin Meese held their famous press conference and confessed that something funny had been going on in the White House basement that the Washington press corps felt emboldened enough to start covering the scandal seriously. Until then, the idea of a secret parallel government had been sneeringly dismissed as some left-wing conspiracy theory.

What is devious about these standards of proof is that they sound so eminently responsible. They are doubly handy because they can be applied after publication, when the heat comes down. Then, as CNN/Time Warner did, lawyers and former government operatives can be called in to produce palliative reports bemoaning the lack of "proof" and the bothersome story can interred without further adieu. (Few will question the validity of these reports because, after all, they come straight from the top.)

But somewhere along the way it's been forgotten that journalism was never meant to be held to courtroom standards of proof. As investigative reporter Pete Brewton once put it: "I'm not in the proof business. I'm in the information business." Unlike police and prosecutors, reporters don't have the power to subpoena records or wiretap phone conversations. We can't conduct 24-hour surveillance, or pay informants for information. We write what we can find on the public record (which becomes less public all the time). Or at least we used to.

Fortunately, there are still some reporters and editors out there who consider an official denial to be a starting point, rather than the end, of a promising story. It is these men and women who are the true journalists, the ones who will carry on where the giants of yesterday—George Seldes, I. F. Stone, and the late Jonathan Kwitny—left off. Though many of them toil in relative obscurity, for little money and even less appreciation, their work contributes more to our lives than the million-dollar celebrity correspondents that we see on the nightly news.

Back in 1938, as fascism was sweeping across Europe, George Seldes presciently observed: "It is possible to fool all the people all the time—when government and press cooperate."

Today, such mass deception is possible on a scale that Seldes never could have imagined. That is why it is more important than ever to support the journalists represented between these covers. If these few bits of illumination flares should ever sputter and disappear, out of neglect or frustration or censorship, we will be enveloped by a darkness the likes of which we've never seen.

Preface

By Peter Phillips

We are honored to dedicate *Censored 2006* to journalist Gary Webb. His exposure of the CIA Contra drug links was an important story adding to documentation of the corruption of the U.S. national security state. His work cost him his career and eventually his life.

Censored 2006's chapter 6 addresses the structural specifics of media censorship in the U.S. Corporate media today is interlocked with the largest, most profitable corporations in the world and serves at the altar of government propaganda. Finding the 25 most important censored news stories (Chapter 1) that the corporate media has failed to cover is a task taking thousands of student and faculty research hours, not because we have to search so hard to find the stories, but rather because we have to sort through thousands, not covered, to select the most critical. Knowing there are so many important new stories unreported has lead Project Censored to expand the frequency of our website postings, where over 30 million people clicked-in over the last twelve months.

Chapter 2, Déjà vu is a review and update on important censored stories from prior years, as most remain uncovered by the corporate media in the U.S.

In contrast to the most important censored news stories, is our annual list of junk food news (Chapter 5), where a review of the frivolous and overdone—Ashton and Demi's love affair and Reality TV stars—are ranked and analyzed.

The now permanent features of the *Censored* yearbook, Fairness and Accuracy in Reporting, PR Watch, and the Index on Censorship provide a comprehensive review of the state of media news in chapters 8, 9, and 10. We much appreciate the research and involvement of Peter Hart & Julie Hollar from FAIR, Laura Miller with PR Watch, and Rohan Jayasekera from the London-based Index on Censorship.

Project Censored interns wrote about their participation in the Media Reform Conference in St. Louis, May 2005, and the importance of the expanding the media democracy movement (Chapter 7). They highlight key independent media groups working worldwide including: Common Dreams.org, BuzzFlash.com, Center for Digital Democracy, A-Infos.ca, The Australian Greens: www.greens.org.au

Each year Project Censored publishes original research work and media commentary from a broad selection of journalists and authors. *Censored 2006* offers chapter-length investigative reports covering: Voter Fraud 2004, Unanswered Questions of 9/11, U.S. Military and the Media, The Firing of Dan Rather, The Economic Hitman Uncovered, Updates on the FCC and Non-Embedded Reporting from Iraq and Haiti. Top scholars, media researchers, investigative reporters, foreign journalists and faculty & students at Sonoma State University have contributed to *Censored 2006*.

Censored 2006 contains a huge amount of information. We recommend you read it slowly, share the information, and use it to guide your democratic actions for human betterment.

On behalf of the over 250 students, faculty and national judges who work on this annual book, welcome to *Censored 2006*.

Acknowledgments

Project Censored is managed through the Department of Sociology in the School of Social Sciences at Sonoma State University. We are an investigative sociology and media analysis project dedicated to journalistic integrity and the freedom of information throughout the United States.

Over 250 people were directly involved in the production of this year's *Censored 2006*. University and program staff, students, faculty, community experts, research interns, guest writers, and our distinguished national judges all contributed time, energy, and money to make this year's book an important resource for the promotion of freedom of information.

I want to personally thank those close friends and intimates who have counseled and supported me through another year of Project Censored. Most important, my wife Mary Lia, who as my lover, friend, and partner provides daily consultative support to Project Censored. The men in the Green Oaks breakfast group, Noel Byrne, Bob Butler, Bob Klose, Derrick West, Colin Godwin, and Bill Simon, are personal advisors and confidants who help with difficult decisions. A special thanks also to Carl Jensen, founder of Project Censored, and director for 20 years. His continued advice and support are very important to the Project. Trish Boreta, Project Censored coordinator is an important daily associate administrator of the Project. Her dedication and enthusiasm are greatly appreciated. Katie Sims, our story coordinator and student advisor, deserves a special thank you, she supervised the processing of over 700 story nominations for this year's book and advises the Project Censored TV news team.

A big thanks goes to the people at Seven Stories Press. They are more than a publishing house, but rather have become close friends, who help edit our annual book in record time, and serve as advisors in the annual release process of the "Most Censored Stories." Publisher Dan Simon is just a cool guy dedicated to building democracy in America through knowledge and literature. He deserves full credit for assembling an excellent support crew including: production director Jon Gilbert, managing editor Phoebe Hwang, associate editors Ria Julien, Anna Lui, and George Mürer, senior editor Greg Ruggiero, academic market director Tara Parmiter, sales manager Lars Reilly, publicists Jessie Kindig and Ruth Weiner, and book designer Cindy LaBreacht.

Thanks also to Bill Mokler and the sales staff at Consortium Books, who will see to it that every independent bookstore, chain store, and wholesaler in the U.S. are aware of *Censored 2006*. Thanks to Publishers Group Canada, our distributors in Canada, as well as Turnaround Publishers Services Ltd. in Great Britain and Tower Books in Australia.

We especially thank and welcome Novi Mondi Media in Italy for translating and distributing the Censored yearbooks in Italian.

Thank you to Norman Solomon who wrote the introduction to the Censored 2006 edition. Norman is a long time Project Censored judge and national media commentator.

Thanks also to the authors of the most censored stories for 2006. Without their often-unsupported efforts as investigative news reporters and writers, the stories presented in *Censored* would not be possible.

Our guest writers this year are Dennis Loo, Norman Solomon, Dahr Jamail, Peter Hart, Julie Hollar, Lisa Parks, David Altheide, Robin Andersen, Geoff Davidian, Lyn Duff, Laura Miller, Anne Strahm, and Rohan Jayasekera. They represent a unique combination of scholars, journalists and activists dedicated to media freedom through a diversity of news and opinion. Thank you to each and all for your unique contribution to *Censored 2006*.

This year's book again features the cartoons of Tom Tomorrow. "This Modern World" appears in more than 90 newspapers across the country. We are extremely pleased to use Tom Tomorrow's wit and humor throughout the book.

Our national judges, some of whom have been involved with the Project for 29 years, are among the top experts in the country concerned with First Amendment freedoms and media principles. We are honored to have them as the final voice in ranking the top 25 best *Censored* stories.

An important thanks goes to our financial donors including; Sonoma State University Instructionally Related Activity Fund, the School of Social Sciences at Sonoma State University, and especially the over 4,000 individuals who purchase books and send us financial gifts each year. You are our financial base who continue to give year after year to this important student-run media research project.

This year we had 111 faculty/community evaluators assisting with our story assessment process. These expert volunteers read and rated the nominated stories for national importance, accuracy, and credibility. In April, they participated with over 100 students in selecting the final top 25 stories for 2006.

Most of all, we need to recognize the Sonoma State University students, in the Spring 2005 Media Censorship class and the Fall 2004 Sociology of Media class, who worked thousands of hours nominating and researching some 700 under-published news stories. Students are the principle writers of the censored news synopses in the book each year. Over 80 students served as interns for the project, working on various teams including: public relations, web design, news story research, office support, events/fund raising, and TV news production. Student education is the most important aspect of Project Censored, and we could not do this work without the dedication and effort of our student interns.

Daryl Khoo is our webmaster. The Project Censored web site, www.projectcensored.org, has expanded under his supervision. We are pleased to announce that over 30,000,000 people logged on to Project Censored in 2004–5.

Lastly, I want to thank our readers and supporters from all over the United States and the world. Hundreds of you nominated stories for consideration as the most censored news story of the year. Thank you very much!

PROJECT CENSORED STAFF

Peter Phillips, Ph.D.	Director
Carl Jensen, Ph.D.	Director Emeritus and Project Advisor
Tricia Boreta	Coordinator/Editor
Katie Sims	Research Coordinator/Bookkeeper
Daryl Khoo	Webmaster
Christopher Cox	Teaching Assistant
Kristine Snyder	Teaching Assistant
Tina Tambornini	Teaching Assistant
Celeste Vogler	Teaching Assistant
Joni Wallent	Teaching Assistant
Phillip Lewis	Student Office Assistant
Jennifer Page	Student Office Assistant

Spring & Fall 2004 & 2005 Interns and Community Volunteers

Sean Arlt, Adam Armstrong, Lisa Badenfort, Dana Balicki, Merle Barron, Collette Blair, Dan Bluthardt, Grace Boreta, Jocelyn Boreta, Sean Brady, Lew Brown, Sandy Brown, J. R. Canko, Megan Charpiot, Alex Childress, Jackie

Christensen, Rebekah Cohen, Christopher Cox, Suze Cribbs, Kenny Crosbie, Nicholas Curran, Cassandra Cyphers, Stephen Dietrich, David Fatemi, Brooke Finley, Jessica Froiland, Bill Gibbons, Thedoria Grayson, Leslie Grimaldi, Matthew Hagan, Margaux Hardy, Larissa Heeren, John Hernandez, Jon Hess, Allison Hunt, Cody Jennings, Matt Johnson, Melissa Jones, Luke Judd, Sita Khalsa, Daryl Khoo, Sarah Kintz, Chris Kyle, Christina Leslie, Melody Lindsay, Lawren Lutrin, Erin Maxwell, Julie Mayeda, David McCuan, Andy Messersmith, Meegan Moonan, Deanna Murrell, Attila Nagy, Michael Oroszi, Ambrosia Pardue, Caitlyn Pardue, Josh Parrish, Ned Patterson, Simon Payne, Mike Persinger, Liz Pope, Christina Reski, Jacob Rich, Brittny Roeland, Sean Roney, Lori Rouse, Dr. Herb Ruhs, Theodora Ruhs, Daniel Sadowski, Michelle Salvail, Ben Sheppee, Troy Silveira, Josh Sisco, Kristine Snyder, David Sonnenberg, Jason Spencer, Tara Spreng, Kendall Sternberg, David Stolowitz, Adam Stutz, Tina Tambornini, Angelica Tercero, Mark Thompson, Bridget Thornton, Joshua Travers, Celeste Vogler, Joni Wallent, Britt Walters, Mike Ward, Chris Williams.

Special Thanks

We would like to include a special thanks to Project Censored alumnus and volunteer Bill Gibbons for his exhaustive research and perusal of online media. Many of our yearly nominations are due to his effort and we are truly in his debt.

Student Researchers in Sociology of Media Class, Fall 2004

Erica Bosque, Sara Brunner, Travis Byrne, Heather Caito, Kaytheena Canepa, Cirilo Cortez, John Ferritto, Brian Fuchs, Christopher Getty, Jonathan Hess, Lorraine Harpen, Matt Holman, Tracy Johnson, Tracy Kauffman, Brent Kidder, Chris Kyle, Allison Lewis, Billy Lo, Natalia Lewis, Audra Link, Emma Moverley, Deanna Murrell, Alisa Nelson, Megan Searcy, Perry Sommer, Emily Petersen, Amanda Pyle, Tami Sheets, Jeanette Staten, Tina Tambornini, Celeste Vogler, Deborah Wallace, Britt Walters.

Student Researchers in Media Censorship Class, Spring 2005

Kathy Baldassari, Cary Barker, Chris Bui, Sandra Brown, Michael Cattivera, Joseph Davis, Vanessa Dern, Paige Dumont, Kiel Eorio, John Ferritto, Jessica Froiland, Theodoria Grayson, Jenifer Green, Danielle Hallstein, Michelle Jesolva, Shatae Jones, Brian Lanphear, Brian Miller, Deanna Murrell, Michael

Osipoff, Ned Patterson, Jason Piepmeier, Christina Reski, Angela Sciortino, Adrienne Smith, David Stolowitz, Joey Tabares, Melissa Waybright.

Project Censored 2005 Broadcast Support

We are indebted to members of Sonoma State and local PBS-affiliate KRCB for their invaluable help and support with our broadcast project throughout 2004 and 2005. This includes KRCB President and CEO Nancy Dobbs, Program Director Stan Marvin, Project Censored Broadcast Team Director David McCuan, KRCB Public Affairs Director Jonathan Blease and KRCB Producer/Director Kara Blair. We would also like to thank Kelley Brogan, Nicole Stahl, Olise Eze, and Greg Thompson.

VINTAGE HIGH SCHOOL, Napa California was active in contributing story nominations for *Censored 2006.* Thanks to class instructor Travis Title and his Political Literature class including: Noel Bates, Kendal Buffington, Daniel Hetzer, Brandy Jinks, Steve Martin, Elizabeth Neuman, Adam Pereira, Stacie Pickett, Thomas Shook, Vanessa Tacoban, Denise Taylor, Alden Underhill

Thanks also to Kenn Burrows' Holistic Health Class at San Francisco State University for story development and spreading the Project Censored message.

PROJECT CENSORED 2005 NATIONAL JUDGES

ROBIN ANDERSEN, associate professor and chair, Department of Communication and Media Studies, Fordham University.

RICHARD BARNET, author of 15 books and numerous articles for the *New York Times Magazine, The Nation,* and *The Progressive.*

LIANE CLORFENE-CASTEN, cofounder and president of Chicago Media Watch, a volunteer watchdog group that monitors the media for bias, distortions, and omissions. She is an award-winning journalist with credits in national periodicals such as *E Magzine, The Nation, Mother Jones, Ms., Environmental Health Perspectives, In These Times,* and *Business Ethics.* She is the author of *Breast Cancer: Poisons, Profits, and Prevention.*

LENORE FOERSTEL, Women for Mutual Security, facilitator of the Progressive International Media Exchange (PRIME).

DR. GEORGE GERBNER, dean emeritus, Annenberg School of Communications, University of Pennsylvania; founder of the Cultural Environment Movement; author of *Invisible Crises: What Conglomerate Media Control Means for America and the World* and *Triumph and the Image: The Media's War in the Persian Gulf.*

ROBERT HACKETT, professor, School of Communications, Simon Fraser University; Co-director of News Watch Canada, Author or co-author of *News and Dessent: The Press and the Politics of Peace in Canada* (Ablex, 1991); *Sustaining Democracy? Journalism and the Politics of Objectivity* (Garamond, 1998), and *The Missing News: Filters and Blind Spots in Canada's Press* (Garamond Press, 2000).

DR. CARL JENSEN, founder and former director of Project Censored; author of *Censored: The News That Didn't Make the News and Why* (1990–1996) and *20 Years of Censored News* (1997).

SUT JHALLY, professor of communications and executive director of the Media Education Foundation, University of Massachusetts.

NICHOLAS JOHNSON,* professor, College of Law, University of Iowa; former FCC Commissioner (1966–1973); author of *How to Talk Back to Your Television Set.*

RHODA H. KARPATKIN, president of Consumers Union, non-profit publisher of *Consumer Reports.*

CHARLES L. KLOTZER, editor and publisher emeritus, *St. Louis Journalism Review.*

NANCY KRANICH, past president of the American Library Association (ALA).

JUDITH KRUG, director of the Office for Intellectual Freedom, American Library Association (ALA); editor of *Newsletter on Intellectual Freedom; Freedom to Read Foundation News;* and *Intellectual Freedom Action News.*

MARTIN LEE, investigative journalist, media critic and author. He was an original founder of Fairness and Accuracy in Reporting in New York and former editor of *Extra Magazine.*

WILLIAM LUTZ, professor of English, Rutgers University; former editor of *The Quarterly Review of Doublespeak;* author of *The New Doublespeak: Why No One Knows What Anyone's Saying Anymore* (1996).

JULIANNE MALVEAUX, PH.D., economist and columnist, King Features and Pacifica radio talk show host.

CYNTHIA MCKINNEY, the first African American woman from Georgia to serve in the United States House of Representatives from 1992 to 2002. And again in 2005.

MARK CRISPIN MILLER, professor of media Ecology, New York University; director of the Project on Media Ownership.

JACK L. NELSON,* professor, Graduate School of Education, Rutgers University; author of 16 books, including *Critical Issues in Education* (1996), and more than 150 articles.

MICHAEL PARENTI, political analyst, a lecturer, and author of several books, including *Inventing Reality; The Politics of News Media; Make Believe Media; The Politics of Entertainment;* and numerous other works.

DAN PERKINS, political cartoonist, pen name Tom Tomorrow, and creator of "This Modern World."

BARBARA SEAMAN, lecturer; author of *The Greatest Experiment Ever Performed on Women: Exploding the Estrogen Myth* (Hyperion 2003); *The Doctor's Case Against the Pill; Free and Female; Women and the Crisis in Sex Hormones;* and other books; cofounder of the National Women's Health Network.

ERNA SMITH, professor of journalism, San Francisco State University, author of several studies on mainstream news coverage on people of color.

NANCY SNOW, professor, author and writer; College of Communications, California State University-Fullerton; Senior Fellow, USC Center on Public Diplomacy; Adjunct Professor, University of Southern California, Annenberg School for Communication; author, *Propaganda, Inc.* (Seven Stories, 2002), *Information War* (Seven Stories, 2004), co-editor with Yahya R. Kamalipour, *War, Media and Propaganda* (Rowman & Littlefield, 2004).

NORMAN SOLOMON, syndicated columnist on media and politics; co-author of *Target Iraq: What the News Media Didn't Tell You* (Context Books, 2003); executive director of the Institute for Public Accuracy.

SHEILA RABB WEIDENFELD,* president of D.C. Productions, Ltd.; former press secretary to Betty Ford.

---

*Indicates having been a Project Censored judge since its founding in 1976

PROJECT CENSORED 2004 AND 2005 FACULTY, STAFF, AND COMMUNITY EVALUATORS

Melinda Barnard, Ph.D.	Communications
Philip Beard, Ph.D.	Modern Languages
Jim Berkland, Ph.D.	Geology
Stephen Bittner, Ph.D.	History
Barbara Bloom, Ph.D.	Criminal Justice Administration
Andrew Botterell, Ph.D.	Philosophy
Maureen Buckley, Ph.D.	Counseling
Elizabeth Burch, Ph.D.	Communications
Noel Byrne, Ph.D.	Sociology
James R. Carr, Ph.D.	Geology
Yvonne Clarke, MA.	University Affairs
Liz Close, Ph.D.	Nursing (Chair)
Lynn Cominsky, Ph.D.	Physics/Astronomy
G. Dennis Cooke, Ph.D.	Zoology
Bill Crowley, Ph.D.	Geography
Victor Daniels, Ph.D.	Psychology
Laurie Dawson, Ph.D.	Labor Education
Randall Dodgen, Ph.D.	History
Stephanie Dyer, Ph.D.	Cultural History
Carolyn Epple, Ph.D.	Anthropology
Gary Evans, MD	
Michael Ezra, Ph.D.	Chemistry
Tamara Falicov, M.A.	Communication Studies
Fred Fletcher,	Community Expert Labor
Dorothy (Dolly) Friedel, Ph.D.	Geography
Susan Garfin, Ph.D.	Sociology
Patricia Leigh Gibbs, Ph.D.	Sociology
Robert Girling, Ph.D.	Business, Economics
Mary Gomes, Ph.D.	Psychology
Myrna Goodman, Ph.D.	Sociology
Scott Gordon, Ph.D.	Computer Science
Karen Grady, Ph.D.	Education
Diana Grant, Ph.D.	Criminal Justice Administration
Velma Guillory-Taylor, Ed.D.	American Multicultural Studies

Chad Harris, M.A.	Communication Studies
Daniel Haytin, Ph.D.	Sociology
Laurel Holmstrom	Academic Programs; MA (English)
Jeffrey Holtzman, Ph.D.	Environmental Sciences
Sally Hurtado, Ph.D.	Education
Pat Jackson, Ph.D.	Criminal Justice Administration
Tom Jacobson J.D.	Environmental Studies & Planning
Sherril Jaffe, Ph.D.	English
Paul Jess	Community Expert, Environmental Law
Cheri Ketchum, Ph.D.	Communications
Patricia Kim-Rajal, Ph.D.	American Culture
Mary King M.D.	Health
Paul Kingsley, MD	
Jeanette Koshar	Nursing
John Kramer, Ph.D.	Political Science
Heidi LaMoreaux, Ph.D.	Liberal Studies
Virginia Lea, Ph.D.	Education
Benet Leigh, M.A.	Communications Studies
Wingham Liddell, Ph.D.	Business. Administration
Jennifer Lillig Whiles, Ph.D.	Chemistry
Thom Lough, Ph.D.	Sociology
John Lund	Business & Political Issues
Rick Luttmann, Ph.D.	Math
Robert Manning	Peace Issues
Regina Marchi, M.A.	Communication Studies
Ken Marcus, Ph.D.	Criminal Justice Administration
Perry Marker, Ph.D.	Education
Elizabeth Martinez, Ph.D.	Modern Languages
David McCuan, Ph.D.	Political Science
Phil McGough, Ph.D.	Business Administration
Eric McGuckin, Ph.D.	Liberal Studies
Robert McNamara, Ph.D.	Political Science
Andy Merrifield, Ph.D.	Political Science
Jack Munsee, Ph.D.	Political Science
Ann Neel, Ph.D.	Sociology
Catherine Nelson, Ph.D.	Political Science

Leilani Nishime, Ph.D.	American Multicultural Studies
Linda Nowak, Ph.D.	Business
Tim Ogburn	International Business
Tom Ormond, Ph.D.	Kinesiology
Wendy Ostroff, Ph.D.	Liberal Studies
Ervand M. Peterson, Ph.D.	Environmental Sciences
Keith Pike, M.A.	Native American Studies
Jorge E. Porras, Ph.D.	Modern Languages
Jeffrey T. Reeder, Ph.D.	Modern Languages
Michael Robinson, Rabbi	Religion
Rick Robison, Ph.D.	Library
R. Thomas Rosin, Ph.D.	Anthropology
Richard Senghas, Ph.D.	Anthropology/Linguistics
Rashmi Singh, Ph.D.	American Multicultural Studies
Cindy Stearns, Ph.D.	Women's Gender Studies
John Steiner, Ph.D.	Sociology
Greg Storino	American Airlines Pilot
Meri Storino, Ph.D.	Counseling
Elaine Sundberg, M.A.	Academic Programs
Scott Suneson, M.A.	Sociology/Political Sci.
Bob Tellander, Ph.D.	Sociology
Laxmi G. Tewari, Ph.D.	Music
Karen Thompson, Ph.D.	Business
Suzanne Toczyski, Ph.D.	Modern Languages
Carol Tremmel, M.A.	Extended Education
Charlene Tung, Ph.D.	Women's Gender Studies
David Van Nuys, Ph.D.	Psychology
Francisco H. Vazquez, Ph.D.	Liberal Studies
Greta Vollmer, Ph.D.	English
Alexandra Von Meier, Ph.D.	Environmental Sciences
Albert Wahrhaftig, Ph.D.	Anthropology
Tim Wandling, Ph.D.	English
Tony White, Ph.D.	History
Rick Williams J.D.	Attorney at Law
John Wingard, Ph.D.	Anthropology
Craig Winston, J.D.	Criminal Justice
Richard Zimmer, Ph.D.	Liberal Studies

Sonoma State University Supporting Staff and Offices

Eduardo Ochoa: Chief Academic Officer and staff

Elaine Leeder: Dean of School of Sciences and staff

William Babula: Dean of School of Arts and Humanities

Barbara Butler and the SSU Library Staff

Paula Hammett: Social Sciences Library Resources

Jonah Raskin and Faculty in Communications Studies

Susan Kashack, Jean Wasp, and staff in SSU Public Relations Office

Colleagues in the Sociology Department: Noel Byrne, Kathy Charmaz, Myrna Goodman, Melinda Milligan, Thom Lough, Elaine Wellin, and department coordinators Lisa Kelley-Roche and Matt Horn

The Project Censored crew (SSU faculty, students, and PC staff).

Introduction

By Norman Solomon

For many years, as a *Newsday* reporter specializing in science and health, Laurie Garrett broke new ground with articles and books. Along the way, she won the Peabody, the Polk and the Pulitzer prizes. But in February 2005, Garrett resigned from the *Newsday* staff, leaving behind a memo to colleagues that noted the recent evolution of the newspaper's ownership, first with management changes at the top of Times Mirror and then the purchase by the Tribune company.

"Ever since the Chandler Family plucked Mark Willes from General Foods, placing him at the helm of Times Mirror with a mandate to destroy the institutions in ways that would boost dividends, journalism has suffered at *Newsday*," Garrett wrote. And she added: "The deterioration we experienced at *Newsday* was hardly unique. All across America news organizations have been devoured by massive corporations, and allegiance to stockholders, the drive for higher share prices and push for larger dividend returns trumps everything that the grunts in the newsrooms consider their missions."

When I began to appear on panels about media during the 1980s, critiques of corporate power in the newsroom were highly controversial. Few mainstream journalists seemed inclined to openly express concern about the effects of consolidated media ownership on their profession. And the managers of news outlets were routinely dismissive. At a forum on a California university campus, a *Sacramento Bee* executive who followed me to the podium was so outraged by my rather restrained comments that he ceremoniously set aside his prepared text to denounce my calumnies.

All I had done was cite the reasoned warnings from insightful media critics who had begun to assess the gathering dangers of what veteran journalist Ben Bagdikian called "The Media Monopoly." That was the title of his book that first appeared twenty-two years before Laurie Garrett wrote her farewell memo.

Like most trailblazers, Bagdikian walked in the footsteps of other visionaries. One of the most significant was a tough and compassionate media critic whose work spanned most of the 20th century.

As a young man, George Seldes covered the First World War and then reported on historic events in Europe for the *Chicago Tribune* from 1919 until 1928. Seldes quit the paper and went on to blaze a trail as an independent journalist—ready, able and eager to challenge media business-as-usual. Naturally, he earned hostility from the kind of media magnates he skewered in *Lords of the Press*. The renowned historian Charles A. Beard called that 1938 book "a grand job."

Forty-five years later, another emigre from newsrooms wrote a book that turned out to have profound effects on critical thinking about media. When *The Media Monopoly* first appeared in 1983, the media establishment and many of its employees shrugged; if they paid any attention, it was usually just long enough to dismiss Ben Bagdikian's warning about consolidation of media ownership as alarmist.

While the media landscape shifted, Bagdikian saw corporate behemoths on the horizon—and *The Media Monopoly* emerged as an illuminating book. During the past two decades, several updated editions of *The Media Monopoly* have been published, including the revised 2004 book titled *The New Media Monopoly*. Meanwhile, an entire generation of media activists has come of age. They understand that centralized dominance of news and information—as a dwindling number of humongous firms control most of the journalistic flow in the United States—undermines the First Amendment and democratic possibilities.

There are a lot of parallels between Seldes and Bagdikian. In the first half of the 20th century, Seldes did some exemplary reporting as a mainstream journalist before opting out of the mass-media system in order to critique it. During the last half of the century, something similar occurred with Bagdikian, who was a high-ranking editor at the *Washington Post* when he played a key role in making possible the newspaper's revelations about contents of the top-secret Pentagon Papers in mid-June 1971.

The strong similarities between George Seldes and Ben Bagdikian include unwavering support for labor. With his books and feisty newsletter "In Fact" (published throughout the 1940s), Seldes fiercely advocated for the rights of unions inside and outside the newspaper industries. *Lords of the Press* was dedicated to "the American Newspaper Guild and others interested in a free press."

After leaving the Post, Bagdikian angered top management because he vehemently critiqued the *Washington Post* Company's vicious suppression of the pressmen's strike in the mid–1970s. At that point, Bagdikian wrote an article for *Washington Monthly* magazine critical of the *Post*'s anti-labor policies.

More than 20 years later, in 1997, when *Washington Post* owner Katharine Graham released her autobiography *Personal History* in hardcover, it quoted a note she'd sent to her son in the midst of the bitter labor dispute, saying that Bagdikian's article "literally takes my breath away it's so insane." And she also quoted a memo that she'd sent to the *Post*'s top editor Ben Bradlee: "I am really embarrassed to think this ignorant biased fool was ever national editor. Surely the worst asps in this world are the ones one has clasped to the bosom." Graham had allowed her mogul mentality to triumph over rationality.

When the paperback edition of *Personal History* appeared in early 1998, it contained the same number of pages and was almost identical to the hardcover. But Graham had quietly removed her idiotic sentences about Bagdikian: an unpublicized move that was, in effect, a tacit retraction of her wacky defamation. The episode underscores just how furious—and arrogant—big media owners can get when journalists challenge their prerogatives and power.

It would be a mistake to hark back to an imagined golden era of journalism in the United States. While styles have changed, economic power and political clout have always skewed media coverage. And there has always been chilling truth to A.J. Liebling's observation that "freedom of the press is guaranteed only to those who own one." Yet even while some standards of accuracy and fairness in news reporting have arguably risen during the past several decades, trends of corporate consolidation have generally had effects of tightening the severe constraints on what newsrooms provide to readers, listeners and viewers.

Shortly after Laurie Garrett's resignation from the *Newsday* staff in early 2005, she was interviewed on the *CounterSpin* radio show, produced by the media watch group FAIR (where I'm an associate). After noting that "there's always been good journalism and bad journalism," a host of the program asked: "What is the primary thing that you think has changed during your tenure, such that it is now so inhospitable?"

"The profit motive," Garrett replied. "I mean, look, when I came into journalism—way back, we're not going to say when—there were still plenty of family-owned newspapers across America, family-owned radio, family-owned television stations, or a small company that maybe owned only two or three outlets. And you still had a sense that there was a hint of a competitive spirit between newspapers in the same town and so on. That's all gone, long gone." She went on: "First of all, the competition's gone.... And secondly, most of the old small-scale businesses have long since been bought up by corporations," many of which have a media portfolio that's just one part of a very big corporate empire. Managers of media outlets increasingly insist on turning very high profits. And, in Garrett's words, "it's just not realistic to have the same profit expectations of news, and to think of news as a product in quite the same way as one would think of an automobile, computer chips, insurance services and so on."

The media intersections of corporate leverage and militarism have usually been obscured—but they're more important than ever. The United States has entered the last half of the 21st century's first decade in the midst of what appears to be perpetual war. Some big media owners, like General Electric, are also major military contractors. Every day, media outlets receive large ad revenues from companies that are entwined with Pentagon contracting. And the powerful forces that have made the news media part of the "war on terror" are also enmeshed with a heavily propagandized culture. If major news outlets really challenged the basic assumptions and terminology of Washington's war-makers, the economic consequences for those media enterprises would probably be severe.

During wartime—and we're now often reminded that the U.S. war effort has no end in sight—corporate media managers see waving the flag as a good business practice. In sharp contrast, offering challenges to militarized mindsets is apt to be viewed as economically hazardous. A lot of this process is unspoken and perhaps even unconscious. But the results can be seen, heard and read every day in the mass media. Tactics and specific politics of war may be hotly debated in major news outlets, but the discourse scarcely raises a peep about the fundamentals of the USA as a supreme warfare state and the prerogatives of pursuing a U.S. global empire.

We can't depend on news media to ask the key questions or to supply meaningful answers. Based on deception, war persists; based on injustice, poverty festers. Under the roof of corporate journalism, and in the ongoing context of a military-industrial-media complex, routine forms of news filtration and censorship help to perpetuate these dire human circumstances. Truly independent journalism can help to challenge them.

Project Censored is in its 29th year of spotlighting such vital independent journalism. The book in front of you lays out information that has rarely gotten through the barriers of corporate media. Focusing on well-documented stories that deserve serious attention, Project Censored goes where the media's conformist angels fear to tread. This year's list deals with such crucial matters as increased secrecy, fraud in the U.S. elections of 2004, obscured stories from Iraq and much more. It's the kind of journalism we need.

Norman Solomon's latest book is *War Made Easy: How Presidents and Pundits Keep Spinning Us to Death*, published by Wiley in 2005. He is the founder and executive director of the Institute for Public Accuracy.

CHAPTER 1

The Top Censored Stories of 2004 and 2005

By Kate Sims, Peter Phillips, Tricia Boreta, Theodora Ruhs, Michelle Salvail, Brooke Finley, Josh Sisco, Marcia Simmons, Chris Cox, Kristine Snyder, Tina Tambornini, Celeste Vogler, Joni Wallent and the students of Project Censored

Most people eat the same things everyday. They have five pairs of the same pants in different colors. They go to the same bar and have "their" place to get away for the weekend. When it's time to inform themselves about what's happening in the world, their source of news is no exception. They consider the closest source of information the best and only one.

Learning from a variety of sources can be a rather overwhelming process for the uninitiated. After all, sorting through the information within many pages, airwaves and digital bytes is no quick and easy task. It's certainly way less so than clicking on the broadcast news or going to CNN's website.

Diversity of news is not something that is widely taught in public schools, or used in abundance in our society. It is not at the forefront of our collective consciousness. When put to the task of collecting an independent and analytical body of information, whether for work or simply our own betterment, our cynical and lazy eye may ask for the one-stop shop.

The independent press is an ever evolving entity filled with oppositions, contradictions, heated arguments and passionate beliefs. It takes ten steps back from the scene one moment and jumps in full-bore, "gonzo-style," the next.

It is not safe, easy or predictable. It is not a one-stop shop with a single filter to remove dangerous, radical or career-damaging facts, theories and ideas. Its participants care about telling the truth and make sure that the decision-makers do as well; and if they don't, they damn well better be held accountable.

Our goal at Project Censored is to further that aim through education and training. It is the students who find, research, and write the stories and updates that comprise many of the chapters. And it is the students who cull through the mountain of stories we get every year looking for the ones that they feel could have made a difference.

We have all heard the phrase, "the best way to learn something is to teach it." And that is what we are doing here. In the process we are honing our powers of focus and critical thinking. By compiling these stories for you, the reader, the students become the media that they want to be. In order to expand the horizons of public perception, we must expand our own. And so we have jumped in, full-bore, to do just that. We hope you appreciate the effort.

—Josh Sisco, researcher, Project Censored

Here are the stories divided by category:

POLITICS
#1 Bush Administration moves to eliminate open government
#3 Another year of distorted election coverage
#25 Homeland Security Was Designed to Fail

MEDIA
#2 Media Coverage Fails on Iraq: Fallujah and the Civilian Death toll
#7 Journalists Face Unprecedented Dangers to Life and Livelihood

FOREIGN POLICY
#6 The Real Oil for Food Scam
#8 Iraqi Farmers Threatened By Bremer's Mandates
#13 Rich Countries Fail to Live up to Global Pledges
#16 US NORTHCOM Plans Integration of Canada

HEALTH
#11 Mandatory Mental Screening Program Usurps Parental Rights
#19 Child Wards of the State used in AIDS Experiments

ENVIRONMENT
#10 Mountaintop Removal Threatens Ecosystem and Economy

ECONOMY
#9 Iran's New Oil Trade System Challenges U.S. Currency
#18 Little Known Stock Fraud Could Weaken U.S. Economy

DOMESTIC POLICY
#4 Surveillance Society Quietly Moves In
#14 Corporations Win Big on Tort Reform, Justice Suffers
#21 New Immigration Plan Favors Business Over People

HUMAN RIGHTS ISSUES
#20 American Indians Sue for Resources Compensation Provided to Others
#23 Plight of Palestinian Child Detainees Highlights Global Problem
#24 Ethiopian Indigenous are Victims of Corporate and Government Resource Aspirations

MILITARY
#5 U.S. Uses Tsunami to Military Advantage in Southeast Asia
#12 Military in Iraq Contracts Human Rights Violators
#17 U.S. Uses South American Military Bases to Expand Control of the Region

SCIENCE
#22 Nanotechnology Offers Exciting Possibilities But Health Effects Need Scrutiny

EDUCATION
#15 Conservative Plan to Override Academic Freedom in the Classroom

1 Bush Administration Moves to Eliminate Open Government

Source:
Common Dreams, September 14, 2004. Press release.
Title: "New Report Details Bush Administration Secrecy"
Author: Karen Lightfoot
<http://www.commondreams.org/news2004/0914-05.htm>
<http://www.democrats.reform.house.gov/story.asp?ID=692&Issue=Open+Go
vernment>

Faculty Evaluator: Yvonne Clarke, MA
Student Researcher: Jessica Froiland

Throughout the 1980s, Project Censored highlighted a number of alarming reductions to government access and accountability (see Censored 1982 #6, 1984 #8, 1985 #3 and 1986 #2). It tracked the small but systematic changes made to existing laws and the executive orders introduced. It now appears that these actions may have been little more than a prelude to the virtual lock box against access that is being constructed around the current administration.

"The Bush Administration has an obsession with secrecy," says Representative Henry Waxman, the Democrat from California who, in September 2004, commissioned a congressional report on secrecy in the Bush Administration. "It has repeatedly rewritten laws and changed practices to reduce public and congressional scrutiny of its activities. The cumulative effect is an unprecedented assault on the laws that make our government open and accountable."

CHANGES TO LAWS THAT PROVIDE PUBLIC ACCESS TO FEDERAL RECORDS

The Freedom of Information Act (FOIA) gives citizens the ability to file a request for specific information from a government agency and provides recourse in federal court if that agency fails to comply with FOIA requirements. Over the last two decades, beginning with Reagan, this law has become increasingly diluted and circumvented by each succeeding administration.

Under the Bush Administration, agencies make extensive and arbitrary use of FOIA exemptions (such as those for classified information, privileged attorney-client documents and certain information compiled for law enforcement purposes) often inappropriately or with inadequate justification. Recent evidence shows agencies making frivolous (and sometimes ludicrous) exemption claims, abusing the deliberative process privilege, abusing the law enforcement exemption, and withholding data on telephone service outages.

Quite commonly, the Bush Administration simply fails to respond to FOIA requests at all. Whether this is simply an inordinate delay or an unstated final refusal to respond to the request, the requesting party is never told. But the effect is the same: the public is denied access to the information.

The Bush Administration also engages in an aggressive policy of questioning, challenging and denying FOIA requesters' eligibility for fee waivers, using a variety of tactics. Measures include narrowing the definition of "representative of news media," claiming information would not contribute to public understanding.

Ten years ago, federal agencies were required to release documents through FOIA—even if technical grounds for refusal existed—unless "foreseeable harm" would result from doing so. But, according to the Waxman report, an October 2001 memo by Attorney General John Ashcroft instructs and encourages agencies to withhold information if there are any technical grounds for withholding it under FOIA.

In 2003, the Bush Administration won a new legislative exemption from FOIA for all National Security Agency "operational files." The Administration's main rationale for this new exemption is that conducting FOIA searches diverts resources from the agency's mission. Of course, this rationale could apply to every agency. As NSA has operated subject to FOIA for decades, it is not clear why the agency now needs this exemption.

The Presidential Records Act ensures that after a president leaves office, the public will have full access to White House documents used to develop public policy. Under the law and an executive order by Ronald Reagan, the presumption has been that most documents would be released. However, President Bush issued an executive order that establishes a process that generally blocks the release of presidential papers.

CHANGES TO LAWS THAT RESTRICT PUBLIC ACCESS TO FEDERAL RECORDS

The Bush Administration has dramatically increased the volume of government information concealed from public view. In a March 2003 executive order, President Bush expanded the use of the national security classification.

The order eliminated the presumption of disclosure, postponed or avoided automatic declassification, protected foreign government information, reclassified some information, weakened the panel that decides to exempt documents from declassification and adjudicates classification challenges, and exempted vice presidential records from mandatory declassification review.

The Bush Administration has also obtained unprecedented authority to conduct government operations in secret, with little or no judicial oversight. Under expanded law enforcement authority in the Patriot Act, the Justice Department can more easily use secret orders to obtain library and other private records, obtain "sneak-and-peek" warrants to conduct secret searches, and conduct secret wiretaps. In addition, the Bush Administration has used novel legal interpretations to expand its authority to detain, try, and deport individuals in secret. Since the September 11, 2001 attacks, the Bush Administration has asserted unprecedented authority to detain anyone whom the executive branch labels an "enemy combatant" indefinitely and secretly. It has authorized military trials that can be closed not only to the public but also to the defendants and their own attorneys. And the Administration has authorized procedures for the secret detention and deportation of aliens residing in the United States.

CONGRESSIONAL ACCESS TO INFORMATION

Compared to previous administrations, the Bush Administration has operated with remarkably little congressional oversight. This is partially attributable to the alignment of the parties. The Republican majorities in the House and the Senate have refrained from investigating allegations of misconduct by the White House. Another major factor has been the Administration's resistance to oversight. The Bush Administration has consistently refused to provide to members of Congress, the Government Accountability Office, and congressional commissions the information necessary for meaningful investigation and review of the Administration's activities.

For example, the Administration has contested in court the power of the Government Accountability Office to conduct independent investigations and has refused to comply with the rule that allows members of the House Government Reform Committee to obtain information from the executive branch, forcing the members to go to court to enforce their rights under the law. It has also ignored and rebuffed numerous requests for information made by members of Congress attempting to exercise their oversight responsibilities with respect to executive branch activities, and repeatedly withheld information from the investigative commission established by Congress to investigate the September 11 attacks.

UPDATE Rep. Waxman's companion bill, HR 5073 IH, the Restore Open Government Act of 2004, was not heard by Congress before the Winter Recess in December, and the bill was not reintroduced in the Opening Session in January 2005. However, on February 16, after the commencement of the 109th Congress, John Cornyn (R-Tex.) and Patrick Leahy (D-Vt.) introduced a bill entitled the Openness Promotes Effectiveness in our National Government Act of 2005, S. 394 (the Cornyn-Leahy bill), which according to their joint statement "is designed to strengthen laws governing access to government information, particularly the Freedom of Information Act." On the same day, an identical bill, H.R. 867, was introduced in the House of Representatives by Rep. Lamar Smith (R-Tex.).[1]

For more information on Rep. Waxman's legislation and work on open government, site, please visit www.democrats.reform.house.gov.

NOTE

1. *St. Petersburg Times* (Florida), February 18, 2005, "Improving access to information."

2 Media Coverage Fails on Iraq: Fallujah and the Civilian Death Toll

PART 1: FALLUJAH—WAR CRIMES GO UNREPORTED

Sources:
Peacework, December 2004–January 2005
Title: "The Invasion of Fallujah: A Study in the Subversion of Truth"
Authors: Mary Trotochaud and Rick McDowell

World Socialist Web Site, November 17, 2004
Title: "U.S. Media Applauds Destruction of Fallujah"
Author: David Walsh

The NewStandard, December 3, 2004
Title: "Fallujah Refugees Tell of Life and Death in the Kill Zone"
Author: Dahr Jamail

Faculty Evaluators: Bill Crowley, Ph. D., Sherril Jaffe, Ph. D.
Student Researcher: Brian K. Lanphear

Over the past two years, the United States has conducted two major sieges against Fallujah, a city in Iraq. The first attempted siege of Fallujah (a city of 300,000 people) resulted in a defeat for Coalition forces. As a result, the United States gave the citizens of Fallujah two choices prior to the second siege: leave the city or risk dying as enemy insurgents. Faced with this ultimatum, approximately 250,000 citizens, or 83 percent of the population of Fallujah, fled the city. The people had nowhere to flee and ended up as refugees. Many families were forced to survive in fields, vacant lots, and abandoned buildings without access to shelter, water, electricity, food or medical care. The 50,000 citizens who either chose to remain in the city or who were unable to leave were trapped by Coalition forces and were cut off from food, water and medical supplies. The United States military claimed that there were a few thousand enemy insurgents remaining among those who stayed in the city and conducted the invasion as if all the people remaining were enemy combatants.

Burhan Fasa'a, an Iraqi journalist, said Americans grew easily frustrated with Iraqis who could not speak English. "Americans did not have interpreters with them, so they entered houses and killed people because they didn't speak English. They entered the house where I was with 26 people, and shot people because [the people] didn't obey [the soldiers'] orders, even just because the people couldn't understand a word of English." Abu Hammad, a resident of Fallujah, told the Inter Press Service that he saw people attempt to swim across the Euphrates to escape the siege. "The Americans shot them with rifles from the shore. Even if some of them were holding a white flag or white clothes over their head to show they are not fighters, they were all shot." Furthermore, "even the wound[ed] people were killed. The Americans made announcements for people to come to one mosque if they wanted to leave Fallujah, and even the people who went there carrying white flags were killed." Former residents of Fallujah recall other tragic methods of killing the wounded. "I watched them [U.S. Forces] roll over wounded people in the street with tanks... ...This happened so many times."

Preliminary estimates as of December of 2004 revealed that at least 6,000 Iraqi citizens in Fallujah had been killed, and one-third of the city had been destroyed.

Journalists Mary Trotochaud and Rick McDowell assert that the continuous slaughter in Fallujah is greatly contributing to escalating violence in other regions of the country such as Mosul, Baquba, Hilla, and Baghdad. The violence prompted by the U.S. invasion has resulted in the assassinations of at least 338 Iraqi's who were associated with Iraq's "new" government.

The U.S. invasion of Iraq, and more specifically Fallujah, is causing an incredible humanitarian disaster among those who have no specific involvement with the war. The International Committee for the Red Cross reported on December 23, 2004 that three of the city's water purification plants had been destroyed and the fourth badly damaged. Civilians are running short on food and are unable to receive help from those who are willing to make a positive difference. Aid organizations have been repeatedly denied access to the city, hospitals, and refugee populations in the surrounding areas.

Abdel Hamid Salim, spokesman for the Iraqi Red Crescent in Baghdad, told Inter Press Service that none of their relief teams had been allowed into Fallujah three weeks after the invasion. Salim declared that "there is still heavy fighting in Fallujah. And the Americans won't let us in so we can help people."

The UN High Commissioner for Human Rights Louise Arbour voiced a deep concern for the civilians caught up in the fighting. Louise Arbour emphasized that all those guilty of violations of international humanitarian and human rights laws must be brought to justice. Arbour claimed that all violations of these laws should be investigated, including "the deliberate targeting of civilians, indiscriminate and disproportionate attacks, the killing of injured persons and the use of human shields."

Marjorie Cohn, executive vice president of the National Lawyers Guild, and the U.S. representative to the executive committee of the American Association of Jurists, has noted that the U.S. invasion of Fallujah is a violation of international law that the U.S. had specifically ratified: "They [U.S. Forces] stormed and occupied the Fallujah General Hospital, and have not agreed to allow doctors and ambulances to go inside the main part of the city to help the wounded, in direct violation of the Geneva Conventions."

According to David Walsh, the American media also seems to contribute to the subversion of truth in Fallujah. Although, in many cases, journalists are prevented from entering the city and are denied access to the wounded, corporate media showed little concern regarding their denied access. There has been little or no mention of the immorality or legality of the attacks the United States has waged against Iraq. With few independent journalists reporting on the carnage, the international humanitarian community in exile, and the Red Cross and Red Crescent prevented from entering the besieged city, the world is forced to rely on reporting from journalists embedded with U.S. forces. In the U.S. press, we see casualties reported for Fallujah as follows: number of U.S. soldiers dead, number of Iraqi soldiers dead, number of "guerillas" or "insurgents" dead. Nowhere were the civilian casualties reported in the first weeks of the invasion. An accurate count of civilian casualties to date has yet to be published in the mainstream media.

PART 2: CIVILIAN DEATH TOLL IS IGNORED

Sources:

The Lancet, October 29, 2004
Title: "Mortality Before and After the 2003 Invasion of Iraq"
Authors: Les Roberts, Riyadh Lafta, Richard Garfield, Jamal Khudhairi and Gilbert Burnham

The Lancet, October 29, 2004
Title: "The War in Iraq: Civilian Casualties, Political Responsibilities"
Author: Richard Horton

The Chronicle of Higher Education, February 4, 2005
Title: "Lost Count"
Author: Lila Guterman

FAIR, April 15, 2004
Title: "CNN to Al Jazeera: Why Report Civilian Deaths?"
Author: Julie Hollar

Faculty Evaluator: Sherril Jaffe, Ph.D.
Student Researcher: Melissa Waybright

In late October, 2004, a peer reviewed study was published in *The Lancet*, a British medical journal, concluding that at least 100,000 civilians have been killed in Iraq since it was invaded by a United States-led coalition in March 2003. Previously, the number of Iraqis that had died, due to conflict or sanctions since the 1991 Gulf War, had been uncertain. Claims ranging from denial of increased mortality to millions of excess deaths have been made. In the absence of any surveys, however, they relied on Ministry of Health records. Morgue-based surveillance data indicate the post-invasion homicide rate is many times higher than the pre-invasion rate.

In the present setting of insecurity and limited availability of health information, researchers, headed by Dr. Les Roberts of Johns Hopkins University, undertook a national survey to estimate mortality during the 14.6 months before the invasion (Jan 1, 2002, to March 18, 2003) and to compare it with the period from March 19, 2003, to the date of the interview, between Sept 8 and 20, 2004. Iraqi households were informed about the purpose of the survey, assured that their name would not be recorded, and told that there would be no benefits or penalties for refusing or agreeing to participate.

The survey indicates that the death toll associated with the invasion and occupation of Iraq is in reality about 100,000 people, and may be much higher. The major public health problem in Iraq has been identified as violence. However, despite widespread Iraqi casualties, household interview data do not show evidence of widespread wrongdoing on the part of individual soldiers on the ground. Ninety-five percent of reported killings (all attributed to U.S. forces by interviewees) were caused by helicopter gunships, rockets, or other forms of aerial weaponry.

The study was released on the eve of a contentious presidential election—fought in part over U.S. policy on Iraq. Many American newspapers and television news programs ignored the study or buried reports about it far from the top headlines. "What went wrong this time? Perhaps the rush by researchers and *The Lancet* to put the study in front of American voters before the election accomplished precisely the opposite result, drowning out a valuable study in the clamor of the presidential campaign." (Lila Guterman, *Chronicle of Higher Education*)

The study's results promptly flooded though the worldwide media—everywhere except the United States, where there was barely a whisper about the study, followed by stark silence. "*The Lancet* released the paper on October 29, the Friday before the election, when many reporters were busy with political stories. That day the *Los Angeles Times* and the *Chicago Tribune* each dedicated only about 400 words to the study and placed the stories inside their front section, on pages A4 and A11, respectively. (The news media in Europe gave the study much more play; many newspapers put articles about it on their front pages.)

In a short article about the study on page A8, the *New York Times* noted that the Iraqi Body Count, a project to tally civilian deaths reported in the news media, had put the maximum death count at around 17,000. The new study, the article said, "is certain to generate intense controversy." But the *Times* has not published any further news articles about the paper. The *Washington Post*, perhaps most damagingly to the study's reputation, quoted Marc E. Garlasco, a senior military analyst at Human Rights Watch, as saying, "These numbers seem to be inflated." Mr. Garlasco says now that he hadn't read the paper at the time and calls his quote in the *Post* "really unfortunate." (Lila Guterman, *Chronicle of Higher Education*).

Even so, nobody else in American corporate media bothered to pick up the story and inform our citizens how many Iraqi citizens are being killed at the hands of a coalition led by our government. The study was never mentioned on television news, and the truth remains unheard by those who may need to hear it most. The U.S. government had no comment at the time and remains silent about Iraqi civilian deaths. "The only thing we keep track of is casualties for U.S. troops and civilians," a Defense Department spokesman told *The Chronicle*.

When CNN anchor Daryn Kagan did have the opportunity to interview the Al Jazeera network editor-in-chief Ahmed Al-Sheik—a rare opportunity to get independent information about events in Fallujah—she used the occasion to badger Al-Sheik about whether the civilian deaths were really "the story" in Fallujah. CNN's argument was that a bigger story than civilian deaths is "what the Iraqi insurgents are doing" to provoke a U.S. "response" is startling. "When reports from the ground are describing hundreds of civilians being killed by U.S. forces, CNN should be looking to Al Jazeera's footage to see if it corroborates those accounts—not badgering Al Jazeera's editor about why he doesn't suppress that footage." (MediaWatch, *Asheville Global Report*)

Study researchers concluded that several limitations exist with this study, predominantly because the quality of data received is dependent on the accuracy of the interviews. However, interviewers believed that certain essential charcteristics of Iraqi culture make it unlikely that respondents would have fabricated their reports of the deaths. The Geneva Conventions have clear guidance about the responsibilities of occupying armies to the civilian population they control. "With the admitted benefit of hindsight and from a purely public health perspective, it is clear that whatever planning did take place was grievously in error. The invasion of Iraq, the displacement of a cruel dictator, and an attempt to impose a liberal democracy by force have, by themselves, been insufficient to bring peace and security to the civilian population.

The illegal, heavy handed tactics practiced by the U.S. military in Iraq evident in these news stories have become what appears to be their standard operating procedure in occupied Iraq. Countless violations of international law and crimes against humanity occurred in Fallujah during the November massacre.

Evidenced by the mass slaughtering of Iraqis and the use of illegal weapons such as cluster bombs, napalm, uranium munitions and chemical weapons during the November siege of Fallujah when the entire city was declared a "free fire zone" by military leaders, the brutality of the U.S. military has only increased throughout Iraq as the occupation drags on.

According to Iraqis inside the city, at least 60 percent of Fallujah went on to be totally destroyed in the siege, and eight months after the siege entire districts of the city remained without electricity or water. Israeli style checkpoints were set up in the city, prohibiting anyone from entering who did not live inside the city. Of course non-embedded media were not allowed in the city.

UPDATE: Since these stories were published, countless other incidents of illegal weapons and tactics being used by the U.S. military in Iraq have occurred.

During "Operation Spear" on June 17th, 2005, U.S.-led forces attacked the small cities of Al-Qa'im and Karabla near the Syrian border. U.S. warplanes dropped 2,000 pound bombs in residential areas and claimed to have killed scores of "militants" while locals and doctors claimed that only civilians were killed.

As in Fallujah, residents were denied access to the city in order to obtain medical aid, while those left inside the city claimed Iraqi civilians were being regularly targeted by U.S. snipers.

According to an IRIN news report, Firdos al-Abadi from the Iraqi Red Crescent Society stated that 7,000 people from Karabla were camped in the desert outside the city, suffering from lack of food and medical aid while 150 homes were totally destroyed by the U.S. military.

An Iraqi doctor reported on the same day that he witnessed, "crimes in the west area of the country…the American troops destroyed one of our hospitals, they burned the whole store of medication, they killed the patient in the ward…they prevented us from helping the people in Qa'im."

Also like Fallujah, a doctor at the General Hospital of al-Qa'im stated that entire families remained buried under the rubble of their homes, yet medical personnel were unable to reach them due to American snipers.

Iraqi civilians in Haditha had similar experiences during "Operation Open Market" when they claimed U.S. snipers shot anyone in the streets for days on end, and U.S. and Iraqi forces raided homes detaining any man inside.

Corporate media reported on the "liberation" of Fallujah, as well as quoting military sources on the number of "militants" killed. Any mention of civilian casualties, heavy-handed tactics or illegal munitions was either brief or non-existent, and continues to be as of June 2005.

FOR ADDITIONAL INFORMATION:

For those interested in following these stories, it is possible to obtain information by visiting the English Al-Jazeera website at http://english.aljazeera. net/HomePage, my website at www.dahrjamailiraq.com, The World Tribunal on Iraq at www.worldtribunal.org, and other alternative/independent news websites.

3 Another Year of Distorted Election Coverage

Source:
In These Times, 02/15/05
Title: "A Corrupted Election"
Authors: Steve Freeman and Josh Mitteldorf

Seattle Post-Intelligencer, January 26, 2005
Title: "Jim Crow Returns To The Voting Booth"
Authors: Greg Palast, Rev. Jesse Jackson

www.freepress.org, Nov. 23, 2004
Title: "How a Republican Election Supervisor Manipulated the 2004 Central Ohio Vote"
Authors: Bob Fitrakis, Harvey Wasserman

Faculty Evaluator: Ann Neel, MA
Student Researcher: Mike Osipoff

Political analysts have long counted on exit polls to be a reliable predictor of actual vote counts. The unusual discrepancy between exit poll data and the actual vote count in the 2004 election challenges that reliability. However, despite evidence of technological vulnerabilities in the voting system and a higher incidence of irregularities in swing states, this discrepancy was not scrutinized in the mainstream media. They simply parroted the partisan declarations of "sour grapes" and "let's move on" instead of providing any meaningful analysis of a highly controversial election.

The official vote count for the 2004 election showed that George W. Bush won by three million votes. But exit polls projected a victory margin of five million votes for John Kerry. This eight-million-vote discrepancy is much greater than the error margin. The overall margin of error should statistically have been under one percent. But the official result deviated from the poll projections by more than five percent—a statistical impossibility.

Edison Media Research and Mitofsky International, the two companies hired to do the polling for the Nation Election Pool (a consortium of the nation's five major broadcasters and the Associated Press), did not immediately provide an explanation for how this could have occurred. They waited until January 19, the eve of the inauguration.

Edison and Mitofsky's "inaugural" report, "Evaluation of Edison/Mitofsky Election System 2004," stated that the discrepancy was "most likely due to Kerry voters participating in the exit polls at a higher rate than Bush voters." The media widely reported that this report proved the accuracy of the official count and a Bush victory. The body of the report, however, offers no data to substantiate this position. In fact, the report shows that Bush voters were more likely to complete the survey than Kerry voters. The report also states that the difference between exit polls and official tallies was far too great to be explained by sampling error, and that a systematic bias is implicated.

The Edison and Mitofsky report dismisses the possibility that the official vote count was wrong, stating that precincts with electronic voting systems had the same error rates as precincts with punch-card systems. This is true. However, it merely points to the unreliability of punch-card and electronic systems, both of which are slated for termination under the Helping America Vote Act of 2002. According to the report, only in precincts that used old-fashioned, hand-counted paper ballots did the official count and the exit poll data fall within the normal margin of error.

Also, the report shows, the discrepancy between the exit polls and the official count was considerably greater in the critical swing states. And while this fact is consistent with allegations of fraud, Mitofsky and Edison suggest, without providing any data or theory to back up their claim, that this discrepancy is somehow related to media coverage.

In precincts that were at least 80 percent for Bush, the average within-precinct error (WPE) was a whopping 10.0 percent—the numerical difference between the exit poll predictions and the official count. Also, in Bush strongholds, Kerry received only about two-thirds of the votes predicted by exit polls. In Kerry strongholds, exit polls matched the official count almost exactly (an average WPE of 0.3).

This exit poll data is a strong indicator of a corrupted election. But the case grows stronger if these exit poll discrepancies are interpreted in the context of more than 100,000 officially logged reports of irregularities and possible fraud during Election Day 2004.

Bush campaign officials compiled a 1,886-name "caging list," which included the names and addresses of predominantly black voters in the traditionally Democratic Jacksonville, Florida. While Bush campaign spokespersons stated that the list was a returned mail log, they did not deny that such a list could be used to challenge voters on Election Day. In fact, the county elections supervisor says that he could see no other purpose for compiling such a list.

In Franklin County Ohio, Columbus voters faced one of the longest ballot lines in history. In many inner city precincts, voters sometimes had three-hour waits to get to the poll before being required to cast ballots within five minutes, as demanded by the Republican-run Board of Elections. Seventy-seven out of the county's 2,866 voting machines malfunctioned on Election Day. One machine registered 4,258 votes for Bush in a precinct where only 638 people voted. At least 125 machines were held back at the opening of the polls, and another 68 were never deployed. While voters were rushed through the process, 29 percent of the precincts had fewer voting machines than in the 2000 election despite a 25 percent increase in turnout.

Taken together, these problems point to an election that requires scrutiny. Even if the discrepancy between exit polls and actual vote counts is simply a fluke, other flaws and questionable practices in the voting process make one wonder whether or not the people's voice was actually heard and if we are truly a working democracy.

UPDATE BY JOSH MITTELDORF: Some news is too important to report. People might get upset, and the smooth functioning of our democracy would be jeopardized. Thus the media has collectively done the responsible thing, and refrained—at great cost to themselves, be assured—from publicizing doubts about the legitimacy of the 2004 election, in order to help assure the "orderly succession of power."

Unfortunately, some internet sites such as Commondreams.org and Freepress.org do not realize their obligations to the commonwealth, and have thus been less responsible in maintaining silence. And there's an upbeat radio voice from Vermont, Thom Hartmann, who would be fun to listen to if only he didn't insist on relating so many discomfiting truths.

But so long as you stay away from these isolated derelicts, you will be gratified to receive a reassuringly consistent story line: George Bush won the 2004 election fair and square. It's time to stop asking pointless questions. Get with the program!

UPDATE BY GREG PALAST AND REVEREND JESSIE JACKSON: There are conspiracy nuts out there on the Internet who think that John Kerry defeated George Bush in Ohio and other states. I know, because I wrote "Kerry Won" for TomPaine.com two days after the election.

"Kerry Won" was the latest in a series coming out of a five-year investigation, begun in November 2000, for BBC Television Newsnight and Britain's Guardian papers, dissecting that greasy sausage called American electoral democracy.

On November 11, a week after TomPaine.com put the report out on the

'Net, I received an email from the *New York Times* Washington Bureau. Hot on the investigation of the veracity of the vote, the Times reporter asked me pointed questions:

Question #1: Are you a "sore loser"?
Question #2: Are you a "conspiracy nut"?

There was no third question. Investigation of the vote was, apparently, complete. The next day, their thorough analysis of the evidence yielded a front-page story, "VOTE FRAUD THEORIES, SPREAD BY BLOGS, ARE QUICKLY BURIED."

Here's a bit of what the Paper of Record failed to record.

In June 2004, well before the election, my co-author of "Jim Crow" Rev. Jesse Jackson brought me to Chicago. We had breakfast with Vice-Presidential candidate John Edwards. The Reverend asked the Senator to read my report of the "spoilage" of Black votes—one million African Americans who cast ballots in 2000 but did not have their votes register on the machines.

Edwards said he'd read it over after he'd had his bagel. Jackson snatched away his bagel. No read, no bagel. A hungry Senator was genuinely concerned—these were, after all, Democrats whose votes did not tally, and he shot the information to John Kerry. A couple of weeks later, Kerry told the NAACP convention that one million African-American votes were not counted in 2000, but in 2004 he would not let it happen again.

But he did let it happen again. More than a million votes in 2004 were cast and not counted.

As a reporter, it's not my job to help the Democratic Party learn to tie its shoes. And, as a nonpartisan journalist, I'm not out to expose the Republican Party's new elaborate campaign to prevent voters from voting—but I must report it. However, editors and news producers in my home country, the USA, seem less than interested. Indeed, they are downright hostile to reporting this story of the shoplifting of our democracy.

America has an apartheid voting system, denying African-Americans, Hispanics and American Natives the assurance their ballots will count. Worse, America has an apartheid media which denies racial disenfranchisement a seat at the front of the news bus.

It was in November 2000 I first ran into the U.S. news lord's benign neglect of the "new Jim Crow" methods of denying citizens of color their vote. While working with the British *Guardian* papers just days before the 2000 presidential election, I discovered that Governor Jeb Bush and his Secretary of State, Katharine Harris, had wrongly purged tens of thousands of Black citizens from voter rolls as "felons"—when in fact their only crime had been V.W.B.: Voting While Black.

Nothing appeared in the U.S. press. However, I admit that the Florida purge story was picked up by the *New York Times* ... fofur years later.

Just before the November 2004 election, BBC television Newsnight discovered new, confidential "caging lists" which we got our hands on from inside the Republican National Committee headquarters. These were rosters of thousands of minority voters targeted to prevent them from voting on election day: a violation of federal law. It was big news in Europe and South America. In the USA, there was nothing except an attack on BBC's report by ABC's web site. ABC's only listed source for their attack on the BBC was the Republican Party.

The story of the purge of Black voters, the million missing Black ballots cast but not counted, the caging lists, and other games used to deny the vote to the dark-skinned and the poor, would have been buried long ago if not for BBC Television, *Harper's Magazine* (may it last a thousand years), Britain's *Guardian* and *Observer*, *The Nation*, the op-ed editors at the *San Francisco Chronicle* and *Seattle Post-Intelligencer* and, provocatively, *Hustler* Magazine. Even if ignored or actively 'dissed by U.S. "mainstream" media, the story will be continue to be reported, due to the passionate insistence of Reverend Jackson, from a thousand pulpits.

Thanks to GeorgeBush.com for capturing the 'caging lists.' And bless the blogs, for they shall set the truth free: TomPaine.com, Buzzflash, Working-for-Change and other Internet sites carried the story over the electronic Berlin Wall.

Finally, my gratitude to our indefatigable investigative team, particularly Oliver Shykles and Matt Pascarella for their work on this story—on which they continue today—and to Meirion Jones, producer nonpareil at BBC television's Newsnight.

For Additional Documentation of Voter Fraud 2004 See Chapters 2 and 3.

4 Surveillance Society Quietly Moves In

Sources:
Information Management Journal, Mar/Apr 2004
Title: "PATRIOT Act's Reach Expanded Despite Part Being Struck Down"
Author: Nikki Swartz

LiP Magazine, Winter 2004
Title: "Grave New World"
Author: Anna Samson Miranda

Capitol Hill Blue, June 7, 2004
Title: "Where Big Brother Snoops on Americans 24/7"
Authors: Teresa Hampton and Doug Thompson

Faculty Evaluator: John Steiner, Ph. D.
Student Researcher: Sandy Brown, Michelle Jesolva

"While the evening news rolled footage of Saddam being checked for head lice, the Intelligence Authorization Act for Fiscal Year 2004 was quietly signed into law."[1]

On December 13, 2003, President George W. Bush, with little fanfare and no mainstream media coverage, signed into law the controversial Intelligence Authorization Act while most of America toasted the victory of U.S. forces in Iraq and Saddam's capture. None of the corporate press covered the signing of this legislation, which increases the funding for intelligence agencies, dramatically expands the definition of surveillable financial institutions, and authorizes the FBI to acquire private records of those individuals suspected of criminal activity without a judicial review. American civil liberties are once again under attack.

History has provided precedent for such actions. Throughout the 1990s, erosions of these protections were taking place. As part of the 1996 Anti-Terrorism bill adopted in the wake of the Oklahoma City bombing, the Justice Department was required to publish statistics going back to 1990 on threats or actual crimes against federal, state and local employees and their immediate families when the wrongdoing related to the workers' official duties. The numbers were then to be kept up to date with an annual report.[2] Members of congress, concerned with the threat this type of legislation posed to American civil liberties, were able to strike down much of what the bill proposed, including modified requirements regarding wiretap regulations.

The "atmosphere of fear" generated by recent terrorist attacks, both foreign and domestic, provides administrations the support necessary to adopt stringent new legislation. In response to the September 11 attacks, new agencies, programs and bureaucracies have been created. The Total Information Office is a branch of the United States Department of Defense's Defense Advanced Research Projects Agency. It has a mission to "imagine, develop, apply, integrate, demonstrate and transition information technologies, components and prototype, closed-loop, information systems that will counter asymmetric threats by achieving total information awareness."³ Another intelligence gathering governmental agency, The Information Awareness Office, has a mission to gather as much information as possible about everyone in a centralized location for easy perusal by the United States government. Information mining has become the business of government.

In November 2002, the *New York Times* reported that the Defense Advanced Research Projects Agency (DARPA) was developing a tracking system called "Total Information Awareness" (TIA), which was intended to detect terrorists through analyzing troves of information. The system, developed under the direction of John Poindexter, then-director of DARPA's Information Awareness Office, was envisioned to give law enforcement access to private data without suspicion of wrongdoing or a warrant.⁴ The "Total Information Awareness" program's name was changed to "Terrorist Information Awareness" on May 20, 2003 ostensibly to clarify the program's intent to gather information on presumed terrorists rather than compile dossiers on U.S. citizens.

Despite this name change, a Senate Defense Appropriations bill passed unanimously on July 18, 2003, expressly denying any funding to Terrorist Information Awareness research. In response, the Pentagon proposed The Multistate Anti-Terrorism Information Exchange, or MATRIX, a program devised by longtime Bush family friend Hank Asher as a pilot effort to increase and enhance the exchange of sensitive terrorism and other criminal activity information between local, state, and federal law enforcement agencies. The MATRIX, as devised by the Pentagon, is a State run information generating tool, thereby circumventing congress' concern regarding the appropriation of federal funds for the development of this controversial database. Although most states have refused to adopt these Orwellian strategies, Ohio, Pennsylvania, Connecticut and Florida have all jumped on the TIA band wagon.

Yet, somehow, after the apparent successful dismantling of TIA, expressed concern by Representatives Mark Udall of Colorado, Betty McCollum of Minnesota, Ron Paul of Texas and Dennis Moore of Kansas, and heightened public awareness of the MATRIX, the Intelligence Authorization Act was signed into law December 13, 2003.⁵

On Thursday, November 20, 2003 Minnesota Representative Betty McCollum stated that, "The Republican Leadership inserted a controversial provision in the FY04 Intelligence Authorization Report that will expand the already far-reaching USA Patriot Act, threatening to further erode our cherished civil liberties. This provision gives the FBI power to demand financial and other records, without a judge's approval, from post offices, real estate agents, car dealers, travel agents, pawnbrokers and many other businesses. This provision was included with little or no public debate, including no consideration by the House Judiciary Committee, which is the committee of jurisdiction. It came as a surprise to most Members of this body."[6]

According to *LiP Magazine*, "Governmental and law-enforcement agencies and MATRIX contractors across the nation will gain extensive and unprecedented access to financial records, medical records, court records, voter registration, travel history, group and religious affiliations, names and addresses of family members, purchases made and books read."[7]

Peter Jennings, in an ABC original report, explored the commercial applications of this accumulated information. Journalist and author Peter O'Harrow, who collaborated with ABC News on the broadcast "Peter Jennings Reporting: No Place to Hide," states "...marketers—and now, perhaps government investigators—can study what people are likely to do, what kind of attitudes they have, what they buy at the grocery store."[8] Although this program aired on prime-time mainstream television, there was no mention of the potential for misuse of this personal information network or of the controversy surrounding the issues of privacy and civil liberties violations concerning citizens and civil servants alike. Again, the sharing of this kind of personal information is not without precedent.

On November 12, 1999, Clinton signed into law the Gramm-Leach-Bliley Act, which permits financial institutions to share personal customer information with affiliates within the holding company. The Intelligence Authorization Act of Fiscal Year 2004 expands the definition of a surveillable financial institution to include real estate agencies, insurance companies, travel agencies, Internet service providers, post offices, casinos and other businesses as well. Due to massive corporate mergers and the acquisition of reams of newly acquired information, personal consumer data has been made readily available to any agency interested in obtaining it, both commercial and governmental.

With the application of emerging new technologies such as Radio Frequency Identification chips or RFIDs, small individualized computer chips capable of communicating with a receiving computer, consumer behavior can literally be tracked from the point of purchase to the kitchen cupboard, and can be monitored by all interested parties.

UPDATE BY ANNA MIRANDA: *The United States is at risk of turning into a full-fledged surveillance society. The tremendous explosion in surveillance-enabling technologies, combined with the ongoing weakening in legal restraints that* *protect our privacy mean that we are drifting toward a surveillance society. The good news is that it can be stopped. Unfortunately, right now the big picture is grim.* —ACLU[9]

THE PATRIOT ACT

Fifteen 'sunset' provisions in the PATRIOT Act are set to expire at the end of 2005. One amendment, the "library provision" went before Congress in June. Despite President Bush's threat to veto, lawmakers, including 38 Republicans, voted 238 to 187 to overturn the provision, which previously allowed law enforcement officials to request and obtain information from libraries without obtaining a search warrant. Although inspectors still have the "right" to search library records, they must get a judge's approval first.

Attorney General Alberto Gonzales informed Congress in April that this provision has never been used to acquire information, although the American Library Association recently reported that over 200 requests for information were submitted since the PATRIOT Act was signed into law in October 2001.

The overturning of the library provision has been seen as a small victory in the fight to reclaim privacy rights. Rep. Saunders, who was responsible for almost successfully having the provision repealed last year, commented that "conservative groups have been joining progressive organizations to call for changes."[10]

THE MATRIX

The fight to the right for privacy continues to wage on with more successes, as the MATRIX program was officially shut down on April 15, 2005. The program, which consisted of 13 states—and only had four states remaining prior to its closure, received $12 million in funding from the Department of Justice and the Department of Homeland Security. By utilizing a system called FACTS (Factual Analysis Criminal Threat Solution), law enforcement officials from participating states were able to share information with one another and utilized this program as an investigative tool to help solve and prevent crimes. According to the Florida Department of Law Enforcement, "Between July 2003 and April 2005, there have been 1,866,202 queries to the FACTS application."[11] However, of these queries, only 2.6 percent involved terrorism or national security.

Although the MATRIX has been shut down, Florida law enforcement officials are pursuing continuing the program and rebuilding it. Officials have sent out a call for information from vendors beginning a competitive bidding process.

RFID TECHNOLOGY AND THE REAL ID ACT

On May 10, 2005, President Bush secretly signed into law the REAL ID Act, requiring states within the next three years to issue federally approved electronic identification cards. Attached as an amendment to an emergency spending bill funding troops in Afghanistan and Iraq, the REAL ID Act passed without the scrutiny and debate of Congress.

One of the main concerns of the electronic identification card is identity theft. The Act mandates the cards to have anti-counterfeiting measures, such as an electronically readable magnetic strip or RFID chip. Privacy advocates argue that RFID chips can be read from "unauthorized" scanners allowing third parties or the general public to gather and/or steal private information about an individual. Amidst growing concerns about identity theft, the REAL ID Act has given no consideration to this drawback.

Other privacy concerns regarding the electronic identification card is the use of information by third parties once they've scanned the cards and accessed the information. At this time, the Act does not specify what can be done with the information. A company or organization scanning your identification card could potentially sell your personal information if strict guidelines on what to do with the information are not mandated.

Inability to conform over the next three years will leave citizens and residents of the United States paralyzed. Identification cards that do not meet the federally mandated standards will not be accepted as identification for travel, opening a bank account, receiving social security checks, or participating in government benefits, among other things.

NOTES

1. *LiP Magazine.* http://www.lipmagazine.org/.
2. The *Washington Post* December 01, 1997, Final Edition.
3. http://en.wikipedia.org/wiki/Total_Information_Awareness.
4. Electronic Privacy Information Center http://www.epic.org/privacy/profiling/tia/. Information Awareness Office, See HR 2417.
5. Ibid.
6. Congressional Record: November 22,2003 pg.E2399.
   http://www.fas.org/irp/congress/2003_cr/h112203.html.
7. *LiP Magazine.* http://www.lipmagazine.org/.
8. *ABC News.* http://abcnews.go.com/Technology/Primetime/story.
9. http://www.aclu.org/Privacy/PrivacyMain.cfm.
10. http://bernie.house.gov/documents/articles/20050406114413.asp.
11. http://www.fdle.state.fl.us/press_releases/20050415_matrix_project.html.

5 U.S. Uses Tsunami to Military Advantage in Southeast Asia

Sources:

Jane's Foreign Report (*Jane's Defence*), February 15, 2005
Title: "U.S. Turns Tsunami into Military Strategy"

The Irish Times, February 8, 2005
Title: "U.S. Has Used Tsunami to Boost Aims in Stricken Area"
Author: Rahul Bedi

Inter Press Service, January, 18 2005
Title: "Bush Uses Tsunami Aid to Regain Foothold in Indonesia"
Author: Jim Lobe

Faculty Evaluator: Tony White, Ph. D., Craig Winston, Ph. D.
Student Researcher: Ned Patterson

The tragic and devastating power of 2004's post holiday tsunami was plastered across the cover of practically every newspaper around the world for the better part of a month. As the death toll rose by the thousands every day, countries struggled to keep pace with the rapidly increasing need for aid across the Indian Ocean Basin.

At the same time that U.S. aid was widely publicized domestically, our coinciding military motives were virtually ignored by the press. While supplying our aid (which when compared proportionately to that of other, less wealthy countries, was an insulting pittance), we simultaneously bolstered military alliances with regional powers in, and began expanding our bases throughout, the Indian Ocean region.

Long viewed as a highly strategic location for U.S. interests, our desire to curtail China's burgeoning economic and military might is contingent upon our control of this area. In the months following the tsunami, writes Rahul Bedi in *The Irish Times*, the U.S. revived the Utapao military base in Thailand it had used during the Vietnam War. Task force 536 is to be moved there to establish a forward positioning site for the U.S. Air Force.

During subsequent tsunami relief operations, the U.S. reactivated its military co-operation agreements with Thailand and the Visiting Forces Agreement with the Philippines. U.S. Navy also vessels utilized facilities in Singapore, keeping with previous treaties. Further, the U.S. marines and the navy arrived in Sri Lanka to bolster relief measures despite the tsunami-hit island's initial reluctance to permit their entry.

The U.S. also stepped up their survey of the Malacca Straits, over which China exercises considerable influence, and through which 90 percent of Japan's oil supplies pass. The United States has had trouble expanding its military influence in the region largely due to suspicions by Indonesia and Malaysia that the U.S. is disguising imperial aims under the goal of waging war against terror. The two countries have opposed an American plan to tighten security in the vital Malacca Straits shipping lanes, which might have involved U.S. troops stationed nearby.

Former Secretary of State Colin Powell declared that U.S. relief to the tsunami-affected region would assist the war against terror and introduce "American values to the region." The Bush Administration is also reviving its hopes of normalizing military ties with Indonesia, writes Jim Lobe for InterPress Service. The world's most populous Muslim nation, its strategically located archipelago, critical sea lanes, and historic distrust of China have made it an ideal partner for containing Beijing.

During a January 2005 visit to Jakarta, Deputy Defense Secretary Paul Wolfowitz told reporters, "I think if we're interested in military reform here, and certainly this Indonesian government is and our government is, I think we need to possibly reconsider a bit where we are at this point in history moving forward."

According to an article in the *Asheville Global Report*, the following month the U.S. State Department made a decision to renew the International Education and Military Training (IMET) program for Indonesia, despite considerable human rights issues.

According to Bedi, Washington has long wanted a navel presence in Trincomalee, eastern Sri Lanka, or alternatively in Galle, further south, to shorten the supply chain from its major regional military base in distant Diego Garcia, which the British Ocean Territory leased to the U.S. in 1966 for the length of fifty years. The use of these bases would ring China, giving the U.S. added control over that country's activities.

Diego Garcia's geostrategic location in the Indian Ocean and its full range of naval, military and communications facilities gives it a critical role supporting the U.S. Navy's forward presence in the North Arabian Sea and the Indian Ocean Region. However, because of the bases' remoteness and the fact that its lease from Britain expires in 2016, the U.S. seeks an alternative location in the region. "Clearly these new bases will strengthen Washington's military logistical support in the region," says Professor Anuradha Chenoy at Delhi's Jawaharlal Nehru University. She went on to emphasize that an alternative to the Diego Garcia base must be found soon, as the lease from Britain will soon expire.

Long before the tsunami struck, an article dated April 21, 2003, by Josy Joseph on Rediff.com explained that a classified report commissioned by the United States Department of Defense expresses a desire for access to Indian bases and military infrastructures. The United States Air Force specifically wants to establish bases in India. The report, entitled "Indo-U.S. Military Relations: Expectations and Perceptions," was distributed amongst high-ranking U.S. officials and a handful of senior members within the Indian government. It continues on about the Defense Department's desire to have "access closer to areas of instability."[1]

The report says, "American military officers are candid in their plans to eventually seek access to Indian bases and military infrastructure. India's strategic location in the centre of Asia, astride the frequently traveled Sea Lanes Of Communication (SLOC) linking the Middle East and East Asia, makes India particularly attractive to the U.S. military."

The report also quotes U.S. Lieutenant Generals as saying that the access to Indian bases would enable the U.S. military "to be able to touch the rest of the world" and to "respond rapidly to regional crisis." A South Asia Area Officer of the U.S. State Department has been quoted as saying, "India's strategic importance increases if existing U.S. relationships with Asia fail."

Post-tsunami U.S. actions in the Indian Ocean illustrate its intention to move this agenda forward sooner rather than later.

NOTE

1. Joseph, Josy; "Target Next: Indian Military Bases"; rediff.com, April 21, 2003; and Lobe, Jim; "Skepticism over renewed military ties with Indonesia"; *Asheville Global Report*, March 10–16, 2005.

6 The Real Oil-for-Food Scam

Sources:
Harper's Magazine, December 2004
Title: "The UN is Us: Exposing Saddam Hussein's Silent Partner"
Author: Joy Gordon
http://www.harpers.org/TheUNisUS.html

Independent/UK, December 12, 2004
Title: "The Oil for Food 'Scandal' is a Cynical Smokescreen"
Author: Scott Ritter
http://www.commondreams.org/views04/1212-23.htm

Faculty Evaluator: Robert McNamara, Ph. D.
Student Researcher: Deanna Murrell

The U.S. has accused UN officials of corruption in Iraq's oil for food program. According to Joy Gordon and Scott Ritter the charge was actually an attempt to disguise and cover up long term U.S. government complicity in this corruption. Ritter says, "this posturing is nothing more than a hypocritical charade, designed to shift attention away from the debacle of George Bush's self-made quagmire in Iraq, and legitimize the invasion of Iraq by using Iraqi corruption and not the now-missing weapons of mass destruction, as the excuse." Gordon arrives at the conclusion that, "perhaps it is unsurprising that today the only role its seems the United States expects the UN to play in the continuing drama of Iraq is that of scapegoat."

According to Gordon the charges laid by the U.S. accounting office are bogus. There is plenty of evidence of corruption in the "oil-for-food" program, but the trail of evidence leads not to the UN but to the U.S. "The fifteen members of the Security Council—of which the United States was by far the most influential—determined how income from oil proceeds would be handled, and what the funds could be used for." Contrary to popular understanding, the Security Council is not the same thing as the UN. It is part of it, but operates largely independently of the larger body. The UN's personnel "simply executed the program that was designed by the members of the Security Council."

The claim in the corporate media was that the UN allowed Saddam Hussein to steal billions of dollars from oil sales. If we look, as Gordon does, at who actually had control over the oil and who's hands held the money, a very different picture emerges. "If Hussain did indeed smuggle $6 billion worth of oil in the 'the richest rip off in world history,' he didn't do it with the complicity of the UN. He did it on the watch of the U.S. Navy." explains Gordon.

Every monetary transaction was approved by the U.S. through its dominant role on the Security Council. Ritter explains, "the Americans were able to authorize a $1 billion exemption concerning the export of Iraqi oil for Jordan, as well as legitimize the billion-dollar illegal oil smuggling trade over the Turkish border." In another instance, a Russian oil company "bought oil from Iraq under 'oil for food' at a heavy discount, and then sold it at full market value to primarily U.S. companies, splitting the difference evenly between [the Russian company] and the Iraqis. This U.S. sponsored deal resulted in profits of hundreds of millions of dollars for both the Russians and the Iraqis, outside the control of 'oil for food.' It has been estimated that 80 percent of the oil illegally smuggled out of Iraq under 'oil for food' ended up in the United States."

Not only were criminals enriched in this nefarious scheme, it also ended up sabotaging the original purpose of "oil for food." Gordon explains, "How Iraq sold its oil was also under scrutiny, and the United States did act on what it perceived to be skimming by Hussain in these deals. The solution that it enacted, however, succeeded in almost bankrupting the entire Oil for Food Program within months."

Harebrained Security Council policy not only succeeded in enriching the dishonest, it also virtually destroyed the program. According to Gordon, the U.S. and UK attempted to prevent kickbacks resulting from artificially low prices: "Instead of approving prices at the beginning of each sales period (usually a month), in accordance with normal commercial practices, the two allies would simply withhold their approval [of the price] until after the oil was sold—creating a bizarre scenario in which buyers had to sign contracts without knowing what the price would be." The result was "oil sales collapsed by forty percent, and along with them the funds for critical humanitarian imports."

What we have here, according to Gordon and Ritter, is a bare-faced attempt by criminals to shift blame to the innocent. Gordon concludes, "Little of the blame can credibly be laid at the feet of 'the UN bureaucracy.' Far more of the fault lies with policies and decisions of the Security Council in which the United States played a central role."

UPDATE BY JOY GORDON: The accusations against the Oil for Food Program have served as a springboard for general attacks on the credibility of the United Nations as a whole, as well as personal attacks on Kofi Annan. For the most part the mainstream media has seized on the accusations and repeated them, without doing any of the research that would give the discussion more integrity. For example, "the United Nations" is criticized for "its" failures, and the Secretary General is then blamed because these events "happened on his watch." What was not mentioned at all for the first year of media coverage is that "the UN" is made up of several different parts, and that the part that designed and oversaw the Oil for Food Program was the Security Council, whose decisions cannot be overridden or modified in any way by the Secretary General. Not only that, while the most vitriolic accusations against the UN have come from the United States, the U.S. is in fact the most dominant member of the Security Council. The U.S. agreed to all the decisions and procedures of the Oil for Food Program that are now being so harshly criticized as "failures of the United Nations."

The mainstream press, for the most part, has repeated that the Oil for Food Program lacked accountability, oversight, or transparency. What is most striking about this is that the elaborate structure of oversight that was in fact in place—and is never mentioned at all—is so easily available. It is on the program's web site in complete detail along with huge amounts of information, making the program in fact highly transparent. Yet the mainstream press coverage reflects none of this.

Last fall we saw the beginnings of some acknowledgement of the U.S. responsibility for Iraq's ongoing smuggling, as some Democrats introduced evidence in hearings that all three U.S. administrations knew of and supported Iraq's illicit trade with Jordan and Turkey, two key U.S. allies. The press picked that up, but little else.

Since my article came out, there has been a good deal of press coverage from public radio stations and from foreign press. In addition, I have testified twice before Congressional committees, where the members of Congress were incredulous to hear that in fact the program operated very differently than they had been told—even though the information I provided them was obvious, basic, publicly available, and easily accessible.

FOR ADDITIONAL INFORMATION:
Organizations actively addressing these issues include the UN Association and the UN Foundation.
Information about the accusations against the program can be found at the following sites: http://www.oilforfoodfacts.org/
UN web site on Oil for Food program: http://www.un.org/Depts/oip/
The Volcker Committee investigating the accusations: http://www.iic-offp.org/

7 Journalists Face Unprecedented Dangers to Life and Livelihood

Sources:
www.truthout.org, Feb. 28, 2005
Title: "Dead Messengers: How the U.S. Military Threatens Journalists"
Author: Steve Weissman
http://www.truthout.org/docs_2005/022405A.shtml

Title: "Media Repression in 'Liberated' Land"
InterPress Service, November 18, 2004
Author: Dahr Jamail
http://www.ipsnews.net/interna.asp?idnews=26333

Faculty Evaluator: Elizabeth Burch, Ph.D.
Student Researcher: Michelle Jesolva

According to the International Federation of Journalists (IFJ)[1], 2004 was the deadliest year for reporters since 1980, when records began to be kept. Over a 12-month span, 129 media workers were killed and 49 of those deaths occurred in the Iraqi conflict. According to independent journalist Dahr Jamail, journalists are increasingly being detained and threatened by the U.S.-installed interim government in Iraq. When the only safety for a reporter is being embedded with the U.S. military, the reported stories tend to have a positive spin. Non-embedded reporters suffer the great risk of being identified as enemy targets by the military.

The most blatant attack on journalists occurred the morning of April 8, 2004, when the Third Infantry fired on the Palestine Hotel in Baghdad killing cameramen Jose Couso and Taras Protsyuk and injuring three others. The hotel served as headquarters for some 100 reporters and other media workers. The Pentagon officials knew that the Palestine Hotel was full of journalists and had assured the Associated Press that the U.S. would not target the building. According to *Truthout*, the Army had refused to release the records of its investigation. The Committee to Protect Journalists, created in 1981 in order to protect colleagues abroad from governments and others who have no use for free and independent media, filed suit under the Freedom of Information Act to force the Army to release its results. The sanitized copy of the releasable results showed nothing more than a Commander inquiry.

Unsatisfied with the U.S. military's investigation, Reporters Without Borders, an international organization that works to improve the legal and physical safety of journalists worldwide, conducted their own investigation. They gathered evidence from journalists in the Palestine Hotel at the time of the attacks. These were eye witness accounts that the military neglected to include in their report. The Reporters Without Borders report also provided information disclosed by others embedded within the U.S. Army, including the U.S. military soldiers and officers directly involved in the attack. The report stated that the U.S. officials first lied about what had happened during the Palestine Hotel attack and then, in an official statement four months later, exonerated the U.S. Army from any mistake of error in judgment. The investigation found that the soldiers in the field did not know that the hotel was full of journalists. Olga Rodriguez, a journalist present at the Palestine Hotel during the attack, stated on KPFA's *Democracy Now!* that the soldiers and tanks were present at the hotel 36 hours before the firing and that they had even communicated with the soldiers.

There have been several other unusual journalist attacks, including:

➤ March 22, 2003: Terry Lloyd, a reporter for British TV station ITN, was killed when his convoy crossed into Iraq from Kuwait. French cameraman Frederic Nerac and Lebanese interpreter Hussein Osman, both in the convoy, disappeared at the same time.[2]

➤ June, 2003: According to Dahr Jamail, within days of the 'handover' of power to an interim Iraqi government in 2003, al-Jazeera had been accused of inaccurate reporting and was banned for one month from reporting out of Iraq. The ban was later extended to "indefinitely" and the interim government announced that any al-Jazeera journalist found reporting in Iraq would be detained. Corentin Fleury, a French freelance photographer, and his interpreter Bahktiyar Abdulla Hadad, were detained by the U.S. military when they were leaving Fallujah before the siege of the city began. They were both held in a military detention facility outside of the city and were questioned about the photos that were taken of bomb-stricken Fallujah. Fleury was released after five days but his interpreter, Bahktiyar Abdulla Hadad, remained.

➤ April 8, 2004: The same day of the attack on the Palestine Hotel, *Truthout* writes, the U.S. bombed the Baghdad offices of Abu Dhabi TV and Al-Jazeera while they were preparing to broadcast, killing Al-Jazeera correspondent Tariq Ayyoub. August 17, 2004: Mazen Dana was killed while filming (with permission) a prison, guarded by the U.S. military in a Baghdad suburb. According to *Truthout's* Steve Weissman, the Pentagon issued a statement one month later claiming that the troops had acted within the rules of engagement.[3]

> March 4, 2005: Nicola Calipari, one of Italyís highest ranking intelligence officials, was shot dead by U.S. troops. He was driving with Italian journalist Guiliana Sgrena, who had just been released from captivity and was on her way to Baghdad's airport. Sgrena survived the attack. She stated in an interview with Amy Goodman on KPFA's *Democracy Now!* that the troops "shot at us without any advertising, any intention, any attempt to stop us before" and they appeared to have shot the back of the car.[4]

In all cases, little investigation has been conducted, no findings have been released and all soldiers involved have been exonerated.

At the World Economic Forum, on a panel titled: "Will Democracy Survive the Media?," Eason Jordan, a CNN news chief, commented that the U.S. commanders encourage hostility toward the media and fail to protect journalists, especially those who choose not to embed themselves under military control. According to *Truthout,* during a discussion about the number of journalists killed during the Iraq war, Jordan stated that he knew of 12 journalists who had not only been killed by U.S. troops, but had been targeted. Jordan also insisted that U.S. soldiers had deliberately shot at journalists. After the forum, Jordan recanted the statements and was forced to resign his job of 23 years at CNN.

As a matter of military doctrine, the U.S. military dominates, at all costs, every element of battle, including our perception of what they do. The need for control leads the Pentagon to urge journalists to embed themselves within the military, where they can go where they are told and film and tell stories only from a pro-American point of view. The Pentagon offers embedded journalists a great deal of protection. As the Pentagon sees it, non-embedded eyes and ears do not have any military significance, and unless Congress and the American people stop them, the military will continue to target independent journalists. Admirals and generals see the world one way, reporters another; the clash leads to the deaths of too many journalists.

UPDATE BY STEVE WEISSMAN: When *Truthout* boss Marc Ash asked me earlier this year to look into the Pentagon's killing of journalists, many reporters believed that the military was purposely targeting them. But, as I quickly found, the crime was more systemic and in many ways worse. As far as anyone has yet proved, no commanding officer ever ordered a subordinate to fire on journalists as such. Not at Baghdad's Palestine Hotel in April 2003. Not at the Baghdad checkpoint where soldiers wounded Italian journalist Giuliana Sgrena and killed her Secret Service protector in March 2005. Andnot anywhere else in Iraq or Afghanistan.

How, then, did the U.S. military end up killing journalists?

It started with a simple decision—the Pentagon's absolute refusal to take any responsibility for the lives of journalists who chose to work independently rather than embed themselves in a British or American military unit. Despite repeated requests from Reuters and other major news organizations, Pentagon officials still refuse to take the steps needed to reduce the threat to independent journalists:

1. The military must be forced to respect the work that independent journalists do, protect them where possible, and train soldiers to recognize the obvious differences between rocket launchers and TV cameras.
2. Commanders need to pass on information about the whereabouts of journalists with a direct order not to shoot at them.
3. When soldiers do kill journalists, the Pentagon needs to hold them responsible, something that no military investigation has yet done.
4. When the military tries to forcibly exclude journalists and otherwise prevent "hostile information" about its operations, such as its destruction of Falujah, Congress and the media need to step in and force the Pentagon to back off.

One other problem needs urgent attention. Military intelligence regularly monitors the uplink equipment that reporters use to transmit their stories and communicate by satellite phone. But, as the BBC's Nik Gowing discovered, the electronic intelligence mavens make no effort to distinguish between journalistic communications and those of enemy forces. All the sensing devices do is look for electronic traffic between the monitored uplinks and known enemies.

In Gowing's view, this led the Americans to order a rocket attack on the Kabul office of the Arab broadcaster Al Jazeera, whose journalists kept regular contact with the Taliban as part of their journalistic coverage.

To date, neither Congress nor the military have done what they need to do to protect unembedded journalists and the information they provide. More shamefully, the mass media continues to underplay the story.

But, for those who want it, reliable information is easily available, either from the Committee to Protect Journalists, Reporters without Borders, or the International Federation of Journalists.

NOTES

1. www.ifj.org.
2. "Missing ITN Crew May Have Come Under 'Friendly Fire,'" www.guardian.co.uk/Iraq/Story/0,2763,919832,00.html, March 23, 2003.
3. *Democracy Now!* March 23, 2005, Wounded Spanish Journalist Olga Rodriguez describes the U.S. Attack on the Palestine Hotel that killed two of her colleagues.
4. *Democracy Now!* April 27, 2005, Giuliana Sgrena Blasts U.S. Cover Up, Calls for U.S. and Italy to leave Iraq.

8 Iraqi Farmers Threatened By Bremer's Mandates

Sources:
Grain, October 2004
Title: "Iraq's New Patent Law: A Declaration of War against Farmers"
Authors: Focus on the Global South and GRAIN

TomPaine.com, October 26, 2004
Title: "Adventure Capitalism"
Author: Greg Palast

The Ecologist, February 4, 2005
Title: "U.S. Seeking to Totally Re-engineer Iraqi Traditional Farming System into a U.S.-style Corporate Agribusiness"
Author: Jeremy Smith

Faculty Evaluator: John Wingard, Ph. D.
Student Researcher: Cary Barker

In his article "Adventure Capitalism," Greg Palast exposes the contents of a secret plan for "imposing a new regime of low taxes on big business, and quick sales of Iraq's banks and bridges—in fact, 'ALL state enterprises'—to foreign operators." This economy makeover plan, he claims, "goes boldly where no invasion plan has gone before."

This highly detailed program, which began years before the tanks rolled, outlines the small print of doing business under occupation. One of the goals is to impose intellectual property laws favorable to multinationals. Palast calls this "history's first military assault plan appended to a program for toughening the target nation's copyright laws."

It also turns out that those of us who may have thought it was all about the oil were mostly right. "The plan makes it clear that—even if we didn't go in for the oil—we certainly won't leave without it."

In an interview with Palast, Grover Norquist, the " *capo di capi* of the lobbyist army of the right," makes the plans even more clear when he responds, "The right to trade, property rights, these things are not to be determined by some democratic election." No, these things were to be determined by the Coalition Provisional Authority, the interim government lead by the U.S.

Before he left his position, CPA administrator Paul Bremer, "the leader of the Coalition Provisional Authority issued exactly 100 orders that remade Iraq in the image of the Economy Plan." These orders effectively changed Iraqi law.

A good example of this business invasion involves agriculture. The details of this part of the "market make-over" are laid out in the *Grain* website article called "Iraq's new Patent Law: a declaration of war against farmers."

"Order 81" of the 100 is entitled "Patent, Industrial Design, Undisclosed Information, Integrated Circuits and Plant Variety." According to *Grain* staff writers, this order "made it illegal for Iraqi farmers to re-use seeds harvested from new varieties registered under the law." Plant Variety Protection (PVP)is the tool used for defining which seeds are re-useable and which are not. PVP "is an intellectual property right or a kind of patent for plant varieties which gives an exclusive monopoly right on planting material to a plant breeder who claims to have discovered or developed a new variety. So the "protection" in PVP has nothing to do with conservation, but refers to safeguarding of the commercial interests of private breeders (usually large corporations) claiming to have created the new plants."

Dovetailing with this order is a plan to "re-educate farmers" in order to increase their production. As part of a $107 million "project" facilitated by Texas A&M, farmers will be given equipment and new high-yielding PVP protected seeds. Jeremy Smith from the *Ecologist* points out that, "After one year, farmers will see soaring production levels. Many will be only too willing to abandon their old ways in favor of the new technologies. Out will go traditional methods. In will come imported American seeds." Then, based on the new patent laws, "any 'client' (or 'farmer' as they were once known) wishing to grow one of their seeds, 'pays a licensing fee for each variety'."

Smith explains that "Under the guise of helping Iraq back on its feet, the U.S. setting out to re-engineer the country's traditional farming system into a U.S.-style corporate agribusiness." In that traditional system, "97 percent of Iraqi farmers used their own saved seed or bought seed from local markets." He continues, "Unfortunately, this vital heritage and knowledge base is now believed lost, the victim of the current campaign and the many years of conflict that preceded it."

Of course, this project will also introduce "new chemicals—pesticides, herbicides, fungicides, all sold to the Iraqis by corporations such as Monsanto, Cargill and Dow."

As *Grain* staff writers point out, "over the past decade, many countries of the South have been compelled to adopt seed patent laws through bilateral treaties" with the U.S. The Iraqi situation, however, is different in that "the adoption of the patent law was not part of negotiations between sovereign countries. Nor did a sovereign law-making body enact it as reflecting the will of the Iraqi people." Essentially, the U.S. has reneged on its promise of freedom for the Iraqi people. The actions of the U.S. clearly show that the will of the Iraqi people is not relevant. Paul Bremer's 100 orders make sure it will stay that way. *Grain* argues "Iraq's freedom and sovereignty will remain questionable for as long as Iraqis do not have control over what they sow, grow, reap and eat." Palast says poignantly, "The free market paradise in Iraq is not free."

UPDATE BY GREG PALAST: In February 2003, White House spokesman Ari Fleisher announced the preparations for "Operation Iraqi Liberation"—O.I.L.

I can't make these things up.

I'm not one of the those people who believes George Bush led us into Iraq for the oil but, from the documents I've obtained, it's clear that we sure as hell aren't leaving without it.

At BBC Television *Newsnight*, which has granted me journalistic asylum from the commercially-crazed madhouse of the American news market, we ran Fleisher's announcement of operation O.I.L. (later corrected to Operation Iraqi Freedom—OIF!). More importantly, we ran a series of stories—which I also developed for *Harper's Magazine* in the USA—on the pre-invasion plans to slice up and sell off Iraq's assets, "especially the oil," in the terms of one State Department secret document.

After we got our hands on the confidential document to "Move Iraq's Economy Forward"—i.e. sell off its oil—we at BBC put General Jay Garner on the air. Garner, whom the president appointed as viceroy over the newly-conquered Iraq, confirmed the plan to sell off Iraq's oil—and his refusal to carry out the deed. U.S. Defense Secretary Donald Rumsfeld fired him and smeared him for his dissent. This was big, big news in Europe where I reported it—but in the U.S. the story was buried.

We later discovered that the plan to sell off Iraq's oil was replaced by another confidential plan. This one, 323 pages long and literally written by oil industry consultants, was obtained by BBC and *Harper's* after a protracted legal war with the State Department. We discovered, interestingly, that this industry plan to create a state oil company favorable to OPEC was first conceived in February 2001. In other words, invasion was in the works, including stratagems for controlling Iraq's oil, within week's of George Bush's first inauguration and well before the September 11 attack.

The discovery of this plan for Iraq's oil, received exactly zero coverage by the U.S. "mainstream" press. Only *Harper's Magazine* gave it full play along with those wonderful internet sites (Buzzflash, Guerrilla News, WorkingFor-Change, CommonDreams, Alternet and more) that cussedly insist on printing news from abroad not approved by the Powers That Be.

Bless them. They, Project Censored, and *Harper's*, have my deepest thanks for bringing my words back home.

Want to see the television you're not supposed to see? The British Broadcasting Corporation has graciously kept my reports available as Internet video archives. Go to www.GregPalast.com and click on the "Watch BBC" buttons for the stories effectively censored by the U.S. news lords and the Bush Administration's chorus of journalist castrati.

Finally, I must give special thanks to our team's special investigator on Iraq, Leni von Eckardt, to brilliant BBC producer Meirion Jones, to the stalwart editors of *Harper's Magazine* who withstood legal threats to publish the story, and to TomPaine.com, which has always provided a refuge for the best investigative reporting American newspapers won't print.

9 Iran's New Oil Trade System Challenges U.S. Currency

Source:
GlobalResearch.ca, October 27
Title: "Iran Next U.S. Target"
Author: William Clark

Faculty Evaluator: Phil Beard, Ph. D.
Student Researcher: Brian Miller

The U.S. media tells us that Iran may be the next target of U.S. aggression. The anticipated excuse is Iran's alleged nuclear weapons program. William

Clark tells us that economic reasons may have more to do with U.S. concerns over Iran than any weapons of mass destruction.

In mid-2003 Iran broke from traditional and began accepting eurodollars as payment for it oil exports from its E.U. and Asian customers. Saddam Hussein attempted a similar bold step back in 2000 and was met with a devastating reaction from the U.S. Iraq now has no choice about using U.S. dollars for oil sales (*Censored 2004* #19). However, Iran's plan to open an international oil exchange marker for trading oil in the euro currency is a much larger threat to U.S. dollar supremacy than Iraq's switch to euros.

While the dollar is still the standard currency for trading international oil sales, in 2006 Iran intends to set up an oil exchange (or bourse) that would facilitate global trading of oil between industrialized and developing countries by *pricing* sales in the euro, or "petroeuro." To this end, they are creating a euro-denominated Internet-based oil exchange system for global oil sales. This is a direct challenge to U.S. dollar supremacy in the global oil market. It is widely speculated that the U.S. dollar has been inflated for some time now because the monopoly position of "petrodollars" in oil trades. With the level of national debt, the value of dollar has been held artificially high compared to other currencies.

The vast majority of the world's oil is traded on the New York NYMEX (Mercantile Exchange) and the London IPE (International Petroleum Exchange), and, as mentioned by Clark, both exchanges are owned by U.S. corporations. Both of these oil exchanges transact oil trades in U.S. currency. Iran's plan to create a new oil exchange would facilitate trading oil on the world market in euros. The euro has become a somewhat stronger and more stable trading medium than the U.S. dollar in recent years. Perhaps this is why Russia, Venezuela, and some members of OPEC have expressed interest in moving towards a petroeuro system for oil transactions. Without a doubt, a successful Iranian oil bourse may create momentum for other industrialized countries to stop exchanging their own currencies for petrodollars in order to buy oil. A shift away from U.S. dollars to euros in the oil market would cause the demand for petrodollars to drop, perhaps causing the value of the dollar to plummet. A precipitous drop in the value of the U.S. dollar would undermine the U.S. position as a world economic leader.

China is a major exporter to the United States, and its trade surplus with the U.S. means that China has become the world's second largest holder of U.S. currency reserves (Japan is the largest holder with $800 billion, and China holds over $600 billion in T-bills). China would lose enormously if they were still holding vast amounts of U.S. currency when the dollar collapsed and assumed a more realistic value. Maintaining the U.S. as a market for their goods is a pre-eminent goal of Chinese financial policy, but they are increasingly dependent on Iran for their vital oil and gas imports. The Chinese government is careful to maintain the value of the yuan linked with the U.S. dollar (8.28 yuan to 1 dollar). This artificial linking makes them, effectively, one currency. But the Chinese government has indicated interest in de-linking the dollar-yuan arrangement, which could result in an immediate fall in the dollar. More worrisome is the potentiality of China to abandon its ongoing prolific purchase of U.S. Treasuries/debt—should they become displeased with U.S. policies towards Iran.

Unstable situations cannot be expected to remain static. It is reasonable to expect that the Chinese are hedging their bets. It is unreasonable to expect that they plan to be left holding devalued dollars after a sudden decline in their value. It is possible that the artificial situation could continue for some time, but this will be due largely because the Chinese want it that way. Regardless, China seems to be in the process of unloading some of its U.S. dollar reserves in the world market to purchase oil reserves, and most recently attempted to buy Unocal, a California-based oil company.

The irony is that apparent U.S. plans to invade Iran put pressure on the Chinese to abandon their support of the dollar. Clark warns that "a unilateral U.S. military strike on Iran would further isolate the U.S. government, and it is conceivable that such an overt action could provoke other industrialized nations to abandon the dollar *en masse*." Perhaps the U.S. planners think that they can corner the market in oil militarily. But from Clarks point of view, "a U.S. intervention in Iran is likely to prove disastrous for the United States, making matters much worse regarding international terrorism, not to mention potential adverse effects on the U.S. economy." The more likely outcome of an Iran invasion would be that, just as in Iraq, Iranian oil exports would dry up, regardless of what currency they are denominated in, and China would be compelled to abandon the dollar and buy oil from Russia—likely in euros. The conclusion is that U.S. leaders seem to have no idea what they are doing. Clark points out that, "World oil production is now flat out, and a major interruption would escalate oil prices to a level that would set off a global depression."

UPDATE BY WILLIAM CLARK: Following the completion of my essay in October 2004, three important stories appeared that dramatically raised the geopolitical stakes for the Bush Administration. First, on October 28, 2004, Iran and China signed a huge oil and gas trade agreement (valued between $70 and $100 billion dollars.)[1] It should also be noted that China currently receives 13 percent of its oil imports from Iran. The Chinese government effectively drew a "line in the sand" around Iran when it signed this huge oil and gas deal. Despite desires by U.S. elites to enforce petrodollar hegemony by force, the geopolitical risks of a U.S. attack on Iran's nuclear facilities would surely create a serious crisis between Washington and Beijing.

An article that addressed some of the strategic risks appeared in the December 2004 edition of the *Atlantic Monthly*.[2] This story by James Fallows outlined the military war games against Iran that were conducted during the summer and autumn of 2004. These war-gaming sessions were led by Colonel Sam Gardiner, a retired Air Force colonel who for more than two decades ran war games at the National War College and other military institutions. Each scenario led to a dangerous escalation in both Iran and Iraq. Indeed, Col. Gardiner summarized the war games with the following conclusion, "After all this effort, I am left with two simple sentences for policymakers: *You have no military solution for the issues of Iran. And you have to make diplomacy work.*"[3]

The third and final news item that revealed the Bush Administration's intent to attack Iran was provided by investigative reporter Seymour Hersh. The January 2005 issue of *The New Yorker* ("The Coming Wars") included interviews with high-level U.S. intelligence sources who repeatedly told Hersh that Iran was indeed the next strategic target.[4] However, as a permanent member of the UN Security Council, China will likely veto any U.S. resolution calling for military action against Iran. A unilateral military strike on Iran would isolate the U.S. government in the eyes of the world community, and it is conceivable that such an overt action could provoke other industrialized nations to abandon the dollar in droves. I refer to this in my book as the "rogue nation hypothesis."

While central bankers throughout the world community would be extremely reluctant to "dump the dollar," the reasons for any such drastic reaction are likely straightforward from their perspective—the global community is *dependent* on the oil and gas energy supplies found in the Persian Gulf. Numerous oil geologists are warning that global oil production is now running "flat out." Hence, any such efforts by the international community that resulted in a dollar currency crisis would be undertaken—not to cripple the U.S. dollar and economy as punishment towards the American *people per se*—but rather to thwart further unilateral *warfare* and its potentially destructive effects on the critical oil production and shipping infrastructure in the Persian Gulf. Barring a U.S. attack, it appears imminent that

Iran's euro-denominated oil bourse will open in March, 2006.[5] Logically, the most appropriate U.S. strategy is compromise with the E.U. and OPEC towards a dual-currency system for international oil trades.

FOR ADDITIONAL INFORMATION: Readers interested in learning more about the dollar/euro oil currency conflict and the upcoming geological phenomenon referred to as Peak Oil can read William Clark's new book, *Petrodollar Warfare: Oil, Iraq and the Future of the Dollar*. Available from New Society Publishers: www.newsociety.com, www.amazon.com or from your local book store.

NOTES

1. "China, Iran sign biggest oil & gas deal," *China Daily*, October 31, 2004. http://www.chinadaily.com.cn/english/doc/2004-10/31/content_387140.htm.
2. James Fallows, "Will Iran be Next?," *Atlantic Monthly*, December 2004, pgs. 97-110.
3. James Fallows, ibid.
4. Seymour Hersh, "The Coming Wars," *The New Yorker*, January 24th-31st issue, 2005, pgs. 40-47. Posted online January 17, 2005. Online: http://www.newyorker.com/fact/content/?050124fa_fact
5. "Oil bourse closer to reality," IranMania.com, December 28, 2004. Online: http://www.iranmania.com/News/ArticleView/Default.asp?ArchiveNews=Yes&NewsCode=28176&NewsKind=BusinessEconomy.

10 | Mountaintop Removal Threatens Ecosystem and Economy

Source:
Earthfirst! Nov-Dec 2004
Title: "See You in the Mountains: Katuah Earth First! Confronts Mountaintop Removal"
Author: John Conner

Faculty Evaluator: Ervand Peterson, Ph. D.
Student Researcher: Angela Sciortino

Mountaintop removal is a new form of coal mining in which companies dynamite the tops of mountains to collect the coal underneath. Multiple peaks are blown off and dumped onto highland watersheds, destroying entire mountain ranges. More than 1,000 miles of streams have been destroyed by this practice in West Virginia alone. Mountain top removal endangers and destroys entire communities with massive sediment dams and non-stop explosions.

According to Fred Mooney, an active member of the Mountain Faction of Katuah Earth First!, "MTR is an ecocidal mining practice in which greedy coal companies use millions of pounds of dynamite a day (three million pounds a day in the southwest Virginia alone) to blow up entire mountain ranges in order to extract a small amount of coal." He goes on to say that "Then as if that wasn't bad enough, they dump the waste into valleys and riverbeds. The combination of these elements effectively kills everything in the ecosystems."

Most states are responsible for permitting and regulating mining operations under the Surface Mining Control Act. Now MTR is trying to break into Tennessee, specifically Zeb Mountain in the northeast. Because Tennessee did such a poor job in the '70s, the state renounced control, and all mining is now regulated under the federal Office of Surface Mining. This makes Tennessee unique because activists have recourse in the federal courts to stop mountaintop removal.

The coal industry has coined many less menacing names for mountaintop removal, such as cross range mining, surface mining and others. But regardless of the euphemism, MTR remains among the most pernicious forms of mining ever conceived. Blasting mountain tops with dynamite is cheaper than hiring miners who belong to a union. More than 40,000 have been lost to MTR in West Virginia alone.

Ninety-three new coal plants are being planned for construction throughout the U.S. Demand for coal will increase as these new facilities are completed. Oil is starting to run out and there are no concrete plans for a transition to renewable resources such as wind and solar energy. Coal companies therefore will be well-positioned to capitalize on their growing market. Katuah Earth First! (KEF!) is one of several groups resisting MTR.

The coal taken from Zeb Mountain is being burned by the Tennessee Valley Authority, and continues to cause environmental damage. KEF! wants to raise awareness and direct attention to the perpetrators—TVA and the Office of Surface Mining (OSM). KEF! emphasized that "the issue of mountain top removal is not just a local one. It is intertwined with many global issues such as corporate domination of communities, the homogenization of local cultures and the over consumption of our wasteful society."

Four federal agencies that review applications for coal mines have entered an agreement that would give state governments an option that could speed up the process. The Army Corps of Engineers, Environmental Protection Agency, Fish and Wildlife Service and Office of Surface Mining said that the agreement was intended to streamline the procedures companies go through when applying for permits to start surface coal mines, including those that remove entire mountaintops to unearth coal.[1]

Environmental groups are beginning to challenge these policies in federal district court. The current program allows the Army Corps of Engineers to issue a general permit for a category of activities under the Clean Water Act if they "will cause only minimal adverse environmental effects" according to federal regulation. Coal companies then also must seek individual "authorizations" from the Corps for the projects for which they have received a general permit.[2]

According to the Bush Administration, the federal judge who blocked the streamline permitting of new mountaintop removal coal mines has overstepped his authority. Lawyers for the Army Corps of Engineers asked a federal appeals court to overturn the July 2004 ruling by U.S. District Judge Joseph R. Goodwin. Industry lawyers criticized Goodwin's decision as the "latest unwarranted and impermissible dismantling" of mountaintop removal regulations by federal judges in Southern West Virginia.[3]

UPDATE BY JOHN CONNER: The destructions of highland watersheds are a crime against the very future. The Appalachian Mountains are some of the most diverse in the world. Areas incredibly rich in biodiversity are being turned into the biological equivalent of parking lots. It is the final solution for 200 million-year-old mountains. Since dynamite is cheaper than people, MTR has broken the back of the mining unions in West Virginia, massive sediment dams threaten to bury entire communities, water tables are destroyed, and wells dry up. It is a form of cultural genocide driving a mountain people from their hills—then destroying the hills themselves.

There has been a direct impact on Marsh Fork Elementary, where a massive sediment dam looms above the elementary school. Over 18 people have been arrested for non-violent civil disobedience trying to protect the children of that school. Additionally, Mountain Justice Summer has begun a campaign modeled on Redwood and Mississippi Summers, where folks from all over North America have come to our region to help us defend our mountains.

When the Martin County coal impoundment burst, it released more than 20 times the waste volume into a community than the Exxon Valdez spill— yet the coal industry successfully suppressed the story. The coal industry is incredibly powerful, and there exists a glass ceiling on how far our stories go. The story of the folks committing civil disobedience for the first time in history in West Virginia to resist Mountain Top Removal was placed on the AP— but virtually no outlets outside of West Virginia picked it up.

People can get more information on this issue at mountainjusticesummer.org.

This site has everything—links, pictures, and state-by-state activities. From there you can sign yourself up for our electronic newsletter and find out what is going on in all the states under attack by Mountain Top Removal.

NOTES

1. *Inside Energy with Federal lands*, February 7, 2005,"Environmentalists sue to block process for Ky. Mountaintop mining operations."
2. Associated Press, February 11, 2005, "Federal agencies will work together to speed up mining permits."
3. *Charleston Gazette* (West Virginia), March 22, 2005, Tuesday, "Bush, Industry seek reversal of mining ruling."

Mandatory Mental Screening Program Usurps Parental Rights

Sources:
Asheville Global Report (British Medical Journal),No. 284, June 24-30, 2004
Title: "Bush Plans To Screen Whole U.S. Population For Mental Illness"
Author: Jeanne Lenzer
http://www.agrnews.org/issues/284/#2
Truth News, September 13,2004
Title: "Forcing Kids Into a Mental Health Ghetto"
Congressman Ron Paul
http://www.truthnews.net/world/2004090078.htm

Faculty Evaluator: David Van Nuys Ph.D.
Student Researchers: John Ferritto, Matt Johnson

In April of 2002, President Bush appointed a 22 member commission called the President's New Freedom Commission on Mental Health in order to "identify policies that could be implemented by Federal, State and local governments to maximize the utility of existing resources, improve coordination of treatments and services, and promote successful community integration for adults with a serious mental illness and children with a serious emotional disturbance."[1] Members of this commission include physicians in the mental health field and at least one (Robert N. Postlethwait) former employee of pharmaceutical giant Ely Lilly and Co.

In July of 2003 the commission published the results of their study. They found that mental health disorders often go undiagnosed and recommended to the President that there should be more comprehensive screening for mental illnesses for people of all ages, including pre-school age children. In accordance with their findings, the commission recommended that schools were in a "key position" to screen the 52 million students and 6 million adult employees of our nation's schools.[2]

The commission also recommended linking the screenings with treatment and support. They recommended using the Texas Medication Algorithm Project (TMAP) as a model treatment system.[3] TMAP, which was implemented in Texas' publicly funded mental health care system while George W. Bush was governor of Texas,[4] is a disease management program that aids physicians in prescribing drugs to patients based on clinical history, background, symptoms, and previous results. It was the first program in the United States aimed at establishing medication guidelines for treating mental health illnesses.[5] Basically, it is an algorithm that recommends specific drugs which should be used to treat specific diseases. Funding for TMAP was provided by a Robert Wood-Johnson Grant as well as several major drug companies. The project began in 1995 as an alliance of individuals from pharmaceutical companies, the University of Texas, and the mental health and corrections systems of Texas.[6]

Critics of mental health screening and TMAP claim that it is a payoff to Pharmaceutical companies. Many cite Allen Jones, a former employee of the Pennsylvania Office of the Inspector General. He was fired when he revealed that many key officials who have influence over the medication plan in his state received monetary perks and benefits from pharmaceutical companies, which benefited from their drugs being in the medication algorithm. TMAP also promotes the use of newer, more expensive anti-psychotic drugs. Results of studies conducted in the United States and Great Britain found that using the older, more established anti-psychotic drugs as a front line treatment rather than the newer experimental drugs makes more sense. Under TMAP, the Ely Lilly drug olanzapine, a new atypical antipsychotic drug, is used as a first line treatment rather than a more typical anti-psychotic medication. Perhaps it is because Ely Lilly has several ties to the Bush family, where George Bush Sr. was a member of the board of directors. George W. Bush also appointed Ely Lilly C.E.O. Sidney Taurel to a seat on the Homeland Security Council. Of Ely Lilly's $1.6 million political contributions in 2000, 82 percent went to Republicans and George W. Bush.[7]

In November of 2004, Congress appropriated $20 million[8] to implement the findings of the New Freedom Commission on Mental Health. This would include mandatory screening by schools for mental health illnesses. Congressman Ron Paul, R-Texas introduced an amendment to the appropriations bills which would withhold funding for mandatory mental health screenings and require parental consent and notification. His amendment, however, was voted down by a wide margin (95-315 in the House of Representatives).[9] Paul, a doctor and long-time member of the American Association of Physicians and Surgeons (AAPS) states, "At issue is the fundamental right of parents to decide what medical treatment is appropriate for their children. The notion of federal bureaucrats ordering potentially millions of youngsters to take psychotropic drugs like Ritalin strikes an emotional chord with American parents." Paul says the allegation "that we have a nation of children with undiagnosed mental disorders crying out for treatment is patently false," and warns that mental health screening could be used to label children whose attitudes, religious beliefs, and political views conflict with established doctrine. Paul further warns that an obvious major beneficiary of this legislation is the pharmaceutical industry. The AAPS has decried this legislation, which they say will lead to mandatory psychological testing of every child in America without parental consent, and "heap even more coercive pressure on parents to medicate children with potentially dangerous side effects."

UPDATE BY JEANNE LENZER: Whether it's the pills we take or the oil we use, it would be reassuring to know that the information used to develop new medicines or to utilize natural resources wisely is based on science—not corporate spin.

But blandishments from Big Pharma to politicians and doctors have a profound effect on health care in the U.S., making medical research closer to propaganda than science at times.

One way drug companies, in collusion with doctors, increase their market share is to expand the definition of diseases. When diagnostic criteria were liberalized for attention deficit disorder in 1991, the number of children diagnosed jumped by about 60 percent.

The American Psychiatric Association (APA) acknowledged in the July 2004 issue of *Advocacy News* that, "The *BMJ* story has gained some traction in derivative reports on the Internet." But, they boasted, "mainstream media have not touched the story, in part thanks to APA's work, for which the [Bush] Administration is appreciative."[10]

The APA's boast is curious. The article was the most downloaded article in the history of the *BMJ*. It clearly struck a nerve with a public wary of doctors and politicians whose pockets are lined with drug company money.

Given the interest in the *BMJ* story, it would seem that the APA, instead of attempting to keep the story out of the mainstream media, would be anxious to counter the widely circulated statements in the article. It would also seem that the mainstream press could provide the Administration and the APA the best possible vehicle to counter these supposed factual errors in the *BMJ* article.

But, the facts might prove difficult to square with the public. More than one in every 100 *toddlers and preschoolers* in the United States are on powerful psychiatric drugs, such as Ritalin and Prozac, according to a study published in the February 2000 issue of the *Journal of the American Medical Association*.

Joseph T. Coyle, M.D., wrote in an accompanying editorial, "It appears that behaviorally disturbed children are now increasingly subjected to quick and inexpensive pharmacologic fixes, as opposed to informed mutimodal therapy." He concluded, "These disturbing prescription practices suggest a growing crisis in mental health services to children and demand more thorough investigation."

But instead of issuing warnings about overmedication or inappropriate prescribing, the experts on the New Freedom Commission warn ominously that *too few* children are receiving treatment for mental illness. They cite escalating numbers of toddlers expelled from daycare as evidence of potentially serious psychological problems—problems to be diagnosed and cured with mental health screening and pills. Social and economic reasons for the rise in kiddie expulsions are left unexamined.

As bad as this is for those put on drugs and labeled "mentally ill," the far bigger concern is the creation of a disease for every drug, a situation made possible by the hand-in-glove relationship between industry and the government.

NOTES

1. http://www.mentalhealthcommission.gov/.
2. http://www.worldnetdaily.com/news/article.asp?ARTICLE_ID=39078.
3. http://www.worldnetdaily.com/news/article.asp?ARTICLE_ID=39078.
4. http://www.worldnetdaily.com/news/article.asp?ARTICLE_ID=39078.
5. http://www.news-medical.net/?id=3084.
6. http://www.worldnetdaily.com/news/article.asp?ARTICLE_ID=39078.
7. http://www.worldnetdaily.com/news/article.asp?ARTICLE_ID=39078.
8. http://www.truthnews.net/world/2004090078.htm.
9. http://www.worldnetdaily.com/news/article.asp?ARTICLE_ID=41606.
10. See Medicating Aliah: http://www.motherjones.com/news/feature/2005/05/medicating_aliah.html.

Alliance for Human Rights Protection "http://www.ahrp.org" www.ahrp.org
http://www.psych.org/join_apa/mb/newsletters/advocacy/AdvNewsJuly2004.htm#21.

12 Military in Iraq Contracts Human Rights Violators

Sources:

Mother Jones, November/December 2004
Title: "Dirty Warriors: How South African Hitmen, Serbian Paramilitaries, and Other Human Rights Violators Became Guns for Hire for Military Contractors in Iraq"
Author: Barry Yeoman

www.corpwatch.org, March 7, 2005
Title: "Intelligence, Inc."
Author: Pratap Chatterjee

www.law.com, May 11, 2004
Title: "Untested Law Key in Iraqi Abuse Scandal"
Author: Jonathan Groner

Faculty Evaluator: Rick Williams, JD
Student Researcher: Danielle Hallstein

The United States government is contracting private firms to recruit, hire, and train civilians to perform duties normally done by military personnel. These corporate employees are sent to fill empty positions as prison guards, military police, and interrogators at United States military bases worldwide, including Iraq, Afghanistan, and Cuba. Independent of the United States military, these employees are not held accountable by military law. Many of the recruits are citizens with prior experience as policemen or soldiers. However, a number of the employees have backgrounds as mercenaries and soldiers who fought for repressive regimes throughout the world, such as in South Africa, Chile, and Yugoslavia. Employees from some of these firms have recently been indicated in prisoner abuse at the Abu Ghraib prison in Iraq.

The Pentagon claims that it can no longer fight the war on terror without enlisting the help of private contractors. The reason for this inability is that the number of active troops in the United States military has dropped from 2.1 million to 1.4 million since the end of the Cold War. This puts a lot of pressure on companies to fill positions as quickly as possible. One negative consequence of this rushed hiring is the lack of in-depth background checks on applicants. Many recruits have been implicated in past human rights violations, including torture and killing. One of these ex-soldier-turned-United States employees was Gary Branfield, who was killed in a firefight with Iraqi soldiers in the spring of 2004. In the 1980s he was a covert operations specialist working for the South African apartheid government. Branfield's mission was to track down and assassinate members of the African National Congress living outside of South Africa. Mysteriously, this information failed to appear during background checks performed by Branfield's employer, Hart Group. Hart Group has been hired by the United States to guard Iraqi energy facilities and to protect the engineers rebuilding Iraq's electricity network. Retired justice of the Constitutional Court of South Africa Richard Goldstone comments, "The mercenaries we're talking about worked for security forces that were synonymous with murder and torture."

The Titan Corporation, which claims to provide "comprehensive information and communications products, solutions, and services for National Security" (www.corpwatch.org), has a contract with the U.S. to supply translators for the Abu Ghraib prison in Iraq. A 2004 military investigation into prisoner abuses at Abu Ghraib concluded that "Titan employees actively participated in detainee abuse, including assault and possibly rape" (*Mother Jones, 2004*). However, the only legal action taken against Titan as of yet is in the U.S. district court for the Southern district of California, where the Abu Ghraib prisoners have filed a class action suit against the employees of Titan. Employees of California Analysis Center Incorporated (CACI) were also found to have participated in the abuse. Plaintiffs in this suit are demanding a jury trial, but the process is moving slowly. Jeffrey Ellefante, executive vice president at CACI, says that CACI has yet to be informed of the specific accusations against its employees. Oddly enough, the soldiers implicated in the abuse have already been court martialed under the Military Code of Conduct.

So why is there a discrepancy between the punishment of soldiers and that of independent employees for the same crime? The answer is legal ramifications. While United States military personnel are subject to the Uniform Code of Military Justice, independent contractors working through the Pentagon as civilians are not. Because of this, Congress passed the Military Extraterritorial Jurisdiction Act (MEJA) in 2000 to enable the prosecution of civilians "employed by or accompanying U.S. armed forces" (www.law.com). Unfortunately, MEJA can only be applied to civilian employees who are contracted through the Department of Defense (DOD), and to crimes committed overseas that would merit a minimum one-year sentence under Federal law. Currently there is an investigation into the deaths of Iraqi prisoners after having been questioned by private interrogators hired by the CIA. If found guilty, these interrogators may be let off on a technicality because they work for the CIA, not the DOD, like MEJA requires.

This begs the question, under whose jurisdiction do these crimes fall? In an attempt to answer this, the Defense Department proposed new regulation earlier this year that "would require DOD contractors to make sure their employees comply with the Uniform Code of Military Justice where applicable" (www.law.com.) Debate over this proposal will open on May 24, 2005. Critic Daniel Guttman, fellow at John Hopkins University, questions the "where applicable" phrase saying, "it says the Uniform Code applies where applicable, but when is that?...They seem to be making policy on the run" (www.law.com). As for now, the Pentagon claims that it, "is not in the business of policing contractors' hiring practices," therefore it may take many more cases like Abu Ghraib before the U.S. government steps in to regulate the unlimited power that these private contractors are brandishing.

UPDATE BY BARRY YEOMAN: This was the first major article to systemically link the issues of military privatization with human rights abuses. We explained how the recent growth of a private security industry, fueled by the invasion of Iraq, necessitated the hiring of former soldiers and police officers trained and experienced in assassination and torture in formerly repressive countries.

Numerous radio stations have interviewed me about this article. Among the radio shows are "Political Thought," WMAR, Poughkeepsie NY; "The Morning Zone," KGAB, Cheyenne WY; and Ian Masters' Background Briefing, KPFK-FM, Los Angeles CA. The last of these interviews can be accessed at http://www.barryyeoman.com/biography.html.

A column called "Coalition of Willing is Dwindling" in the *Paradise Post* (CA) quoted from it. I have done extensive interviews with a European television network, which is producing a documentary on the subject.

Amnesty International has a petition drive seeking accountability for private contractors at Abu Ghraib: http://takeaction.amnestyusa.org/action/index.asp?step=2&item=10897.

There are several excellent resources on the growth of this industry: Peter Singer's book "Corporate Warriors: The Rise of the Privatized Military Industry" (Cornell University Press, 2003) and the Center for Public Integrity's 11-part investigation "Making a Killing: The Business of War" http://www.publicintegrity.org/bow/ are but a few.

13 Rich Countries Fail to Live Up to Global Pledges

Sources:
Oxfam Press Release, December 6, 2004
Title: "Poor Are Paying the Price of Rich Countries' Failure"
Author: Caroline Green
http://www.oxfam.org/eng/pr041206_MDG.htm

InterPress Service, OneWorld U.S., December 6, 2004
Title: "45 Million Children to Die in Next Decade Due to Rich Countries' Miserliness"
Author: Jim Lobe
http://us.oneworld.net/article/view/99063/1/

Faculty Evaluator: Maureen Buckley, Ph. D.
Student Researcher: Paige Dumont

Forty-five million children will needlessly die between now and the year 2015, reveals the report by Oxfam, "Poor Are Paying the Price of Rich Countries' Failure." According to this report, 97 million more children will be denied access to an education by the year 2015 and 53 million more people will lack proper sanitation facilities. Ending poverty will require assistance on many levels. For third world countries, economic growth is undermined by unfair trade rules. Without finance and support, these countries will not be able to take advantage of global trade, investment opportunities, or protect basic human rights.

Wealthy countries such as the U.S., Germany, Japan, and the UK have promised to provide a very small fraction of their wealth to third world countries. By offering .7 percent of their gross national income, they could reduce poverty and end the burden of debt that makes low income countries pay up to $100 million per day to creditors. In the years 1960-65, wealthy countries spent on average 0.48 percent of their combined national incomes on official development assistance but by the year 2003 the proportion had dropped to 0.24 percent. Vital poverty-reduction programs are failing for the lack of finance. Cambodia and Tanzania are among the poorest countries in the world, yet they will require at least double the level of external financing that they currently receive if they are to achieve their poverty-reduction targets.

Global initiatives to enable poor countries to develop provisional education and combat HIV/AIDS are starved of cash. Despite the fact that HIV infection rates are rising in sub-Saharan Africa, the global fund to fight AIDS, Tuberculosis, and Malaria is assured of only one quarter of the funds that it needs for 2005. Poor countries continue to spend more paying back their creditors than they do on essential public services. Low-income countries paid $39 billion in debt payments and interest in 2003, while they received only $27 billion in aid.

Wealthy countries can easily afford to deliver the necessary aid and debt relief. For wealthy countries such as the U.S. to spend merely 0.7 percent of gross national income on humanitarian aid is equal to one-fifth of its expenditure on defense and one half of what it spends on domestic farm subsidies. The U.S., at just 0.14 percent, is the least generous provider of aid in proportion to national income of any developed country. By comparison, Norway is the most generous provider at 0.92 percent. The U.S. is spending more than twice as much on the war in Iraq as it would cost to increase its aid budget to 0.7 percent, and six times more on its military program. Canceling the debts of the 32 poorest countries would be small change for the wealthy nations.

Millions of children are now in school in Tanzania, Uganda, Kenya, Malawi, and Zambia, thanks to money provided by foreign aid and debt relief. Because of these relief funds, Ugandans no longer have to pay for basic health care. A policy was implemented that resulted in an increase of 50 to 100 percent in attendance at Ugandan health clinics and doubled the rate on immunities. History also shows that aid has been necessary in eradicating global diseases as well as rebuilding countries devastated by war.

The wealthiest of nations have continuously signed international statements pledging to increase foreign aid to 0.7 percent of their gross national income in order to eliminate the crippling debts of third world countries. Repeatedly, they have broken their promises.

14 Corporations Win Big on Tort Reform, Justice Suffers

Sources:
Dollars and Sense, Issue #252, March/April 2004
Title: "Supremes Limit Punitive Damages"
Author: Jamie Court
http://www.dollarsandsense.org/0304court.html

Democracy now! Feb 4, 2005
Title: "Tort reform: The Big Payoff for Corporations, Curbing the Lawsuits that Hold Them Accountable"
Author: Amy Goodman et al (Juan Gonzalez interview with Joanne Doroshow)
http://www.democracynow.org/article.pl?sid=05/02/04/1537236

Faculty Evaluator: Perry Marker, Ph. D.
Student Researcher: Chris Bui

On February 18, 2005, President Bush signed into law the most sweeping federal tort reform measure in more than a decade. The Class Action Fairness Act puts into effect a tort reform that will take away people's access to the courts, undermining the constitutional right to trial by jury. These reforms weaken consumer and worker protections, denying due process of law in civil cases to all but the wealthiest in our society. The act will move many civil lawsuits from state to federal courts in an attempt to end so-called "forum shopping" by trial lawyers seeking districts most hospitable to multi-party suits against companies.

What has been lost in all the partisan rhetoric is the fact that class action suits are most often lawsuits brought by people who have been hurt by HMO abuses, civil rights violations, or workplace injuries and violations. These are the suits that allow for compensation when large numbers of people are hurt by companies in the pursuit of profit. Although, at times, individual injuries may be relatively small, they represent a pattern of behavior on the part of the defendant. While legal recourse may not be available on an individual level, by joining together at the state level, people have been able to affect responsible change in the conduct of corporations. Federal courts are not expert in these cases, are already overburdened, and are much smaller than state courts. Critics claim that the real intention of this law is to make sure these cases get buried quickly and are ultimately dismissed.

Attached to this bill is a mass tort section that will severely restrict large class action suits against pharmaceutical companies and paves the way for medical malpractice reform, effectively immunizing abusive or negligent corporations from liability.

The reform sets a cap of $250,000 per lawsuit while shielding drug companies from responsibility for punitive damages and lawsuits where the drug had been approved by the FDA. One woman who was taking the FDA approved drug Vioxx, for example, had a stroke and continued taking the drug because she wasn't warned of its major side effect—stroke. She went on to have a second stroke. The new reform would limit her settlement to $250,000 for a lifetime of disabilities. Under this new legislation corporations will not be held accountable for their faulty products and will only be punished with a slap on the wrist in terms of financial payment.

UPDATE BY JAMIE COURT: The Supreme Court ruling in Campbell seems to be an eye-glazing experience for the mainstream media. For example, the press ignored the significance of the ruling in covering the Congressional debate over 2005 legislation signed into law by President Bush that created new hurdles to class action lawsuits. Given the Campbell ruling's limits, the new class action restrictions give a virtual guarantee to banks, insurers, drug makers, and other big industries that no matter how egregious their conduct, the penalty will always be financially manageable. Indeed if the media had taken more notice of the ruling, President Bush's campaign plank of limiting lawsuits of all kind would be seen in a far different light.

Read the State Farm v. Campbell case at http://www.supremecourtus.gov/.

15 Conservative Plan to Override Academic Freedom in the Classroom

Source: *The Nation*
Title: "The New PC"
Author: Russell Jacoby
Date of Publication: April 4, 2005
Student Researchers: Vanessa Dern, Theodora Ruhs

For centuries, the higher education classroom has been a haven for honest debate and protected academic freedom. The college professor, one of the last "rugged individualists," had the freedom to teach a given subject in his or her own manner, as he or she saw it. The interpretation of the subject matter was the professors own, not a representation of a "liberal" or "conservative" dogma.

The halls of academia have included a wide variety of perspectives, from Newt Gingrich and William F. Buckley Jr. to Noam Chomsky and Albert Einstein.

In his article "The New PC," Russell Jacoby addresses a new extremist conservative movement to bring what they say is "political balance" to higher education. These conservatives see academia as a hotbed of liberal activity that is working to indoctrinate America's youth with leftwing ideology, citing studies that conclude that faculty of most universities are overwhelmingly liberal. They fear that these liberal faculty members are abusing students who profess conservative belief systems, and to remedy this they are pushing for regulation of the academic world to monitor professors' expression of theory and opinion.

At the forefront of this movement is David Horowitz and his academic watchdog organization, Students for Academic Freedom (SAF). SAF counsels its student members that, when they come across an 'abuse' like controversial material in a course, they are to write down the date, class and name of the professor. They are advised to accumulate a list of incidents or quotes, obtain witnesses, and lodge a complaint. Many in the academic world see these actions as a new McCarthy-ism—an effort to sniff out those who do not subscribe to the 'dominant' belief structure of the nation.

Beyond his student watch group, Horowitz is also championing a "Student Bill of Rights." Ironically, this bill claims to protect academic freedom. It proposes some ideas that are commonsense, such as, "students will be graded solely on the basis of their reasoned answers and appropriate knowledge of the subjects and disciplines they study, not on the basis of their political or religious beliefs."[1] But Jacoby warns that academic freedoms extended to students easily turn into the end of freedom for teachers. In Horowitz's society of rights, students would have the right to hear all sides of all subjects all the time. Principle #4 of Horowitz's academic bill of rights states that curricula and reading lists "should reflect the uncertainty and unsettled character of all human knowledge," and provide "students with dissenting sources and viewpoints where appropriate." The bill does not, however, distinguish when or where dissenting viewpoints are, or are not, appropriate.

The SAF website has a section for students to post 'abuses' and complaints about their academic experiences. Perusing these postings, Jacoby found one student reporting an 'abuse' in an introductory Peace Studies and Conflict Resolution class, "where military approaches were derided. The student complained that 'the only studying of conflict resolution that we did was to enforce the idea that non-violent means were the only legitimate sources of self-defense." Jacoby points out the irony, "presumably the professor of 'peace studies' should be ordered to give equal time to 'war studies.' By this principle, should the United States Army War College be required to teach pacifism?" From this point the movement seems to be rendered ridiculous.

Several authors, including Jacoby, point out the hypocrisy of Horowitz's focus on the humanities and education in general. The conservatives who feel such an urgency to protect the freedoms of conservative students in the humanities and to balance out the ratio of liberal to conservative faculty are in no rush to sort out the inequalities in business schools where the trend often appears to be the opposite, with the liberals in the minority. And as Jacoby points out, "of course, they do not address such imbalances in the police force, Pentagon, FBI, CIA, and other government outfits where the stakes seem far higher and where, presumably, followers of Michael Moore are short in supply."

Despite the apparent circus, this movement poses a real threat to the academic world. Whether or not the Student Bill of Rights passes in any of the state legislatures, where it stands as of Spring 2005, is not as important as how it influences public opinion. Already this movement has led to attacks and firings of a number of professors for their left leaning viewpoints. Ward Churchill, from the University of Colorado, was threatened with termination for using the term "little Eichmanns" to describe World Trade Center workers.[2] Oneida Mernato, a political science professor at Metropolitan State College of Denver, was also harassed for her liberal bias in class.[3] And more recently, self-proclaimed anarchist David Graeber was fired, he believes, for his personal political activity, and for standing up for a student organizer who he felt was being treated unfairly.[4,5]

Horowitz also aims to affect other areas of government involvement in academia, specifically funding. Proclaiming that academics are "a privileged elite that work between six to nine hours a week, eight months a year for an annual salary of about $150,000 a year,"[6] Horowitz further claims that he is "dedicated to exposing the cowards who run our universities to the alumni and taxpayers who pay their salaries. State Senator Larry Mumper argues, "Why should we, as fairly moderate to conservative legislators, continue to support universities that turn out students who rail against the very policies that their parents voted us in for?"[7]

NOTES

1. Students for Academic Freedom. "The Student Bill of Rights." http://www.studentsforacademicfreedom.org/essays/sbor.html.
2. ibid.
3. ibid.
4. http://www.villagevoice.com/people/0523,interview,64691,24.html.
5. "Early Exit" http://www.insidehighered.com/news/2005/05/18/yale.
6. Mattson, Kevin.
7. Mattson. Kevin.

16 U.S. Plans for Hemispheric Integration Include Canada

Sources:

Centre for Research on Globalisation, November 23, 2004
Title: "Is the Annexation of Canada Part of Bush's Military Agenda?"
Author: Michel Chossudovsky
http://globalresearch.ca/articles/CHO411C.html

Canadian Dimension, Jan/Feb 2005, Winnipeg: Vol.39, Iss.1; pg. 12
Title: "Canada's Chance to Keep Space for Peace"
Author: Bruce K. Gagnon
space4peace.org

Faculty Evaluator: Sherril Jaffe, Ph. D.
Student Researcher: Christina Reski

The U.S. and Canada have been sharing national information since the creation of NORAD (North American Aerospace Defense Command) in 1958. This bi-national agreement to provide aerospace warning and control for North America is scheduled to expire in May 2006. In preparation for the renewal of this contract, the U.S. and Canadian commanders are proposing to expand the integration of the two countries, including cooperation in the "Star Wars" program, cross-national integration of military command structures, immigration, law enforcement, and intelligence gathering and sharing under the new title of NORTHCOM, U.S. Northern Command.

Former Canadian Prime Minister Jean Chretien refused to join NORTH-COM. To circumvent his decision, this "illusive transitional military" (aka NORAD/NORTHCOM) formed an interim military authority in December 2002, called the Bi-National Planning Group (BPG.) The command structure is fully integrated between NORAD, NORTHCOM and the BPG. The BPG is neither accountable to the U.S. Congress nor the Canadian House of Commons. The BPG is also scheduled to expire in May 2006. Hence, the push for Canada to join NORTHCOM.

Donald Rumsfeld said that U.S. Northern Command would have jurisdiction over the entire North American region. NORTHCOM's jurisdiction, outlined by the U.S. Department of Defense (DoD), includes all of Canada, Mexico, parts of the Caribbean, contiguous waters in the Atlantic and Pacific oceans up to 500 miles of the Mexican, U.S. and Canadian coastlines as well as the Canadian Artic.

Under NORTHCOM, Canada's military command structures would be subordinated to those of the Pentagon and the DoD. In December 2001, the Canadian government reached an agreement with the head of Homeland Security Tom Ridge, entitled the "Canada-U.S. Smart Border Declaration." This agreement essentially hands over confidential information on Canadian citizens and residents to the U.S. Department of Homeland. It also provides U.S. authorities with access to tax records of Canadians. The National Intelligence Reform Act of 2004, currently debated in the U.S. Senate, centers on a so-called 'Information Sharing Network' to coordinate data from 'all available sources.'"

The BPG is the interim military for NORTHCOM. Part of the BPG's agenda is the Civil Assistance Plan (CAP) which supports the ongoing militarization of the civilian law enforcement and judicial functions in both the U.S. and Canada. Military commanders would "provide bi-national military assistance to civil authorities." The U.S. military would have jurisdiction over Canadian territory from coast to coast, extending from the St. Laurence Valley to the Parry Island in the Canadian Arctic.

It appears that some Canadian leaders are in full support of this program. In the summer 2004, Canada agreed to amend the NORAD treaty to allow sharing satellite and radar data with the ballistic missile defense program based in Colorado. This operation center will control the 40 interceptor rockets planned for Alaska, California and at sea.

On February 22, 2005, at the NATO summit in Brussels, Canadian Prime Minister Paul Martin declared that his people would not participate in the controversial Missile Defense Shield. Contradicting this message, Canadian Ambassador to the U.S. (and former board member of the Caryle Group) Frank McKenna, said "We are part of it now."

On August 2, 2004, the U.S. Air Force quietly published a new doctrine called "Counterspace Operations." The development of offensive counterspace capabilities provides combatant commanders with new tools for counterspace operations…that may be utilized throughout the spectrum of conflict and may achieve a variety of effects from temporary denial to complete destruction of the adversary's space capability. It has also been noted that Canadian Military personnel are taking part in large scale American space war games designed to prepare for combat in orbit.

Under an integrated North American Command, Canada would be forced to embrace Washington's pre-emptive military doctrine, including the use of nuclear warheads as a means of self defense, which was ratified by the U.S. Senate in December 2003.

Similar bi-national negotiations are being conducted with Mexico. U.S. military could exert strategic control over air space, land mass and contiguous territorial waters extending from the Yucatan peninsula in southern Mexico to the Canadian Arctic, representing 12 percent of the world's land mass. The militarization of South America under the "Andean Trade Preference Act" as well as the signing of a "parallel" military cooperation protocol by 27 countries of the Americas (the so-called Declaration of Manaus) is an integral part of the process of hemispheric integration (see story #17).

Richard N. Haass, of the U.S. Department of State, said at the 2002 Arthur Ross Lecture, "In the 21st century, the principal aim of American foreign policy is to integrate other countries and organizations into arrangements that will sustain a world consistent with U.S. interests and values, and thereby promote peace, prosperity and justice as widely as possible. Integration reflects not merely a hope for the future, but the emerging reality of the Bush Administration's foreign policy."

17 U.S. Uses South American Military Bases to Expand Control of the Region

Sources:
Bulletin of the Atomic Scientists, Jan/Feb 2005
Title: "What's the Deal at Manta"
Author: Michael Flynn

NACLA Report on the Americas, Nov/Dec 2004
Title: "Creeping Militarization in the Americas"
Authors: Adam Isacson, Lisa Haugaard and Joy Olson

Z Magazine, December 29, 2004
Title: "Colombia—A Shill (proxy) Country For U.S. Intervention In Venezuela"
Authors: Sohan Sharma and Surinder Kumar

Faculty Evaluator: Jorge Porras, Ph. D.
Student Researchers: Adrienne Smith, Sarah Kintz

The United States has a military base in Manta, Ecuador, one of the three military bases located in Latin America. According to the United States, we are there to help the citizens of Manta, but an article in the *Bulletin of Atomic Scientists* says that many people tell a different story.

According to Miguel Moran, head of a group called Movimiento Tohalli, which opposes the Manta military base, "Manta is part of a broader U.S. imperialist strategy aimed at exploiting the continent's natural resources, suppressing popular movements, and ultimately invading neighboring Colombia." Michael Flynn reported that the military base in Ecuador is an "integral part of the U.S. counterinsurgency strategy in Colombia—and is a potential staging ground for direct American involvement in the conflict there. Ecuadorians worry that the U.S. could ultimately pull their country into conflict." Flynn goes on to say that "the base is also at the center of a growing controversy regarding the U.S. efforts to block mass emigration from Ecuador [to the U.S.]." Policy makers have diminished the difference between police roles and military roles, stating that a police force is a body designed to protect a population through minimal use of force and the military, which aims to defeat an enemy through use of force.

According to a ten-year lease agreement between Ecuador and the United States, "... U.S. activities at the base are to be limited to counter-narcotics surveillance flights (the agreements for the other two Latin American Forward Operating Locations contain similar restrictions)." Ecuadorian citizens are not pleased with the lease or the way the U.S. has abused it. "A coalition of social and labor organizations has called for the termination of the U.S. lease in Manta on the grounds that the United States has violated both the terms of the agreement and Ecuadorian law."

The U.S., says Flynn, is intervening in Colombia through private corporations and organizations. Most of the military operations and the spraying of biochemical agents are contracted out to private firms and private armies. In 2003, according to the article in *Z Magazine*, the U.S. State Department said, "...there are seventeen primary contracting companies working in Colombia, initially receiving $3.5 million." One of these private American defense contractors, DynCorp, runs the military base at Manta. "The Pentagon's decision to give DynCorp—a company that many Latin Americans closely associate with U.S. activities in Colombia—the contract to administer the base reinforced fears that the United States had more than drug interdiction in mind when it set up shop in Manta," says Flynn.

In addition, say Sharma and Kumar, DynCorp was awarded a "$600 million contract to carry out aerial spraying to eliminate coca crops which also contaminates maize, Yucca, and plantains-staple foods of the population; children and adults develop skin rashes." The chemical, the foundation for the herbicide Roundup, is sprayed in Ecuador in a manner that would be illegal in the United States.

According to the NACLA report, in 2004, the Pentagon began installing 3 substitute logistics centers (now under construction) in the provinces of Guayas, Azuay, and Sucumbios, and is currently militarizing the Ecuadorian police who are receiving "anti-terrorist" training by the FBI. The U.S. military is also aiding Colombia's "war on drugs." Isacson, Haugaard and Olson write that, "increased militarization of antinarcotics operation is a pretext for stepped up counterinsurgency action and extending the war against them by the U.S." Washington also has seven security offices in Ecuador: defense (DAO), drug enforcement (DEA), military aid (MAAG), internal security, national security (NSA), the U.S. Agency for Internal Development (USAID), the Peace Corps, and the Central Intelligence Agency (CIA). According to the Bush Administration they are mixing military and police roles to "...govern its counter-terror efforts in the hemisphere."

Michael Flynn offers this quote from an Ecuadorian writer as another example of the United States intervening in the operations of another country to further its own agenda: "The U.S. invasion of Iraq and the pressure on Ecuador to sign the interdiction agreement form part of a policy aimed at consolidating a unipolar world with one hegemonic superpower."

UPDATE BY MICHAEL FLYNN: I think one important aspect of my story about the Manta base is that it shows the arrogance that often characterizes U.S. relations with its southern neighbors. This arrogance comes with a heavy price, which the U.S. is paying now as South American leaders express an ever greater willingness to take an independent path in their affairs and reject the U.S. lead. This fact was clearly revealed recently when the Organization of American States soundly rejected a U.S. proposal to set up a mechanism to review the state of democracy in the Americas. Manta is a small part of this much larger picture. U.S. ambassadors, the head of Southcom, even representatives in Congress have shown a disregard for Ecuadorian concerns about operations at the Manta base, which has helped fan criticism of the base, and has turned into a lightning rod of criticism of U.S. policies. And this is only one of among dozens of similar bases spread out across the globe—what impact are they having on U.S. relations?

An equally important issue touched on in my story is the U.S. reaction to the migration crises that has gripped several Latin countries in recent years. Manta is a sort of quasi-outpost of the U.S. southern border, which has shown remarkable flexibility in recent years. The fact is, the border itself ceased long ago to be the front line in the effort to stop unwanted migration. The United States uses military bases located in host countries as staging grounds for detention efforts. It has funded detention centers in places like Guatemala City, and it has teamed up with law enforcement officials from other countries to carry out multi-lateral operations aimed at breaking up migrant smuggling activities. Manta is one piece in this larger puzzle.

To my knowledge, the mainstream press has not picked up on the precise story lines covered in my article. On the other hand, the press has not altogether ignored these issues either. Ginger Thompson of the *New York Times* has tracked the plight of migrants in several Latin American countries, and last year she teamed up with an Ecaudorean journalist to produce a remarkable story about the harrowing experience of migrants who dare to board the smuggling vessels leaving Ecuadorean shores. They did not, however, scrutinize Manta's role in interdicting these migrants, or address the many problematic aspects of U.S. overseas interdiction practices. Regarding U.S. overseas military bases, the recent turmoil in Uzbekistan has drawn the attention of the U.S. press to contradictions in U.S. policy that have emerged between its desire to have bases in strategic spots around the world and President Bush's promise to advocate democratic change across the globe. Also, Dana Priest of the *Washington Post* has done excellent work reporting on the role of U.S. bases and military commanders around the globe. See, for example, Priest's *The Mission: Waging War and Keeping Peace with America's Military* (New York: Norton, 2003). Several alternative press outlets have also tracked this issue, including for example *Mother Jones* magazine, which ran a story by Chalmers Johnson on this issue, and the Nation Institute's Tom Engelhardt, who has run a number of pieces in his *TomDispatch* touching on U.S. overseas bases.

FOR ADDITIONAL INFORMATION: For those interested in following up on the Manta base, the best source of information online is the web site of the Ecuadorean daily: *El Universo* at http://www.eluniverso.com/.

I would also suggest looking at the studies about U.S. forward operation locations published by the Amsterdam-based Transnational Institute at http://www.tni.org/.

To find out more about U.S. cross-border interdiction policies, a story that has been woefully under-reported in the United States, I suggest taking a look at other stories I have written on this subject, some of which are available on the web site of the International Reporting Project: http://www.pewfellowships.org/index.htm.

Finally, to get a global perspective of U.S. basing ambitions, I suggest perusing the May 2005 report of the U.S. Overseas Basing Commission, which is available online at http://www.fas.org/irp/agency/dod/obc.pdf.

UPDATE BY LISA HAUGAARD: While the nation is focused on events in Iraq and Afghanistan, 9/11 has also had a disturbing impact on U.S. policy toward Latin America. But the growth in U.S. military programs towards Latin America and the unfortunate emphasis by the United States on encouraging non-defense related roles for militaries is part of a more general trend that the Center for International Policy, Latin America Working Group Education Fund and Washington Office on Latin America have been documenting since 1997. Latin American civil society organizations, individuals and governmental leaders have struggled hard to strictly limit their militaries' involvement in civilian affairs, given that many militaries in the region had exercised severe repression, carried out military coups and maintained political control during several turbulent decades. After this painful history, it is troubling for the United States to be encouraging militaries to once again adopt non-defense related roles, as is the growing weight of U.S. military, rather than regional development aid in U.S. relations.

We are seeing a continuation of the general trend of declining U.S. development assistance and stable military aid to the region as well as the United States encouraging actions that blur the line between civilian police and military roles. We are also witnessing efforts by the Defense Department to exercise greater control over "security assistance"(foreign military aid programs) worldwide, which were once overseen exclusively by the State Department. This almost invisible shift-—by no means limited to Latin America—is disturbing because it removes the State Department as the lead agency in deciding where foreign military aid and training is appropriate as part of U.S. foreign policy. It will lead to less stringent oversight of military programs and less emphasis upon human rights conditionality.

Our report, which we published in Spanish, received good coverage from the Latin American press. Mainstream U.S. newspapers regularly use our military aid database. The larger story about the general trends in U.S. military aid in Latin America and changes in oversight of foreign military programs, however, is one that has been covered by only a few major media outlets.

To see our military aid database, reports and other information (a collaborative project by the three organizations) see our "Just the Facts" website, http://www.ciponline.org/facts. See also our organizations' websites: Washington Office on Latin America, www.wola.org; Center for International Policy, www. ciponline.org; and Latin America Working Group Education Fund, www.lawg.org.

We welcome efforts by journalists, scholars and nongovernmental organizations to insist upon greater transparency and public oversight of U.S. military training programs, not just in Latin America but worldwide.

18 Little Known Stock Fraud Could Weaken U.S. Economy

Sources:

San Antonio Express-News—March 2, 2005
Title: "Naked Short Selling Is A Plague For Businesses And Investors"
Author: David Hendricks

TheMotleyFool.com—March 30, 2005
Title: "Who's Behind Naked Shorting?"
Author: Karl Thiel

Financial Wire—Stockgate Today Series
Title: "SEC's Donaldson Addresses Liquidity Fraud," September 20, 2004;
"Dateline NBC Cancelled and Attorney Accuses DTCC of Cheap Thuggery,"
April 7, 2005
Author: Dave Patch

Faculty Evaluator: Wingham Liddell, Ph.D.
Student Researcher: David Stolowitz

The negligence of government regulatory agencies and the media is becoming worrisome as a major scandal, unknown outside the financial community, is bankrupting small businesses and investors and having a negative effect on the economy.

While the balance of supply and demand is a fairly well known principle of economic health, a related and similar relationship exists between liquidity—the availability of liquid, spendable assets such as cash, stocks and bonds—and security—the stability, endurance and trustworthiness of more long-term financial mechanisms.

A healthy economy requires both enough access to liquid assets to ensure a smooth and flexible flow of money *and* a system that guarantees enough stability, protection and security for investors to take a reasonable measure of risk without having excessive fears of losing their money. Unreasonable emphasis on the first requirement and not enough attention to the second is a trend that has developed in the last decade and may have more to do with ideology than sound economic policy. Liquidity fraud and naked shorting abuses as described in this article are a symptom of a greater problem within our economic culture. This lopsided philosophy of economic regulation is a significant factor in creating the kind of climate that has produced company scandals like Enron and WorldCom, as well as a careless attitude towards free trade and globalization that may create more costs than benefits in the name of "economic growth."

The scandal coined "Stockgate" by the *Financial Wire* involves the abuse of a practice called "short selling." As opposed to a traditional approach to investing in which stocks are researched and bought on the hope they will rise over the "long" term, going "short" involves a bet that a stock is about to go down in value. In a short sale, an investor sells stock that he or she technically doesn't own. The investor borrows these shares of stock from their broker, who in turn may likely borrow the shares himself from a financial clearinghouse like a brokerage firm or hedge fund. Hoping that the price of the stock will drop, the investor is obligated to eventually "close" the short by buying back the sold shares at a hopefully lower price, thus making a profit from the fall of the stock. When the time runs out for "covering" the short and the price hasn't dropped, the investor is forced to buy back the shares at a loss and take a financial hit. The short sale of stocks is a risky bet, usually not recommended except for speculation or hedging—to protect long-term financial positions with short-term offsets. As short-selling is a sale of stocks not owned, but loaned, it is an example of buying on margin—a category of practices whose abuses stand out clearly in many people's minds as a significant factor in the Stock Market Crash of 1929 which ushered in the Great Depression.

Naked shorting is an illegal abuse of short selling in which investors short-sell stock that they have no intention or ability to ever cover. When allowed to occur, naked shorting drives the stock value of a company down by creating more stock shares flowing around the market than actual shares of stock that the company can back with their current earnings. Companies, their shareholders, and indeed the entire economy are hurt financially by naked shorting, as it reduces the money available to support economic growth. According to activist Dave Patch, "Naked shorting steals some of the greatest ideas, products, and services in America. Small micro-cap companies are driven out of business by this abuse and we are left with the unknowns of what these companies and their employees had to offer our futures. The opportunities for the next Microsoft may never be felt as naked shorting snuffed out that creativity before it was ever brought to fruition. Ultimately, naked shorting steals from the very foundation of our nation as it steals the American dream of opportunity."

Patch and other investors hurt by or concerned about the consequences of naked shorting organized, petitioned and investigated the background surrounding the Stockgate scandal. What they found was not merely a series of noteworthy cases of extravagant abuse by individual investors and professionals, but a systemic pattern of negligence by regulators that allowed the abuse to go by largely unchecked. A whole series of checks and balances was originally designed to prevent abuses like naked shorting. Yet, as their research has shown, every regulator along the way has failed its duty and led to both widespread and high-figure abuse. While investors have lost hundreds of billions of dollars in savings, the Wall Street Firms responsible for the abuse saw negligible fines that had no appreciable impact on their stock values. Some executives were even given raises in the midst of their negligence and fraud!

As more pressure has been brought against regulatory agencies to stop the fraud and enforce rules, an opposition has come forth that actually favors allowing the illegal practice to continue unchecked. These critics argue that all short sales, including illegal naked shorts, help bust the hype that can surround micro-cap companies. Excitement over new but untried ideas can artificially inflate stock prices, causing eventual losses to companies and investors when the bubble bursts, as in the case of the dot-com boom of the '90s.

While it is true, as the critics argue, that removing naked shorting could in some cases allow hyped prices to climb further, such an effect is vastly overrated. The argument does not take many other financial factors into account, such as the increased efficiency in the flow of information and shares that eliminating naked shorting would create or the fact that legal short selling could provide the same protections. Many securities analysts say it is fallacious to assert that the only recourse to the adjustment in hype and price securities is to allow an illegal practice to continue.

The same enforcement of already existing rules by regulators could curb hype just as much as it curbs naked shorts. A proactive stance by the financial community in informing and educating the public could also prevent the pump and dump schemes that such critics say would be the consequence of ending naked shorting.

Often it is the very organizations that did little to stop the dot-com problem from getting out of hand while it was occurring that now cry out at the prospect of the SEC stepping up to protect small investors from naked shorting. Of particular interest is the fact that much of this criticism comes out of the Depository Trust Commission (DTCC), which takes a share of profits from every short sale and is currently fighting off lawsuits accusing it of impropriety in a number of areas. The DTCC is also alleged to have brought pressure to bear on media corporations such as General Electric to suppress the story from being reported. GE's NBC *Dateline* program obtained an exclusivity contract to cover the Stockgate scandal over a year ago, and then postponed the episode indefinitely. Officially, *Dateline* claims that a slew of more important stories than this widespread financial scandal have caused the delay. At the time of this writing, however, they are preparing to air an Al Roker interview with an *American Idol* finalist.

ADDITIONAL REFERENCES:

David Sedore, "Hedge Fund Assets Frozen": March 4, 2005; "Hedge Fund Virtually Bare": March 12, 2005; etc. *The Palm Beach Post*—KL Financial fraud series.

PrimeZone Media Network, "First American Scientific Corp. Takes Counter Measures to Stop 'Naked Shorting' of its Stock"—December 17, 2004.

19 Child Wards of the State Used in AIDS Experiments

Sources:
UK Observer
Title: "GlaxoSmithKline Allegedly Used Children as Laboratory Animals"
Author: Antony Barnett

Democracy Now! December 2004
Title: "Guinea Pig Kids: How New York City is Using Children to Test Experimental AIDS Drugs."

Mainstream Media Coverage: Fox News Network, *The O'Reilley Factor*, March 10, 2004, *CBS Morning News*, February 2, 2005.

Faculty Evaluator: Jeanette Koshar, Ph. D.
Student Researcher: Mike Cattivera, Kiel Eorio

Orphans as young as three months old were used as test subjects in AIDS drug trials in New York's Incarnation Children's Center. The Center, which is run by Catholic Charities, specializes in treating HIV sufferers, and the drug trials were performed on children with HIV or who were born to HIV-positive mothers. The New York City Health Department is looking into claims that more than 100 children at Incarnation were used in as many as 36 experiments. Most of these experiments were sponsored by federal agencies such as the National Institute of Allergy and Infectious Diseases.

Documents obtained by the *UK Observer* have implicated British pharmaceutical giant GlaxoSmithKline's involvement in at least four experiments conducted at Incarnation since 1995 using black and Hispanic children. Several trials were conducted to test the toxicity of AIDS drugs. In one trial, children as young as four received a high-dosage cocktail of seven drugs; another tested the reaction of six-month-olds to a double dosage of a measles vaccine. Other studies conducted on children included testing AZT, which can carry dangerous side effects, as well as testing the long term safety of anti-bacterial drugs on six-month old babies. GlaxoSmithKline also used children to "obtain tolerance, safety and pharmacokinetic data" for Herpes drugs.

These trials were conducted by Columbia University Medical Center doctors. A spokesperson for Columbia University said that there have been no trials at Incarnation since 2000, and that the consent for using the children as test subjects was provided by the Administration for Children's Services. Consent was based upon a panel of doctors and lawyers who decided whether or not the benefits of allowing the child to receive the drugs outweighed the risks (although it was unclear what recipient "benefits" referred to). Though GlaxoSmithKline has acknowledged their involvement in the trials at Incarnation, they deny any wrongdoing. According to their spokesperson: "These studies were implemented by the U.S. Aids Clinical Trial Group, a clinical research network paid for by the National Institutes of Health. Glaxo's involvement in such studies would have been to provide study drugs or funding but we would have no interactions with the patients."

The medical community has defended these studies, saying it enabled children, normally without access to treatment, the opportunity to receive AIDS drugs. However, many, outraged at these studies, argue there is a difference between providing children with the latest AIDS drugs and using them for experimentation. According to Antony Barnett, several experiments were considered to be Phase 1 trials, which are among the most dangerous. These drugs are similar to those used in chemotherapy and carry serious side effects. Critics also argue that it is difficult to test babies for HIV, and results are often incorrect; therefore many of these trials may have been conducted on babies or children not actually infected with HIV.

These trials at New York's Incarnation Children's Center were part of a broader series of HIV and AIDS drug trials that were conducted in at least seven states on foster children. Some children died during the trials. However, government officials have so far found no evidence that their deaths could be directly connected to the experiments.[1]

NOTE

1. http://washingtontimes.com/metro/20050511-103959-2907r.htm.

20 American Indians Sue for Resources; Compensation Provided to Others

Sources:

LiP, Winter 2004
Title: "Trust Us, We're the Government: How to Make $137 Billion of Indian Money Disappear."
Author: Brian Awehali

News from Indian Country, March 8, 2004
Title: "Despite Wealth of Resources, Many Tribes Still Live in Poverty"
Author: Angie Wagner

Mainstream Media Coverage: *New York Times*, April 7, 2004, and the *Washington Post*, March 14, 2004

Community Evaluator: Keith Pike MA
Student Researcher: Kiel Eorio

Native Americans, after more than two centuries, are still being cheated by the government and U.S. companies. Oil companies operate at Montezuma Creek in Utah. Montezuma Creek lies on a Navajo Reservation. The companies have under-compensated the Native Americans for the right to their natural resources since the 1950s. District court-appointed invesigator Alan Balaran discovered that non-Native Americans in the same area received royalties that amounted to more than 20 times the amount of the Native Americans on the reservation.

Native American reservations are filled with natural resources, but the government has routinely allowed energy companies to short-change the tribes. In Balaran's findings it shows that the government owes Native Americans as much as $137.5 billion in back royalties. The issue of the government keeping funds from Native Americans dates back to the Dawes Act of 1887. The Dawes act created a trust fund for Native Americans over the years; since then the government has grossly mismanaged revenues from oil, timber and mineral leases on tribal land.

According to Elouise Cobell, a member of the Blackfeet tribe, many Native Americans depend on these royalty checks for the bare necessities. The Navajo Nation has more than 140,000 members and is the country's largest tribe. It is also one of the poorest. More than 40 percent of its people live in poverty while the median household annual income is $20,000, less than half of the national median. Mary Johnson, a Navajo tribe member, who lives in a one bedroom stone house off the main highway, once received a royalty check for $5.30. These required checks are commonly paid out in sporadic intervals.

Johnson Martinez, a 68-year-old Navajo, lives out of a trailer that is pulled by his pickup truck. His "home" is just yards away from where gas pipelines sit on the family land. He has no running water and sometimes no electricity. There are even times when he doesn't have any food. At night he builds a fire to keep him and his dogs warm. Sometimes he has received checks for only a few cents.

In 1994, Congress passed the American Indian Trust Reform Act. This required the Interior Department to account for all the money in the trust fund and clean up the accounting process. The Individual Indian Monies case, also known as Cobell V. Norton, is the largest class action suit ever filed against the federal government. Filed in 1996, Elouise Cobell is at the center of the suit that involves more than 100 years of revenues generated by government leases on Native American land held "in trust" for mining as well as oil and gas exploration. For years she has tried to get an accurate accounting of funds held in trust by the U.S. Government for individual Native American land leased by the federal government for natural resource stripping. The defendant in the Cobell V. Norton case is Interior Department Secretary Gale Norton. She has been held in contempt by Federal Judge Royce C. Lamberth for ignoring his orders to account for the fund. Lamberth stated that he had never seen greater government incompetence than the Interior Department had shown in administrating the money and representing itself in court.

In early of 2001, Alan Balaran, the investigator in the case, made a surprise visit to the Government's warehouse. There he found papers from a shredder, which had records concerning the money paid out of the trust fund. The Bureau of Indian Affairs, which resides under the Interior Department, stated that similar documents were being shredded every day.

In March of 2004, Lamberth ordered a shutdown for the Interior Department's internet connections due to security holes that could have allowed hackers to access hundreds of millions of dollars in royalties from Native American lands managed by the agency, according to Balaran's findings. This was the third internet shutdown in three years. This particular shutdown was ordered after the Interior Department refused to sign sworn certificates that it had fixed major security flaws. This is the same system that processes hundreds of millions of dollars annually for Native Americans.

In April of 2004, Alan Balaran resigned under pressure as the investigator in the case. He states that the Bush Administration has been pursuing his refusal to silence criticisms of the Interior Department's handling of individual Native American accounts. Balaran's findings show that the Bush Administration knowingly allowed energy companies to continue to pay Native Americans far less than non-Native Americans for natural resources. Judge Royce C. Lamberth has ordered the government to complete a historic accounting for all funds in the case by January 6, 2008.

REFERENCES:

Rocky Mountain News, August 21, 2003 "Indians Underpaid for Land Leases, Official Charges; Appraisal Program Under Norton Targeted" by M.E. Sprengelmeyer.

Bismarck Tribune, April 7, 2004, "Investigator: Interior Favored Companies" by Robert Gehrke.

PR Newswire, February 24, 2005 "Cobell Litigation Team: U.S. District Court Reissues Structural Injunction in Cobell V. Norton Indian Trust Case-Full Accounting to Be Complete by January 6, 2008."

UPDATE BY BRIAN AWEHALI: The Cobell v. Norton case is important because the government is colossally and obviously wrong. This is evident in light of the success of Eloise Cobell's team in successive court victories. The sheer scope of the case, its possible precedent-setting resolution, and the ways in which it highlights the current limitations of Native Americans' dependent-yet-sovereign status, all provide opportunities for real reform and long-term re-examination of the terms of U.S.-to-Native, government-to-government relations.

Media coverage of this story has largely suffered from two main challenges. The first challenge has been the massive bureaucratic complexities of the case, which I believe insulated it from quite a lot of daily news coverage. The second, and subtler, challenge is the average American's lack of understanding of Native sovereignty. Without a clear understanding of this, Americans literally have no meaningful framework to fit the story into, and it simply disappears.

Ongoing security flaws in the Department of the Interior's trust accounting systems have continued for a ridiculously long time. Despite failure after failure to amend security flaws that allow for manipulation of records, and in spite of repeated documented instances of bureaucratic ill will resulting in massive theft and "loss" from trust accounts, the Department of the Interior is still in charge of them. Another investigative story on SmartMoney.com (December 3, 2004) reported that "officials in the Bush Administration had detailed knowledge of fraudulent practices that allowed energy companies to cheat impoverished Native Americans out of vast sums over dozens of years."

Indian Country Today also reported that behind the scenes negotiations might already be happening between the White House and Congress—but not with the plaintiffs in the case. The piece also warns of the possibility of another "midnight rider" on an appropriations bill that would effectively defer justice for yet another year.

Because recent developments in this case have centered mostly around court motions and abstruse legal machinations, there hasn't been much hard "news" for the mainstream press to grab onto. Without new and breaking "hooks," I think the perception is that this is an old story, rather than the very urgent and pressing one that it is. I also believe the government's strategy—stall, obfuscate and deceive—is a deliberate attempt to keep media attention largely surface and scattershot.

The best places to go for information about the case are the following sites: http://www.indiantrust.com, *Indian Country Today*: http://www.indiancountry.com, The Friends Committee on National Legislation: http://www.fcnl.org/issues/item.php?item_id=1266&issue_id=112

21 New Immigration Plan Favors Business Over People

Sources:
Interhemispheric Resource Center IRC,
November 16, 2004,

Washington Free Press, Nov/Dec, 2004
Title: How U.S. Corporations Won the Debate Over Immigration
Author: David Bacon
www.americaspolicy.org

MotherJones.com, November 11, 2004
Title: "Migrants No More"
Author: Maggie Jones
www.motherjones.com/news/feature/2004/11/11_404

Faculty Evaluator: Francisco Vazquez, Ph.D.
Student Researchers: Joseph F. Davis

A bi-partisan effort from the Federal government is emerging to close the borders with Mexico by increasing barriers that keep "illegal" immigrants from traveling to and from Mexico, and in turn creating a guest worker program with specific time limits for residency. Reminiscent of the defunct bracero program, the status of "guest worker" has reappeared as the preferred name for Mexican nationals working in this country.

The leading organization behind the guest worker legislation is The Essential Worker Immigration Coalition (EWIC), which was organized in 1999, while Bill Clinton was still president. The group quickly grew to include 36 of the country's most powerful employer associations, headed by the U.S. Chamber of Commerce. The National Association of Chain Drug Stores—including Wal Mart (which was sanctioned for employing undocumented workers last year)—belongs, as do the American Health Care Association, the American Hotel and Lodging Association, the National Council of Chain Restaurants, the National Restaurant Association, and the National Retail Federation. Each of these associations represents employers who depend on a workforce almost entirely without benefits and working at (or below) minimum wage.

Edward Kennedy, Democrat, and John McCain, Republican, are promoting a bi-partisan bill that would create the designation of "guest worker" for a three-year period. About half a million workers would be eligible for the status if they are sponsored by American businesses and pay five hundred dollars. The over ten million undocumented workers residing in the United States who are not sponsored by businesses would be encouraged to come forward and pay a two-thousand-dollar fine to receive the new status. The guest worker category can be renewed after three years, or businesses could sponsor workers for green cards.

The proposed legislation does not address the growing problem of undocumented workers residing in the United States. Because of the nature of the work being offered under this program, most guest workers will be left with little more than minimum wage employment. There are no benefits or health care offered under the new program. The two-thousand-dollar price tag for uninvited potential guest workers means that most of the more than ten million undocumented workers will be unwilling to come forth. Historically, millions of Mexican laborers would return to Mexico during off-seasons to visit family. Today, with tighter border restrictions and the cost of paying a labor smuggler up to $300, few people return to Mexico, resulting in permanent under-class poverty communities spread out throughout the country.

There has been no serious discussion on Capitol Hill on realistically dealing with the undocumented worker situation in this country because U.S. corporations will continue to benefit from cheap labor sources from outside and inside the borders of the United States.

The official bracero program, negotiated in 1942 between the U.S. and Mexican governments was ended in 1964. Ernesto Galarza, a labor organizer, former diplomat and early hero of the Chicano movement, was its greatest opponent in Washington. But Cesar Chavez was also an early voice calling for abolition. Chavez later said he could never have organized the United Farm Workers until growers could no longer hire braceros during strikes. In fact, the great five-year grape strike in which the UFW was born began the year after the bracero program ended. According to the UFW's Mark Grossman, "Chavez believed agribusiness' chief farm labor strategy for decades was maintaining a surplus labor supply to keep wages and benefits depressed, and fight unionization."

The organization of veterans of the bracero program, with chapters in both the U.S. and Mexico, was even more critical. "We're totally opposed to the institution of new guest worker programs," explained Ventura Gutierrez, head of the Union Sin Fronteras. "People who lived through the old program know the abuse they will cause." One former bracero, Manual Herrera, told the Associated Press's Julianna Barbassa, "they rented us, got our work, then sent us back when they had no more use for us." Thousands of former braceros are still trying to collect money deducted from their pay during the 1940s and 1950s.

Money that was supposedly held in trust to ensure they completed work contracts, but never turned over to them. Bush's proposal contains a similar provision. "If we accept, then our grandsons and great-grandsons will go through what we went through," ex-bracero Florentino Lararios told Barbassa. U.S. labor opposition focused on the lack of a real amnesty. Eliseo Medina, executive vice president of the Service Employees International Union, and one of the AFL-CIO's key policy makers on immigration, said, "Bush tells immigrants you have no right to earn citizenship, but tells corporations you have the right to exploit workers, both American and immigrant...." This proposal allows hard-working, tax-paying immigrants to become a legitimate part of our economy, but it keeps them from fully participating in our democracy— making immigrants a permanent sub-class of our society.

UPDATE BY DAVID BACON: "How Corporations Won the Debate over Immigration" broke a story of national importance—how the largest U.S. corporations, dependent on a steady supply of immigrant workers, got the President and Congress to introduce legislation giving them a vastly expanded guest worker program. This program, like the old "bracero" program of the 1940s and '50s, used a system of contract labor to exploit immigrant workers and deny them their rights, while creating an oversupply of labor to drive down wages for all workers, immigrant and non-immigrant alike.

The story was originally published in the fall of 2004. By the spring of 2005, corporate pressure for expanded guestworker programs had grown so strong that even bipartisan proposals for immigration reform included them. The word in Washington DC is now that no immigration reform is worth discussing unless corporate America gets what it wants. In mid-May, a new bill was introduced by Senators Edward Kennedy and John McCain, which includes a program even larger than that proposed by Bush.

The President's program calls for 300,000 people to be given temporary visas for three years, renewable for another three. The Kennedy/McCain bill calls for 400,000 temporary visas. In addition, the bill calls for requiring the 9 million currently undocumented immigrants in the U.S. to enroll as guestworkers for six years to qualify for making application for a green card, and to pay a $2000 fine. Increased enforcement of employer sanctions, the law that makes it a federal crime for an undocumented worker to hold a job, would be used to force people into the program by making it even more risky to try to work without becoming a guest worker.

Despite these draconian provisions, the bill won the sponsorship of many Democrats, and almost no Republicans. In the meantime, Texas Senator Cornyn announced his intention to introduce an even more conservative bill in mid-July. The Cornyn bill is regarded as the legislative embodiment of the President's program. It is a straight temporary worker bill, with no provisions for legalization.

No matter whether sponsored by Democrats or Republicans, the corporate lobby for temporary workers has legislation which corresponds to its program.

In the meantime, however, a much more liberal bill has been introduced by Congresswoman Sheila Jackson Lee and members of the Congressional Black Caucus. Instead of increasing job competition and pitting one group of low-wage workers against another, the bill tries to balance the needs of all low-wage workers. African-American and other minority communities suffering high unemployment would receive job training and creation programs. The bill would set up a legalization program for undocumented immigrants based on their residency, rather than employment status. It has provisions to strengthen protection for the rights of immigrant workers, ends discrimination against immigrants from countries like Haiti and Liberia, and has no guest worker program.

Republicans and many Democrats have derided the Jackson Lee bill as incompatible with the atmosphere in Congress, which seeks both to reward corporations and increase punitive measures against immigrants, especially the undocumented. But a rising tide of protest in immigrant communities and other communities of color around the country has criticized the growing wave of anti-immigrant legislation, and is callling for a movement to defend their rights instead.

Generally, the story of corporate sponsorship of the guest worker proposals has been ignored by the mainstream media. Reports on the Kennedy-McCain and Bush proposals have treated them as "pro-immigrant" because they would allow workers to cross the border legally. They've ignored the actual conditions for immigrants under current guest worker programs, as well as the money and influence trail leading back from these proposals to the corporate lobby, the Essential Worker Immigration Coalition. They have also ignored the Jackson-Lee bill, even though it presents the unprecedented political situation in which the country's most progressive immigration legislation is being proposed by African-American Congress members.

Readers who want more information about the overall situation of immigrants and legislation which affects them can contact the National Network for Immigrant and Refugee Rights, at 510-465-1984, www.nnirr.org. More information on pending immigration legislation and the Jackson Lee bill is available from Nolan Rappaport, minority counsel to the House Immigration Subcommittee, 202-225-2329.

22 Nanotechnology Offers Exciting Possibilities But Health Effects Need Scrutiny

Source:
The Chronicle of Higher Education September 10, 2004
Title: "The Dark Side of Small"
Author: Richard Monastersky

Faculty Evaluator: Scott Gordon, Ph. D., Jennifer Lillig Whiles, Ph. D.
Student Researcher: Jason Piepmeier

The science of nanotechnology is rapidly advancing, but there is little research to show whether or not nano-sized molecules are safe for people and the environment.

Nanotechnology is the science of using molecules that are virtually impossible to see; one blood cell measures at 7,000 nanometers in width. Nanotechnology has virtually unlimited potential. Products such as stainless, wrinkle free pants use nanotechnology as well as transparent sunscreens and tennis balls that keep their bounce. The U.S. government spent close to $1 billion in 2004 on research and development in nanotechnology.

However, only 1 percent of it is going towards research for risk assessment, despite the fact that nanotechnology also has the potential to cause harm to people and the environment. The nano-sized molecules can damage, or kill, the skin cells of humans and also kill valuable bacteria in water. The reason little money is given to research the risks is nanotechnology's huge upside; some estimates predict that the nanotech market will reach $1 trillion in a decade.

Thousands of papers have come out touting different developments in nanoscience, but fewer than fifty have examined how engineered nanoparticles will affect people and the environment. The studies that have been conducted to determine if nano-molecules are safe paint a grim picture for nanotechnology. In the spring of 2004, Eva Oberdorster, an adjunct scientist at Duke University, made headlines with potentially disturbing news about highly praised a nanoparticle called "fullerness," named for the inventor R. Buckminister Fuller.

The "fullerness" is made of 60 carbon atoms, bonded together like a molecular soccer ball. Oberdorster put a solution of "fullerness" into a tank with large-mouthed bass and later examined different organs in the fish. She found signs of oxidative damage in their brains and speculated that the nanoparticles had stimulated the production of free radicals, highly reactive compounds that can cause cellular damage. "Normally," she said, "particles can't get into the brains of fish or people because a protective structure called the blood-brain barrier keeps out harmful materials." But Oberdorster's, and other experiments show that nano-size particles can slip through that barrier by traveling up nerve cells into the brain.

Oberdorster's father also studies the effects of nanoparticles. Dr. Gunter Oberdorster, a professor of toxicology in environmental medicine at the University of Rochester, received a $5.5 million, five-year grant from the Department of Defense to study the effects of nanoparticles. Scientists at the University of Rochester looked at the titanium dioxide nanoparticles that are used as pigments in white paint. Rats and mice inhaled particles ranging in size from 12 nanometers up to 250 nanometers. The smaller particles were found to cause more inflammation than an equal amount of larger particles. "The smaller particles react differently from the larger ones," he says, "because nano-size materials evade the normal defense system in the lungs, the macrophage cells that gobble up the irritants and clear them out." Once nanoparticles get deep into the lungs, they can cross over into the blood stream and from there can into any organ in the body. Inhaling the nano-sized particles in titanium dioxide, which is on the market now, is unlikely because they are captured in liquid substances. However, Dr. Oberdoester suggests that it may be possible for nanoparticles to cross over through the skin.

Another study, run by Anna A. Shevedova, an adjunct associate professor at West Virginia and a senior staff scientist at the National Institute for Occupational Safety and Health (NIOSH), found that carbon nanotubes generated dangerous free radicals in cultures of human skin cells. Her research team reported that the nanotubes caused oxidative damage that triggered the deaths of cells.

Almost everybody involved in nanotechnology says it is too soon to tell whether and how these materials might harm people or the environment. But early studies show that this is something that should be looked into more seriously. In a survey conducted by North Carolina State University, public perception of nanotechnology remains fairly positive. As has happened with new technologies in the past, this optimism may become accusations and lawsuits if the side effects of nanotechnology outweigh the benefits.

23 Plight of Palestinian Child Detainees Highlights Global Problem

Sources:
Left Turn, December 2004
Title: "Control & Resistance: Palestinian Child Prisoners"
Authors: Catherine Cook, Adah Kay, Adam Hanieh

The Guardian, August 28, 2004
Title: "Palestinians Want an End to Their Solitary Confinement"
Author: Karma Nabulsi

Faculty Evaluator: Carolyn Epple, Ph. D. Maureen Buckley, Ph. D.
Student Researcher: Shatae Jones

According to Catherine Cook, Adah Kay, and Adam Hanieh, approximately 350 Palestinian children ages 12-18, are currently being held in Israeli prisons. Over 2,000 children have been arrested since the beginning of the second Intifada, a Palestinian uprising against the Israeli occupation. This number corresponds with number given in a report by the human rights organization Defense for Children International, which adds that another 170 children are held in military detention centers.

Looking at the testimonies from hundreds of detained children, Cook et al found a pattern in the children's experience of arrest, interrogation, sentencing and prison conditions. The children overwhelmingly reported abuse during their experience in either prison or detention camp. The consistency of these reports reveals that these patterns of abuse are not just the actions of a few bad soldiers, but perhaps reveals a broader policy. Virtually every child interviewed describes a deliberate pattern of behavior by Israeli soldiers or police characterized by violence, physical and psychological threats, and overwhelming force, often in the middle of the night. Cook, Kay and Hanieh believe that the similarity in testimonies from child prisoners points to a systematic approach to child abuse, calculated to exploit children's vulnerability and create feelings of fear, intimidation and helplessness.

One testimony in their study states, "Because there was no one I could talk to and I felt incredibly frightened and scared, I tried to commit suicide while being in solitary confinement. On October 12, 2003, I was moved to Ofer Military Prison Camp. When I arrived the soldiers asked me to take off my clothes. They used a metal detector on my naked body. One hand was holding the metal detector, while the other hand touched my naked body, concentrating mainly on my back and bottom."

Even without the abuses by personnel, the living conditions that children are put in are bad enough. The report by Karma Nabulsi tells us that children are "locked in cells for hours on end with, in some cases, only 45 minutes outdoor exercise allowed every two days. Many are forced to sleep on the floor due to overcrowding. Windows are boarded up with iron panels, which block out the light and intensify the heat in the rooms." Practices, such as these, have been well documented in other troubled areas around the world, but are only beginning to be documented within occupied territories.

Also noticeable is a lack of decent healthcare. Cook, Kay and Hanieh see the abuse of children during interrogation, the notoriously poor sanitary conditions within Israeli prisons, and denial of adequate medical treatment as ways to pressure child detainees into collaboration. When conducting a series of interviews with 60 ex-prisoners from Bethlehem in 1994, the authors found that "90 percent of those interviewed claimed that the administration used the denial of medical treatment as a way of recruiting collaborators." One former child prisoner asserted that prisoners were well aware that the prison hospitals were using the threat of withholding treatment to force detainees to collaborate. According to the DCI report, "In many areas, Israel does not reach the standards demanded by the minimum rules [of the UN Convention of the Rights of a Child]. For instance, it is not possible for a youth in detention to work, and there are no educational facilities. In the territories, the situation is even worse." This statement implies that the rights of all children (Israeli as well as Palestinian) are not being attended to by Israeli authorities. It seems that in Israel there is a problem in the attitude toward child welfare in general. But, according to Project Censored evaluator Maureen Buckley, "this story represents just a small piece of the larger picture of the ongoing, worldwide failure to protect the rights of children."

REFERENCE:
DCI Israel Children's Rights Monitor, 2004 Report "International Standards."

UPDATE BY CATHERINE COOK, ADAH KAY AND ADAM HANIEH: In the 15 months since this article was written in spring 2004, little has changed for child prisoners, and the issue has been largely boycotted by the mainstream press. But the thousands of Palestinian political prisoners, including children under 18, in Israeli detention centers and jails remain high on the political agenda. The Israeli government still uses prisoners as a key bargaining chip in the so called "peace process." But relevant human rights and international standards play no part in this ritual; Palestinian negotiators could not secure the unconditional release of all child prisoners as an issue separate from negotiations over adult prisoners. So the recent second tranche of prisoners released at the end of May included only 14 children. As in the past, most of the other 384 prisoners, had almost completed their sentences.

Last year saw the revelations of U.S. torture of Iraqi prisoners including children dubbed the biggest story of the Iraqi war by William Rivers Pitt in his article "Torturing Children."[1] Like Israel, the U.S. administration and military attempted to present this as rogue practice, but the evidence pointed to systemic abuse. We and others tried at the time to highlight the striking similarities to the abuse meted out over decades to Palestinian prisoners including children.[2] But again, these parallels largely escaped the mainstream press.

Currently, out of around 7,500 Palestinian detainees, about 280 are children (including 30 boy administrative detainees held indefinitely without formal trial or charge). DCI/PS,[3] who represent the majority of child prisoners, report a dramatic increase in arrests of 12-14 year-olds, most for throwing stones last year. There has also been an increase last year in the numbers of children arrested from the northern West Bank (e.g.Nablus and Jenin), in part reflecting the continued use of mass arrests as a method of control. They also note harsher sentencing policies, such as doubling of sentences of more than three years compared with 2003—only partly due to some of the charges being more serious.

There has been no improvement in detention conditions with particularly poor provision in detention/interrogation centers—bare cells and inadequate food served on bits of paper with no cutlery. In prisons,[4] girls are still housed in cells with adult women prisoners with little natural light, and they get no formal education. Boys also receive no education, except in one of the prisons; many are still beaten and punished by having family visits refused or solitary confinement.

In August 2004, in protest against harsh prison conditions, Palestinian prisoners launched their largest hunger strike in decades. The Israeli prison administration did their best to undermine this by confiscating liquids and salts, setting up barbeques outside cells, raiding cells, beating up prisoners, placing them in isolation and refusing medical treatment until the strike ended. Eventually the strike petered out. As with so many other Palestinian issues, this action was largely ignored by the mainstream press.

This last year has seen Israel's position, tacitly supported by the U.S. government, strengthened against the Palestinians. Under cover of its promise of unilateral disengagement from Gaza, Israel continues to entrench itself in the West Bank and extends its system of suppression and control in which arrest and prison play such a key role.

FOR ADDITIONAL INFORMATION:

Defence for Children International/Palestine Section, Research and International Advocacy Unit, RIA@dci-pal.org, www.dci-pal.org

Adameer Prisoners' Support and Human Rights Association, www.addameer.org, addameer@p-ol.com

Sumoud http://sumoud.tao.ca; Email sumoud@tao.ca

NOTES

1. William Rivers Pitt, "Torturing Children," *Truthout* July 20, 2004.
2. Catherine Cook, "Torture of Iraqi Prisoners Spotlights Israeli Treatment of Palestinian Prisoners," Information Brief # 106, May 11, 2004.
3. *Defence for Children International (Palestine Section) Annual Review* 2004.
4. DCI/PS's Legal department regularly visits prisons, detention and interrogation centres in the West Bank and in Israel to monitor prison conditions for children and intercede on their behalf with the Israeli prison administration.

24 Ethiopian Indigenous Victims of Corporate and Government Resource Aspirations

Sources:
World War 4 Report, Issue 97, April 2004
"State Terror in Ethiopia: Another Secret War for Oil?"
http://www.ww4report.com/97.html

Z Magazine Online, May 2004
Author: keith harmon snow

Faculty Evaluator: Tom Lough, Ph.D.
Student Researcher: Thedoria Grayson

According to a report by keith harmon snow, after conducting Field observations in January, the U.S.-based organizations Genocide Watch and Survivor's Rights International released a conclusive report on February 22, 2004. This report provides evidence that Ethiopian People's Revolutionary Defense Front (EPRDF) soldiers and "Highlander" militias in the Anuak territory of Ethiopia have killed thousands of native civilians. The Highlanders are predominantly Tigray and Amhara peoples who resettled in Anuak territory in 1974. The Highlanders are on a quest to force the Anuak from the region. Ethiopia is the latest U.S. ally in the "War on Terror" to turn its back on its own indigenous peoples. The Annuak territory is a zone coveted by corporate interests for its oil and gold. EPRDF soldiers and settlers from Ethiopian highlands initiated a campaign of massacres, repressions, and mass rape, deliberately targeting the Anuak minority.

According to Snow, the U.S. government was informed about the unfolding violence in the Gambella region as early as December 16, 2003. Massacres were reportedly ordered by the commander of the Ethiopian army in Gambella, Nagu Beyene, with the authorization of Gebrehad Barnabas, Regional Affairs Minister of the Ethiopian government.

According to Anuak sources relying on sympathetic oppositionists within the regime, the EPRDF plans to procure the petroleum of Gambella were laid out at a top-level cabinet meeting in Addis Ababa (the capital of Ethiopia) in September 2003. Prime Minister Meles Zenawi chaired the meeting, at which the militant ethnic cleansing of the Anuaks was reportedly openly discussed. December 13, 2003 marked the start of a coordinated military operation to systematically eliminate Anuaks. Sources from inside the military government's police and intelligence network say that the code name of the military operation was: "OPERATION SUNNY MOUNTAIN."

The killing of eight UN officials and Ethiopian government officials whose van was ambushed on December 13, 2003 sparked the recent conflict. Although there is no specific evidence about the ethnicity of the killers, the targets of the attacks have been mainly Anuaks. After this attack, EPRDF soldiers used automatic weapons and hand grenades, then attacked the Anuak villages, summarily executing civilians, burning dwellings (sometimes with people inside), and looting property. Some 424 Anuak people were reportedly killed, with over 200 more wounded. Numerous sources report that there have been regular massacres of the Anuak since 1980. Discrimination against the Anuak has been detailed in six reports published in the *Cultural Survival Quarterly* beginning in 1981(see e.g.: "Oil Development in Ethiopia: A Threat to the Anuak of Gambella," Issue 25.3, 2001). There is no evidence to support claims of previous communal violence between the two indigenous groups(Anuaks and the local Nuer), according to the *New York Times* and other media, and by the EPRDF government.

As of November 4, 2004, at least 1,500 and perhaps as many as 2,500 Anuak civilians have died in the recent fighting. Intellectuals, leaders, students and other educated classes have been intentionally targeted. Hundreds of people remain unaccounted for and many have mysteriously "disappeared." Thousands and perhaps tens of thousands of Anuak homes have reportedly been burned.

The Anuak men have been killed, arrested, or displaced, leaving thousands of women and children vulnerable. Anuak women and girls are routinely raped, gang-raped and kept as sexual slaves by EPRDF forces, often at gunpoint. Girls have been shot for resisting rape, and summary executions for girls held captive for prolonged periods as sexual slaves have been reported. Reports from non-Anuak police officials in Gambella indicate an average of up to seven rapes per day. Due to the isolation of women and girls in rural areas, rapes remain underreported. Some 6,000 to 8,000 Anuak remain at refugee camps in Pochalla, Sudan, and there are an estimated 1,000 annual refugees in Kenya. In August 2004, approximately 25 percent (roughly 50,000 people) of Gambella's population had been displaced.

To the Anuak and other indigenous peoples of southwestern Ethiopia, the government of Prime minister Meles Zenawi is a ruthless military dictatorship. Almost everyone links "the problem" to Gambella's oil. "Since the problem, we are not able to farm or to fish," said one Anuak survivor who was shot three times. He is shy, but he will show you where one bullet entered and exited his wrist. He was shot December 13, 2003—the day the EPRDF and local highlander militias launched their genocidal war on the Anuaks. "Many men ran away into the bushes and were killed since the problem began," says one witness. "They are raping many girls. They keep some women by force." The violence has almost completely disrupted this year's planting season, and people believe that famine in the coming winter months (October-March, 2005) will be exacerbated by the destruction of milling machines and food stores.

In August 2003, the U.S. committed $28,000,000 to international trade enhancements with Ethiopia. Beginning July 2003, forces from the Pentagon's Combined Joint Task Force-Horn of Africa (CJTF-HOA) held a three-month bilateral training exercise with Ethiopian forces at the Hurso Training Camp, northwest of Dire Dawa. The U.S. Army's 10th Mountain Division recently completed a three-month program to train an Ethiopian army division in counter-terrorism attacks. Operations are coordinated through the CJTF-HOA regional base in Djibouti, where the Halliburton subsidiary KBR is the prime contractor.

Because Ethiopia is considered to be an essential partner of the U.S. in its "War on Terrorism," the U.S. provided some $1,835,000 in International Military and Educational Training (IMET) to Ethiopia between 1995–2000. Some 115 Ethiopian officers were trained under the IMET program from 1991–2001. Approximately 4,000 Ethiopian soldiers have participated in IMET and Foreign Military Sales and Deliveries programs. The U.S. also equipped, trained, and supported Ethiopian troops under the Africa Regional Peacekeeping program. Ethiopia has remained a participant of the IMET program in 2000–2004. A U.S. AID representative asked Congress to approve some $80,000,000 in funding for Ethiopia's programs in the Fiscal Year of 2005. Ethiopia was described as a "top priority" of the Bush Administration.

In 2000, Texas-based Sicor Inc. signed a $1.4 billion dollar deal with Ethiopia for the "Gazoil" joint venture to exploit oil and gas in the southeast Ogaden Basin. Hunt Oil Company of Dallas, Texas is also involved in the Ogaden Basin through the subsidiary Ethiopia Hunt Oil Company. Hunt Oil's chairman of the board and CEO Ray L. Hunt is also director of Halliburton Company. U.S. Cal Tech International Corp. is also reportedly negotiating a joint venture with the China National Petroleum Corp. to operate in the same regions. The Anuak are also gold miners in the Gambella district. U.S. based Canyon Resources has gold operations in southern Ethiopia. The interest of multinational gold and oil corporations indicate alterior motives in the terror campaign against the Anuaks.

Anuak sources in Gambella state: "The Anuak people have not been involved in the discussions about the oil, our leaders have not agreed on these projects, and they will not hire any Anuaks for these jobs. If any Anuaks say anything about the oil, he will be arrested."

UPDATE BY KEITH HARMON SNOW: It is important to recognize that the U.S. public is subject to an ongoing institutionalization of "truth" and "reality" that is premised on *total information warfare*. This is nowhere so starkly evident as with the stereotypes, mythologies and deceptions doled out to the U.S. public on the subject of Africa (the Arab world, and all things Islamic, run a close second). This includes mainstream reportage, policy debates, scholarly journals, tabloids, radio shows, and print magazines—from *WIRED* to *National Geographic*. This is also evident in supposed "alternative" media sources like *The Nation* and films like *Hotel Rwanda*.

Alternative? To what? Virtually all available media fall on a spectrum that serves up topics and frameworks that are tolerated and allowed, where "healthy debate," "exposés" and (perceived) "hostility" (to what people in other countries are calling EMPIRE), are even *encouraged*. Hence we have Seymour Hersh offering us revealing exposés on torture in Abu Ghraib, but saying nothing about the profits being made over the dead bodies due to U.S. sponsored covert operations and destabilization in Congo during and since the Clinton regime.

Nation editor Katrina Van de Heuvel will steer sharply away from any challenge to the "humanitarian" actions of the International Rescue Committee (IRC), a strong proponent of military intervention—allied with the other two big humanitarian agencies CARE and Refugees International—in the recent massive lobbying effort to "stop genocide" in Darfur, Sudan. Is there genocide in Darfur? If so, or even not so, why has it received overwhelming press attention while the Anuak genocide has received none? What about nearby Congo? And Rwanda?

Van de Heuvel has ties with Henry Kissinger, a member of an IRC board, and one of the few U.S. officials to be publicly labeled as a war criminal. The IRC is a powerful faction in Congo, Rwanda and Sudan, and the Congolese accused them of espionage. CARE's "partners" include aerospace and defense corporation Lockheed-Martin, who is also a major underwriter of Seymour Hersh's regular print venue, the war advocacy journal *Atlantic Monthly*.

A truly "investigative" journalist might hack through the propaganda of *Hotel Rwanda* to get to United Artists parent company Metro Goldwyn Meyer, whose directors, not surprisingly, given what the film does not tell you about the U.S.-sponsored invasion of Rwanda (1990–1994), include current United

Technologies director and U.S. General (Ret.) Alexander Haig. Recall that "I'm in charge here" Al Haig served under a Hollywood actor named Ronald Reagan. *Hotel Rwanda* took off from the now celebrated but wholly mythologized book *We Regret To Inform You That Tomorrow We Will Be Killed* by Philip Gourevitch, the *New Yorker*'s premier Africanist, and whose brother-in-law, Jamie Rubin, was Madeleine Albright's leading man. *The Nation* runs the standard nonsense on Rwanda, usually by Victoria Britain. Another pro-military interventionist on Darfur, Samantha Power could surely satisfy *The Nation*, given her selective and patriotic journalism on Rwanda and the Balkans, for which she won a Pulitzer.

Behind the mass hysteria whipped up in the post-September 11th America are the dirty little and not-so-little but secret wars whipped up in defense of predatory capitalism and empire in "uncivilized" and "savage" places like Djibouti, Sudan, Sierra Leone, Liberia, Congo and (Gambella) Ethiopia.

By February 21, 2002, the U.S. DOD had already purchased 79 RQ-1 Predators from General Atomics, for a per unit price of about $7 million, or some $553 million dollars. "State Terror in Ethiopia" was the first report, and *WW4 Report* the first venue, to illuminate the U.S. military alliance with the Ethiopian regime and the regional base of U.S. covert operations in Hurso, Ethiopia as well as the presence of RQ-1 Predator Drones being operated over the entire Horn region by the Central Intelligence Agency. Smith College students recently working to "stop genocide" in Darfur held a letter-writing campaign demanding that George Bush authorize that unmanned Predator drones—impersonal, indiscriminate killing robots—be launched against Arabs on horses, and other "undefined" targets, in Darfur.

It takes more than one party to wage a war. From Chad, Uganda and Ethiopia come weapons and logistical support for the enemies of the Islamic regime in Khartoum. At the same time, the Bush gang has reportedly "allied" with the Sudan government in its "war on terror"—if we believe the Ken Silverstein "exposé" in the *L.A. Times* (which is merely being *expedient* in its truth-telling). Off the agenda are any discussions of the U.S. regimes of terror in Uganda or Cameroon, for example, or U.S. support for the Sudan People's Liberation Army and other warring militias and factions in Darfur, Chad, Ethiopia, Somalia, and Congo.

Like nearby Chad, Ethiopia has become a favored territory from which transnational corporate interests can be served by launching clandestine terror operations against Islamic governments, Al Queda phantoms, and other hostile enemies. The latter category, of course, includes Arabs on horseback, machete-wielding Hutus, Mai-Mai "wearing bathroom fixtures" on their heads, innocent men, women and children all over Africa, and, of course, the Anuaks of Ethiopia who, like the Ogonis in Nigeria and the Fur of Darfur, have the audacity to be living over someone else's oil.

Shortly after "State Terror in Ethiopia" appeared in *WW4 Report* and *Z Magazine*, Marc Lacey, Nairobi Bureau Chief for the *New York Times*, ran some damage control, and reported from Gambella with a nasty little blame-the-victims story that deflected attention from the undesirable details: "Amid Ethiopia's Strife, a Bathing Spot and Peace" (*New York Times*, 6/11/04). There was hardly a word about oil or U.S. interests, and Lacey framed the story to suggest that peace had returned to Gambella, an area rife with ancient tribal animosity, he declared, where the Anuaks "once went naked and ate rats." (Curiously, not one *New York Times* link to this story is active today, perhaps because it has been widely noted for its racism, and so it is being electronically erased.)

Doug McGill of the *McGill Report* has done some wonderful and consistent work to report on the Anuak story. *World War 4 Report* also published a second follow-up story titled "Ethnic Cleansing in Ethiopia." Soon after this appeared, Human Rights Watch finally published a major report on the Anuak genocide based on the field investigations "Today is the Day of Killing Anuaks" and "Operation Sunny Mountain?" (undertaken for Survivor's Rights International and Genocide Watch by this author, as an unpaid volunteer). While their researcher received a copy of "Operation Sunny Mountain?" several months prior to its formal release and before traveling to Ethiopia, Human Rights Watch never cited their sources or contacts. Survivor's Rights International and Genocide Watch (also a proponent of "stopping genocide" through U.S. or NATO military intervention in Darfur, Sudan) soon severed their ties with this investigator, apparently offended by the *WW4 Report* and *Z Magazine* stories on Ethiopia and Rwanda, which point to U.S. military involvement.

The U.S.-supported regime of Meles Zenawi in Ethiopia is going to fall, imminently, as widespread domestic dissent and protest, which remain underreported, further escalate. June 2005 saw massive government repression, troops firing on crowds, and torture spreading across Ethiopia after the people protested obvious election-rigging (sanctioned by Jimmy Carter and election monitors). Ethiopia's secret U.S.-sponsored war (2000) against Eritrea has destabilized the border region, causing untold death and despair. Murder, extrajudicial execution, rape, disappearances, arrest and imprisonment of Anuaks, Oromos, Nuers and other indigenous Ethiopian people continue. What makes "State Terror in Ethiopia" so poignant is its sharp juxtaposition to the stories of genocide and crimes against humanity in Darfur, which received widespread attention, and to Congo, which is mostly off the media agenda.

With Darfur, what is really at issue is not genocide, and it is not about "humanitarian" anything, or there wouldn't be so many people dead already—and still dying. It is about regime change, and some people will do anything to get us to support that. In Congo, the death toll has struck seven million since the U.S. invasion began, and the war rages on while both Clinton and Bush factions profit from diamond and gold and other hundreds-of-multimillion-dollars-a-month material thefts. Next to the holy wars of Congo and Darfur, the Anuaks are a mere thorn in the side of Empire. Such is the political economy of genocide.

25 Homeland Security Was Designed to Fail

Sources:
Mother Jones, September/October 2004
Title: "Red Alert"
Author: Matthew Brzezinski

NPR, September 24, 2004
Title: "Fortress America: On the Front Lines of Homeland Security" (an interview with Matthew Brzezinski)
Author Matthew Brzezinski

Faculty Evaluators: Greg and Meri Storino
Student Researcher: Joey Tabares

It was billed as America's frontline defense against terrorism. But badly underfunded, crippled by special interests, and ignored by the White House, the Department of Homeland Security (DHS) has been relegated to bureaucratic obscurity. Unveiled on March 1, 2003, the Department of Homeland Security had been touted as the Bush Administration's bold response to the new threats facing America in the post-Cold War world of global terrorism. It is currently composed of 22 formerly separate federal agencies and it boasts 186,200 employees. Its operations are funded by a budget of nearly $27 billion.

There are 15,000 industrial plants in the United States that produce toxic chemicals. According to the Environmental Protection Agency(EPA), about 100 of these plants could endanger up to a million lives with poisonous clouds of ammonia, chlorine, or carbon disulfide that could be released into the atmosphere over densely populated areas by a terror attack. Unprotected chemical plants are possible candidates for future attacks by terrorists. These are some of the most vulnerable pieces of infrastructure in America.

Following 9/11 there was a big push to increase security at all chemical plants in the United States. Democrats put forth a Chemical Security Act, the purpose of which was to codify parameters for site security, ensure safe transport of toxic materials, and prevent further accidents from happening. But Republicans defeated the bill after oil companies pumped millions of dollars into lobbying campaigns to stop it.

Matthew Brzezinski's article in *Mother Jones* asserts that President Bush doesn't put much importance, if any at all, on Homeland Security reports. Security spending has risen just 4 percent since 9/11, and most of that increase was only to cover higher insurance programs. There are many chemical plants that have no fencing requirements, cameras, and no guards. The article points out the spending needed to insure the safety of U.S. citizens and compares it (unfavorably) to the amount spent in Iraq over the same time period.

Aside from being hamstrung by its reluctant architects, DHS simply has not been able to compete with Iraq in the battle for resources. With the President's tax cuts trimming government revenues, and budget deficits reaching levels not seen since the Vietnam War, money is tight for programs the White House does not see as top priorities. The truth of the matter is that Homeland Security is very much a shoestring operation—so much so that worried Democrats in Congress keep trying to throw more money at it.

Brzezinski, recent author of "Fortress America" and former Wall Street correspondent, suggests the Department of Homeland Security needs a serious reassessment of its goals and operations to better protect Americans. He says the White House has decided that the Homeland Security intelligence unit should rank lower than the FBI and the CIA. Seven Republican Senators that had previously endorsed the Chemical Security Act later withdrew their support. $5.7 million in contributions from the petrochemical campaign (led by the American Petroleum Institute) helped to ensure that Republicans took the Senate in the 2002 midterm elections and that the Chemical Security Act die out. People opposing the act emphasized the economic impact of the Security Act. The argument was that Chlorine and its derivatives went into products that account for 45 percent of the nations GDP, and reductions to its production would hurt the economy.

Three years after 9/11 almost anybody can still gain entry into thousands of chemical sites across the country. If a factory spends lots of money on security spending upgrades, its products can't compete with other factories that spend nothing. Only legislation can level the playing field.

The failure of the mainstream media to acknowledge the fact that Homeland Security has been a complete washout further signifies the cozy relationship it enjoys with the halls of power. Protection of the homeland has been an area where the president has received consistently high marks from the country—ostensibly because this is the one area where he has stayed strong and focused. It would have been helpful for the country to know if this wasn't true.

REFERENCES:
Judy Clark, *Oil and Gas Journal*, June 23, 2003, "Government, Industry Forge Partnerships for Security Enhancement."
Primedia, August 1, 2003, "An Overlooked Vulnerability?"

Censored 2006 Runners-Up
Compiled by Christina Reski

GUATEMALAN WOMEN MURDERED FOR DEMOCRATIC ACTIVISM
Source: *Indymedia.org*, July/August 2004
Title: "Guatemala: 1,300 Women Murdered in Just Over Three Years"
Author: Diego Cevallos

Over 1,300 women have been killed since 2001 in Guatemala. Because of previous U.S. involvement, the country lacks the law enforcement mechanisms to prevent the murders of women, and many may be targeted due to their pro-democracy and worker's rights activism. Police and judicial authorities are implicated in some of the killings in Guatemala, where one woman a day is killed on average as a victim either of domestic violence or, more commonly, of ordinary criminal violence. Patricia Pinto, a member of the Latin American and Caribbean Committee for the Defense of Women's Rights and the Collective for the Defense of Women in Guatemala, pointed out that of the 19,000 reports of domestic violence received by prosecutors in 2002, just 10 were fully resolved in favor of the women reporting the violence.

PUBLIC BROADCASTING IN BIG DANGER
Sources:
Common Cause, commoncause.org, June 14, 2005
Title: "Public Broadcasting Under Fire"

Asheville Global Report, No. 260, Jan. 8-15, 2004
Title: "Public Broadcasting Under Siege: $800,000 Buys Two Seats on the Corporation for Public Broadcasting's board"

Republican majority in congress and new Bush appointments have targeted the Corporation for Public Broadcasting for de-funding. The House subcommittee voted to cut funding for public radio and television. They also voted to eliminate all Federal money for the CPB within 2 years.

FEDERAL LAW HINDERS STATES ABILITY TO PROTECT FOOD SAFETY

Source: *consumerunion.org,* Oct. 1, 2004
Title: "Committee Passes Bill Hindering States Ability to Protect Food Safety"
Author: Jean Halloran

The House Energy and Commerce Committee passed H.R. 2699, the National Uniformity for Food Act, paving the way for a possible vote in the full House of Representatives before Congress adjourns for the year. The measure would prevent states from enforcing their own food safety laws unless they are "identical" to federal law. Since few states laws are identical, the bill would take state and local health departments out of food safety enforcement.

SCIENTIST CONVENTION IN ESSEX ENGLAND ISSUES ENVIRONMENTAL WARNING

Source: *The Independent UK,* Feb. 6, 2005
Title: "Apocalypse Now: How Mankind is Sleepwalking to the End of the Earth"
Author: Geoffrey Lean

Floods, storms and droughts. Melting Arctic ice, shrinking glaciers, oceans turning to acid. The world's top scientists met in Essex in February of 2005 to warn that dangerous climate change is taking place today and to urge leaders to respond.

PROFITING OFF OF SENIOR AILMENTS

Source: *Public Citizen News,* May/June 2004
Title: "Greedy Rx Drug Companies Raise Prices to Discount Savings From Cards"
Author: Joan Claybrook

The Medicare discount card prohibits the government from negotiating better drug prices, giving drug companies free reign to raise prices. The Medicare discount card was proposed in 2001 to save senior citizens an average 10-25 percent off the price of most medications. The law, finalized by a Republican majority Congress and signed by Bush, prohibits the government from negotiating better drug prices. Not surprisingly, many drug companies raised their prices on the most commonly prescribed medications, which makes the discount card of little benefit. The real victors of this bill are the insurance and drug companies who will be making hundreds of billions of dollars. The full benefit doesn't even kick in until 2006. A web site that was constructed to allow seniors to determine which of the 73 different drug discount cards available were right for them (based on the medications they take), revealed that the prices were no better than what's already available at online pharmacies and generally higher than what Canadians pay for the same prescriptions. It is yet another victory for big business in the Bush Administration, promising that private markets can deliver health benefits more cheaply and efficiently than the Medicare program. Many seniors feel they have been tricked and are justifiably outraged.

ALL THE PRESIDENT'S MEN
Source: *New Progressive Institute Inc.*, Feb. 21, 2005
Title: "Secret Society: Just Who is the Council for National Policy, and Why Aren't They Paying Taxes?"
Author: Sarah Posner

The Council for National Policy (CNP) was established in 1981 by the right-wing, evangelical political motivator, Tim LaHaye. CNP holds a tax-exempt status, is not required to reveal the names of its members, membership is by invitation only and the CNP policy is to keep membership confidential and not to speak to the press or public about organizational business. In 2003, CNP received almost a million dollars in contributions from members who received tax deductions. CNP has been noted as the most influential gathering of conservatives in America. "A private meeting of 400 leading conservatives" is often code for CNP in the conservative press.

BALLOT INITIATIVES HAVE BECOME CORRUPTED BY CORPORATIONS
Source: reclaimdemocracy.org, March 7, 2004
Title: "Ballot Initiatives Hijacked by Corporations"
Authors: Jeffrey Kaplan, Jeff Milchen

The ballot initiative process has become corrupted by the influx of corporate millions. Corporations are aided by the poor construction of the law. Corporations use company funds to hire petitioners who gather signatures to get initiatives on the ballot that rescind the law and overturn ordinances. Undermining democracy can be lucrative for corporations but costly for the rest of us.

U.S. UNDERMINES INITIATIVE TO PROVIDE POOR COUNTRIES WITH ACCESS TO AIDS MEDICINE

Source: *New Internationalist,* 2005
Title: "Dollar Diplomacy"
Author: Sanjay Basu

HIV treatment requires a number of different types of medications, and these types are patented by different companies in the U.S. and UK. Ideal combination medications cannot be produced as one company owns the patent to a necessary chemical and another company owns the patent to a secondary component. The patents are argued to be necessary in order to give inventors a fixed time in a marketplace to recoup costs on research and development (R&D). But the R&D claim ignores the fact that most AIDS drugs were produced through public financing (even through the clinical trials stages), and 85 percent of the basic and applied research for the top five selling drugs on the market were produced through taxpayer funding.

U.S.-FINANCED ORGANIZATION PROMOTES THE OVERTHROW OF ELECTED LEADERS ABROAD

Source: *Mother Jones,* Dec. 2004
Title: "Outfront: The Coup Connection"
Author: Joshua Kurlantzick
The International Republican Institute, financed by the government, has been promoting the overthrow of elected leaders abroad. Despite USAID guidelines, which require working with people across political spectrums, the IRI almost always chooses sides with dictators—and against democratizing forces.

NATIONAL ID CARD ALLOWS GOVERNMENT TO TRACK ANYONE, ANYTIME

Source: *Babylonrising* 11/08/04
Title: "The New National ID Card"
Author: Steve Jones

The National ID Card will allow the government to keep track of people in ways it never has before. DNA will be encoded into birth certificates and driver's licenses.

NEW EARLY WARNING RULE WOULD ONLY WARN AUTOMAKERS, NOT THE PUBLIC

Source: *bushsecrecy.org*, Feb. 26, 2005
Title: "New 'Early Warning' Rule Would Still Keep Auto Defects Secret"
Author: Public Citizen, citizen.org

Under a rule announced in July 2003, the only information pertaining to auto defects that will be publicly available is the data on injuries and deaths. Quarterly information submitted by automakers to the National Highway Traffic Safety Administration, including consumer complaints to manufacturers, warranty claims and field reports from dealers, will be kept secret.

GOT MILK? AT WHAT COST?

Source: *Dollars & Sense*, Issue #225 Sept/Oct 2004
Title: "Hidden Horrors California Dairy Workers Face Danger and Abuse"
Author: R. M. Arrieta

California has a huge dairy industry. To keep labor costs down, dairies are hiring illegal immigrants. Many workers with an illegal immigration status are dependent upon their employers for housing, which makes them vulnerable. The workers slave for 12 to 16 hours a day to make less than a living wage. Meal breaks are few or non-existent, there is no overtime pay, and some owners abuse their workers mentally and physically. In 2001 the death of two workers did prompt a visit from Cal OSHA who started to dole out fines to dairies in the Central Valley. According to the California Department of Food and Agriculture, California provides 19 percent of the nation's milk supply. The workers are beginning to organize and have formed California Rural Legal Assistance(CRLA), a farm worker advocacy group. However, this group can only represent those who are documented, permanent residents possessing green cards. Most of the dairies are tied up in appeals and have not paid.

PRIVATIZATION OF MILITARY HEALTH CARE IS BIG BUSINESS

Source: *People's Weekly World Newspaper Online*, Sept. 9, 2004
Title: "Bush to Privatize Military Health Staff"
Author: Phil E. Benjamin

Medical and dental professionals provide care to over 8.9 million active military personnel, their dependents, and retirees. Turning these health-related functions over to private contractors would be a major financial boon to many Bush supporters. For example, Senate Majority Leader Bill Frist runs the largest chain of for-profit hospitals in the U.S.: Columbia/HCA, which is a major player in the recently enacted Bush Medicare drug fiasco. There are now 40,648 civilians and 91,917 military personnel employed by this program. The privatization process alone has been allocated a budget of $35.8 million. Privatization of these services would mean the end of almost all public accountability.

SUICIDAL TROOPS IN THE WAR ON TERROR
Source: *Frontline,* March, 2004
Title: "Coming to Grief"
Author: Hans Johnson

Mental health problems are contributing to an increased suicide rate among U.S. service members in Iraq. From a survey conducted by *Stars and Stripes* of 2,000 service members, 34 percent reported their morale as low or very low. Nearly 1,000 troops from the occupied territory have been transported to Germany to be treated for mental health problems. According to William Winkenwerder, a director of mental health policy at the Pentagon, the official rate of 13.5 suicides per 100,000 troops on the ground is about 20 percent higher than the recent average of 11. Hospital records from the Landstuhl Regional Medical Center in Germany report that 12,000 soldiers (10,000 from Iraq, and 2,000 from Afghanistan) are receiving care. Army Colonel Rhonda Cornum, who oversees the medical center, estimates that nearly 10 percent of those troops are hospitalized for mental health injuries. Carl Rising-Moore, a U.S. activist, is trying to urge Canadian armed forces veterans to help him construct a "Freedom Underground." This system would aid U.S. service members who go AWOL from combat in Iraq by crossing the border into Canada. This would serve as a last resort for soldiers who are considering pulling the trigger on themselves.

OVERSEAS WORKERS CAN POST OUR PERSONAL RECORDS WITH IMPUNITY
Source: *Public Citizens News,* Nov/Dec. 2004
Title: "Outsourcing Your Privacy: Protections Are Lost When Records are Sent Overseas"
Author: Megan Farrington

Companies are sending the personal records of U.S. citizens overseas to be processed by low-income workers in countries that have no laws against or punishment for posting them in public or online. This was discovered when some consumers found their personal information had, indeed, been posted online.

CHEMICAL COMPANIES USE NEW LEGAL TACTICS TO HIDE PAST MISDEEDS

Source: *The Nation,* Feb. 7, 2005
Title: "Cancer, Chemicals and History"
Author: Jon Wiener

Companies are using new tactics to insure past misdeeds are not revealed in court by attempting to discredit academic research on vinyl chloride and cancer. Twenty of the biggest chemical companies in the United States have launched a campaign to discredit two historians who have studied the industry's efforts to conceal links between their products and cancer. In an unprecedented move, attorneys for Dow, Monsanto, Goodrich, Goodyear, Union Carbide and others have subpoenaed and deposed five academics who recommended that the University of California Press publish the book *Deceit and Denial: The Deadly Politics of Industrial Pollution,* by Gerald Markowitz and David Rosner.

PLAN COLOMBIA KILLING THOUSANDS OF NON-COMBATANTS

Source: *Earthisland.org,* Autumn 2004
Title: "Chronicle of a Disaster Foretold"
Author: Brad Miller

U.S. aid, known as Plan Colombia, is now being openly used for counter-insurgency and the protection of U.S. oil corporations' assets. Four hundred U.S. soldiers now occupy Colombia; the Bush Administration hopes to double this number in 2005. In 2003, Colombian President Alvaro Uribe and the Colombian Congress passed an "anti-terrorist" measure that gave the military judicial powers to tap phones, conduct searches and raids without warrants and arrest subjects solely on the basis of accusation. Further, any member of the security forces who commits human rights violations while battling terrorists will be immune from prosecution. Over four thousand non-combatants are killed in Colombia every year.

COLOMBIAN COCA-COLA MAFIA

Source: *Conscious Choice*, March 2004
Title: "Coke's Campaign of Terror"
Author: Kari Lydersen

In Carepa, Colombia where a Coca-Cola bottling plant operates, the managers employed members of one of the brutal, armed paramilitary groups, the United Self-Defense Forces of Colombia, to oppose the union workers. Coca-Cola does not own the bottling plants, but contracts with the companies that do. As the union at the bottling plant began organizing, the paramilitary group began threatening the union organizers. The Colombian Trade Union Federation reports that 45 trade unionists were murdered in the first eight months of 2003, and 117 or more were murdered in 2002. Fearing for their lives, about 60 out of 100 plant workers quit and fled the area. The union was crushed and the new workers were hired at wages less than half of what the union members were making. The union wage of about $380 per month dropped to $130.

SHIELD FROM MANDATORY GOVERNMENT DISCLOSURE

Source: *News Media Update*, Sept. 16, 2004
Title: "Satellite Images Protected from Release Under Defense Bill"
Author: Kirsten B. MItchell

A Senate provision in the National Defense Authorization Act for 2005 would make acquiring unclassified satellite images impossible. The provision would allow agencies to protect satellite images and any unclassified reports or information derived from the images. It was intended to shield information from mandatory government disclosure under the Freedom of Information Act. This new provision, however, falls under one of the nine exemptions in the FOI Act, which protects information made confidential by other federal laws. The usefulness of such imagery is readily apparent. These satellite images are used by news organizations in covering wars, refugee movements, natural disasters, genocides, and illicit weapons. The Senate has already passed the measure and a congressional committee is working to iron out the differences in the House and Senate versions of the bill.

RADIOACTIVE DUMP TO BE SOLD TO PUBLIC AS NATURE PARK

Source: *Truth Out*, Jan. 22, 2005
Title: "The Radioactive Cover-up at Rocky Flats"
Author: Amanda Griscom Little

An FBI agent alleges the government is lying about radioactive material dumped at Colorado weapons plant. The site is now being turned into a park. The FBI agent exposed deadly contamination at the old nuclear-weapons plant, but the federal government has concealed the findings. Congress has voted to convert the tract into a wildlife refuge and open it to school field trips and public recreation.

PETTY THEFT FOR LIFE

Source: *The Guardian*
Title: "Buried Alive Under California's '3 Strikes and You're Out' Law"
Author: Dan Glaister

Sixty-five percent of those imprisoned under three strikes in California were convicted of non-violent crimes; 354 of them received 25-years-to-life sentences for petty theft of less $250. The cost of keeping these people in jail is boiling over to more than $1 billion a year. California is one of a few states that do not restrict the initiative to violent crimes.

WOMEN'S ADVANCES IN PAY NOT AS ROBUST AS WAS THOUGHT

Source: *BusinessWeek*, June 14, 2004
Title: "Women's Pay: Why the Gap Remains a Chasm"
Author: Aaron Bernstein

A new study spells out the costly impact of family obligations. Women who drop out of the workforce risk derailing their career and permanently slashing their pay. Just one year off cuts a woman's total earnings over 15 years by 32 percent, while two years slice it by 46 percent and three by 56 percent.

CORPORATE WAR PROFITEERS UNDERMINING RECONSTRUCTION OF IRAQ

Source: *Center for Corporate Responsibility*, Dec. 31, 2004
Title: "Top Ten War Profiteers of 2004: You know it's Bad When Halliburton is #7"
Author: corporatepolicy.org

In December, Congressman Henry Waxman (D-CA) announced that "a growing list of concerns about Halliburton's performance" on contracts that total $10.8 billion have led to multiple criminal investigations into overcharging and kickbacks. At the beginning of the Iraq war, Andrew Natsios, head of the U.S. Agency for International Development (AID), proclaimed that the reconstruction of Iraq would look like a modern-day Marshall Plan. But a year and a half later, fierce resistance to the occupation, combined with bureaucratic ineptitude and corporate corruption, threaten to undermine the Bush Administration's grand designs.

BUSH ADMINISTRATION HAS BIG PLANS FOR IRAQI OIL
Source: *The Toronto Star*, Sept. 20, 2004
Title: "Crude Dudes"
Author: Linda McQuaig

A Cheney Task Force document released under court order, titled: "Foreign Suitors for Iraqi Oilfields" identifies 63 oil companies from 30 countries and specifies which Iraqi oil fields each company is interested in, as well as the status of the company's negotiations with Saddam Hussein's regime. Among the companies are Royal Dutch/Shell of the Netherlands, Russia's Lukoil and France's Total Elf Aquitaine, which was identified as being interested in the 25-billion-barrel Majnoon oil field.

BUSH'S SPACE PROGRAM: IS IT WORTH THE COST?
Source: *The Ecologist*, July/August 2004
Title: "Bush Lightyear"
Author: Karl Grossman

Bush Administration is gearing up to launch nuclear weapons into space. In a time of social poverty, the Bush Administration is engaging NASA in an extremely expensive, dangerous and unreliable space program.

PENTAGON TO BEGIN BROADCASTING ON TELEVISION
Source: BigNewsNetwork.com, Feb 27, 2005
Title: "Pentagon to Broadcast to Millions of U.S. Homes"

The Pentagon will now produce and disseminate the news itself. The service will emanate from what is known as the Pentagon Channel, an internal public relations television unit within the Department of Defense.

MAKING THE BIG BUCKS

Source: *Impact Press,* June/July 2004
Title: "Why Have Corporate Reforms Failed to Control CEO Pay?"
Author: Scott Klinger

In 2003 the average U.S. manufacturing worker made $517 a week compared to the average large company CEO who made $155,769 a week. This 301:1 ratio was up from 282:1 in 2002 and just 42:1 in 1982. There have been minor reforms to improve this inequality, but the vast majority of large company corporate directors are current or retired CEOs of other large businesses. For one CEO to challenge another CEO's pay would challenge their own status. The Security and Exchange Commission (SEC) is currently considering another change of policy that would give shareholders direct access to nominate Director candidates to a proxy ballot.

UKRAINIAN PRESIDENTIAL CANDIDATE CORRUPTED BY US/IMF INFLUENCE

Source: *Global Research,* Nov. 28, 2004
Title: "IMF Sponsored 'Democracy' in The Ukraine"
Author: Michel Chossudovsky

Victor Yushchenko was backed by the U.S. and IMF with the promise that he would break unions and institute "austerity policies" in Ukraine. He is not only supported by the IMF and the international financial community, he also has the endorsement of The National Endowment for Democracy (NED), Freedom House and George Soros' Open Society Institute, which played a behind-the-scenes role last year in helping "topple Georgia's president Eduard Shevardnadze by putting financial muscle and organizational metal behind his opponents." (New Statesman, 29 November 2004).

"HUMAN RIGHTS ACT" AIMS TO SABOTAGE NORTH/SOUTH KOREAN PEACE TALKS

Sources: *People's Weekly World,* Dec. 11-17, 2004
Title: "New Law Aims to Destabilize North Korea"
Author: Dan Margolis

And
The Guardian, Dec. 15, 2004
Title: "U.S. Law Aimed at North Korea
Author: Dan Margolis

In 2004, President Bush signed the "North Korea Human Rights Act of 2004" (NKHRA), which earmarks over $23 million dollars a year for what many see as interference in the internal affairs of the Democratic People's Republic of Korea (DPRK). Critics and supporters alike (including the architect of the bill) say it is aimed not at human rights, but at destabilizing and overthrowing the DPRK government.

CIA FUNDS PROMISED STUDENTS
WHO TAKE THE RIGHT COURSES
Source: *CounterPunch*, 2005 Vol. 12, No. 01
Title: "Exposing the Pat Roberts Intelligence Scholars Program: The CIA's Campus Spies"
Author: David H. Price

The Pat Roberts Intelligence Scholars Program is using universities as covert training grounds for the CIA and other agencies. Students are not allowed to tell fellow students or professors about their arrangement. The secrecy surrounding the current use of university classrooms as covert training grounds for the CIA and other agencies now threatens the fundamental principles of academic openness as well as the integrity of a wide array of academic disciplines.

ENERGY ALTERNATIVES MOVING AHEAD
DESPITE LACK OF GOVERNMENT SUPPORT
Source: *Mother Jones*, Dec. 2004
Title: "One Roof at a Time"
Author: Bill McKibben

Despite mountains of evidence from other countries and local areas of the U.S. that show the possibilities of alternative energy, the Bush Administration is committed to a nuke/oil-power-only policy. However, with no help from the Bush Administration—but plenty from Europe, Japan, New York, and California—solar power is edging into the mainstream.

THIS MODERN WORLD

by TOM TOMORROW

DO-IT-YOURSELF FUNNIES

SPECIAL PRE-ELECTION DEADLINE EDITION!

INSTRUCTIONS: 1. CIRCLE THE OPTIONS WHICH MOST ACCURATELY REFLECT THE ACTUAL OUTCOME OF THE ELECTION. 2. GUFFAW HEARTILY.

GOSH, BIFF--THE OUTCOME OF *THIS* ELECTION DEFINITELY (is/is not) SUBJECT TO *DISPUTE!*

THAT'S *TRUE*, BETTY! (George Bush/John Kerry/neither man) WON AN *UNDENIABLY* (legitimate/questionable) VICTORY!

YES, IT IS CERTAINLY (fortunate/unfortunate) THAT THIS ELECTION (was not/was) MARRED BY VOTING IRREGULARITIES AS A RESULT OF (hacked voting machines/confusion and incompetence/outright fraud)!

THINGS DEFINITELY (could/could not) HAVE GONE WORSE!

OF COURSE, WE *CAN'T* FORGET THE EMOTIONS WE ALL FELT WHEN FEARS OF A LAST-MINUTE (terrorist attack/October Surprise/completely unpredictable event) TURNED OUT TO BE UTTERLY (prophetic/misguided)!

IT'S HARD TO *IMAGINE* HOW DIFFERENTLY THINGS MIGHT HAVE TURNED OUT IF IT (had/had not) REALLY *HAPPENED!*

AT *ANY* RATE--I'LL BET MOST AMERICANS ARE EXPERIENCING A SENSE OF (overwhelming relief/sickly despair) NOW THAT A REPEAT OF THE 2000 ELECTION DEBACLE (has been avoided/seems inevitable)!

WE SURE HAVE A LOT TO BE (grateful for/enraged by) *THIS* YEAR!

WE SURE *DO!* THIS ELECTION WAS *TRULY* PROOF THAT THE SYSTEM IS (in great shape/broken beyond any possibility of repair)!

I (could/couldn't) AGREE *MORE!*

THIS MODERN WORLD--THE CARTOON THAT'S ALWAYS TIMELY--EVEN WHEN IT'S *NOT!*

TOM TOMORROW©2004... www.thismodernworld.com

CHAPTER 2

Déjà vu: Updates on Prior Censored News

HAITI: DIPLOMACY BY DEATH SQUAD, U.S. AND GLOBAL
WEALTH INEQUALITY, ALIEN TORT CLAIMS ACT, BUSH CEN-
SORS SCIENTISTS, DANGERS OF DEPLETED URANIUM, THE
FEDERALIST SOCIETY & THE CHRISTIAN LEGAL SOCIETY, 9/11
RICO LAWSUIT, NEW NUKE PLANTS, FOX NEWS CAN LEGALLY
LIE, REINSTATING THE DRAFT, VOTER FRAUD & THE SALE OF
ELECTORAL POLITICS

By Peter Phillips, Lyn Duff, Kate Sims, Dora Ruhs, David Stolowitz,
Brittny Roeland, Lori Rouse, Bridget J. Thornton, Ambrosia Pardue,
Rebekah Cohen, Brooke Finley, Josh Parrish and Michele Salvail

CENSORED #12 2005
THE DESTABILIZATION OF HAITI

Original Sources:
KPFA RADIO-FLASHPOINTS, April 1, 2004
Title: "Interview with Aristide's Lawyer, Brian Concannon"
Reporter: Dennis Bernstein

GLOBALRESEARCH.CA, February 29, 2004
Title: "The Destabilization of Haiti"
Author: Michel Chossudovsky

DOLLARS AND SENSE, September/October 2003
Title: "Still Up Against the Death Plan in Haiti"
Author: Tom Reeves

KPFA—DEMOCRACY NOW!, March 17, 2004
Title: "Aristide Talks with Democracy Now! About the Leaders
of the Coup and U.S. Funding of the Opposition in Haiti"
Reporter: Amy Goodman

And *Censored 2005*, Chapter 10—Haiti: The Untold Story.

On February 29, 2004, President Jean-Bertrand Aristide was forced into exile by U.S. military. While the Bush Administration and the corporate press implied that Aristide left willingly, Aristide was able to give a detailed account of his U.S. military led kidnapping to a Haitian journalist in the United States via cell phone who, in turn, broadcast his speech on Pacifica Radio's Flashpoints News, KPFA. While the U.S. was forced to acknowledge the kidnapping allegations, they were quick to discredit them and deny responsibility. The circumstances underlying the current situation in Haiti, as well as the history of U.S. involvement is being ignored by U.S. officials and mainstream media.

HAITI: DIPLOMACY BY DEATH SQUAD CONTINUES

UPDATE BY LYN DUFF: It was February 29, 2005, one year to the day since a U.S.-backed group of disbanded soldiers violently overthrew the popularly elected democracy in Haiti, when Adele was attacked by a group of masked men affiliated with an anti-democracy militia.

The 16-year-old lived in a highly populated and impoverished neighborhood in Port-au-Prince that was known for its support of Aristide and Haiti's fledgling democratic movement. When attackers broke down the door of her one-room concrete-block house, Adele says she was sure that they were going to kill her.

She had good reason to make this assumption. Three weeks earlier a group of armed men, two of whom she recognized as newly inducted members of the Haitian National Police, arrived looking for her parents whom the police accused of being gang members. Both of Adele's parents were at work but unfortunately, she says, her father walked in right as the men were about to leave. The men shackled her father, Adele says, and then they forced him to kneel down outside the front door before shooting him in the back of the head.

The body of Adele's father body was discovered a week later in a ravine in the neighboring suburb of Carreforre. His body was naked, had been set on fire, and was being eaten by wild dogs, she says. Adele went to the offices of MINUSTAH (United Nations Stabilization Mission in Haiti) requesting help but was referred by them to the National Coalition for Haitian Rights (NCHR), a U.S. funded human rights organization that refuses to aid known or suspected supporters of Aristide and, according to independent international human rights groups, has played a repressive and colluding role with the coup government.

On the evening when the armed men returned to her home, they decided not to kill Adele. Instead, she says, they raped her.

Over the course of five hours inside her home and in the presence of her uncle and ten-year-old brother, more than a dozen men raped Adele. At one point, she says, her attackers forced her to have sexual contact with her uncle and, in an act reminiscent of the New York police abuse of Haitian immigrant Abner Louima, she was sodomized with a broom handle and a piece of metal pipe.

Sitting in a church sanctuary months later, Adele breaks into tears and rocks back and forth while telling her story. The American missionary who introduced us, Ann Lautan, says that Adele's story is far from unusual. Girls as young as eight or nine have been raped by members of anti-democracy militias, the Haitian National Police, and the disbanded Haitian military, she says.

One of the other young victims is Marjory, a 15-year-old from the northern port town of Cap Haitian who has become a vocal spokesperson for the rights of child victims of rape after armed gangs of disbanded Haitian soldiers in the north attacked her last year.

It was the middle of the night when masked men armed with semi-automatic assault rifles burst into Marjory's home. Then only 14, Marjory was the oldest daughter of a local trade unionist. When they discovered that her father, who the political opposition sought because of his support for the pro-democracy movement, was in hiding, they raped Marjory, her mother and an 11-year-old cousin.

It's been a year since she was attacked but Marjory remembers every moment of that night. She describes her attackers in detail, down to the scars on one man's hands and the smell of cigarettes on another's jacket.

"They violated me. [When it was happening] I closed my eyes and waited for them to finish... One of the men told me to open my eyes and look at him while he [raped me]. I didn't want to look at him. They hit me when I cried."

Today Marjory and her mother live with Christian missionaries who took them in after her father was arrested and disappeared five months ago. Marjory speaks openly now about her ordeal and has met with human rights delegations, several journalists and representatives of the United Nations. "Too many women are being violated. The victims need to come together, they need to speak on the radio about the crimes being committed against us," she says. "We are telling the United Nations, the foreigners, and George Bush that we will not allow the situation to continue. Children should not be raped. Women should not be raped. People should not be forced from their homes. We are asking for our rights which will only come with the return of democracy to Haiti."

Marjory and Adele are part of a growing number of young girls and women who human rights investigators say have been victims of mass rape committed by members of the disbanded military and their compatriots who patrol the countryside and Haiti's cities, hunting down supporters of Haiti's pro-democracy movement.

Marjory says she was targeted because her father's trade union organized against a wealthy businessman and because her parents are members of Lavalas, the political party led by ousted president Jean Bertrand Aristide. Other victims say they were targeted because they or their family members belong to other pro-democracy political organizations or because they work with peasant unions or local women's groups.

"Rape is becoming a common tool of oppression," explains attorney Mario Joseph whose organization Bureau des Avocats Internationaux (BAI) has investigated hundreds of human rights cases in the past year. Joseph, who assisted in the prosecution of the human rights crimes committed during the 1991-94 coup says that it is discouraging to see the number of convicted human rights violators who are now walking free and serving in the new U.S.-installed interim government.

"Women and girls are raped because their father or another relative is a member of Lavalas or is targeted [by the political opposition]. They are raped as a form of punishment. The victims do not feel they can go to the police for help with their problems because in many areas the people who victimized them are the ones running the show; they are the ones patrolling the streets as if they are police, committing crimes with impunity under the eyes of the UN. And even in Port-au-Prince, the former military has been hired into the national police force."

According to Leon Charles, chief of the Haitian National Police, 2000 former members of the Haitian Army have been integrated into the police force, with plans for an additional 1000 former soldiers to be hired by 2006. Aristide disbanded Haiti's army in 1994 after soldiers committed numerous human rights violations, including mass rapes, during the 1991-94 coup. United Nations soldiers have also been accused of participating in sexual attacks. In one case, high school student Diamanta Jean Paul, 17, said she was sodomized by Jordanian soldiers who were on patrol in the Delmas neighborhood of Port-au-Prince. The day after she came forward with her story the Jean Paul home was ransacked by police and her father and brother were arrested. The family fled to the Dominican Republic where they are now living in hiding.

In another case, Pakistani soldiers were accused of raping a 23-year-old woman at a banana plantation in the northern town of Gonaives.

"The foreigners grabbed me and pulled my pants down, had me lie on the ground and then raped me," said the woman who asked that her name be withheld. She says two soldiers raped her while a third watched.

Damian Onses-Cardona, spokesperson for the UN mission in Haiti, initially claimed MINUSTAH was "aggressively" investigating the case but later backed down and released statements to the press accusing the victim of being a prostitute, saying that she went willingly into the banana grove to exchange sex for money and only accused the soldiers of rape after they refused to pay her.

More than 7,000 UN troops from countries including China, Brazil and the United States, among others, are stationed in Haiti. One of the American military units currently stationed in Haiti is the Army Reserve 372nd Military Police Company. The unit became internationally known after photos leaked to the press exposed their abuse of Iraqis at the Abu Ghraib prison.

Capt. Michael Rauh, the unit's commander, said that none of the soldiers convicted of charges in the prisoner-abuse scandal would be transferred to Haiti. The announcement has done little to soothe the concerns of human rights monitors who note that U.S. troops have been responsible for guarding leading figures of the former government, including ousted Prime Minister Yvon Neptune who was arrested by the coup government and has been held without charge or trial for nearly a year. In March and April 2004, U.S. marines were responsible for the deaths of nearly dozens of Haitian civilians, including numerous children, some of whom where shot in the back while fleeing street fighting in Port-au-Prince.

"These American soldiers sexually molested and abused hundreds of

Iraqi prisoners and what does President Bush do to them? He sends them to Haiti. What kind of a message is the American government trying to convey to us?" asks Marie Baptiste, a survivor of mass rape who advocates for other victims through a women's community group in her neighborhood.

"Dispatching the Abu Ghraib abusers to monitor the Haitian National Police (HNP), who are themselves committing atrocities similar to the ones committed in Abu Ghraib, this sends a clear message that the American government supports the brutal oppression of the ordinary Haitian people," she said.

"George Bush might as well give the Boca Raton regime [of interim prime minister Gerald Latortue] a blank check with a signed note of permission reading 'go ahead, beat and kill all the supporters of democracy, we're behind you 100 percent.'"

Nearly 1500 civilian police have been dispatched to Haiti in recent months. Canadian commissioner David Beer oversees civilian police, who have a dual role as both UN soldiers and trainers or monitors of the HNP. The civilian police dress in riot gear and accompany HNP on raids or other police actions targeted at pro-democracy neighborhoods. In one recent raid on Bel Air, residents, including several children, were shot and killed by both civilian police and HNP police. Beer told the press that only two people, both of whom were "gang members" were killed.

However, on a visit to Bel Air just hours after the shooting, pools of blood lay thickening on the dusty streets throughout the neighborhood. In one was a child's sandal, with part of the foot still strapped inside. Neighbors said it belonged to a toddler who was shopping with her mother and that as far as they knew she was still alive and had been taken by a local priest to a health clinic for treatment.

On Rue des Fronts Forts the body of a high school student, still in his parochial uniform, lay covered by fabric and green branches. In an alley near the Port-au-Prince cathedral an English grammar textbook and a bag of avocados lay in another pool of blood. The items belonged to a girl who was shot at close range by civilian police, say residents. She died shortly thereafter and UN soldiers removed her body.

In one alley, 9mm bullet casings lay scattered over the ground and an elderly man pointed to the bullet holes in the wall of his house. "The police and the foreign soldiers came here today and they killed my wife," he told reporters. "They shot her and she was 75-years-old."

Later, when Lautan visited the man, she discovered that his murdered wife was Emele Lisette, a survivor of mass rape who led a women's advocacy group. Ironically Lautan says, Lisette had recently approached the civilian police to ask that they take action to curb politically motivated rapes in Bel Air. "Emele thought that if the civilian police would step up their patrols and more closely monitor the HNP, that it would both force the HNP begin to crackdown on paramilitary groups who were committing rapes in the area at night, and that the civilian police could prevent the HNP officers from also participating in sexual assaults."

In the two weeks following the murder of Emele Lisette, Lautan says that there has been a sharp increase in politically motivated rapes in Bel Air. "It's as if the actions of the civilian police were paramount to a stamp of approval for the HNP and the militias," she says.

No one knows how many women and girls have been victims of politically motivated rapes since the coup violence began in late 2003, say human rights advocates. NCHR refuse to investigate human rights reports in the poorer neighborhoods, where most of the attacks have occurred, "because those zones are all Aristide-supporter, it's not safe for us to go there," says NCHR's Pierre Esperance. In what critics say is an odd statement coming from a human rights advocate, Esperance has publicly declared that human rights crimes are now non-existent in Haiti and that reports of politically motivated attacks are "fairy tales."

NCHR has received extensive funding from the United States Agency for International Development (USAID) including a large chunk of the 1.4 million dollars that was distributed primarily to anti-Aristide organizations in the year prior to the February 2004 coup, according to USAID area director Pamela Callen. In an ironic twist, critics say that NCHR only focus their energies on the few human rights violations they say were committed by members of the pro-democracy movement.

Meanwhile, the handful of attorneys who are investigating Haiti's devolving human rights situation are swamped with reports of atrocities including illegal arrests, torture, murder, and rape. "And what we are seeing more often is that after a woman is raped, the attackers force her son or brother to have sexual relations with her as they watch, so that both she and her family are violated again," explains Joseph.

That was the case with Joesephina Helicaux, 66, whose son is a member of a peasant union that has called for the return of democracy to Haiti. Although they would not consider themselves Aristide supporters, the family believes that the coup and his removal from power by foreign forces was illegal and that Aristide should be allowed to finish his term as president. Josephina's son said as much during a demonstration earlier this year, where he was interviewed on a local radio station.

The next day the Helicaux family was eating dinner when a group of armed men burst into their home. The men were not masked and Joesephina Helicaux says that two were in police uniforms. "I told the children to be quite and to stop crying. The men searched our room. Afterwards they raped all of us [women], even the girls, and made the men stand and watch," she says. The youngest girl who was attacked was then 9 years old.

Although the son who had spoken on the radio was not home, another one was, as well as a 28-year-old nephew. The attackers forced Joesephina Helicaux to have intercourse with her nephew and son, she says. "They laughed [while it was happening]. They told us 'move here, do this,'" she remembers.

After their attackers left, a neighbor contacted Lautan who came to the home with Alfred Desslieanes, pastor of the New Life Church in Delmas. The pair transported the family to Port-au-Prince's General Hospital where doctor's refused to treat them, reportedly because they feared reprisals from the government.

"The doctors told us outright, they don't treat *chimeres* and if this family was victimized by the police or by the former military then they are *chimeres*," says Lautan. *Chimere* is a derogatory term for the unemployed that has become synonymous with both "gangster" and "Aristide-supporter."

The family was taken to a private clinic where doctors treated them for bleeding, contusions, vaginal tearing, and, in the case of the nephew, several broken bones from a beating he received after he initially refused to follow the men's orders to have sexual relations with his grandmother, says Desslienanes.

Human rights advocates say members of the disbanded Armed Forces of Haiti (FADH) have committed many of the rapes. President Jean Bertrand Aristide disbanded FADH in 1994 after soldiers committed numerous atrocities during the 1991–1994 coup including gang rape and the mass execution of peasants in northern Haiti.

FADH ex-General Herard Abraham now serves as the Minister of the Interior in the U.S.-created interim government of Haiti, which is led by American Gerald Latortue. Latortue, of Boca Raton, Florida, was installed as Prime Minister of Haiti by American ambassador James B. Foley in March 2004. Both Latortue and Abraham have publicly called for the reinstatement of the Haitian army. In the meantime they have begun to pay former soldiers millions in "back pay" for the past ten years since the army was disbanded, and they have been responsible for the plan to integrate thousands of former soldier, including convicted human rights violators, into the ranks of the Haitian National Police.

Victims of human rights abuses argue that they now have nowhere to turn for help. International observers say both the UN and the HNP has done little to investigate human rights crimes, including the most heinous violations such as murder, rape and torture by paramilitary forces. Some victims say the police have arrested them after they reported a human rights crime. One women's advocate says she forbids her clients from reporting their rapes to police saying, "a woman who reports that she has been victimized is very likely to then be raped again by the police when she goes to police station to make a complaint."

Judges who prosecuted human rights violators under the former, democratic government have themselves also become victims of human rights violations.

Magistrate Napela Saintil, who presided over the Raboteau massacre trial five years ago, was severely beaten in his home by heavily armed men and was threatened with death because he convicted Louis Jodel Chamblain the former leader of the paramilitary organization FRAPH (Front for the Advancement and Progress of Haiti) of human rights crimes several years ago. Judge Jean Senat Fleury, who also participated in the Raboteau massacre trial, appealed to international organizations to protect the judiciary after he too was threatened. Lawyer Leslie Jean-Louis was beaten and nearly lynched by a paramilitary militia while walking home from his office in the rural city of Leogane, about 20 miles west of Port-au-Prince.

Meanwhile, observers say that Minister of Justice Bernard Gousse has systematically removed pro-democracy judges from office through intimidation, firings, and in some cases, by having the judges arrested or deported from the country. Judges who order pro-democracy supporters released due to a lack of evidence or charges against them have found their orders ignored by the National Penitentiary, which incarcerates both men and boys. One judge, speaking on the condition of anonymity, said that when he wants someone released he has to "stroke the warden's ego" and give bribes, even though the prisoner whose liberation he has ordered is innocent.

An investigation by Amnesty International found widespread evidence of both judicial and police misconduct. The report details specific cases of police abuse including an example of the breadth and scope of violence taking place in an average week in Port-au-Prince. The London-based human rights group found that just during one week in October, 2004, HNP officers murdered of a family of seven in their home in Fort National, killed four young men in broad daylight in Carrefour Péan, tortured a 13-year-old street child after he refused to give them the names of Aristide supporters, and covered the head of a man with a plastic bag and severely beat him on the street before incarcerating him at a local police station indefinitely and without charging him with a crime.

An estimated 50,000 human rights victims have fled Haiti for neighboring Dominican Republic. Most entered the country illegally and live in hiding. In May 2005, Dominican authorities began the largest mass expulsion in recent history by rounding up, arresting and deporting Haitian nationals and Dominicans of Haitian descent in the northeast section of the country. Although military authorities and officials from the Dominican Republic's Migration Office claim they are deporting only undocumented Haitian migrants, thousands of Dominican citizens who are suspected of being Haitian or have dark skin, have been deported. Some report that Dominican soldiers tore up their state identification cards before arresting them and forcing them across the border. Relief workers on the Haitian side of the border say that buses are arriving daily with dozens of unaccompanied children, many of whom don't even speak Kreyol because they are second or third generation Dominican.

"We have mothers here without their children. We have children without their families. We have some children who were deported that are so young they don't even know their last name or the name of the city where they are from," said one aid worker. "I asked one [unaccompanied] child what his mother's name was and he said in Spanish 'mommy.' I asked him how old he was and he held up three fingers."

Towns on the Haitian side of the border have been overwhelmed with deportees and are running low on food and water, say relief workers. At night thousands sleep on the ground of the town squares and churches. Many of the deportees are those who fled to escape political repression and have been victims of rape or torture says aid worker Christian Johanstan. "Everyone we work with has been traumatized. The Dominicans who were illegally deported have been traumatized by the military and police who uprooted them. The Haitians have been doubly traumatized by those who staged the coup and committed human rights abuses against them and then by the country in which they sought refuge."

The mass expulsions, which were reportedly authorized at the highest levels of the Dominican government, have led the human rights organization Minority Rights Group International to threaten action under international law against the country. Saying that the Dominican Republic is practicing "ethnic cleansing," an MRG spokesperson confirmed that the group would seek sanctions against the Dominican Republic on the basis of ongoing and widespread discrimination against Haitians and Dominicans of suspected Haitian descent. "Mass arbitrary expulsions are a violation of numerous civil, political, economic, and social rights under international law," said a statement from the group.

Meanwhile, ordinary Haitians say they continue to live in fear of abuse, imprisonment, torture and death. Some say that abuse will only stop if and when Aristide, who is currently in exile in South Africa, is allowed to return to Haiti. A minority of Haitians say that because the United States will never allow Aristide to return to Haiti, the country's only hope lies in electing a less repressive dictator to replace Latortue.

National elections have been set for November 2005, however Fanmi Lavalas, the party to which both Aristide and the vast majority of Haitians belong, has said they will boycott the elections if they are not allowed to participate fully and Aristide is not allowed to return to Haiti.

Lyn Duff <LynDuff@aol.com> first traveled to Haiti in 1995 to help establish that country's first children's radio station. During the past ten years she has covered Haiti extensively for both Pacific News Service and Pacifica Radio's Flashpoints on KPFA-FM.

CENSORED #1 2005
WEALTH INEQUALITY IN 21ST CENTURY THREATENS ECONOMY AND DEMOCRACY

Original sources:
MULTINATIONAL MONITOR, May 2003, Vol. 24, No. 5
Title: "The Wealth Divide" (An interview with Edward Wolff)
Author Not Listed

BUZZFLASH, March 26 and 29, 2004
Title: "A Buzzflash Interview, Parts I & II" (with David Cay Johnston)
Author: Buzzflash Staff

LONDON GUARDIAN, October 4, 2003
Title: "Every Third Person Will Be a Slum Dweller Within 30 years, UN Agency Warns"
Author: John Vidal

MULTINATIONAL MONITOR, July/August, 2003
Title: "Grotesque Inequality"
Author: Robert Weissman

Since the 1970s, a gap has grown in the United States between the rich and the poor, gradually eliminating middle classes and forcing people into more and more divergent levels of income. Based on data accumulated over the last thirty years, most economists now agree, 95 percent of the American population's incomes are falling, while a mere 5 percent is quickly amassing unprecedented wealth. This trend is hardly the natural result of the workings of the economy, but is the product of a series of carefully crafted legislative policies authored by and for the super-rich over the last 25 years. These policies have, over time, transferred more and more of the tax burden off of the rich and onto working people.

The ramifications of this radical inequality are not limited to the United States. The transfer of the world's wealth that allows the top 400 income earners in the U.S. to earn as much in a year as the entire population of the 20 poorest countries in Africa is fueled by the exploitation of the labor and resources of poor countries. The spread of urban growth—owing to the conversion of the world's economy to cash crops—has led the UN to warn that if changes are not made 1/3 of the world's population will be slum dwellers by 2030 living on $1 a day.

UPDATE BY DAVID STOLOWITZ: Sociologists have observed for some time that the United States, unlike Europe, places more emphasis on differences of race as opposed to differences of social class. To even acknowledge that different socio-economic classes exist in America is often seen at odds with the American ethos that the United States gives everyone the opportunity necessary to pull themselves up by their bootstraps. The Democratic Party justifiably attacked George Bush's tax cuts for the wealthiest 1 percent, yet beyond this they have done little to garner attention to wealth inequality in the United States.

The corporate media, as well as National Public Radio, did recently feature and discuss the results of a landmark study by the Pew Hispanic Center showing a disproportionate amount of poverty among U.S. racial minorities—especially Latino and African Americans. This study rocked the boat of a complacent media who had posited the question, "Is racism disappearing in America?" and prematurely concluded that racism was on its way out, and even that it was respectable to begin to speak of so-called "reverse racism."

An interesting finding in the corporate media's coverage is that it was considered safer and more tenable to address this issue within the bounds of the financial, business or economic press. Just as I found in my story on Naked Shorting, the business press, usually thought of as "conservative," actually provided coverage on the issue that the rest of the corporate media wouldn't touch. In 2004–05 *Business Week*, *The Economist*, and *Industry Week* featured excellent articles on the wealth gap and related issues, criticizing the Bush Administration for its role in the problem and defending the validity of a debate on free trade, international lending, and their consequences.

International media are taking wealth inequality more seriously as well. British papers like *The Guardian* have not only informed their readers about the problem, but encouraged a debate about the Blair government's role in it. The poverty and corruption of Russia's oligarchy is becoming better known in Europe, while the U.S. maintains its own iron curtain when it comes to the image of "democratically reformed" Russia and the former Soviet states.

Over the last few years, the U.S. has particularly increased its criticism of China for all kinds of policies, while it hypocritically pursues agendas that are just as dangerous and often identical. In the case of wealth inequality, the U.S. government and a compliant corporate media have been especially critical of poverty and related issues in China but generally avoid the topic in the U.S.

SOURCES:

"Blair does mind the wealth gap," *The Guardian*, 24 March 2005.

Yvette Cooper, "Now we must narrow the wealth gap," *The Guardian*, 22 March 2005.

Laura D'Andrea Tyson, "How Bush widened the Wealth Gap; Not since the '20s has income inequality been this great," *BusinessWeek*, 1 November, 2004.

"Ever higher society, ever harder to ascend—Meritocracy in America," *The Economist*, 1 January 2005.

Patricia Panchak, "Take the Demon Out of the Debate; Questions on free trade deserve to be answered, not scorned," *IndustryWeek*, July 2004.

Michael J. Mandel and Richard S. Dunham, "Where Wealth Lives," *BusinessWeek*, April 19, 2004.

CENSORED # 2 2005

ASHCROFT VS. THE HUMAN RIGHTS LAW THAT HOLDS CORPORATIONS ACCOUNTABLE

Ashcroft goes after 200-year-old human rights law

Source: One World
Author: Jim Lobe

During his reign as attorney general, John Ashcroft sought to strike down one of the world's oldest human rights laws, the Alien Tort Claims Act (ATCA). This law holds government leaders, corporations, and senior military officials liable for human rights abuses taking place in foreign countries.

This attack on the ATCA came after Ninth Circuit Court of Appeals ruled that Unocal Corporation could be held liable for human rights abuses committed against Burmese peasants near a pipeline the company was building. By attempting to throw out this law, the Bush Administration effectively opened the door for human rights abuses to continue under the veil of foreign relations. According to a *Wall Street Journal* article, upholding the law could jeopardize aspects of the war on terrorism.

UPDATE BY BRITTNY ROELAND: At the end of 2004, two closely watched cases brought under the Alien Tort Claims Act ended with a whimper. On the day they were set to be heard by the Ninth Circuit U.S. Court of Appeals, Roe v. Unocal and Doe v. Unocal settled on confidential terms.

In response to its involvement in a human rights violation case, Unocal said that it would provide funds for improving living conditions, health care and education in the region where the pipeline was built. They also reaffirmed their commitment to human rights. However this statement infers no original wrongdoing.

In January 2005, New York judge John Sprizzo's decision to throw out a $20 billion lawsuit brought in the U.S. against 35 corporations that did business in apartheid-era South Africa. This was a blow for the human rights lobbyists who have, in the past decade, increasingly used the centuries-old Alien Tort Claims Act (ATCA) to try to hold big business accountable for alleged human rights violations overseas.

The plaintiffs filed a notice of appeal "[The case] tries to identify specific companies that tried to willingly and knowingly assist apartheid."

The Departments of State and Justice submitted an amicus brief in the Unocal case in August arguing, much as Sprizzo had done, that the Supreme Court's ruling in June 2004 showed there is no aiding and abetting liability under ATCA. "There is no indication in either the language or history of the Alien Tort that Congress intended such a vast expansion of suits in this sensitive foreign policy area," the brief reads.

Whether or not "aiding and abetting" is covered by the Supreme Court ruling, corporate involvement in human rights abuses still is a serious problem. Human Rights Watch released a report this year, stating that in the Niger Delta, the struggle for oil revenue and government funds has lead to violent outbreaks between rival-armed groups. This violence has resulted in the death of many innocent people, but oil production continues.

A case against the Royal Dutch/Shell in Nigeria, a court refused to dismiss the lawsuit brought by surviving relatives of Saro-Wiwa and Kpuinen, victims of the violence. In denying Shell's motion to dismiss the case, the court found that the alleged actions of Shell and Anderson constituted participation in crimes against humanity, torture, summary execution, arbitrary detention, and other violations of international law.

In a case concerning Exxon Mobil's involvement in Indonesia alleges that the security forces that partook in the crimes are either employees or agents of Exxon Mobil, and thus it is liable for their actions. Exxon Mobil filed a routine motion to dismiss these claims, and a response against this motion was filed on December 14, 2001. The court has not yet ruled on the motion to dismiss, leaving the Acehnese victims of abuse in a state of legal limbo.

SOURCES:
www.laborrights.org
Talk of the Nation National Public Radio (NPR)
Deseret Morning News (Salt Lake City) February 19, 2005
Jim Washer, *Greenwire* January 28, 2005 Friday

CENSORED #3
BUSH ADMINISTRATION MANIPULATES SCIENCE AND CENSORS SCIENTISTS

Original sources:
The Nation, March 8, 2004
Title: "The Junk Science of George W. Bush"
Author: Robert F. Kennedy Jr.

Censorship News: The National Coalition Against Censorship Newsletter, Fall 2003, #91
Title: "Censoring Scientific Information"

Oneworld.net, February 20, 2004
Title: "Ranking Scientists Warn Bush Science Policy Lacks Integrity"
Author: ENS Correspondents

Office Of U.S. Representative Henry A. Waxman, August 2003

Title: "Politics And Science In The Bush Administration"
Prepared by: Committee on Government Reform—Minority Staff
(Updated November 13, 2003)

Critics charge that the Bush Administration is purging, censoring, and manipulating scientific information in order to push forward its pro-business, anti-environmental agenda. In Washington, D.C. more than 60 of the nation's top scientists, including 20 Nobel laureates, leading medical experts, and former federal agency directors, issued a statement on February 18, 2004 accusing the Bush Administration of deliberately distorting scientific results for political ends and calling for regulatory and legislative action to restore scientific integrity to federal policymaking.

Princeton University scientist Michael Oppenheimer states, "If you believe in a rational universe, in enlightenment, in knowledge and in a search for the truth, this White House is an absolute disaster."

UPDATE BY MICHELE SALVAIL: Last year, we reported that the Bush Administration was receiving flack for distorting the data from scientific research for political ends and then calling for regulatory and legislative action to restore scientific integrity to federal policymaking.

Unfortunately, although there is wider coverage in the corporate media about the issues, the trend continues. Since last year, Union of Concerned Scientists issued a report citing the abuses of the Bush Administration. The report says that White House officials have asked nominees for scientific advisory panels to disclose whether or not they had voted for Bush.

Over two hundred scientists employed by the Department of the Interiors Fish and Wildlife Service admitted that they were directed to alter findings to decrease the protection of plants and animals. According to a survey conducted by the Union of Concerned Scientists and Public Employees for Environmental Responsibility, the U.S. Fish and Wildlife staff of 1,400 scientists, there was a 30 percent response rate. The scientists admitted that they were forced to alter data or withhold the findings of their research that would give them cause to provide greater protection of endangered species.

The FDA admitted to withholding the data from the research of the risks of giving antidepressants to children. The FDA restrained it's foremost expert from giving testimony at a conference formed to determine what proper guidance that the FDA is responsible for giving to the public about recent studies that link anti-depressants to suicide in children. The expert has concluded that children, when given anti-depressants, were close to twice as likely to become suicidal as those given a placebo.

A White House staff member crossed out the words "Confirmed public health risk" that described the findings on mercury and changed the sentence to "warrants regulation." A toxicologist within the Office of Management and Budget recommended changes to a sentence saying children exposed to mercury while they are in their mother's womb "are at increased risk of poor performance and no behavioral tests." This particular sentence was changed for publication to say that children "may be at increased risk."

According to "independent scientists, retired Livermore Lab physicists and community organizations," the findings of a study conducted by the Agency for Toxic Substances and Disease Registry (ATSDR) is flawed and does not draw well supported conclusions that are consistent with commonly accepted knowledge of the principles of exposure to radiation. The Federal agency is being accused of inadequately assessing the impacts on public health at the Livermore Lab's main site. According to this group of core witnesses, the report misrepresents the actual risks posed by radioactive and toxic releases at the plant. The ATSDR's report asserts that there is "no apparent health hazard" from the hazardous materials used at the Livermore Lab. The report does not warn the public of health concerns related to the amount of plutonium that is being found in the ground water, public parks, home gardens. Toxic wastes have been dumped into the "groundwater aquifer and radioactive tritium plumes in the air, rain water and plants." The report does not state that there is any need for public concern from these activities implemented by the Livermore Lab.

The Energy Department concluded that Yucca Mountain water flow studies are scientifically sound although scientists who conducted the research have admitted to falsifying these documents. The USGS scientists emailed each other between 1998 and 2000. In these e-mails, they discussed altering data for the quality assurance requirements of their research. Bob Loux, of the Nevada Agency for Nuclear Projects, a critic of the proposal, said, "It was going to be a white wash from square one." While many lawsuits against the project to store nuclear waste at the Yucca Mountain site are still pending, Congress approved of a $10 million provision for the storage of nuclear waste at interim surface sites. The very same day, The Nuclear Regulatory Commission's Atomic Safety and Licensing Board rejected the appeal by the State of Utah seeking to halt the plan to store nuclear fuel rods on the Skull Valley Goshute Indian Reservations Land. Four thousand nuclear waste caskets are to be temporarily stored at the Private Fuel Storage Facility approximately 50 miles southwest of Salt Lake City pending the completion of the Yucca Mountain Project.

SOURCES:

Greenwire, "Yucca Mountain: Nevada petitions for NRC copy of license application" June 8, 2005.

Greenwire, "Yucca Mountain: DOE finds contested water studies technically sound," June 7, 2005.

Associated Press, "NRC staff told data cited in Yucca Mountain e-mails is sound," June 7, 2005.

Greenwire, "Nuclear Waste: Industry, Congress eye casks for surface storage," June 6, 2005.

Mary O'Driscoll, "Nuclear Waste: Nevadans target Yucca funding over document falsification," *Environment and Energy Daily*, May 11, 2005.

Las Vegas Review Journal, "DOE: Water studies sound," June 7, 2005.

Los Angeles Times, "U.S. Scientists Say They are Told to Alter Findings," February 10, 2005.

U.S. Newswire, "Once Again, Whitehouse silences a Scientist; FDA Admits It Barred Experts From Testifying About Impact of Anti-Depressants on Children," April 16, 2004.

San Francisco Chronicle, "Wildlife Scientists Feeling Heat; Species Protection data suppressed, many report," February 10, 2005.

Dee Ann Divis, *UPI*, "PoliSci; Trust in science hurt in 2004, December 28, 2004.

New York Times April 7, 2004.

U.S. Newswire, "Once Again, White House Silences a Scientist; FDA Admits it Barred Experts from Testifying About Impact of Anti Depressants on Children," April 16, 2004.

CENSORED #4 2005

HIGH URANIUM LEVELS FOUND IN TROOPS AND CIVILIANS

Original Sources:
Uranium Medical Research Center, January 2003
Title: "UMRC's Preliminary Findings from Afghanistan & Operation Enduring Freedom"
and
"Afghan Field Trip #2 Report: Precision Destruction— Indiscriminate Effects"
Author: Tedd Weyman, UMRC Research Team

Awakened Woman, January 2004
Title: "Scientists Uncover Radioactive Trail in Afghanistan"
Author: Stephanie Hiller

Dissident Voice, March 2004
Title: "There Are No Words...Radiation in Iraq Equals 250,000
Nagasaki Bombs"
Author: Bob Nichols

New York Daily News, April 5,2004
Title: "Poisoned?"
Author: Juan Gonzalez

Information Clearing House, March 2004
Title: "International Criminal Tribune For Afghanistan At Tokyo,
The People vs. George Bush"
Author: Professor Niloufer Bhagwat J.

Civilian populations in Afghanistan and Iraq and occupying troops have
been contaminated with astounding levels of radioactive depleted and non-
depleted uranium as a result of post-9/11 United States' use of tons of uranium munitions.

Uranium dust will be in the bodies of our returning armed forces. Nine
soldiers from the 442nd Military Police serving in Iraq were tested for DU
contamination in December 2003. Conducted at the request of *The New York
Daily News*, as the U.S. government considers the cost of $1,000 per affected
soldier prohibitive, the test found that four of the nine men were contaminated with high levels of DU, likely caused by inhaling dust from depleted
uranium shells fired by U.S. troops. Several of the men had traces of another
uranium isotope, U-236, that are produced only in a nuclear reaction
process.

Most American weapons (missiles, smart bombs, dumb bombs, bullets,
tank shells, cruise missiles, etc.) contain high amounts of radioactive uranium. Depleted or non-depleted, these types of weapons, on detonation,
release a radioactive dust which, when inhaled, goes into the body and stays
there. It has a half-life of 4.5 billion years. Basically, it's a permanently
available contaminant, distributed in the environment, where dust storms
or any water nearby can disperse it. Once ingested, it releases subatomic
particles that slice through DNA.

UPDATE BY JOSH PARRISH: There is national dispute on the dangers of Depleted Uranium (DU). The Depart of Defense has continually claimed that DU munitions are safe. At the same time, veterans groups and various scientists and doctors say that DU is the cause of Gulf War Syndrome and responsible for a sharp rise in birth defects among Iraqis and returning U.S. servicemen. The information coming from the Department of Defense has, at best, been contradictory. Dr. Michael Kilpatrick, the deputy director of the Deployment Health Support Directorate and Pentagon spokesman on Depleted Uranium, has said "as long as this (DU exposure) is exterior to your body, you're not at any risk and the potential of internalizing it from the environment is extremely small." Several studies, commissioned by the Pentagon, have supported this assertion. One in particular, The Presidential Advisory Committee on Gulf War Veterans' Illnesses, that reported to President Clinton in 1996 stated that "current scientific evidence does not support a causal link" between veterans symptoms and chemical exposures in the Persian Gulf. This committee goes on to say that stress "is likely to be an important contributing factor to the broad range of physical and psychological illnesses currently being reported by gulf war veterans."

However, these Pentagon studies contradict an Army report from 1990 that stated DU is "linked to cancer when exposures are internal, [and] chemical toxicity causing kidney damage." Here the U.S. government acknowledges that internal exposure to DU is likely to be harmful. It is only after the 1991 Gulf War, where DU munitions were used for the first time, the government began to claim they were harmless.

The main point of contention between the U.S. government and those who oppose the use of DU is what constitutes internal exposure and how does this exposure occur. The military insists that only soldiers who had shrapnel wounds from DU or who were inside tanks shot by DU shells and accidentally breathed radioactive dust were at risk. This ignores the findings of Leonard Dietz who, in 1979, found that DU contaminated dust could travel great distances through the air. Dietz accidentally discovered that air filters he was experimenting with had collected radioactive dust from a lead plant that was producing DU 26 miles away. "The contamination was so heavy that they had to remove the topsoil from 52 properties around the plant," Dietz said.

When they were in Iraq, the soldiers of the 442nd Military Police Company performed duties such as providing security for convoys, running jails and training Iraqi police. The fact that some of these soldiers have DU in their bodies is proof that one need not be directly exposed to a DU explo-

Another conservative group from whom President Bush receives suggestions for Federal Court nominations is the Christian Legal Society. A recent *Washington Times* article quoted a director of the organization as saying, "There's a normal process that the White House has definitely been pursuing for at least six months where they are soliciting views and recommendations," said Samuel B. Casey, executive director of the Christian Legal Society (CLS). "We have submitted our views." (*Washington Times*, May 20, 2005)

This is the only mention in the United States press referring to the organization's important role in suggesting Federal Court nominees. However, there are many more reports in the past year about the CLS's legal activism. Campus chapters of the CLS sued several law schools and colleges around the country alleging that the colleges' non-discrimination policies violated their First Amendment rights which prohibited the organization's activities that refused membership to homosexuals or those who supported homosexuals. In addition, the CLS chapters required that each member sign a declaration of faith. Ohio State amended their non-discrimination policy in light of the lawsuit. The Columbus Dispatch reported, "Ohio State University will allow student religious organizations to exclude people who don't hold a given group's religious beliefs."

According to their website, the Christian Legal Society has 165 law student ministry chapters. They promote biblical conflict resolution and state that they advance religious freedom "By writing and submitting "friend of the court" briefs to federal and states courts, particularly the United States Supreme Court, on behalf of ourselves and many other organizations interested in defending the inalienable rights of life and religious liberty."

A footnote at the bottom of their mission statement page boasts their prominence in government, "CLS' Center for Law and Religious Freedom is one of the most respected religious liberty advocates in the Christian community, providing Christian-perspective administrative, legislative or litigation-related public interest advocacy services in every type of legal forum from Oregon to Congress and the Oval Office."

The Christian Legal Society received one article in the Washington Times, with a brief reference to their influence in judicial nominations. Their goal is to dominate the legal institution. Interestingly, this organization that promotes religious ethics in law, has board members that work for Bank of America, sit on the North District Court of Appeals, and a board member that works with a firm specializing in business and estate law as well as church not-for-profit law. Interestingly, the board members have more ties to corporate America than religious America.

The Christian legal Society and the Federalist Society have the ear of the president. These organizations have the organizational power and governmental influence to continue the push for conservative control of the Federal Judiciary.

CENSORED # 9 2005

WIDOW BRINGS RICO CASE AGAINST U.S. GOVERNMENT FOR 9/11

Original Sources:
www.scoop.co.nz, November 2003
Title: 9/11 Victim's Wife Files RICO Case Against GW Bush
Author: Philip J. Berg

www.scoop.co.nz, December 2003
Title: Widow's Bush Treason Suit Vanishes
Author: W. David Kubiak

Ellen Mariani lost her husband, Louis Neil Mariani, on 9/11 and is refusing the government's million-dollar settlement offer. Her husband Louis Neil Mariani died when United Airlines flight 175 was flown into the South Tower of the World Trade Center.

Ellen Mariani has studied the facts of the day for nearly two years, and has come to believe that the White House "intentionally allowed 9/11 to happen" in order to launch the "War on Terrorism." Her lawyer, Phillip Berg, former Deputy Attorney General of Pennsylvania, who filed a 62-page complaint in federal district court charging that President Bush and officials, including but not limited to, Cheney, Rumsfeld, Rice and Ashcroft, (1) had adequate foreknowledge of 9/11 yet failed to warn the country or attempt to prevent it; (2) have since been covering up the truth of that day; (3) have therefore abetted the murder of plaintiff's husband and violated the Constitution and multiple laws of the United States; and (4) are thus being sued under the Civil Racketeering, Influences, and Corrupt Organization (RICO) Act for malfeasant conspiracy, obstruction of justice and wrongful death.

UPDATE BY BRIDGET J. THORNTON: Ellen Mariani settled her case against the U.S. government on December 1, 2004. The attorney for Mariani continues his work on the RICO case with a new plaintiff, William Rodriguez. Rodriguez, a maintenance worker at the World Trade Center during the 9/11 attacks, testified before the 9/11 panel that he encountered Mohand Alsheheri during the summer of 2001.

The RICO case claims the government failed to prevent the 9/11 attacks. More families have similar sentiments. The RICO case is one of about 80 independent lawsuits filed against the government, airlines, and airports by families of 9/11 victims, according to Charles Miller, Department of Justice spokesman. A group of 12 individuals formed the Family Steering Committee to lobby for an independent 9/11 commission and demand answers to questions still not addressed. Finally, a group of families of NYC firefighters killed in the WTC, sued the City when it denied a *New York Times* reporter access to emergency calls placed that day. These families forfeited their right to compensation under the 9/11 Victims Fund in pursuing independent lawsuits. The Fund precludes the families who accept compensations from filing future lawsuits concerning the 9/11 attacks.

Many questions remain unanswered for the victim's families and the people of the United States. To view a list of the questions submitted to the 9/11 panel by the Family Steering Committee, the web site is http://911independentcommission.org. also see Chapter 4 The Unanswered Questions of 9/11.

CENSORED #10 2005
NEW NUKE PLANTS: TAXPAYERS SUPPORT, INDUSTRY PROFITS

Original sources:
Nuclear Information and Resource Service, November 17, 2003
Title: "Nuclear Energy Would Get $7.5 Billion in Tax Subsides, U.S. Taxpayers Would Fund Nuclear Monitor Relapse If Energy Bill Passes"
Authors: Cindy Folkers and Michael Mariotte

WISE/NIRS Nuclear Monitor, August 2003
Title: "U.S. Senate Passes Pro-Nuclear Energy Bill"
Authors: Cindy Folkers and Michael Mariotte

In 2002, the Bush Administration was looking to give the industry a huge boost through the new Energy Policy Act. HR-6, a House of Representatives bill sponsored by Senator Peter Domenici (R-NM), would have given nuclear power plants a production credit for each unit of energy produce, costing taxpayers an estimated $7.5 billion. This money was to be used to build six new privately owned, for-profit reactors across the country. The bill would have created more incentives for nuclear power, giving $1.1 billion for the production of hydrogen fuel and $2.7 billion for research and development of new reactors under the Nuclear Power 2010 Program despite widespread fears that nuclear plants are extremely dangerous terrorist targets.

The Domenici sponsored bill would have establish "a preferred equity investment" provision that would have required "taxpayers to back private investment in the new facilities up to $200 million." HR-6 was defeated in 2003, but Domenici reintroduced it as S2095, little changed. The main change was that the nuclear tax production credits (PTC) were excluded. However, because S2095 "did not have the support to pass the Senate, Domenici split the bill in two, attempting to pass the policy and tax sections separately." Since the nuclear PTC was not part of S2095 Domenici "threatened to add it separately." The tax credit would amount to at least $6 billion, and could possibly go to $15 or $19 billion.

UPDATE BY AMBROSIA PARDUE: "America must have an energy policy that plans for the future, but meets the needs of today. I believe we can develop our natural resources and protect our environment," said President George W. Bush. (www.whitehouse.gov) On March 9, 2005 President Bush visited Battelle Memorial Institute in Columbus, Ohio saying that "America hasn't ordered a nuclear power plant since the 1970s, and it's time to start building again." Also stating that nuclear power can generate electricity without emitting air pollution or greenhouse gases, and it is the only way of providing "reliable, affordable, and environmentally sound energy for America's future." (www.inl.gove/featurestories/2005-03-14.shtml) Bush spoke to a crowd at Calvert Cliffs Nuclear Power Plant in Maryland on June 22, 2005 once again proclaiming that "it is time for this country to start building nuclear power plants again." He said that the nuclear industry is much safer since the Three Mile Island incident. (www.nydailynews.com/news/wn_report/v-pfriendly/story/321527p-274953c.html) Nothing could be farther from the truth. George W. seems to have monetary profits on his mind when it comes to energy policy—not the future of our environment, or the safety of the American people. The Administration has continued to back nuclear energy and has ignored or opposed measures that would insure Americans would be protected from potentially horrific terrorist attacks against nuclear plants.

According to a new *Public Citizen* report this is "an inaction that reflects officials' aversion to regulating private industry and allegiance to key campaign contributors." The main reasons seem to be monetary—according to *Homeland Unsecured*, the industries representing the five homeland security areas have raised at least $19.9 million for the Bush campaigns, the

Republican National Committee or the Bush inauguration since 2000. They have provided 30 individuals who raise at least $100,000 to $200,000 to the Bush presidential campaigns. They have also spent at least $201 million lobbying the White House from 2002 to June 2004. This continued tie, support, and inaction remains despite twenty-seven state attorney generals warning Congress in October 2002 that attacks against one of the current 103 nuclear plants would be "simply incalculable." The Administration and the Nuclear Regulatory Commission (NRC) have ignored congressional efforts for more security regulation.

In November 2004 the Energy Department announced funding for a Nuclear Regulatory Commission licensing process for new commercial reactors, a process that could lead to the construction of new nuclear plans within a decade. The Bush Administration has a goal of creating new nuclear power, and under the Nuclear Power 2010, the Energy Department is allowing $13 million to be given to a two-industry consortium. The Energy Department has provided NuStart energy with $4 million for fiscal year 2005 and $9 million to a group lead by Dominion energy. The DOE said that this will "demonstrate the untested combined Construction and Operating License regulatory process and will enable the power generation companies to make firm business decisions on ordering and building new nuclear power plants." (Environment and Energy Publishing, LLC 11/5/04 "Nuclear Power: DOE pushes ahead on reviving nuclear power")

Domenici successfully included provisions in the fiscal year 2005 bill HR4818 that will increase funding for the DOE programs which will aid new nuclear plant construction; the bill was passed by Congress on November 20, 2004. (Foster Electric "New Nukes Get Funding Boost" 11/30/04)

The energy bill Bush is pushing will not even ensure lower gasoline prices, as said in his own words on June 22. Bush said that by addressing the issue now, and signing a bill now, gas prices will not drop, but life will be better for America's children and grandchildren. (www.nydailynews.com/news/wn_report/v-pfriendly/story/321527p-274953c.html)

According to the Union of Concerned Scientists, "an accident at a U.S. nuclear power plant could kill more people than were killed by the atomic bomb dropped on Nagasaki. The financial repercussions could also be catastrophic." They stated that a risk of nuclear power plants is the potentially massive releases of radioactivity into the atmosphere with devastating harm to people and the environment. One must ask themselves why nuclear power is being pushed for so hard, if gasoline prices will not even be lowered, and if a possible meltdown could occur (because there is no guarantee that it will not happen). One must also ask if environmentally sound energy is the key reason for this push. America also currently lacks protection against terrorist threats, and yet the Administration is backing the expansion of nuclear power; obviously Bush's words only go so far, and the interest of his pocket book runs deeper.

CENSORED #11
THE MEDIA CAN LEGALLY LIE

Original Sources:
CMW REPORT, Spring 2003
Title: "Court Ruled That Media Can Legally Lie"
Author: Liane Casten

ORGANIC CONSUMER ASSOCIATION, March 7, 2004
Title: "Florida Appeals Court Orders Akre-Wilson Must Pay Trial Costs for $24.3 Billion Fox Television; Couple Warns Journalists of Danger to Free Speech, Whistle Blower Protection"

In 1996, Jane Akre and her husband Steve Wilson were hired at WTVT, a Fox network affiliate in Tampa Bay, Florida. The couple worked as a part of an investigative reporting team and in 1997, uncovered a story disclosing controversial information regarding the big agriculture company Monsanto. Akre and Wilson revealed Monsanto's use of Bovine growth hormone (BGH) in dairy cows. This hormone has been scientifically linked to cancer and banned throughout Europe and several other countries.

This story created a problem for Akre and Wilson when Monsanto threatened Fox with a lawsuit if the story was to run. In order for Fox to avoid a conflict, they chose special interest over public welfare and asked the reporters to slant the story and dismiss the facts.

Akre and Wilson disputed with Fox executives over the revisions, and threatened to report the broadcaster to the FCC. This threat and their refusal to change their story, led Fox to fire them both. Akre and Wilson won an initial suit under whistle blower law in the State of Florida and were awarded $425,000 settlement.

Fox appealed the court's decision on February 14, 2003. A Florida Appellate court overturned the settlement, ruling that the whistleblower law only applies to companies that are in violation of a "law, rule, or regulation." Because falsifying, slanting, or distorting news violated only policy, Akre and Wilson were not protected under the Whistleblower law.

Fox argued that that they are protected under the first amendment, thus implying that all broadcasters have the right to be dishonest on public airwaves if they choose.

UPDATE BY REBEKAH COHEN: After the Appellate court ruling, Fox sued Akre and Wilson for over $2,000,000 in legal costs. In August of 2004 the court ruled that Jane Akre and Steve Wilson "filed their 1998 lawsuit against WTVT-Channel 13 in good faith." Akre and Wilson escaped the steep legal fees of nearly $2 million, but ended up paying, in settlement, approximately 10 percent of Fox's costs.

The couple faded out of the news for a few months, but in January 2005, filed a petition with the FCC to deny Fox WTVT in Tampa a license for renewal.

The couple's saga continues as they resume their fight against the station for "intentionally airing false and distorted news reports." They have been waiting to bring forward the license challenge fight as renewals under the FCC only occur every eight years.

In the petition, Akre and Wilson state that in 1997, WTVT's general manager David Boylan, told them that the owners of stations have the right to determine the news that is delivered, thus allowing them the privilege of falsifying news.

Bob Linger, present general manager of WTVT, felt the couple was trying to resurface issues that were already settled in court. However, Akre and Wilson feel their efforts against WTVT are serving a greater purpose. Akre believes that the Tampa station has violated the FCC policies that prohibit broadcasters from "rigging or slanting the news." The couple is prepared to go as far as they can in an effort to prevent broadcasters from airing slanted coverage on public airwaves. "If the FCC is concerned about obscenity, there is nothing more obscene than lying to the public," said Akre.

The stations shouldn't be allowed to hide behind a misinterpretation of the first amendment. "The first amendment is not a license to lie," said Wilson.

Both Akre and Wilson agree that fighting against the station's license renewal is going to be a great challenge. "It's definitely an uphill battle, considering that no station has ever lost its license over news distortion." Despite the odds, Akre and Wilson continue to be optimistic and hopeful about the future.

For updates see: http://www.foxbghsuit.com/

SOURCES:
Al Krebs "Florida Appeals Court Orders Akre-Wilson Must Pay Trial costs

for $24.3 Billion Fox television warns journalists of danger to free speech, whistle blower protection" Organic Consumer Association, March 7, 2004.

CENSORED #14

NEW BILL THREATENS INTELLECTUAL FREEDOM IN AREA STUDIES

Yale Daily News, November 6, 2003
Title: "New Bill Threatens Intellectual Freedom in Area Studies"
Author: Benita Singh

Christian Science Monitor, March 11, 2004
Title: "Speaking in 'Approved' Tongues"
Author: Kimberly Chase

The International Studies in Higher Education Act of 2003 threatens the freedom of education and classroom curriculum. On September 17 of 2003 Congress passed House Resolution 3077, the "International Studies in Higher Education Act of 2003."

The Bill was first proposed in a June 2003 congressional hearing called "International Programs in Higher Education and Questions about Bias." It was authored by Rep. Peter Hoekstra R-Mi, Chairman of the House of Subcommittee on Select Education and Chairman of the House Subcommittee on Technical and Tactical Intelligence. The bill portrays academic institutions as hotbeds for anti-American sentiment, specifically area studies programs. It proposes an advisory board that would be responsible for evaluating the curricula taught at Title VI institutions, course materials assigned in class, and even the faculty who are hired in institutions that accept Title VI funding. The advisory board would report to the Secretary of Education and make funding recommendations based on their findings.

UPDATE BY JACOB RICH: International Studies in Higher Education Act was reintroduced in the new Congress as HR 509 and is still pending in 2005. If the campaign to silence dissent on college campuses looks familiar, maybe that's because it is reminiscent of America's experience with McCarthyism and other attempts to silence dissent on campuses. Capitalizing on people's fear of Communism, McCarthy intimidated, threatened, blacklisted, and attacked people's reputations and livelihood. Under the guise of national security it is estimated that several hundred, and up to one thousand university professors lost their jobs. According to Ellen Schrecker, a professor at Yeshiva

University, author of "The Age of McCarthyism," education was a "main area of concern" and was thought to "harbor populations with cosmopolitan lifestyles and liberal politics that apparently threatened the traditional values so many conservative state politicians claimed to cherish."

On February 28, 2005, ten professors at the Santa Rosa Junior College in Santa Rosa (SRJC), California found anonymous postings of red stars and a reference to communist indoctrination on their office doors. The stars were accompanied by a copy of a state Education Code section prohibiting the teaching of communism with the "intent to indoctrinate" students. Molly McPherson of Rohnert Park came forward to acknowledge her action on behalf of the SRJC Republicans Club claiming she had only intended to start a discussion about the personal politics of humanities instructors by posting the stars. SRJC instructor Marco Giordano disagrees. In his opinion, "This is a grave attack" on the character of his colleagues.

The post 9/11 environment has created an opportunity for conservatives to push their academic reform agenda in the name of national security. The International Studies Act of 2003(HR 509) is a part of this effort.

In the meantime, a bill that passed the Georgia Senate to create what has been called an "an Academic Bill of Rights" is being introduced in 19 state legislatures. According to Sarah Roy, a senior research scholar at Harvard, "The purpose of the bill appears to be the same as that of HR 509: to authorize official interference with the content and conduct of university classes."

On March 24 2005 in Florida a so called Academic Freedom Bill of Rights, sponsored by Rep. Dennis Baxley, R-Ocala, was approved by a Florida House committee despite strenuous objections from the only two Democrats on the committee. The bill sets a statewide standard that students cannot be punished for professing beliefs with which their professors disagree. Professors would also be advised to teach alternative "serious academic theories" that may disagree with their personal views. According to a legislative staff analysis of the bill, "the law would give students who think their beliefs are not being respected legal standing to sue professors and universities."

Students who believe their professor is singling them out for "public ridicule"—for instance, when professors question students' theories in class—would also be given the right to sue. Rep. Dan Gelber, D-Miami Beach, warned that students enrolled in Holocaust history courses who believe the Holocaust never happened could file lawsuits. Students who don't believe the earth is round or that humans have been to the moon could file similar suits. "This is a horrible step," he said. "Universities will have to hire lawyers so our curricula can be decided by judges in courtrooms.

Professors might have to pay court costs—even if they win—from their own pockets. This is not an innocent piece of legislation."

In Ohio, Senator Larry A. Mumper, has introduced the "Academic Bill of Rights for Higher Education." Revealingly, Senator Mumper sounded like Joseph McCarthy, when he said, in regards to college professors, "Eighty percent or so of them are democrats, liberals or socialists or card-carrying Communists." Senator Teresa Fedor, a Democrat from Toledo Ohio, shared her fears about the "Academic Bill of Rights" by saying, "Can we say 21st century witch hunt and book burning?" The proposed legislation in Ohio demands that, "Faculty and instructors shall not infringe the academic freedom and quality of education of their students by persistently introducing controversial matter into the classroom or coursework that has no relation to their subject of study and that serves no legitimate pedagogical purpose."

Who, would decide what's controversial or not? "The enforcement could be random and biased," said Joe White, a political science professor at Case Western Reserve University in Cleveland. Many are concerned by the involvement of legislators in deciding what can and can be said in colleges and universities.

The wording of the Ohio bill is a cut-and-paste version of a bill written Students for Academic Freedom (SAF), which purports to fight anti-conservative bias on the nation's college campuses. The president of SAF is David Horowitz. Horowitz says professors "teach students to identify with America's terrorist enemies and to identify America as a Great Satan oppressing the world's poor and causing them to go hungry."

In March of 2004, the Organization of American Historians created an ad hoc Committee on Academic Freedom; the committee's mandate was "to investigate reports of repressive measures having an impact on historians' teaching, research, employment and freedom of expression." The ad hoc committee report describes how right-wing groups such as SAF, Campus Watch and others "mount systematic and often vituperative campaigns" that call upon college and university administrators to censure or dismiss faculty who have expressed publicly their opposition to the war in Iraq. Their tactics include denunciations sent to the faculty member and campus newspapers "as well as harassing telephone calls late into the night."

Did the students that posted red stars on the doors of professors want to create genuine dialogue, or did they hope to intimidate professors from sharing ideas that are contrary to particular political beliefs? This is not the first time the outside world has tried to gain control over what can be said on college campuses.

CENSORED #24 2005
REINSTATING THE DRAFT

Original Sources:
Salon, November 3, 2003
Title: "Oiling Up the Draft Machine?"
Author: Dave Lindorff

Buzzflash.com, November 11, 2003
Title: "Would a Second Bush Term Mean a Return to Conscription?"
Author: Maureen Farrell

War Times, October-November, 2003
Title: "Military Targets Latino Youth"
Author: Jorge Mariscal

In the spring of 2004, several million dollars were added to the Pentagon's budget to prepare for the activation of the Selective Service System (SSS) By August 2003, thirty-two states, two territories, and the District of Columbia enacted legislation that required driver's license information to be sent to the SSS. Violation of this legislation would restrict access to federal employment and student loans. Also, draft dodging would be much more difficult due to the "Smart Border Declaration," signed by the U.S. and Canada, which involved a "pre-clearance agreement" of people entering or departing each country and a provision aimed at eliminating higher education as a shelter.

Not waiting for the institution of a draft, the Pentagon, in 2003 stepped up their aggressive recruitment of Latinos and other minority groups. The Pentagon preys on the fact that Latinos are the fastest growing group of military-age individuals in the United States. These young people are also particularly likely to enter the military in search of "civilian skills" that they can apply in the workforce. However, 2001 Department of Defense (DOD) statistics showed that while 10 percent of military forces are comprised of Latinos, 17.7 percent of this group occupies "front-line positions," meaning: "infantry, gun crews, and seamanship." These are positions that, beside put these young people in particular danger, are not likely to give them skills translatable to their post military lives.

UPDATE BY BROOKE FINLEY: The activation of SSS began on June 15, 2005. At this time, the Pentagon has begun a campaign to fill 10,350 draft board positions and 11,070 appeals board slots nationwide.

In October 2004, at a campaign stop in Daytona Beach, Florida, President George W. Bush mistakenly said to his supporters: "After standing on the stage, after the debate, I made it very plain we will not have an all-volunteer army. Hearing the alarmed shouts of his supporters, he continued quickly, "And yet this week...will have an all-volunteer army. Let me restate that: we will not have a draft."

The president's quick back-pedaling was understandable considering the polls at the time, which showed that even the slightest mention of a draft would be a form of political suicide for either of the candidates. But despite the reassuring words, it is becoming more apparent that, in order for the Administration to continue to pursue its aggressive foreign policy, the draft is quickly becoming a military necessity.

The Bush Administration has claimed time and again that they will never reinstate the draft and the U.S. House voted 402-2 against S.89 and H.R.163, which would've required all young people, including women, ages 18-26 to serve two years of military service. But an internal Selective Service memo made public under the Freedom of Information Act shows that, in February 2003, a meeting was held with two of Defense Secretary Donald Rumsfeld's undersecretaries and the Selective Services' acting director, to debate and discuss a return of the draft. The memo notes the Administration's reluctance to launch a full scale draft but states, "defense manpower officials concede there are critical shortages of military personnel with certain skills, such as medical personnel, linguists, computer network engineers, etc." The potentially prohibitive costs of "attracting and retaining such personnel for military service has led some officials to conclude that, while a conventional draft may never be needed, a draft of men and women possessing these critical skills may be warranted in a future crisis."

Following this memo, the Health Care Personnel Delivery System (the HCPDS or "Special Skills Draft") was developed for the Selective Service System at the request of Congress and is currently in standby mode. Initially, HCPDS will be used to draft men and women, ages 20-45, who are skilled doctors, nurses, medical technicians and those with "certain other health care skills." But, Richard Flahavan, a spokesman for the Selective Service, admits that this legislation provides a perfect launching pad for a future full-scale draft. "Our thinking," says Flahavan, "was that if we could run a health-care draft in the future, then with some very slight tinkering we could change that skill to plumbers or linguists or electrical engineers or whatever the military was short."

The National Guard and the Army Reserve now make up almost half of the fighting force in Iraq. The Pentagon is demanding that these volunteer soldiers extend their service, and the military, without legal ratification by Congress, has enforced the "stop loss" provision, which forces reservists and guardsmen to remain on active duty for an indeterminate amount of time. Many have been informed that their enlistment has been extended until December 24, 2031.

U.S. Rep. Lloyd Doggett, D-Austin, claims that this extension is already one type of "draft" being used by the military. "People are being forced to stay beyond their commitment, and that's an indication of being overextended."

Another sign of the Administration's predicament is the lowered standards for Marine and Army recruits. The Army has allowed 25 percent more high school drop-outs into their program, and the Marines have offered $30,000 rewards for anyone who re-enlists. Almost $300 million has been spent on incentives alone for new recruits since the war in Iraq began and the advertising costs per new recruit have increased from $640 in 1990 to almost $1,900 in 2004. Recruitment is still focused on attracting the economically disadvantaged. Recruiters are continuously targeting high unemployment areas with flashy marketing campaigns and enlistment bonuses of thousands of dollars.

President Bush signed an executive order allowing legal immigrants to apply for citizenship immediately if they volunteer for active duty, rather than waiting the usual five years. Lt. Gen. James Helmly, the commander of the Army Reserve, sums up the military and President Bush's seduction of potential soldiers with one statement; "We must consider the point at which we confuse 'volunteer to become an American soldier' with 'mercenary'."

Through the No Child Left Behind Act, as well as the National Defense Authorization Act it is required that every high school receiving federal funding hand over the names, addresses and phone numbers of every junior and senior to local military recruitment offices. The public schools predominately targeted are located in poor communities.

With the neo-conservatives' aggressive foreign policy agenda: the possibility of a long commitment in the Middle East; the war on terror coupled with the need to maintain troop levels internationally and the decline in new recruits; a draft seems not only feasible, but at some point irrefutably necessary under current U.S. policy.

CENSORED #6 2005

THE SALE OF ELECTORAL POLITICS

Original Sources:
In These Times, December 2003
Title: "Voting Machines Gone Wild"
Author: Mark Lewellen-Biddle

Independent/UK, October 13, 2003
Title: "All The President's Votes?"
Author: Andrew Gumbel

DEMOCRACY NOW!, September 4, 2003
Title: "Will Bush Backers Manipulate Votes
to Deliver GW Another Election?"
Reporter: Amy Goodman and the staff of Democracy Now!

As reported in *Censored 2005* article, *The Sales of Electoral Politics*, the privatization and manipulation of America's voting process is staying the course. Diebold, Sequoia Voting Systems, Elections Systems & Software (ES&S), along with Accenture, Scientific Applications Information Corporation (SAIC) and Northrup Grumman, all companies with deep connections to the military industrial complex and right wing politics, are forging ahead to bring computerized voting to every precinct in the country as a result of Help America Vote Act of 2002 (HAVA). In the November 2004 election, roughly sixty-five percent of the 116,517,062 votes cast were made through Diebold's, Sequoia's and ES&S' electronic voting machines. With claims like "our reliable systems accurately and securely capture each vote," or motto's such as "maintaining voter confidence, enhancing the voting experience," the end user should be able to trust these companies to do their job objectively with integrity. The reality is these companies failed in delivering to the voters reliability, accuracy and security during the last election which fundamentally dishonored the very core of American democracy.

Reliability and Accuracy in Question

Voters in Florida, Indiana, Nebraska, North Carolina, Ohio, Utah, Wyoming, and many others experienced a myriad of problems on Election Day. A sampling of the documented problems include:

➤ **FLORIDA**—Baker County reported districts that were predominantly democrat voted mostly republican. Orange and Broward County had voting number thresholds of 32, 767 when the threshold was met it began to count backwards (this pattern repeats in areas where optical scanners were used).

➤ **INDIANA**—Laporte County listed 300 registered voters per precinct for a total of 22,200 registered voters when there were actually 79,000; in some counties votes were switched from Democrat to Libertarian.

➤ **NEBRASKA**—Sarpy County ended up with 10,000 phantom votes.

➤ **NEW MEXICO**—votes changed to the opponent.

➤ **NORTH CAROLINA**—Guillford County a computer threw away 22,000 votes for Kerry.

➤ **OHIO**—Cuyahoga County included more votes than voters in many precincts reporting 93,136 extra votes; Franklin County, 638 ballots were cast—Bush was awarded 4,258 votes, Kerry received 260 votes; Perry County reported an 124 percent turnout in some precincts.

➤ **UTAH**—Utah County punch-card machines dropped votes 33,000 votes.

➤ **WYOMING**—voter turnout was 106 percent.

➤ In six states wrong candidates appeared on the screen.

➤ Scripps Howard News Service reviewed votes from 10 counties nationwide and found that 12,000 votes were not counted or a 1 in 10 chance that your vote would be counted.

According to the Election Incident Reporting System, there were 2,115 reported machine problems; not to mention more than 20,000 other reported difficulties people had with waiting in extremely long lines for hours, inadequate voting machine allocation, poorly trained voting personnel, missing absentee ballots, voters who were kept from the polls, and confusing ballot design.

SOURCES:
www.votersunite.org/inof/mapflyer2004.pdf
http://www.wanttoknow.info/electionsproblems

False Security Claims

A report from the Caltech-MIT Voting Technology Project states that an "estimated 1.5 million presidential votes were not recorded in 2000 because of difficulties using voting equipment and that electronic machines have the second highest rate of unmarked, uncounted and spoiled ballots in presidential, Senate, and governor elections over the last 12 years."

In July 2003, a technical report issued by Johns Hopkins University and Rice University in reference to Diebold Systems stated that the systems were far below "minimal security standards applicable in other contexts." They reported problems including "unauthorized privilege escalation, incorrect use of cryptography, vulnerabilities to network threats, and poor software development threats." Diebold refuted these allegations.

In February 2005, under the supervision of appropriate officials, Black Box Voting, computer experts and videographers, were able to hack into a live Diebold voting machine that was used on Election Day, November 2004. "The hack that worked was unsophisticated enough that many high school students would be able to achieve it. This hack altered the election by 100,000 votes, leaving no trace at all in the central tabulator program. It did not appear in any audit log." The hack could have been done by one person and in similar studies they were able to hack into the system from a remote location. This brings into question the "results of 40 million votes in 30 states." This is one example of many security issues that are of concern with the e-voting machine vendors.

SOURCES:
http://web.mit.edu/newsoffice/2001/voting2facts.html
http://avirubin.com/vote.pdf
http://www.bbvforums.org/cgi-bin/forums/board-auth.cgi?file=/1954/3826.html

Privatization of the Voting Process—Who Is Counting?

DIEBOLD INC.—One of the top three privatized voting companies, has gone through serious scrutiny over the course of the past two years and for good reason. They have consistently been reluctant to disclose information regarding voting machine equipment. One important question is, Who are we trusting to create the software? According to Bev Harris of Black Box Voting, in January 2002 Diebold purchased General Elections Systems. On the payroll at the time of the purchase three members of their senior management were convicted felons Jeffrey Dean, Head of Research and Development, Michael K. Graye, Director; and John Elder who oversees the making of paper ballots and punch-cards.

➤ Jeffrey Deanówas in charge of the GEMS central tabulator system that counted 50 percent of the votes in 30 states during the 2004 election, "(by his own admission) is subject to blackmail; but more critically, his embezzlement charges in the police record indicate he was involved in 'sophisticated' manipulation of computer accounting records,' and that 'he was embezzling in order to pay blackmail over a fight he was involved in, in which a person died.'" He pleaded guilty to 23 counts of embezzlement. Diebold claims that he did not work for them after the purchase, However, sources state that he worked for them as a consultant and that he was "sent the passwords to the GEMS files months after Diebold took over the election company."

➤ Michael K. Graye, was arrested in 1996 in Canada on tax-fraud and money-laundering charges that involved $18 million. He was also indicted in the U.S. on stock fraud, and spent 18 months in Canadian and U.S. prisons before pleading guilty to tax fraud in Canada. He has served four years in prison for the stock fraud and was sent to Canada in April 2003 for tax fraud where he was sent back to jail.

➤ Jeffrey Dean's friend John Elderóa convicted cocaine trafficker who served nearly five years in the same prison where Dean was incarcerated—joined Dean at Diebold's GEMS operation not long after Dean signed on with the company." John Elder is still on the payroll for Diebold.

Not surprisingly Diebold has also been in the hot seat for installing uncertified voting software in seventeen counties in the State of California. The most significant problem was that Diebold stated they were using a GEMS version that was certified, but when the audit was done they found at least five counties using another version. The State of California requires systems be "qualified by Independent Testing Authorities at the federal level and certified by the National Association of State Election Directors before the state can certify them for use."

SOURCES:
www.blackboxvoting.org
http://www.wired.com/news/evote/0,2645,61637,00.html?tw=wn_tophead_2

ELECTION SYSTEMS & SOFTWARE, INC. (ES&S)—According to their website they are "the world's largest and most experienced provider of total election management solutions with over 74,000 systems installed worldwide. Over the past decade, ES&S has handled more than 30,000 of the world's most important events—elections. In the U.S. 2000 General Election, ES&S systems counted over 100 million ballots." The primary stockholders in ES&S are the McCarthy Group (35 percent) and *Omaha World-Herald* (45 percent) who also is owner of the McCarthy Group, making *Omaha World-Herald* the primary stockholder of ES &S at this level. The largest stockholder in both of these companies is Peter Kiewit Son & Inc. "Kiewit has connections with both ES&S parent companies and has a track record of hiding ownership when it wants to, it has powerful profit motive for getting the people it wants into office and it has broken the law in the past to achieve its goals." They also are "tied to a string of bid-rigging cases in as many as 11 states and two countries."

A vice president of ES&S, Tom Eschberger, was entangled in a bribery prosecution regarding voting machines—he took an immunity plea and a Georgia official went to jail. (Wired News) http://www.wired.com/news/evote/0,2645,62790,00.html

For others, joining voting equipment companies has proven lucrative. Former Florida Secretary of State Sandra Mortham scored a $172,000 bonus from ES&S after helping the Nebraska-based company win a $17 million contract from Broward County, Fla. She also earned undisclosed amounts from sales of electronic voting systems to Miami-Dade and 10 other counties.

Broward and Miami-Dade both experienced severe problems the first time they used the new ES&S touch-screen machines. According to the American Civil Liberties Union of Florida, as many as one out of 12 voters did not have their votes counted in 31 precincts because poll workers were not able to set up the voting machines or did not verify votes had been properly cast. (Mercury News)

SEQUOIA VOTING SYSTEMS—In May 2002 Great Britain's De La Rue Company, the "world's largest commercial security printer and papermaker, involved in the production of over 150 national currencies and a wide range of security documents such as traveler cheques and vouchers" purchased Sequoia Voting Systems. De La Rue's parent company is Madison Dearborn a private equity firm who is partners with The Carlyle Group, a private investment firm that invests in military, industry, and politics. In March of 2005, De La Rue sold Sequoia Voting Systems to Smartmatic Corporation for $16 million. The CEO of Smartmatic Corporation, Antonio Mugica, "founded Smartmatic in 2000 with three other Venezuelans. The software firm handles its finance and sales in Boca Raton, Florida but does most research and development in Venezuela." The President and Vice-President of Smartmatic both worked with Unisys, a U.S. defense contractor, before moving to Smartmatic. Smartmatic's debut onto the election scene was the 2004 Venezuela Recall Election of Hugo Chavez. Although the company was able to provide a verifiable paper receipt, there were cases of alleged voter fraud due to voting machine irregularities and concerns of conflict of interest.

In addition to having many ownerships over the past two years, Sequoia has been hiring election officials including former California Secretary of State Bill Jones who began working for Sequoia, after giving a thumbs up to Sequoia voting equipment to Santa Clara County, ultimately ending in a $19 million transaction; Kathryn Ferguson, the election official who helped the purchase of Sequoia voting machines for Clark County, Nevada and Santa Clara County, California; and "Michael Frontera, former executive director of the Denver Election Commission, who went to work for Sequoia after awarding it $6.6 million in contracts from his own department." These examples represent the revolving door between elected officials and election software companies is a persistent concern. Andy Draheim, a spokesman for the political advocacy group California Common Cause states "it raises the question whether decisions made in office 'were made with the best of interest of the public in mind or with the best interest of the industry in mind.'"

SOURCES:
http://66.102.7.104/search?q=cache:zb6hiV2DthIJ:www.cnn.com/2004/TE
    CH/07/13/venezuela.e.voting.ap/+bitza,+smartmatic&hl=en&start=14
http://www.delarue.com/DLR_Content/CDA/Pages/Home/home/0,1641,,00.html
http://www.eluniversal.com/2004/08/19/en_revo_art_19A485227.shtml
http://www.ballotintegrity.org/DCForumID74/2.html
http://www.wheresthepaper.org/MercuryNews06_16RegulatorsJoinOther-
    Side.htm

SCIENTIFIC APPLICATIONS INTERNATIONAL CORPORATION (SAIC) was hired by Diebold to test the election software's reliability and security functions in the State of Maryland, appears to have more involvement in the elections business than previously noted. In 1998, SAIC was hired by Diversified Dynamics (recently purchased by Northrop Grumman) to provide them with engineering and software capabilities. Diversified Dynamics, Inc. was co-founded in 1997 by former Virginia Governor L. Douglas Wilder and Thomas G. Davis, to develop electronic voting technology.

SAIC is also linked to ES&S. In 2000, Venezuela fired ES&S for failing to count 5 percent to 15 percent of the ballots, which lead to a delay in the election. The supplier of the ES&S electronic voting software was SAIC. SAIC also has ties to VoteHere, an emerging company, which "aspires to provide cryptography and computer software security for the electronic election industry," Former president, chief operating officer, and vice chairman of SAIC Admiral Bill Owens was Chairman of the Board for VoteHere until 2003 and former SAIC board member ex-CIA Director Robert Gates is on the board.

So who exactly is this background player in the electronic voting business? SAIC, "the Pentagon's number one supplier of computer services," is an information technology, research and engineering firm. They ranked 8th overall in defense contracts from 1998 to 2003, collecting more defense contract dollars than any other company whose main job is providing services rather than products." Their total defense contracts between 1998 and 2003 were $10,598,835,883. Current sampling of contracts include:

➤ SAIC has won multiple contracts for Defense Advanced Research Projects Agency (DARPA).
➤ SAIC was awarded a $30 million contract from the pentagon to put on their payroll 150 Iraqi exiles to plan the new Iraqi government.
➤ Launched a post Sadam T.V. Network under an $82 million contract under the Psychological Warfare Division of the Pentagon.
➤ In November 2004, SAIC signed a two-task contract with the Saudi Arabia Saudi Royal Navy for updating their communications systems; total contract potential is $195,675,067.
➤ Yucca Mountain Project in partnership with Bechtel, LLC, authorized by President Bush in 2002, primary objective is to create "a repository for the disposal of spent nuclear fuel and high-level radioactive waste." Located 100 miles Northwest of Las Vegas, NV, the repository is planned to be open for business by 2010.
➤ Partnering with Northrup Grumman, SAIC was given the task of assisting in training the new Iraqi Army.

SOURCES:
http://www.chronogram.com/issue/2003/11/roomforaview/.
Lynn Landes "Voting Machine Fiasco: SAIC, VoteHere and Diebold," *Online Journal.*

http://www.saic.com/contractcenter/viewcon.html#d.
http://www.publicintegrity.org/pns/list.aspx?act=top.
http://www.alia2.net/article1510.html.

NORTHRUP GRUMANN—In a press release dated October 30, 2002, Northrup Grumann stated they have "entered the worldwide electronic election services market by signing an agreement with !Paper, LLC, Richmond, Va., to exclusively license and manufacture !Paper's electronic voting systems." !Paper, LLC, founded by Thomas G. Davis of Diversified Dynamics (now owned by Northrup Grumman) is a separate company founded to develop "patented' audio ballot technology and other patented 'paper-based' computerized data collection technologies for use in next generation absentee voting systems." Northrup Grumann plans on offering a complete voting system and implementing third-party regional election service providers to implement their election systems. Northrup Grumann is the fourth largest defense contractor. Between 1998 and 2003 they attained $33,829,847,656 in contracts with approximately 73 percent from the Pentagon. Their fiscal year contract revenue went from $5 billion in 2000 to $11 billion in 2003.

SOURCES:
http://intelligence.house.gov/Media/PDFS/BushBio110503.pdf.
http://www.publicintegrity.org/pns/list.aspx?act=top.
http://www.it.northropgrumman.com/press/archive.asp?pid=1422.

ACCENTURE LTD.—formerly known as Arthur Anderson Consulting, a company convicted of destroying evidence in the Enron scandal, is incorporated in British territory of Bermuda where they are exempt from taxes. They split from Arthur Anderson in July 2001 and created a new image. Accenture defines themselves as a "global management consulting, technology services and outsourcing company." They are one of the top 100 public federal contractors. In 2004 they were awarded a $10 billion contract, one of the largest contracts in history, for Homeland Security. This contract has created a heated debate in Congress for the use of off-shore contractors.

The Chairman of the Board of Directors is Sir Mark Moody-Stuart who was previously was chairman of the Royal Dutch/Shell Group of companies and chairman of the "Shell" Transport and Trading Company from 1997 to 2001, after having served six years as both managing director of Shell Transport and managing director of the Royal Dutch/Shell Group of Companies. Accenture is also partners with Halliburton, Vice President Cheney's former employer. They have a total of 110 offices in 48 different countries. According to Black Box Voting, in July 2003, Accenture bought Election.com from Osan Ltd., a private Saudi Firm, which prior to purchasing Election.com Accenture had an equity investment. In a press release August 2003, Accenture stated that they were "working with the Department of Defense's Federal Voting Assistance Program (FVAP) and several states and counties to design and build a new voting technology system for the SERVE project, which stands for Secure Electronic Registration and Voting Experiment." SERVE will provide Internet service that will count the votes of the U.S. military and other civilians.

Bev Harris reported that according to the Canadian Polaris Institute, "Accenture is heavily involved in projects to privatize public services, especially welfare programs in the U.S. Canada and the EU. The company's short history is rife with cost overruns and scandals, the most recent being a possible violation of the U.S. Foreign Corrupt Practices Act. She also reports that Accenture's political contributions (2000–2002) totaled $220,000, with the GOP getting 57 percent. Soft money contributions were $86,000, with the GOP enjoying a 3:1 advantage in contributions."

SOURCES:
http://www.accenture.com/xd/xd.asp?it=enweb&xd=aboutus\governance\governance_home.xml.
http://www.opednews.com/landes_how_we_lost_the_vote.htm.
http://www.blackboxvoting.com/modules.php?name=News&file=article&sid=55.
http://www.polarisinstitute.org/corp_profiles/public_service_gats/corp_profile_ps_accenture.html.
http://www.internetnews.com/bus-news/article.php/3369561.

INFORMATION TECHNOLOGY ASSOCIATION OF AMERICA (ITAA)—is a lobbying group for technology firms. The ITAA established the Election Systems Task Force, consisting of defense contractors and procurement agencies, with the primary objective of pushing the HAVA legislation through Congress. There are twelve companies involved in the task force, of the twelve there are only four that are known: Northrup Grumman, Lockheed Martin, Accenture, and EDS. However, on the Board of Directors for ITAA includes a litany of defense and procurement agencies such as SAIC, Unisys, Raytheon and General Dynamics. The following is a time line of activity regarding ITAA:

AUGUST 22, 2002—The Task Force's top agenda item was simply: "How do we get Congress to fund a move to electronic voting?" The discussion was about the importance of getting the HAVA legislation enacted as a means of creating more business for them as integrators.

SEPTEMBER 6, 2002—ITAA demanded that House and Senate conferees resolve their differences over their respective versions, and pass HAVA.

OCTOBER 12, 2002—HAVA was signed into law by President Bush.

AUGUST 23, 2003—A phone conference to negotiate "lobbying" fees in order to help promote the image of the e-voting machines after their image was tarnished by "activists" and "academic" reports regarding the quality of the systems. The call was attended by ITAA, voting industry companies, and R. Doug Lewis, the head of the Election Center, a non-profit organization whose purpose is to "promote, preserve and improve democracy" primarily through "voter registration and election administration."

DECEMBER 9, 2003—Election Technology Council (ETC) was formed. This group is comprised of Advanced Voting Systems, Diebold, ES&S, HartInterCivic, Sequoia and Unilect. The goal is to "raise the profile" and sell the machines to the American public.

"ITAA says the ETC builds on the work of its Voting Reform Task Group, the which lobbies for HAVA funding." (*Executive Intelligence Review*)

SOURCES:
http://www.larouchepub.com/other/2004/3107repeal_hava.html.
www.blackboxvoting.org.

Validity of Exit Polls

Exit polls are a resource for checking the validity of an election by asking someone after the walk out of an election booth who they voted for. There is a 1 in 456,000 chance that exit polls could have had such a large sampling error. The exit polls had predicted that John Kerry would win by 3 percent with 316 Electoral votes, yet Bush won by 2.5 percent—creating a 5.5 percent difference. The official explanation for the large discrepancy after the election was that Kerry voters were more likely to participate in exit polls.

Using the same data as the National Exit Poll (NEP), the U.S. Counts Votes, National Data Archive Project issued March 31, 2005 came up with a strikingly different case. They found that the Bush supporters actually had a higher rate of participation in the polls so this initial explanation was incorrect. The report also found "statistically significant discrepancies of exit poll results from reported election outcomes were concentrated in five states, four of which were battleground states" i.e. Ohio, Pennsylvania, Florida. The reports hypothesis is that the "voters' intent was not accurately recorded or counted."

U.S. Counts Votes, The National Election Data Archive Project, is an organization that plans to create the first-ever nation-wide database of election results, voter registration information, demographic data, to be analyzed by their core project team's mathematicians, computer programmers, pollsters, and statisticians, as well as by their independent outside peer-review board.

SOURCES:

http://uscountvotes.org/index.php?option=com_content&task=view&id=17
&Itemid=45

www.commondreams.org/headlines05/0401-06.htm

http://itmanagement.earthweb.com/columns/executive_tech/article.php/3495176

Current Legislation in Progress

In October 2002, HAVA was set into action as a result of the 2000 Election fiasco in Florida, which ironically was due to the very machines that HAVA endorses. The deadline for all states to be in compliance with HAVA is January 1, 2006. As reported, there are many issues with the machines and the voting process that need to be addressed before full implementation takes place. Currently, there are several bills that are being voted on in Congress to increase the reliability, accuracy and security of these machines. VerfiedVoting.org, founded by Computer Science Professor, Dr. David Dill, of Stanford University, has put together an excellent resource for reviewing the results of the 2004 Election, current legislation that is in progress and resources to take action. The three HAVA amendments that are reported as the strongest are:

➤ H.R.550 VOTER CONFIDENCE AND INCREASE ACCESSIBILITY ACT OF 2005 which promotes accuracy, integrity and security through voter-verified permanent record or hard copy, prohibits undisclosed software in voting systems, prohibits wireless devices in voting systems, requires certification of software and hardware, ensures instruction of election officials, prohibits connection or transmission of system over internet, prohibits conflicts of interest with certification laboratories and that results are available to the commission and public.

➤ H.R. 704 & S. 330 VOTING INTEGRITY AND VERIFICATION ACT OF 2005 (VIVA

2005) which emphasizing the paper voter-verified permanent record.
➤ H.R. 939 & S. 450 COUNT EVERY VOTE ACT OF 2005, which includes much of H.R. 550 and expands into additional requirements.

"Every citizen of this country who is registered to vote should be guaranteed that their vote matters, that their vote is counted, and that in the voting booth of their community, their vote has as much weight as the vote of any Senator, any Congressperson, any President, any cabinet member, or any CEO of any Fortune 500 Corporation."—Senator Barbara Boxer, January 6, 2005

SOURCE:
www.verfiedvoting.org.

Election Reform Committee

In a press release dated March 2005, the Carter-Baker Commission on Federal Election Reform, co-chaired by former U.S. President Jimmy Carter and former Secretary of State James A. Baker, III began hearing testimony from panels on April 18, 2005; the next panel is scheduled for June 30, 2005. The commission will meet in August to draft a report that will be submitted September 19, 2005 in Washington D.C.

Carter stated, "The overall concern is that 40 percent of the American people don't vote. Secondly, that there's a great deal of doubt in our country about the integrity of the electoral process. Those are the two basic issues. What ca we do to address them? Obviously we want to have more access by American to the voting both. And secondly, we want to make sure that the electoral processes has integrity—that it is not shot with fraud."

The initial members of the panel that testified were: Hon. Gracia Hillman, Chair, U.S. Election Assistance Commission; Chellie Pingree, President, Common Cause; Kay J. Maxwell, President, League of Women Voters; Prof. Henry Bradley, Professor of Political Science and Public Policy, University of California Berkeley; Barbara Arnwine, Executive Director, Lawyers Committee for Civil Rights; Arturo Vargas, Executive Director, National Association of Latino Elected and Appointed Officials; John Fund, *Wall Street Journal* Editorial Board Member and Author of *Stealing Elections*; Colleen McAndrews, Partner, Bell, McAndrews & Hiltchak; Jim Dickenson, Vice President of Governmental Affairs, American Association of People with Disabilities; David Dill, Professor of Computer Science, Stanford University and Found of VerifiedVoting.org; Hon. Ron Thornburgh, Secretary of Sate, State of Kansas; Richard L. Hasen, William H. Hannon Distinguished Professor of Law, Loyola Law School and Co-Editor of *Election Law Journal*.

CHAPTER 3

No Paper Trail Left Behind: The Theft of the 2004 Presidential Election

by Dennis Loo, Ph.D.

Alice laughed: "There's no use trying," she said; "one can't believe impossible things." "I daresay you haven't had much practice," said the Queen. "When I was younger, I always did it for half an hour a day. Why, sometimes I've believed as many as six impossible things before breakfast."
—Lewis Carroll, *Through the Looking Glass*

In order to believe that George Bush won the November 2, 2004 presidential election, you must also believe all of the following extremely improbable or outright impossible things.[1]

1. A big turnout and a highly energized and motivated electorate favored the GOP instead of the Democrats for the first time in history.[2]
2. Even though first-time voters, lapsed voters (people who didn't vote in 2000), and undecideds went for John Kerry by big margins, and Bush *lost* people who voted for him in the cliffhanger 2000 election, Bush *still* received a 3.5 million vote surplus nationally.[3]
3. The fact that Bush far exceeded the 85 percent of registered Florida Republicans' votes that he got in 2000, receiving in 2004 more than

100 percent of the registered Republican votes in 47 out of 67 Florida counties, 200 percent of registered Republicans in 15 counties, and over 300 percent of registered Republicans in 4 counties merely shows Floridians' enthusiasm for Bush. Somehow he managed to do this despite the fact that his share of the cross-over votes by registered Democrats in Florida did not increase over 2000 and he lost ground among registered Independents, dropping 15 points.[4]

4. Florida's reporting of more presidential votes (7.59 million) than the actual number of people who voted (7.35 million), a surplus of 237,522 votes, does not indicate fraud.

5. The fact that a number of predominately Republican Ohio precincts recorded more votes than there were registered voters while many heavily Democratic strongholds reported less than 10 percent participation rates does not indicate a rigged election.[5]

6. Bush won re-election despite approval ratings below 50 percent—the first time in history this has happened. Truman has been cited as having also done this, but Truman's polling numbers were trailing so much behind his challenger, Thomas Dewey, pollsters stopped surveying two months before the 1948 elections, thus missing the late surge of support for Truman. Unlike Truman, Bush's support was clearly eroding on the eve of the election.[6]

7. Harris' last-minute polling indicating a Kerry victory was wrong (even though Harris was exactly on the mark in their 2000 election final poll).[7]

8. The "challenger rule"—an incumbent's final results won't be better than his final polling—was wrong.[8]

9. On election day the early-day voters picked up by early exit polls (showing Kerry with a wide lead) were heavily Democratic instead of the traditional pattern of early voters being heavily Republican.

10. Bush "won" Ohio by 51-48 percent, but this was not matched by the court-supervised hand count of the 147,400 absentee and provisional ballots in which Kerry received 54.46 percent of the vote.[9]

11. Florida computer programmer Clinton Curtis (a life-long registered Republican) must be lying when he said in a sworn affidavit that his employers at Yang Enterprises, Inc. (YEI) and Tom Feeney (general counsel and lobbyist for YEI, GOP state legislator and Jeb Bush's 1994 running mate for Florida Lt. Governor) asked him in 2000 to create a computer program to undetectably alter vote totals. Curtis, under the initial impression that he was creating this soft-

ware in order to forestall possible fraud, handed over the program to his employer Mrs. Li Woan Yang, and was told: "You don't understand, in order to get the contract we have to hide the manipulation in the source code. This program is needed to control the vote in south Florida."[10]

12. Diebold CEO Walden O'Dell's declaration in a August 14, 2003 letter to GOP fundraisers that he was "committed to helping Ohio to deliver its electoral votes to the president next year" and the fact that Diebold is one of the three major suppliers of the electronic voting machines in Ohio and nationally, didn't result in any fraud by Diebold.

13. There was no fraud in Cuyahoga County, Ohio where the number of recorded votes was more than 93,000 larger than the number of registered voters and where they admitted counting the votes in secret before bringing them out in public to count (see appendix at the end of this chapter).

14. CNN reported at 9 p.m. EST on election evening that Kerry was leading by 3 points in the national exit polls based on well over 13,000 respondents. Several hours later at 1:36 a.m. CNN reported that the exit polls, now based on a few hundred more—13,531 respondents—were showing Bush leading by 2 points, a 5-point swing. In other words, a swing of 5 percentage points from a tiny increase in the number of respondents somehow occurred despite it being mathematically impossible.[11]

15. Exit polls in the November 2004 Ukrainian presidential elections, paid for in part by the Bush Administration, were right, but exit polls in the U.S., where exit polling was invented, were very wrong.[12]

16. The National Election Pool's exit polls[13] were so far off that since their inception twenty years ago, they have never been this wrong, more wrong than statistical probability indicates is possible.

17. In *every* single instance where exit polls were wrong the discrepancy favored Bush, never Kerry, even though statistical probability tells us that any survey errors should show up in both directions. Half a century of polling and centuries of mathematics must be wrong.

18. It must be merely a stunning coincidence that exit polls were wrong only in precincts where there was no paper ballot to check against the electronic totals and right everywhere there was a paper trail.

THE EMPEROR (AND THE ELECTORAL PROCESS) HAVE NO CLOTHES

The preceding list recounts only some of the irregularities in the 2004 election since it ignores the scores of instances of voter disenfranchisement that assumed many different forms (e.g., banning black voters in Florida who had either been convicted of a felony previously or who were "inadvertently" placed on the felons list by mistake, while not banning convicted Latino felons; providing extraordinarily few voting machines in predominately Democratic precincts in Ohio; disallowing Ohio voters, for the first time, from voting in any precinct when they were unable to find their assigned precincts to vote in; and so on). A plethora of reasons clearly exists to conclude that widespread and historic levels of fraud were committed in this election.

Indeed, any *one* of the above highly improbables and outright impossibles should have led to a thorough investigation into the results. Taken as a whole, this list points overwhelmingly to fraud. The jarring strangeness of the results and the ubiquity of complaints from voters (e.g., those who voted for Kerry and then saw to their shock the machine record their votes as being for Bush), require some kind of explanation, or the legitimacy of elections and of the presidency would be imperiled.

The explanations from public officials and major media came in three forms. First, exit polls, not the official tallies, were labeled spectacularly wrong. Second, the so-called "moral values" voters expressed in the now ubiquitous "red state/blue state" formula, were offered as the underlying reason for Bush's triumph. And third, people who brought forth any of the evidence of fraud were dismissed as "spreadsheet-wielding conspiracy theorists" while mainstream media censored the vast majority of the evidence of fraud so that most Americans to this day have never heard a fraction of what was amiss. I will discuss each of these three responses, followed by a discussion of the role of electronic voting machines in the 2002 elections that presaged the 2004 election irregularities, and then wrap up with a discussion of these events' significance taken as a whole.

KILLING THE MESSENGER: THE EXIT POLLS

Exit polls are the gold standard of vote count validity internationally. Since exit polls ask people as they emerge from the polling station who they just voted for, they are not projections as are polls taken in the months, weeks or days before an election. They are not subject to faulty memory, voter capriciousness (voters voting differently than they indicated to a pollster previously), or erroneous projections about who will actually turn up to vote. Pollsters know who turned up to vote because the voters are standing there in front of the exit pollsters. Because of these characteristics, exit polls are exceptionally accurate. They are so accurate that in Germany, for example, they are used to decide elections, with the paper ballots being counted in the days afterwards as a backup check against the exit polls. Exit polls are used, for this reason, as markers of fraud.[14]

Significant, inexplicable discrepancies between exit polls and official tallies only started showing up in the U.S. in 2000 and only in Florida (and notably, nowhere else). The discrepancy was not the exit polls' fault, however, but in the official tallies themselves. Although the mainstream media fell on their swords about their election's evening projections calling Florida for Gore in 2000, their projections were right. In analyses conducted by the National Opinion Research Center in Florida after the U.S. Supreme Court aborted the vote recount, Gore emerged the winner over Bush, no matter what criteria for counting votes was applied.[15] The fact that this is not widely known constitutes itself a major untold story.

Exit polling's validity is further affirmed by GOP pollster Dick Morris. Immediately after the 2004 election he wrote:

> Exit polls are almost never wrong. They eliminate the two major potential fallacies in survey research by correctly separating actual voters from those who pretend they will cast ballots but never do and by substituting actual observation for guesswork in judging the relative turnout of different parts of the state...
>
> To screw up one exit poll is unheard of. To miss six of them is incredible. It boggles the imagination how pollsters could be that incompetent and invites speculation that more than honest error was at play here.[16]

Confounded and suspicious of the results, Morris resorted to advancing the bizarre theory that there must have been a conspiracy among the networks to suppress the Bush vote in the west by issuing exit poll results that were so far off from the final tallies.

A number of different statisticians have examined the 2004 election results. University of Pennsylvania statistician Steve Freeman, Ph.D., most notably, analyzed the exit polls of the swing states of Pennsylvania, Ohio and Florida and concluded that the odds of the exit polls being as far off as they were are 250 million to one.[17] Exit polls in Florida had Kerry leading by 1.7 points and by 2.4 points in Ohio. These exit poll figures were altered at 1:30 a.m. November 3, 2004 on CNN to conform to the "official" tally. In the end, Kerry lost Florida by 5 percent and Ohio by 2.5 percent. This is a net shift of 6.7 points in Florida and 4.9 points in Ohio in Bush's favor, well beyond the margin of error. By exit poll standards, this net shift was unbelievable.

A team at the University of California at Berkeley, headed by sociology professor Michael Hout, found a highly suspicious pattern in which Bush received 260,000 more votes in those Florida precincts that used electronic voting machines than past voting patterns would indicate compared to those precincts that used optical scan read votes where past voting patterns held.[18]

The Edison-Mitofsky polling group that conducted the National Exit Poll (NEP) issued a 77-page report on January 19, 2005 to account for why their exit polls were so unexpectedly far off.[19] Edison-Mitofsky rule out sampling error as the problem and indicate that systemic bias was responsible. They concluded that their exit polls were wrong because Kerry voters must have been more willing to talk to their poll workers than Bush voters and because their poll workers were too young and inexperienced. Edison-Mitofsky offer no evidence indicating that their conclusion about more chatty Kerry voters actually occurred, merely that such a scenario would explain the discrepancy. In fact, as nine statisticians[20] who conducted an evaluation of the Edison-Mitofsky data and analysis point out, Bush voters appeared to be slightly *more* willing to talk to exit pollsters than Kerry voters. This would make the exit polls' discrepancy with the official tallies even more pronounced. In addition, the Edison-Mitofsky explanation fails to explain why exit polls were only exceptionally wrong in the swing states.

RED STATE/RED HERRING: THE "MORAL VALUES" VOTERS

A plausible explanation still needs to be offered for the startling 2004 election outcome—how did Bush, caught in a lie about why we went to war with Iraq, racked by prison abuse and torture scandals at Abu Ghraib and Guantanamo, bogged down in Iraq, failing to catch Osama Bin Laden, embarrassed during the debates, and so on, manage to win a big victory? Enter here the "moral values" rationale. As Katharine Q. Seelye of the *New York Times* wrote in a November 4, 2004 article entitled "Moral Values Cited as a Defining Issue of the Election:"

Even in a time of war and economic hardship, Americans said they were motivated to vote for President Bush on Tuesday by moral values as much as anything else, according to a survey of voters as they left their polling places. In the survey, a striking portrait of one influential group emerged—that of a traditional, church-going electorate that leans conservative on social issues and strongly backed Mr. Bush....

In the same issue, another article by Todd S. Purdum entitled "Electoral Affirmation of Shared Values Provides Bush a Majority" cited 1/5 (more precisely, 22 percent) of the voters as mentioning "moral values" as their chief concern. This was echoed throughout major media.[21] The only person in the mainstream media to challenge this was New York Times columnist Frank Rich, on November 28, 2004 in an opinion piece entitled "The Great Indecency Hoax":

The mainstream press, itself in love with the "moral values" story line and traumatized by the visual exaggerations of the red-blue map, is too cowed to challenge the likes of the American Family Association. So are politicians of both parties. It took a British publication, The Economist, to point out that the percentage of American voters citing moral and ethical values as their prime concern is actually down from 2000 (35 percent) and 1996 (40 percent).[22]

As Rich correctly points out, no American media outlet repeated this statistic. Instead, the widely mentioned and oft-repeated "moral values" vote took on the status of an urban—or in this instance, rural—legend.

Shocked by the election results, many people took out their anger at the perceived mendacity of Bush voters, especially those in the so-called "red states." This fury, while understandable given Bush's record, badly misses the point. Voters did not heist this election. As others have pointed out eloquently, many of the people who really did vote for Bush did so because they were misled through systematic disinformation campaigns.[23]

"SPREADSHEET WIELDING CONSPIRACY THEORISTS"

In November 2004 major U.S. media gave headline news treatment to the Ukrainian Presidential election fraud, explicitly citing the exit polls as definitive evidence of fraud. At the very same time major U.S. media dismissed anyone who pointed out this same evidence of likely fraud in the U.S. elections as "conspiracy theory" crazies. A November 11, 2004 Washington Post article, for example, described people raising the question of fraud as "mortally wounded party loyalists and... spreadsheet-wielding conspiracy theorists."[24] Tom Zeller, Jr. handled it similarly, writing in the November 12,

2004 issue of the *New York Times* ("Vote Fraud Theories, Spread by Blogs, Are Quickly Buried"): "[T]he email messages and Web postings had all the twitchy cloak-and-dagger thrust of a Hollywood blockbuster. 'Evidence mounts that the vote may have been hacked,' trumpeted a headline on the Web site CommonDreams.org. 'Fraud took place in the 2004 election through electronic voting machines,' declared BlackBoxVoting.org."[25]

Both of these articles don't even bother to address a fraction of the evidence of irregularities. They do both, however, dismiss the 93,000 excess votes in Cuyahoga County, Ohio as merely an error in how the votes were reported, the *Washington Post* article offering the strange explanation that in "even-numbered years" the county posts vote totals from *other districts outside* the county in the Cuyahoga totals. The *Washington Post* passed off the exit polls discrepancy as "not being based on statistics" since the exit polls "are not publicly distributed." Both of these statements were untrue. The *New York Times* article failed to even mention exit polls. Both articles explain away the glaring and unbelievable totals for Bush in hugely Democratic districts as due to the "Dixiecrat" vote. This would be plausible except for the fact that these votes far in excess of Republican registered voters numbers occurred primarily in non-rural areas. In just one example of this, Baker County, Florida, out of 12,887 registered voters, of whom 69.3 percent were Democrats and 24.3 percent Republicans, Bush received 7,738 votes while Kerry only received 2,180.[26] As Robert Parry of Consortiumnews.org points out:

Rather than a rural surge of support, Bush actually earned more than seven out of 10 new votes in the 20 largest counties in Florida. Many of these counties are either Democratic strongholds—such as Miami-Dade, Broward, and Palm Beach—or they are swing counties, such as Orange, Hillsborough, and Duval.

Many of these large counties saw substantially more newly registered Democrats than Republicans. For example, in Orange County, a swing county home to Orlando, Democrats registered twice as many new voters than Republicans in the years since 2000. In Palm Beach and Broward combined, Democrats registered 111,000 new voters compared with fewer than 20,000 new Republicans.[27]

The only person in major media to treat these complaints seriously and at any length was Keith Olbermann at MSNBC who ran two stories on it, citing Cuyahoga County's surplus 93,000 votes over the registered voter count, and the peculiar victories for Bush in Florida counties that were overwhelmingly Democratic scattered across the state.[28] For his trouble, media conservatives attacked him for being a "voice of paranoia" and spreading "idiotic conspiracy theories."[29]

THE OH-SO LOYAL OPPOSITION: THE DEMOCRATIC PARTY

An obvious question here is: why haven't the Democrats been more vigorous in their objections to this fraud? The fact that they haven't objected more (with a few notable individual exceptions) has been taken by some as definitive evidence that no fraud must have happened because the Democrats have the most to gain from objecting. In part the answer is that the Democrats don't fully understand what has hit them. The Kerry campaign's reaction to the Swift Boat Veterans attack ads that damaged them so much are a good illustration of this. The right wing media hammered away at Kerry through their by now very heavy presence over talk radio, the Internet, Fox News, and other outlets. The mainstream media such as ABC, CBS, NBC, CNN and major newspapers and magazines, still adhering to the standards of "objective" journalism, which the right wing media consider "quaint,"[30] legitimated these false allegations about Kerry by presenting "the two sides" as if one side made up entirely of lies and half-truths could be considered a legitimate "side." The Kerry campaign concluded that these ads were all lies and wouldn't have any effect, thus they took too long to respond to them. By the time they did, the damage had been done. In a CBS/*New York Times* poll taken September 12-16, 2004, 33 percent said they thought that the Swift Boast Veterans' charges against Kerry were "mostly true."[31] A remarkable feat given that Kerry volunteered and was multi-decorated for heroism while Bush used his father's connections to dodge real service.

The Democrats' meek acceptance of other races' extremely peculiar outcomes prior to the 2004 elections illustrates this point further. As a result of the 2000 Florida debacle, Congress passed the "Help America Vote" Act in October 2002. While this act introduced a number of reasonable reforms, it also resulted in the widespread introduction of paperless electronic voting machines. This meant that there was no way to determine if the votes recorded by these computers were accurate and tamper-free. Efforts subsequently by a few Democratic Congresspeople, led by Michigan Rep. John Conyers, to rectify this and ensure a paper ballot, have been stalled by the GOP majority.

The following is a partial list of 2002 discrepancies that can be understood as dress rehearsals for the stolen presidential election of 2004:

On Nov. 3, 2002, the *Atlanta Journal-Constitution* poll showed Democratic Sen. Max Cleland with a 49-to-44 point lead over Republican Rep. Saxby Chambliss. The next day, Chambliss, despite trailing by 5 points, ended up winning by a margin of 53 to 46 percent. This was, in other words, an unbelievable 12-point turn around over the course of one day!

In the Georgia governor's race Republican Sonny Perdue upset incumbent Democratic Gov. Roy Barnes by a margin of 52 to 45 percent. This was especially strange given that the October 16-17, 2002 Mason Dixon Poll (Mason Dixon Polling and Research, Inc. of Washington, D.C.) had shown Democratic Governor Barnes ahead 48 to 39 percent, with a margin of error of plus or minus 4 points. The final tally was, in other words, a jaw dropping 16-point turn-around! What the Cleland "defeat" by Saxby and the Barnes "defeat" by Perdue both have in common is that nearly all the Georgia votes were recorded on computerized voting machines, which produce no paper trail.

In Minnesota, after Democrat Sen. Paul Wellstone's plane crash death,[32] ex-vice-president Walter Mondale took Wellstone's place and was leading Republican Norm Coleman in the days before the election by 47 to 39 percent. Despite the fact that he was trailing just days before the race by 8 points, Coleman beat Mondale by 50 to 47 percent. This was an 11-point turn around! The Minnesota race was also conducted on electronic voting machines with no paper trail.[33]

Welcome to a world where statistical probability and normal arithmetic no longer apply! The Democrats, rather than vigorously pursuing these patently obvious signs of election fraud in 2004, have nearly all decided that being gracious losers is better than being winners,[34] probably because—and this may be the most important reason for the Democrat's relative silence—a full-scale uncovering of the fraud runs the risk of mobilizing and unleashing popular forces that the Democrats find just as threatening as the GOP does.

The delicious irony for the GOP is that the Help America Vote Act, precipitated by their theft of the Florida 2000 presidential vote, made GOP theft of elections as in the preceding examples easy and unverifiable except through recourse to indirect analysis such as pre-election polls and exit polls. This is the political equivalent of having your cake and eating it too. Or, more precisely: stealing elections, running the country, and aggressively, arrogantly and falsely claiming that the people support it.

Flavor Flav of the rap group Public Enemy used to wear a big clock around his neck in order to reminder us all that we'd better understand what time it is. Or, as Bob Dylan once said: "Let us not speak falsely now, the hour's getting late." To all of those who said before the 2004 elections that this was the most important election in our lifetimes; to all of those who plunged into that election hoping and believing that we could throw the villains out via the electoral booth; to all of those who held their noses and voted for Democrats thinking that at least they were slightly better than the theocratic fascists running this country now, this must be said: VOTING REALLY DOESN'T MATTER. If we weren't convinced of that before these last elections, then now is the time to wake up to that fact. The simple fact of the matter is that public policies are not now, nor have they ever been, settled through elections.

THE ROLE OF MASS MOVEMENTS AND ALTERNATIVE MEDIA

What can be done? The George McGovern campaign in 1972 didn't end the war in Vietnam. The Vietnamese people and the anti-war movement ended the war. Civil rights weren't secured because JFK and LBJ suddenly woke up to racial discrimination. The Civil Rights Movement and Black Power Movement galvanized public opinion and rocked this country to its foundations. Men didn't suddenly wake up and realize that they were male chauvinist pigs—women formed the women's movement, organized, marched, rallied, demanded equality and shook this country to the core. The Bush Administration is bogged down and sinking deeper in Iraq not mainly because the top figures of the Bush Administration consist of liars, blind (and incompetent) ideologues, international outlaws and propagators of torture as an official policy, but because the Iraqi people have risen up against imperialist invasion. Prior to the war, the international anti-Iraq war movement brought out millions of people into the streets, the largest demonstrations in history, denying the U.S. imperialists the UN's sanction and leading to Turkey denying U.S. requests to use their land as a staging area. These are major, world-historic feats.

The 2000, 2002 and 2004 elections fraud underscores the critical importance of building a mass movement, a movement of resistance that doesn't tie itself to the electoral road and electoral parties. In addition, as Robert Parry has eloquently argued, a counterforce to the right wing media empire must be built by the left and by progressive-minded people. As it stands today, the right can get away with nearly anything because they have talking heads on TV, radio, the Internet and other outlets who set the tone and the political agenda, with mainstream media focusing on sex and sensationalism and taking their political cues to a large extent from the right.[35]

Like a bridge broken by an earthquake, the electoral road can only lead to plunging us into the sea—which is precisely what happened in the 2004 election.

Dennis Loo, Ph.D. is an Associate Professor of Sociology at California State Polytechnic University, Pomona. He graduated with honors from Harvard with a B.A. in Government and received his M.A. and Ph.D. in Sociology from the University of California at Santa Cruz. His research interests include social problems, media, criminology, and social movements. He can be reached at ddloo@csupomona.edu.

NOTES

1. Several of the items in this list feature Ohio and Florida because going into the election it was universally understood that the outcome hinged on these swing states.

   "Truth Is All" on the DemocraticUnderground.com offered a list that is similar in format to my highly improbables and utterly impossibles list of the 2004 election results and I have drawn directly from their list for items #7 and 8. (http://www.democraticunderground.com/discuss/duboard.php?az=view_all&address=203x22581), retrieved June 4, 2005.

2. High turnout favors Democrats and more liberal-left candidates because the groups who participate the least and most sporadically in voting are from lower socio-economic groups who generally eschew more conservative candidates.

3. Seventeen percent of election 2004 voters did not vote in 2000. Kerry defeated Bush in this group 54 percent to 45 percent. (Katharine Q. Seelye, "Moral Values Cited as a Defining Issue of the Election," The *New York Times*, November 4, 2004). This contradicts the widely held belief that Bush owes his victory wholly or largely to the evangelical vote and "getting out the Republican base" (the newly voting elements of which would have had to have been either first-time or lapsed voters).

4. Gore carried the 2000 Florida Independent vote by only 47 to 46 percent whereas Kerry carried them by a 57 percent to 41 percent margin. In 2000 Bush received 13% of the registered Democratic voters votes and in 2004 he got the virtually statistically identical 14% of their votes. Sam Parry, "Bush's 'Incredible' Vote Tallies," Consortiumnews.com, November 9, 2004.

   See also Colin Shea's analysis: "In one county, where 88% of voters are registered Democrats, Bush got nearly two-thirds of the vote—three times more than predicted by my model. In 21 counties, more than 50% of Democrats would have to have defected to Bush to account for the county result; in four counties at least 70% would have been required. These results are absurdly unlikely." http://www.freezerbox.com/archive/article.asp?id=321

5. "[C]ertified reports from pro-Kerry Cleveland, in Cuyahoga County, [showed] … precincts with turnouts of as few as 22.31 percent (precinct 6B), 21.43 percent (13O), 20.07 percent (13F), 14.59 percent (13D), and 7.85 percent (6C) of the registered voters. Thousands of people in these precincts lined up for many hours in the rain in order, it would appear, not to vote.

"Meanwhile, in pro-Bush Perry County, the voting records certified by Secretary of State Blackwell included two precincts with reported turnouts of 124.4 and 124.0 percent of the registered voters, while in pro-Bush Miami County, there were precincts whose certified turnouts, if not physically impossible, were only slightly less improbable. These and other instances of implausibly high turnouts in precincts won by Bush, and implausibly low turnouts in precincts won by Kerry, are strongly suggestive of widespread tampering with the vote-tabulation processes."

Michael Keefe, "The Strange Death of American Democracy: Endgame in Ohio," http://globalresearch.ca/articles/KEE501A.html, retrieved May 31, 2005.

6. "Bush's job approval has slipped to 48% among national adults and is thus below the symbolically important 50% point." "Questions and Answers With the Editor in Chief," Frank Newport, Editor in Chief, The Gallup Poll, November 2, 2004, http://www.gallup.com/poll/content/?ci=13948&pg=1, retrieved on May 27, 2005.

As Newport further notes, referring to the final Oct. 29-31, 2004 CNN/*USA Today*/Gallup poll, "Among all national adults, 49% now choose Kerry as the candidate best able to handle Iraq, while 47% choose Bush. This marks a significant pickup on this measure for Kerry, who was down nine points to Bush last week. In fact, Kerry has lost out to Bush on this measure in every poll conducted since the Democratic convention."

"Bush's margin over Kerry as the candidate best able to handle terrorism is now seven points. 51% of Americans choose Bush and 44% choose Kerry. This again marks a significant change. Last week, Bush had an 18-point margin over Kerry, and the 7-point advantage is the lowest yet for Bush." In other words, momentum was on Kerry's side, with Bush losing 9 points of support on Iraq and 11 points on handling terrorism over the course of one week! This was hardly a sign of someone about to win by 3.5 million votes.

7. http://www.harrisinteractive.com/harris_poll/index.asp?PID=515 , dated November 2, 2004, retrieved on June 1, 2005: "

Both surveys suggest that Kerry has been making some gains over the course of the past few days (see Harris Polls #83 http://www.harrisinteractive.com/harris_poll/index.asp?PID=512, and #78 http://www.harrisinteractive.com/harris_poll/index.asp?PID=507).

If this trend is real, then Kerry may actually do better than these numbers suggest. In the past, presidential challengers tend to do better against an incumbent President among the undecided voters during the last three days of the elections, and that appears to be the case here. The reason: undecided voters are more often voters who dislike the President but do not know the challenger well enough to make a decision. When they decide, they frequently split 2:1 to 4:1 for the challenger." For Harris' last minute poll results before the 2000 election, see http://www.harrisinteractive.com/harris_poll/index.asp?PID=130, dated November 6, 2000 in which they call the election between Bush and Gore too lose to call and predict that the result will depend upon the turnout.

8. As Gallup explains, challengers tend to get the votes of those saying they are undecided on the eve of an election: "[B]ased on an analysis of previous presidential and other elections… there is a high probability that the challenger (in an incumbent race) will receive a higher percentage of the popular vote than he did in the last pre-election poll, while there is a high probability that the incumbent will maintain his share of the vote without any increase. This

has been dubbed the 'challenger rule.' There are various explanations for why this may occur, including the theory that any voter who maintains that he or she is undecided about voting for a well-known incumbent this late in the game is probably leaning toward voting for the challenger." "Questions and Answers With the Editor in Chief," Frank Newport, Editor in Chief, The Gallup Poll, November 2, 2004, http://www. gallup.com/poll/content/?ci=13948&pg=1, retrieved on May 27, 2005. See also footnote 7 herein.

9. Bob Fitrakis, Steve Rosenfeld and Harvey Wasserman, "Ohio's Official Non-Recount Ends amidst New Evidence of Fraud, Theft and Judicial Contempt Mirrored in New Mexico," The Columbus Free Press, 31 December 31, 2004, at http://www.freepress.org/departments/display/19/2004/1057, retrieved June 6, 2005.

10. Curtis states in his affidavit that he met in the fall of 2000 with the principals of Yang Enterprises, Inc.,—Li Woan Yang., Mike Cohen, and Tom Feeney (chief counsel and lobbyist for YEI). Feeney became Florida's House Speaker a month after meeting with Curtis. Curtis says that he initially thought he was being asked to make such a program in order to prevent voter fraud. Upon creating the program and presenting it to Yang, he discovered that they were interested in committing fraud, not preventing it. Curtis goes on to say: "She stated that she would hand in what I had produced to Feeney and left the room with the software." As the police would say, what we have here is motive and opportunity—and an abundance of evidence of criminal fraud in the Florida vote, together with Feeney's intimate connection to Jeb Bush. Curtis, on the other hand, as a life-long registered Republican—as of these events at least—has no discernible motive to come forward with these allegations, and only shows courage for the risk to himself by doing so. For his full affidavit, see http://fairnessbybeckerman.blogspot.com/2004/12/affidavit-of-vote-fraud-software.html#110243131597922449, retrieved June 1, 2005.

11. Michael Keefer, "Footprints of Electoral Fraud: The November 2 Exit Poll Scam," http://www.glorbalresearch.ca/articles/KEE411A.html, retrieved May 31, 2005.

12. In the Ukraine, as a result of the exit polls' variance from the official tally, they had a revote. In the U.S., despite the exit polls varying widely from the official tally, we had... an inauguration!

13. The NEP was a consortium of news organizations that contracted Edison Media Research and Mitofsky International to conduct the national and state exit polls. Warren Mitofsky created exit polling.

14. "So reliable are the surveys that actually tap voters as they leave the polling places that they are used as guides to the relative honesty of elections in Third World countries. When I worked on Vicente Fox's campaign in Mexico, for example, I was so fearful that the governing PRI would steal the election that I had the campaign commission two U.S. firms to conduct exit polls to be released immediately after the polls closed to foreclose the possibility of finagling with the returns. When the [exit] polls announced a seven-point Fox victory, mobs thronged the streets in a joyous celebration within minutes that made fraud in the actual counting impossible." GOP consultant and pollster Dick Morris, "Those Exit Polls Were Sabotage," http://www.thehill.com/morris/110404.aspx, dated November 4, 2004, retrieved June 4, 2005.

15. "Gore Won Florida," http://archive.democrats.com/display.cfm?id=181, retrieved May 28, 2005.

16. Dick Morris, "Those Exit Polls Were Sabotage," http://www.thehill.com/morris/110404.aspx, dated November 4, 2004, retrieved June 4, 2005.

17. Steven Freeman, "The Unexplained Exit Poll Discrepancy," November 10, 2004, election04.ssrc.org/research/ 11_10,unexplained_exit-poll.pdf.

18. Ian Hoffman, "Berkeley: President Comes Up Short," *The Tri-Valley Herald*, November 19, 2004. The Berkeley report itself is at http://www.yuricareport.com/Election-Aftermath04/, retrieved June 7, 2005.

19. Evaluation of the Edison/Mitofsky Election System 2004 prepared by Edison Media Research and Mitofsky International for the National Election Pool (MEP), January 19, 2005, http://www.exit-poll.net/faq.html, retrieved April 2, 2005.
    MSNBC publicized this report (inaccurately) under the headline "Exit Polls Prove That Bush Won." (Steve Freeman and Josh Mitteldorf, "A Corrupted
    Election: Despite what you may have heard, the exit polls were right," February 15, 2005, *In These Times*, www.inthesetimes.com/site/main/article/1970/, retrieved April 4, 2005.

20. Warren Mitteldorf, Ph.D., Temple University Statistics Department; Kathy Dopp, MS in mathematics, USCountVotes President; Steven Freeman, Ph.D., University of Pennsylvania; Brian Joiner, Ph.D. Professor of Statistics and Director of Statistical Consulting (ret.), University of Pennsylvania; Frank Stenger, Ph.D., Professor of Numerical Analysis, University of Utah; Richard Sheehan, Ph.D. Professor of Finance, University of Notre Dame; Paul Velleman, Ph.D. Assoc. Professor, Dept. of Statistical Sciences, Cornell University; Victoria Lovegren, Ph.D., Lecturer, Dept. of Mathematics, Case Western University; Campbell B. Read, Ph.D., Professor Emeritus, Dept. of Statistical Science, Southern Methodist University. http://uscountvotes.org/ucvAnalysis/US/USCountVotes Re Mitofsky-Edison.pdf.

21. An alternative theory which was advanced by a few was that fears about terrorism and the ongoing war in Iraq made many reluctant to kick out a sitting president. This theory has the benefit, at least, of having some evidence. However, while it explained why so many ignored the fact that WMD was never found in Iraq, the given rationale for launching war on a country that had not attacked us, and a host of other scandals such as torture and murder at Abu Graib, and why Bush did manage to receive a lot of votes, it didn't explain why he won by a 3.5 million margin.

22. *The Economist*, "The triumph of the religious right," November 11, 2004 http://www.economist.com/printedition/displayStory.cfm?Story_ID=3375543, retrieved April 5, 2005.

23. See, for example, ex-conservative David Brock's *The Republican Noise Machine: Right-Wing Media and How It Corrupts Democracy* and Robert F. Kennedy, Jr., "How Washington Poisoned the News," *Vanity Fair*, May 2005.

24. Manuel Roig-Franzia and Dan Keating, "Latest Conspiracy Theory—Kerry Won—Hits the Ether, " *Washington Post*, November 11, 2004, A-02, reprinted at http://www.washingtonpost.com/wp-dyn/articles/A41106-2004Nov10.html, retrieved June 7, 2005

25. Available in its entirety at http://www.yuricareport.com/ElectionAftermath04/Vote-FraudTheoriesNixed.html, retrieved June 6, 2005.

26. Greg Guma, "Election 2004: Lingering Suspicions," United Press International, November 15, 2004, http://www.upi.com/view.cfm?StoryID=20041112-010916-6128r, retrieved June 7, 2005.

27. Robert Parry, "*Washington Post*'s Sloppy Analysis," consortiumnews.com, November 12, 2004 at http://www.consortiumnews.com/2004/111204.html, retrieved June 7, 2005.

28. "Liberty County—Bristol, Florida and environs—where it's 88 percent Democrats, 8 percent Republicans) but produced landslides for President Bush. On Countdown, we cited the five biggest surprises (Liberty ended Bush: 1,927; Kerry: 1,070), but did not mention the other 24." at http://www.truthout.org/docs_04/111004B.shtml#1, retrieved June 7, 2005. See also David Swanson, "Media Whites Out Vote Fraud," January 3, 2005: http://www.truthout.org/docs_05/010405Y.shtml for a good summary of this media white out.

29. Media Matters for America, "Conservatives rail against MSNBC's Olbermann for reporting election irregularities," http://mediamatters.org/items/2004111600006, retrieved June 7, 2005.

30. The Fairness Doctrine governed broadcasters from 1949 to 1987. It required broadcasters, as a condition for having their FCC license, to provide balanced views on controversial questions. The elimination of the Fairness Doctrine was successfully lobbied for by well-heeled conservative groups during the Reagan Administration and paved the way for the creation of a right wing media empire that operates free of any need to provide opposing viewpoints to their own.

31. LexisNexis Academic database, Accession No. 1605983, Question No. 276, number of respondents 1,287, national telephone poll of adults.

32. Wellstone voted against the authorization to go to war on Iraq requested by the second Bush Administration.

33. I owe this summary to "The Theft of Your Vote Is Just a Chip Away," Thom Hartmann, AlterNet. Posted July 30, 2003, retrieved February 8, 2005: http://www.alternet.org/story/16474.
    Chuck Hagel's story is worth mentioning here as well. As former conservative radio talk show host and current Senator from Nebraska Chuck Hagel (who is seriously considering a run for the White House) demonstrated back in 1996, being the head of the company that supplies the voting machines used by about 80% of the voters in Nebraska does not hurt you when you want to be the first Republican in 24 years to win a Senate seat in Nebraska. The fact that Hagel pulled off the biggest upset in the country in the 1996 elections by defeating an incumbent Democratic governor, that he did so through winning every demographic group, including mainly black areas that had never voted Republican before, might have nothing to do with the paperless trail generated by the electronic voting machines his company provides, installs, programs and largely runs. But then again, maybe it does have something to do with his stunning and totally unexpected victories (Thom Hartmann, "If You Want to Win An Election, Just Control the Voting Machines," January 31, 2003, http://www.commondreams.org/views03/0131-01.htm, retrieved April 10, 2005).

34. By contrast, the GOP has decided that being "sore winners," as John Powers so aptly puts it in his book *Sore Winners (and the Rest of Us) in George Bush's America*, beats the hell out of being gracious losers.

35. Robert Parry, "Solving the Media Puzzle," May 15, 2005, http://www.consortiumnews.com/2005/051305.html, retrieved June 7, 2005.

APPENDIX: Cuyahoga County, OH

PRECINCT	REGISTERED VOTERS	BALLOTS CAST
Bay Village	13,710	18,663
Beachwood	9,943	13,939
Bedford	9,942	14,465
Bedford Heights	8,142	13,512
Brooklyn	8,016	12,303
Brooklyn Heights	1,144	1,869
Chagrin Falls Village	3,557	4,860
Cuyahoga Heights	570	1,382
Fairview Park	13,342	18,472
Highland Hills Village	760	8,822
Independence	5,735	6,226
Mayfield Village	2,764	3,145
Middleburg Heights	12,173	14,854
Moreland Hills Village	2,990	4,616
North Olmstead	25,794	25,887
Olmstead Falls	6,538	7,328
Pepper Pike	5,131	6,479
Rocky River	16,600	20,070
Solon (WD6)	2,292	4,300
South Euclid	16,902	16,917
Strongsville (WD3)	7,806	12,108
University Heights	10,072	11,982
Valley View Village	1,787	3,409
Warrensville Heights	10,562	15,039
Woodmere Village	558	8,854
Bedford (CSD)	22,777	27,856
Independence (LSD)	5,735	6,226
Orange (CSD)	11,640	22,931
Warrensville (CSD)	12,218	15,822

CHAPTER 4

Unanswered Questions of 9/11

911 PREWARNINGS, BUILDING 7 COLLAPSE, FLIGHT 77 AND THE PENTAGON, ISRAELI INVOLVEMENT, UNITED AIRLINES PUT-OPTIONS, WAR GAMES, ATTA AND THE $100,000, 9/11 TERRORISTS STILL ALIVE

By Peter Phillips, Ambrosia Pardue, Jessica Froiland, Brooke Finley, Chris Kyle, Rebekah Cohen, and Bridget Thornton with Project Censored and Guest Writer Jack Massen

For many Americans, there is a deep psychological desire for the 9/11 tragedy to be over. The shock of the day is well remembered and terrorist alerts from Homeland Security serve to maintain lasting tensions and fears. The *9/11 Commission Report* gave many a sense of partial healing and completion—especially given the corporate media's high praise of the report. There is a natural resistance to naysayers who continue to question the U.S. government's version of what happened on September 11, 2001. This resistance is rooted in our tendency toward the inability to conceive of people we know as evil; instead evil ones must be others, very unlike ourselves.

We all remember, as young children, scary locations that created deep fears. We might imagine monsters in the closet, dangers in a nighttime backyard, and creepy people in some abandoned house down the street. As we get older we build up the courage to open the closet, or walk out into the backyard to smell the night air. As adults there are still dark closets in our socio-cultural consciousness that make it difficult to even consider the possibility of certain ideas. These fearful ideas might be described as threshold concepts, in that they may be on the borders of discoverability, yet we deny even the potentiality of implied veracity—something so evil that it is completely unimaginable.

A threshold concept facing Americans is the possibility that the *9/11 Commission Report* was on many levels a cover-up for the failure of the U.S. government to prevent the tragedy. Deeper past the threshold is the idea that the report failed to address sources of assistance to the terrorists. Investigations into this area might have led to a conclusion that elements of various governments—including our own—not only knew about the attacks in advance, but may have helped facilitate their implementation. The idea that someone in the Government of the United States may have contributed support to such a horrific attack is inconceivable to many. It is a threshold concept so frightening that it conjures up a state of mind akin to complete disbelief.

Philosophy/Religion professor David Ray Griffin has recently published his findings on the omissions and distortions of the *9/11 Commission Report*. Griffin notes that the 9/11 Commission failed to discuss most of the evidence that seems to contradict the official story about 9/11—for example, the report by Attorney David Schippers that states that some FBI agents who contracted him had information about attacks several weeks prior to 9/11, along with evidence that several of the alleged hijackers are still alive. Griffin's book brings into question the completeness and authenticity of the 9/11 Commission's work. Griffin questions why extensive advanced warnings from several countries were not acted upon by the Administration, how a major institutional investor knew to buy put-options on American and United Airlines before the attack, and how an inexperienced terrorist pilot could have conducted a complicated decent into an unoccupied section of the Pentagon.

Additionally, Griffin notes questions remain on why the 9/11 Commission failed to address the reports that $100,000 was wired to Mohammed Atta from Saeed Sheikh, an agent for Pakistan's Inter-Service Intelligence (ISI), under the direction of the head of ISI General Mahmud Ahmed. General Ahmed resigned his position less than one month later. The *Times of India* reported that Indian intelligence had given U.S. officials evidence of the money transfer ordered by Ahmad and that he was dismissed after the "U.S. authorities sought his removal."

Also, the *9/11 Commission Report* failed to address the reasons for the collapse of World Trade Center (WTC) building 7 more than six hours after the attack. WTC-7 was a 47-story, steel frame building that had only small fires on a few floors. WTC buildings 5 and 6 had much larger fires and did not collapse. This has led a number of critics to speculate that WTC 7 was a planned demolition.

Overall concerns with the official version of 9/11 have been published and discussed by scholars and politicians around the world including: Jim Marrs, Nafeez Ahmed, Michael Ruppert, Cynthia McKinney, Barrie Zwicker, Webster Tarpley, Michel Chossudovsky, Paul Thompson, Eric Hufschmid and many others (see: http://www.911forthetruth.com). The response to most has been to label these discussions as "conspiracy theories" unworthy of media coverage or further review. Pursuit of a critical analysis of these questions is undermined by the psychological barrier about 9/11 issues as threshold concepts—too awful to even consider.

We may be on the borders of discovery regarding the possibility of a great evil within our own government, and perhaps within others outside as well. We must step past the threshold and have the courage to ask the questions, demand answers, and support research into all aspects of this American tragedy. Perhaps the closet isn't as dark and as fearful as we envision. If we don't courageously look and search into the deepest regions of our fears how can we assure our children and ourselves a safe and honest future?

In *Censored 2003*, Project Censored lists the most important unanswered questions about 9/11. Most of those questions remain unanswered today. Since 2001, researchers have expanded the depth of concerns and the reliability of information that continue to encourage the questioning of the official government version of the 9/11 tragedy. The following is Project Censored's effort to cross the threshold and address the questions that are so difficult to imagine.

9/11 Pre-Warnings

BY JESSICA FROILAND

Paul Thompson's *Terror Timeline,* as well as his updated version of the 9/11 timeline located at www.cooperativeresearch.org, was the key reference material used. For further information regarding the information presented, see original articles used in Thompson's research, mentioned throughout.

In a press conference on April 13, 2004, President Bush stated, "We knew he [Osama bin Laden] had designs on us, we knew he hated us. But there was nobody in our government, and I don't think [in] the prior government, that could envision flying airplanes into buildings on such a massive scale." (*Guardian,* 4/15/04) He also said, "Had I any inkling whatsoever that the people were to fly airplanes into buildings, we would have moved heaven and earth to save the country." (*White House*, 4/13/04; *New York Times*, 4/18/04) This statement is in direct conflict with a May 15, 2002 statement wherein the White House admitted that Bush had been warned about bin Laden's desire to attack the U.S. by hijacking aircraft in August 2001. (*New York Times*, 5/16/02, *Washington Post*, 5/16/02, *Guardian*, 5/19/02). There is a massive and growing body of evidence that asserts that the United States government was not only aware of the possibility of the specific scenario of a terrorist air strike/suicide attack, but that it had also received dozens of credible warnings from both international and domestic sources.

Many countries warned the U.S. of imminent terrorist attacks: Afghanistan, Argentina, Britain, Cayman Islands, Egypt, France, Germany, Israel, Italy, Jordan, Morocco, and Russia. Warnings also came from within the United States. Information from our own communications intercepts regarding particular individuals with foreknowledge, previous similarly attempted attacks, and from our own intelligence agents in charge of the investigations of al-Qa'eda.

While many of these warning have been covered in the world media a collective analysis and summary context has been avoided by the U.S. corporate media.

THE ACTUAL 9/11 PRE-WARNINGS

1993: An expert panel commissioned by the Pentagon raised the possibility that an airplane could be used to bomb national landmarks. (*Washington Post*, 10/2/01)

1994: Two attacks took place that involved using hijacked planes to crash into buildings, including one by an Islamic militant group. In a third attack, a lone pilot crashed a plane at the White House. (*New York Times*, 10/3/01)

1996-1999: The CIA officer in charge of operations against al-Qa'eda from Washington writes, "I speak with firsthand experience (and for several score of CIA officers) when I state categorically that during this time senior White House officials repeatedly refused to act on sound intelligence that provided multiple chances to eliminate Osama bin Laden." (*Los Angeles Times*, 12/5/04)

1996-2001: Federal authorities had known that suspected terrorists with ties to bin Laden were receiving flight training at schools in the U.S. and abroad. An Oklahoma City FBI agent sent a memo warning that "large numbers of Middle Eastern males" were getting flight training and could have been planning terrorist attacks. (*CBS*, 5/30/02) One convicted terrorist confessed that his planned role in a terror attack was to crash a plane into CIA headquarters. (*Washington Post*, 9/23/01)

DEC 1998: A *Time* magazine cover story entitled "The Hunt for Osama," reported that bin Laden may be planning his boldest move yet—a strike on Washington or possibly New York City. (*Time*, 12/21/98)

FEBRUARY 7, 2001: CIA Director Tenet warned Congress in open testimony that "the threat from terrorism is real, it is immediate, and it is evolving." He said bin Laden and his global network remained "the most immediate and serious threat" to U.S. interests. "Since 1998 bin Laden has declared that all U.S. citizens are legitimate targets," he said, adding that bin Laden "is capable of planning multiple attacks with little or no warning." (Associated Press, 2/7/01; *Sunday Herald*, 9/23/01)

JUNE 2001: German intelligence warned the CIA, Britain's intelligence agency, and Israel's Mossad that Middle Eastern terrorists were planning to hijack commercial aircraft and use them as weapons to attack "American and Israeli symbols which stand out." A later article quoted unnamed German intelligence sources, stating that the information was coming from Echelon surveillance technology, and that British intelligence had access to the same warnings. However, there were other informational sources, including specific information and hints given to, but not reported by, Western and Near Eastern news media six months before 9/11. (*Frankfurter Allgemeine Zeitung*, 9/11/01; *Washington Post*, 9/14/01; Fox News, 5/17/02)

JUNE 28, 2001: George Tenet wrote an intelligence summary to Condeleezza Rice stating: "It is highly likely that a significant al-Qa'eda attack is in the near future, within several weeks" (*Washington Post*, 2/17/02). This warning was shared with "senior Bush Administration officials" in early July. (*9/11 Congressional Inquiry*, 9/18/02)

JULY 5, 2001: Richard Clark gave a direct warning to the FAA, to increase their security measures. The FAA refused to take such action. (*New Yorker*, 1/14/02; www.cooperativeresearch.org)

JUNE-JULY 2001: President Bush, Vice President Cheney, and national security aides were given briefs with headlines such as "Bin Laden Threats Are Real" and "Bin Laden Planning High Profile Attacks." The exact contents of these briefings remain classified, but according to the 9/11 Commission, they consistently predicted upcoming attacks that would occur "on a catastrophic level, indicating that they would cause the world to be in turmoil, consisting of possible multiple—but not necessarily simultaneous—

attacks." CIA Director Tenet later recalled that by late July, he felt that President Bush and other officials grasped the urgency of what they were being told. (*9/11 Commission Report*, 4/13/04 (B)) But Deputy CIA Director John McLaughlin, later stated that he felt a great tension, peaking within these months, between the Bush Administration's apparent misunderstanding of terrorism issues and his sense of great urgency. McLaughlin and others were frustrated when inexperienced Bush officials questioned the validity of certain intelligence findings. Two unnamed, veteran Counter Terrorism Center officers deeply involved in bin Laden issues, were so worried about an impending disaster, that they considered resigning and going public with their concerns. (*9/11 Commission Report*, 3/24/04 (C)) Dale Watson, head of counter terrorism at the FBI, wished he had "500 analysts looking at Osama bin Laden threat information instead of two." (*9/11 Commission Report*, 4/13/04 (B))

JULY 5, 2001: At issue is a July 5, 2001 meeting between Ashcroft and acting FBI Director Tom Pickard. That month, the threat of an al-Qa'eda attack was so high; the White House summoned the FBI and domestic agencies and warned them to be on alert. Yet, Pickard testified to the 9/11 commission that when he tried to brief Ashcroft just a week later, on July 12, about the terror threat inside the United States, he got the "brush-off. "(MSNBC, 6/22/04)

JULY 10, 2001: A Phoenix FBI agent sent a memorandum warning of Middle Eastern men taking flight lessons. He suspected bin Laden's followers and recommended a national program to check visas of suspicious flight-school students. The memo was sent to two FBI counter-terrorism offices, but no action was taken. (9/11 Congressional Inquiry, 7/24/03) Vice President Cheney said in May 2002, that he was opposed to releasing this memo to congressional leaders or to the media and public. (CNN, 5/20/02)

JULY 16, 2001: British spy agencies sent a report to British Prime Minister Tony Blair and other top officials warning that al-Qa'eda was in "the final stages" of preparing a terrorist attack in the West. The prediction was "based on intelligence gleaned not just from [British intelligence] but also from U.S. agencies, including the CIA and the National Security Agency." The report stated that there was "an acute awareness" that an attack was "a very serious threat." (*Times of London*, 6/14/02)

JULY 2001: President Bush took the unusual step of sleeping on board an aircraft carrier off the coast of Italy after receiving a warning from the Egyptian government that the summit of world leaders in the city of Genoa would be targeted by al-Qa'eda. (*New York Times*, 9/26/01) The Italians meanwhile highly publicized their heightened security measures of increased police presence, antiaircraft batteries, and flying fighter jets. Apparently the press coverage of defenses caused al-Qa'eda to cancel the attack. (BBC, 7/18/01, CNN, 7/18/01, *Los Angeles Times*, 9/27/01)

JULY 26, 2001: Attorney General Ashcroft stopped flying commercial airlines due to a threat assessment. (CBS, 7/26/01) The report of this warning was omitted from the *9/11 Commission Report*. (Griffin 5/22/05)

LATE JULY 2001: CBS reported, "Just days after [Mohammed] Atta return[s] to the U.S. from Spain, Egyptian intelligence in Cairo says it received a report from one of its operatives in Afghanistan that 20 al-Qa'eda members had slipped into the U.S. and four of them had received flight training on Cessnas." Egypt passed on the message to the CIA but never received a request for further information. (CBS News, 10/9/02)

LATE JULY 2001: Taliban Foreign Minister Wakil Ahmed Muttawakil was given information regarding a large attack on targets inside America, from the leader of the rebel Islamic Movement of Uzbekistan (IMU), Tahir Yildash. Muttawakil relayed this information to the U.S. consul general, yet wasn't taken seriously. One source blamed this on the Administration's "warning fatigue." (*Independent*, 9/7/02; Reuters, 9/7/02)

AUG 6, 2001: President Bush received a classified intelligence briefing at his Crawford, Texas ranch, warning that bin Laden might be planning to hijack commercial airliners. The memo was titled "Bin Laden Determined to Strike in U.S." The entire memo focused on the possibility of terrorist attacks inside the U.S. and specifically mentioned the World Trade Center. Yet Bush later stated that the briefing "said nothing about an attack on America." (*Newsweek*, 5/27/02; *New York Times*, 5/15/02, *Washington Post*, 4/11/04, White House, 4/11/04, Intelligence Briefing, 8/6/01) .

EARLY AUGUST 2001: Britain gave the U.S. another warning about an al-Qa'eda attack. The previous British warning on July 16, 2001, was vague as to method, but this warning specified multiple airplane hijackings. This warning was said to have reached President Bush. (*Sunday Herald*, 5/19/02)

AUGUST 2001: Russian President Vladimir Putin warned the U.S. that suicide pilots were training for attacks on U.S. targets. (Fox News, 5/17/02) The head of Russian intelligence also later stated, "We had clearly warned them" on several occasions, but they "did not pay the necessary attention." (*Agence France-Presse*, 9/16/01)

LATE SUMMER 2001: Jordanian intelligence (the GID) made a communications intercept and relayed it to Washington. The message stated that a major attack, code-named "The Big Wedding," had been planned inside the U.S.

and that aircraft would be used. "When it became clear that the information was embarrassing to Bush Administration officials and congressmen who at first denied that there had been any such warnings before September 11, senior Jordanian officials backed away from their earlier confirmations." (*International Herald Tribune*, 5/21/02; *Christian Science Monitor*, 5/23/02)

SEPTEMBER 10, 2001, a group of top Pentagon officials received an urgent warning which prompted them to cancel their flight plans for the following morning. (Newsweek, 9/17/01) The *9/11 Commission Report* omitted this report. (Griffin, 5/22/05)

Given all the pre-warnings and information available before 9/11 it seems unconscionable that on May 16, 2002, National Security Advisor Condoleezza Rice could still claim to the press: "I don't think anybody could have predicted that these people would take an airplane and slam it into the World Trade Center, take another one and slam it into the Pentagon, that they would try to use an airplane as a missile." She added that "even in retrospect" there was "nothing" to suggest that. (White House, 5/16/02) On June 7, 2002, President Bush stated, "Based on everything I've seen, I do not believe anyone could have prevented the horror of September the 11th." (*Sydney Morning Herald*, 6/8/02)

With so many warnings, it is difficult to explain inaction as mere incompetence. The existence of all of these warnings suggests, at least, that people within the U.S. government knew the attacks were coming and deliberately allowed them to happen. This evidence would, however, be consistent with an even more frightening scenario—that the attacks were orchestrated by, or with the help of, people within our government.

ADDITIONAL SOURCES:

Paul Thompson, *The Terror Timeline: Year by Year, Day by Day, Minute by Minute: A Comprehensive Chronicle of the Road to 9/11—and America's Response*, Regan Books, September 1, 2004.

Jim Marrs, *Inside Job: Unmasking the Conspiracies of 9/11*, Origin Press, June 2004.

The 9/11 Commissioners, *The 9/11 Commission Report: Final Report of the National Commission on Terrorists Attacks Upon the United States*, W.W Norton & Company, Inc.

Griffin, David Ray, "*The 9/11 Commission Report*: A 571-page lie," www.911truth.org/index.php?topic=911commission, May 22, 2005

THE BUILDING 7 COLLAPSE MYSTERY

BY JOSH PARRISH

The collapse of World Trade Center Building 7 is one of the more mysterious events that occurred on September 11, 2001. It was not struck by an aircraft as the Twin Towers were and video of the collapse appears to resemble those of buildings brought down by a controlled demolition. These facts have led to speculation that the building was brought down deliberately. Deficient investigations that followed only served to fuel this speculation.

The Federal Emergency Management Agency (FEMA) conducted the first official inquiry into the collapse the World Trade Center buildings. The report is merely a collection of supposition and hypotheses arrived at through the examination of photographic evidence and eyewitness interviews.[1] FEMA's reasoning behind the collapse of Building 7 is as follows: Debris from the collapse of the Twin Towers caused structural damage to Building 7 and ignited fires on several different floors; including floors 6, 7, 8, 10, 11, and 19.[2] There were diesel generators located throughout the building to supply electricity in the event of a power outage. These generators were fed by pressurized fuel lines from large tanks on the lower floors. The falling debris also damaged these pressurized lines and provided a continuous source of fuel for the fires. According to FEMA, neither fire nor structural damage alone would have been sufficient to cause the building's collapse. It was the combination of the structural damage, which diminished the load bearing ability of the structure, and the fire, which weakened the steel, that brought the building down.[3]

While this explanation may sound plausible, it is not based on an examination of any physical evidence. Specifically, the investigators were unable to confirm how much, if any, diesel fueled the fires. "There is no physical, photographic, or other evidence to substantiate or refute the discharge of fuel oil from the piping system. The following is, therefore, a hypothesis based on potential rather than demonstrated fact."[4] The investigators seem to have little faith in their own theories, "Although the total diesel fuel on the premises contained massive potential energy, the best hypothesis has only a low probability of occurrence."[5] When subjected to critical analysis, the investigation by FEMA appears to be nothing more than an attempt to formulate theories that conform to the official version of the events of September 11th, rather than a rigorous scientific study.

One of the ways in which the FEMA investigation was hampered was by the destruction of evidence. Almost immediately following the disaster, the structural steel was removed from the site and placed on ships headed for Asia to be recycled.[6]

The *New York Times* reported on 12/25, 2001 that, "In calling for a new investigation, some structural engineers have said that one serious mistake has already been made in the chaotic aftermath of the collapses: the decision to rapidly recycle the steel columns, beams and trusses that held up the buildings. That may have cost investigators some of their most direct physical evidence with which to try to piece together an answer.... Dr. Frederick W. Mowrer, an associate professor in the fire protection engineering department at the University of Maryland, said he believed the decision could ultimately compromise any investigation of the collapses. 'I find the speed with which potentially important evidence has been removed and recycled to be appalling,' Dr. Mowrer said.... Interviews with a handful of members of the [FEMA funded] team, which includes some of the nation's most respected engineers, also uncovered complaints that they had at various times been shackled with bureaucratic restrictions that prevented them from interviewing witnesses, examining the disaster site and requesting crucial information, like recorded distress calls to the police and fire departments."[7]

Even if one accepts the Bush Administration's official version of the events of that day, there were still compelling reasons to study the evidence. The engineering and construction community could have greatly benefited from a thorough examination of the structural steel. Prior to September 11th, there had never been a fire-induced collapse of a steel framed building. If Building 7 did actually collapse due to fire and falling debris, then a careful examination of the evidence would certainly be warranted; if for no other reason than to learn some valuable lessons about the safety of high-rise buildings in general. Destroying evidence of a disaster of this magnitude is unprecedented.[8] The fact that it occurred raises questions about the motives of those involved in making the decision.

As incomplete and inadequate as FEMA's investigation was, theirs was not the only one conducted. The World Trade Center was heavily insured, and the companies that were due to pay those claims commissioned their own private investigation. The difference between the insurance investigation and FEMA's study is quite remarkable. The insurance companies had unfettered access to the site of the collapse beginning on the very afternoon of September 11th. They were also granted access to powerful computer programs used by the Pentagon for classified research; the FEMA investigators were not. The insurance companies have produced thousands of pages of analysis and an equally staggering number of diagrams and photographs. However, the results of these investigations have remained private.[9] It is interesting to note that a shareholder in Allianz Group proposed denying payment due to evidence of insurance fraud. Allianz Group carried a significant portion of the insurance policy on the World Trade Center. In response to the shareholders' claim, the company made the following statement: "When the company makes insurance payments it does so on the basis of careful scrutiny—especially with payments in the order of magnitude referred to here. Two official commissions in the USA have examined the incidents of 11 September 2001 in detail. Their findings provided no indication that the allegations submitted by the proposer are correct."[10]

The mission of Project Censored is not to draw conclusions in the field of structural engineering; it is to examine mainstream media coverage of newsworthy events. In the case of World Trade Center Building 7, there has been very little coverage of the surrounding issues. The collapse of Building 7 had the appearance of a perfectly executed controlled demolition; it fell straight down into its own footprint, at virtually free-fall speed, yet this issue has hardly been raised in the mainstream media, and was completely ignored by the 9/11 Commission.

The lack of news coverage coupled with the destruction of key evidence and the lack of a credible investigation has given rise to numerous questions and accusations of government complicity in the attacks of that day. The list of tenants that occupied the building lends itself to these theories. Occupants of the building included: The Securities and Exchange Commission (SEC), The FBI, CIA, Secret Service, Department of Defense, IRS, and Mayor Rudolph Giuliani's Office of Emergency Management.[11] Some detractors claim that the building was brought down to destroy evidence against Enron and Ken Lay that was contained in the SEC offices. Others claim that the CIA offices housed the evidence of government involvement in the attacks and thus needed to be destroyed.

Investigations into the destruction of Building 7 have been performed and conclusions have been reached. Those who are not inclined to trust the current administration will inevitably find fault with the investigation, but the fact that the Administration directed the evidence to be destroyed leaves them open to this criticism. The facts surrounding the destruction of Building 7 will likely remain a mystery, unless there is a full and truly independent investigation, using subpoena power.

NOTES

1. *World Trade Center Performance Study*, May 2002, pg. 5-1.
2. *World trade Center Building Performance Study*, May 2002, pg. 5-20.

3. Chertoff, Benjamin, et al. "9/11: Debunking the Myths," *Popular Mechanics*, March 2005. 8 April 2005, http://www.popularmechanics.com/science/defense/1227842.html?page=&c=y.

4. *World Trade Center Building Performance Study*, May 2002, pg. 5-28.

5. *World Trade Center Building Performance Study*, May 2002, pg. 5-31.

6. Manning, Bill, "$elling Out the Investigation," *Fire Engineering*, January 2002, Apr. 2005, http://fe.pennet.com/Artilces/Article_Display.cfm?Section=ARCHI&ARTICLE_ID=1332 37&VERSION_NUM=1.

7. *New York Times*, December 25, 2001.

8. Manning, Bill, "$elling Out the Investigation," *Fire Engineering*, Jan. 2002 8 Apr. 2005, http://fe.pennet.com/Artilces/Article_Display.cfm?Section=ARCHI&ARTICLE_ID=1332 37&VERSION_NUM=1

9. Glanz, James, and Eric Lipton, "Vast Detail on Towers' Collapse May Be Sealed in Court Filings," *New York Times*, 30 Sept. 2002 8 Apr. 2005

10. Allianz Group—Shareholder Proposals, 20 Apr. 2005 13 May 2005, http://www.allianz-group.com/Az_Cnt/az/_any/cma/contents/750000/saObj_750776_05_04_20_Gegenantr_ge_ENGLISH.pdf

11. World Trade Center Performance Study, May 2002, pg. 5-2

CONCERNS ABOUT FLIGHT 77 AND THE PENTAGON

BY BRIDGET THORNTON

At 8:20 a.m. on September 11, 2001, American Airlines Flight 77 left Dulles Airport en route to Los Angeles. Between 8:51 and 8:54, four men hijacked the plane. At 9:38, Flight 77 crashed into the Pentagon. Minutes before impact, the 757, headed for the White House, made a 330 degree turn, while descending 2200 feet, flew over a highway packed with rush hour cars and crashed into the least populated area of the Pentagon which was under construction at the time. This, at least, is the official report as stated in the *9/11 Commission Report*.

In the days and months that followed the Pentagon attack, questions arose about the veracity of the investigation and the amount of information available to the public. How could the alleged pilot, with no commercial plane experience, and complaints from his flight school about poor performance, maneuver the airplane with such precision? Why did the White House oppose an independent investigation? Why did mainstream media fail to provide investigative coverage of the attack? Could the government be complicit?

The main question is whether the government knew about or assisted in the attacks. In fact, a Zogby International Poll in August 2004 revealed that 66 percent of New Yorkers want a new probe of unanswered questions by Congress or New York's Attorney General.[1] Many people believe the official investigation lacked public scrutiny and suffered from uncooperative behavior by the White House. The media also failed to provide the American public with significant investigative journalism. Here lie some of the questions concerning the attack on the Pentagon.

Where were our air defenses?

The *9/11 Commission Report* states that American Airlines Flight 77 crashed into an area of the Pentagon that was under construction, and therefore the least populated area of the complex. This crash occurred at 9:38.[2] The report explains that North American Aerospace Defense Command (NORAD) never heard about Flight 77 and Northeast Air Defense Sector (NEADS) concentrated instead on American Airlines Flight 11, which was mistakenly still thought to be aloft.[3] The report goes on to say that the Indianapolis air traffic controller reported the missing flight to Langley Air Force Base at 9:08 and that a C-130 cargo plane followed, identified, and witnessed the crash.[4] This same cargo plane happened upon the smoking wreckage of Flight 93 in Pennsylvania.[5] The report concludes that Flight 77 crashed into the Pentagon, likely flown by Hani Hanjour and that fighter jets were called to assistance only four minutes before the impact.

Within this confused document, inconsistencies exist. An audio recording reveals that Langley jets did not follow explicit instructions given to them by their mission crew commander. Based on audio reports, the mission crew commander discovered at 9:34 that the jets headed east, not north as instructed by their crew commander. The reason places blame on lack of information about the position of Flight 77, incorrect assumptions, and generic flight plans that allowed the pilots to follow a due east path.[6] However, the mission commander immediately orders the planes to "crank it up" and goes on to say, "I don't care how many windows you break." Could this mean the commander ordered the planes to fly at top speed? If so, did they follow the command? The report does not address this.

How did an inexperienced pilot perform an intricate crash landing?

How did the pilot maneuver the plane with such skill that experienced military aviation experts noted skills similar to a 'crack' military pilot?[7] How did Hani Hanjour, the alleged hijacker who flew Flight 77, make a 330 degree turn, away from the White House and south towards the Pentagon, while descending 2200 feet, advance to full throttle and perform a crash landing with exact precision into the Pentagon? *CBSNews* reported, "And the complex maneuver suggests the hijackers had better flying skills than many investigators first believed."[8] There is serious doubt that Hani Hanjour possessed the ability to maneuver a commercial plane in such an experienced fashion. According to another *CBSNews* report, managers at the flight school placed five complaints with the FAA expressing serious concern about his ability to fly safely.[9] The Commission Report acknowledges his performance but does not acknowledge a possible problem with this information. The question remains unanswered by the United States government and invisible on mainstream media.

Where are the media?

The media could have played an important role in the investigation of the Pentagon attack. In the months following the attack, few reports surfaced that questioned the validity of the independent investigation.[10] Investigative reports emerged that addressed the skills of the alleged pilot and why Langley jets did not respond to the crisis. Rena Golden, executive vice-president and general manager of CNN International says, "Anyone who claims the U.S. media didn't censor itself is kidding you."[11]

Mainstream media reported the official theory, that four Muslim fundamentalists controlled the plane that hit the Pentagon. The media portrays most deviating explanations as conspiracy theories. A recent article in the March 2005 edition of *Popular Mechanics* featured an article in which they "debunked the 9/11 myths." CNN interviewed Jim Meigs; editor-in-chief of the magazine, on the *Anderson Cooper Show* and the exchange that followed proves there are biases and an unwillingness to investigate the attacks. Mr. Meigs told Anderson Cooper, "Well, you know, one thing that conspiracy theorists do is they ignore mounts of evidence that support the ordinary view, then they seize on one or two little inconsistencies and they say, see, how do you explain this?" Mr. Meigs states further, "What we did at *Popular Mechanics* was to actually take those claims by the conspiracy theorist, and subject them to ordinary journalistic fact checking. None of them add [sic] up."[12] Mr. Meigs and CNN exemplify the type of news Americans receive. Questions that search beyond the common theory suffer ridicule and therefore, lack credibility with the public.

Is our government capable of this?

Michael Ruppert includes a document in his book *Crossing the Rubicon* called the Northwoods Project. This was a report to the Kennedy Administration from his National Security Advisors that outlined a similar attack in which the government would shoot down commercial aircraft, blame it on Cuba and use it as a pretext to war.[13] Ruppert does not claim that this document is inspiration to the current administration but that we have in our possession historical evidence that proves our government considers covert and complicit attacks.

David Griffin mentions a document by the Project for the New American Century released in September 2000 entitled "Rebuilding America's Defenses." The document states that "...the process of transformation, even if it brings revolutionary change is likely to be a long one, absent some catastrophic and catalyzing event—like a New Pearl Harbor."[14] Professor Griffin asserts that 9/11 gave the Bush Administration a pretext to war and the unquestioned authority to change fundamental institutions in this country. In *Crossing the Rubicon*, Michael Ruppert offers compelling historical analysis as to why our government has interests in a Middle East war.

The government refuses to examine valid questions and denies information to the American public under the guise of national security. The attack on the Pentagon contains too many unanswered questions about the pilot, the forensics evidence, and the lack of defense for America's military headquarters.

There is an overwhelming amount of information about the Pentagon attack and the 9/11 Commission did not provide it to the public. For this reason, the Pentagon attack deserves thoughtful media attention and open investigation by our government.

NOTES

1. SCOPE: The poll covered five areas of related interest: 1) Iraq—do New Yorkers think that our leaders "deliberately misled" us before the war (51.2 percent do); 2) the 9/11 Commission—did it answer all the "important questions" (36 percent said yes); 3) the inexplicable and largely unreported collapse of the third WTC skyscraper on 9/11—what was its number (28 percent of NYC area residents knew); 4) the question on complicity; and 5) how many wanted a new 9/11 probe. All inquiries about questions, responses and demographics should be directed to Zogby International. SPONSOR: 911truth.org is a coalition of researchers, journalists and victim family members working to expose and resolve the hundreds of critical questions still swirling around 9/11, especially the nearly 400 questions that the Family Steering Committee filed with the 9/11Commission which they fought to create. http://www.zogby.com/news/ReadNews.dbm?ID=855 (Accessed May 8, 2005).
2. *9/11 Commission Report*, 1st ed. W.W. Norton: New York, 26.
3. *9/11 Commission Report*, 26.
4. *9/11 Commission Report*, 26.
5. *9/11 Commission Report*, 30.
6. *9/11 Commission Report*, 27.
7. Michael C. Ruppert *Crossing the Rubicon*, New Society Publishers, British Columbia, 2004.
8. http://www.cbsnews.com/stories/2001/09/11/national/main310721.shtml.
9. David Griffin, *The New Pearl Harbor*, Olive Branch Press: Massachusetts, 41.
10. This is based on a Lexis-Nexis search of 9/11 Pentagon coverage in U.S. news sources from September 2001 to February 2005.
11. Griffin, xiv.
12. *Anderson Cooper 360 Degrees*, CNN, February 21, 2005.

13. Northwoods document located at http://aztlan.net/lavoz_northwoods/northwoods2.htm. (Accessed 29 April 2005).
14. Rebuilding America's Defenses: A report of The Project for the New American Century," September 2000, www.newamericancentury.org.

RUMORS OF ISRAELI INVOLVEMENT IN 9/11

BY BROOKE FINLEY

After the attacks of September 11, 2001, many stories circulated about Israeli involvement. There was the story of the five Israelis filming the burning of the World Trade Center and the "art student" spy ring that warned of the attacks. While most of this information has been glossed over by mainstream media, the reports remain extremely important to understanding the overall picture of what happened on September 11, 2001. As the writer, I attempt to cover the facts without any bias and hope to be able to present them as clearly as possible to the reader. I used Paul Thompson's book *The Terror Timeline*, as a guide for the dates and incidents reported and then used his reference articles and any others that I could find, as research.

In January 2000, a Drug Enforcement Agency (DEA) document was leaked to the press suggesting that a large Israeli spy ring had congregated in the United States. (DEA Report, 6/01) In April of that same year, *USA Today* reported that certain DEA documents revealed that the Israeli spy ring, now commonly called the Israeli "art student" spy ring, "has been linked to several ongoing [Ecstasy] investigations in Florida, California, Texas and New York." (*Insight*, 3/11/02) Members of the "art student spy ring" would go door-to-door, claiming that they were selling artwork. Many of their areas of interest were offices and homes of DEA officials.

Between December 2000 and April 2001, Germany reported that Israeli counter-terror investigators were posing as art students and following terrorist cells within the United States. These "art students" identified Atta and Marwan Alshehhi as possible terrorists, while living within several feet of them in the town of Hollywood, Florida. The "art students" were discovered in April and were immediately deported, supposedly terminating the investigation of Atta and Alshehhi. (*Der Spiegel*, 10/01/02) It was later reported by Fox News that an additional 80 agents were taken into custody between the months of June and December 2001. (Fox News, 12/12/01)

In related foreign press reports, the Mossad learned of four terrorists, living in the U.S., who appeared to be planning an attack in the near future, on the U.S., through information gathered by its "art student" spy ring. (*Die Zeit*, 10/01/02; *Der Spiegel*, 10/01/02; BBC, 10/02/02; *Ha'aretz*, 10/03/02)

By June 2001, close to 120 Israeli "art students" were apprehended. (*le Monde*, 3/05/02; *Salon*, 5/07/02) A leaked DEA document titled "Suspicious Activities Involving Israeli Art Students at DEA Facilities," described dozens of reports of the "apparent attempts by Israeli nationals to learn about government personnel and office layouts." (DEA Report, 6/01) "The report connects the spies to efforts to foil investigations into Israeli organized crime activity involving the importation of the drug Ecstasy. The spies also appear to be snooping on top secret military bases." (www.cooperativeresearch.org)

At some point, between August 8 and 15, 2001, two high-ranking agents from the Mossad came to Washington and warned the FBI and the CIA that an al-Qa'eda attack on the United States was imminent. (Fox News, 5/17/02) On September 20, 2001, the *Los Angeles Times* reported that Mossad officials stated that indications point to a "large scale target" and that Americans would be "very vulnerable." (*Telegraph*, 9/16/01; *Los Angeles Times*, 9/20/01; *Ottawa Citizen*, 9/17/01) The *Los Angeles Times* retracted this story on September 21, 2001, because a CIA spokesman stated, "there was no such warning" and that the allegations were "complete and utter nonsense." (*Los Angeles Times*, 9/21/01) Israel denied that there was ever a meeting between agents of the Mossad and the CIA. (*Ha'aretz*, 10/03/02) The United States has denied knowing about Mohammed Atta prior to the 9/11 attacks. (www.cooperativeresearch.org)

Between December 12 and 15, 2001, the FBI, the DEA and the INS informed Fox News that there were no connections between the "art students" and the incidents of 9/11. They told Fox News that to continue pursuing this topic would be a form of "career suicide." On December 16, 2001, Fox News pulled any information regarding the "art student spy ring" from its website. Fox never made a formal correction. (www.cooperativeresearch.org)

The mainstream media continued to deny any information about the Israeli spy ring, which turned the original stories into "conspiracy theories" and myths. *Jane's Intelligence Digest* blatantly stated on March 13, 2002, "It is rather strange that the U.S. media seems to be ignoring what may well be the most explosive story since the 11 September attacks—the alleged breakup of a major Israeli espionage operation in the USA." (*Jane's Intelligence Digest*, 3/13/02)

On March 11, 2002, the *Palm Beach Post* mentioned the DEA report about the Israeli "art students." The newspaper stated that the DEA determined that all of the students had "recently served in the Israeli military, the majority in intelligence, electronic signal intercept or explosive ordnance units." (*Palm Beach Post*, 3/11/02)

On March 15, 2002, *Forward* published the claim that "the incidents in question appear to represent a case of Israelis in the United States spying on a common enemy, radical Islamic networks suspected of links to Middle East terrorism." (*Forward*, 3/15/02)

On May 7, 2002, *Salon* carried a story on the "art student" spy ring, mentioning that a government source suggested that the majority of the "art students" were a "smoke screen." The source suggested that while most were getting caught up in the DEA's Ecstasy case, others could complete other missions, such as the monitoring of potential terrorists, without being noticed. (*Salon*, 5/07/02)

There are other Israeli incidents revolving around September 11, 2001 that should be mentioned. On September 4, 2001, an Israeli-owned shipping company entitled Zim-American Israeli Shipping Co., moved their North American headquarters from inside the World Trade Center, to Norfolk, Virginia—one week before the 9/11 attacks. (*Virginian-Pilot*, 9/04/01) Zim had announced its move 6 months before the attacks, (*Virginian-Pilot*, 4/03/01) yet 10 employees were still in the building on Sept. 11, taking care of the final moving arrangements. They were able to escape, unharmed. (*Jerusalem Post*, 9/13/01; *Journal of Commerce*, 10/18/01) A year later, a Zim-American ship was caught attempting to ship Israeli military equipment into Iran. (AFP, 8/29/02)

About 2 hours before the first plane hit the World Trade Center on Sept. 11, 2002, Odigo, one of the world's largest instant messaging firms, received warnings of "an imminent attack in New York City." Odigo's headquarters are located two blocks from the World Trade Center but the warnings were received in their Israel location. The FBI was notified immediately after the attacks began. (*Ha'aretz*, 9/26/01; *Washington Post*, 9/27/01) The internet address of the instant message was given to the FBI by Odigo in an attempt to find the name of the sender. (*Deutsche Presse-Agentur*, 9/26/01) Two months after the attacks, the FBI reported that they were still in the process of investigating the instant message and reports have been nonexistent ever since. (*Courier Mail*, 11/20/01)

A Federal Aviation Administration (FAA) memo written on Sept 11 explained a situation where a passenger on Flight 11 was shot and killed by a gun prior to the plane crashing into the World Trade Center. The passenger who was killed was Daniel Lewin. On September 17, the Israeli newspaper, *Ha'aretz*, identified Lewin as a former member of the Israeli special-operations unit, the Israeli Defense Force Sayeret Matkal. (UPI, 3/06/02) The gun story has been denied by officials, claiming that Lewin was most likely stabbed to death. (UPI, 3/06/02; *Washington Post*, 3/02/02)

On June 21, 2002, *ABC News* reported that five Israelis were arrested on Sept 11, 2001 after being caught filming the burning of the World Trade Center from the roof of the "Urban Moving Systems" building, shouting cries of joy. The police found them driving in the company van. (*Bergen Record*, 9/12/01) Investigators said that there were maps of the city with certain places highlighted, found in the van. The FBI confirmed that two of the five men were Mossad agents and that all five were on a Mossad assignment. (*Forward*, 3/15/02) They were held on immigration violations, questioned excessively and then released after 71 days in custody. (*ABC News*, 6/21/02) The owner of Urban Moving System, fled the United States to Israel on Sept 14, 2001. The FBI later told *ABC News* that the company "may have been providing cover for an Israeli intelligence operation." (*Forward*, 3/15/02; New Jersey Department of Law and Public Safety, 12/13/01; *ABC News*, 6/21/01)

While little has been mentioned in the mainstream press about the "art student" spy ring, the questions still remain as to their involvement with the events of 9/11. Were they helping the U.S. government track information regarding the possibilities of an attack within the United States, or were there deeper connections of which the public is unaware? Mainstream media began this story as an investigation, but immediately stopped when officials claimed that it was a farce.

ADDITIONAL SOURCES:

Paul Thompson, *The Terror Timeline: Year by Year, Day by Day, Minute by Minute*, Regan Books, September 1, 2004.

For the online version of Paul Thompson's 9/11 Timeline: The Center for Cooperative Research, "Complete 9/11 Timeline: Israeli spy ring, Israeli foreknowledge," http://www.cooperativeresearch.org/timeline.jsp?timeline=complete_911_timeline&theme=israel

DEA Report, "Suspicious Activities Involving Israeli Art Students of DEA Facilities," http://cryptome.org/dea-il-spy.htm, No date available.

Transcript of Fox News four part Israeli spy ring series, http://cryptome.org/fox-il-spy.htm, no date available.

Michael C. Ruppert, *Crossing the Rubicon: The decline of the American empire at the end of the age of oil*, New Society Publishers, 2004.

Nafeez Mosaddeq Ahmed & The Institute for Policy Research & Development, "The War On Freedom: How and Why America Was Attacked September 11, 2001," *Tree of Life Publications*, 2002.
Intelligence Online, "Israeli Spy Operation Confirmed," *http://www.
911truth.org/readingroom/whole_document.php?article_id=136*, March
14, 2002.

UNANSWERED QUESTIONS ABOUT THE PUT-OPTIONS AND 9/11

BY AMBROSIA PARDUE

It was widely reported immediately after 9/11 that insider trading
occurred in which trading skyrocketed on put-options that bet on a drop in
UAL Corp. and AMR Corp. (parent company to American Airlines) stock
in the days before the attacks. According to Bloomberg data, Morgan Stanley Dean Witter & Co. and Merrill Lynch & Co. also experienced pre-attack
trading twelve to more than twenty-five times the usual volume of put-
options. Morgan Stanley put-options jumped to 2,157 contracts between September 6 and September 10—almost twenty-seven times a previous daily
average of twenty-seven contracts. Merrill Lynch's daily activities previous to September 11th were 252. 12,215 contracts were traded from September 5 to September 10th. Citigroup Inc. had a jump in trading of about
45 percent. One day before the American Airlines planes were hijacked
and crashed, 1,535 contracts were traded on options that let investors profit
from the American Airlines stock falls.[1] All companies were linked to the
hijacked airplanes or to the World Trade Center. Morgan Stanley occupied
twenty-two stories of the WTC and Merrill Lynch had offices nearby.[2] Christian Berthelsen and Scott Winokur of the *San Francisco Chronicle* wrote
on September 29, 2001 that as of that date investors had yet to collect more
than $2.5 million in profits made in these put stock options of United Air-
lines, and "the uncollected money raises suspicions that the investors—
whose identities and nationalities have not been made public—had
advanced knowledge of the strikes."[3]

A put-option is a contract that gives the holder the right to sell a specified number of shares in a particular stock, usually at a predetermined
price, called the strike price, on or before the option's expiration date—
these are the stock index or dollar face value of bonds. The buyer (holder)
pays the seller (writer) a premium and the buyer profits from the contract
if the stock price drops. If the buyer decides to exercise the option, as
opposed to selling it, the seller must buy the security. The seller profits when

the underlying security's price remains the same, rises or drops by less than the premium received.[4] A short sale is where an investor borrows stock from a broker and sells it, hoping to buy it back at a lower price.[5] A put-option bets that a stock will fall, and a call-option bets that stock will rise; there were far more put-options than call-options in the days proceeding September 11th.[6] *Cooperative Research* states that "assuming 4,000 of the options were bought by people with advance knowledge of the imminent attacks, these 'insiders' would have profited by almost $5 million."

Of interest to note is that the firm that handled the purchase of many of the put-options on United Airlines, the Bank of Alex Brown, was headed by 'Buzzy' Krongard until 1998. Krongard was the deputy director of the CIA during G.W.Bush's first four years. Tom Flocco reported on July 16, 2002 that European reporters found most of the suspicious pre-September 11th trading "passed through Deutsche Bank and Alex Brown investment division by means of a procedure called portage, which assures the anonymity of individuals making the transactions."[7]

Cooperative Research reported that the Securities and Exchange Commission published a list that included some thirty-eight companies whose stocks may have been traded prior to September 11th by people who had "advanced knowledge" of the attacks. *From the Wilderness* reported that the CIA, the Israeli Mossad, and many other intelligence agencies monitor stock trading in real time using highly advanced programs. Stock trading irregularities could be used to alert national intelligence services of possible terrorist attacks.

CIA spokesman Tom Crispell denied that the CIA was monitoring U.S. equity markets trading activity prior to September 11th. Tom Flocco has found growing evidence that the FBI and other government intelligence agencies were more closely linked to the pre-September 11th insider trading.[8] A *San Diego Union-Tribune* January 5, 2005 article stated that "a former FBI agent admitted that he gave online stock traders confidential details of federal investigations, including a probe of the Sept. 11 terror attacks."[9]

The *New York Times*, on September 28, 2001, reported that the "short positions and volume of put-options rose sharply across the travel industry—which has been cited repeatedly in news reports as possible evidence of illegal trading." *The London Telegraph* quoted Ernst Weltek, president of Bundesbank, on September 23, 2001 as saying that "there are ever clearer signs that there were activities on international financial markets that must have been carried out with the necessary expert knowledge."[10] Dylan Ratigan of *Bloomberg Business News* said that "this could very well be insider trading at the worst, more horrific, most evil use you've ever seen in your entire life. This would be one of the most extraordinary coincidences in the history of mankind if it was a coincidence."[11] CBSNews.com quoted McLucas, former Securities and Exchange Commission Enforcement Director, as saying that "the options trading in particular suggests to me that somebody, somewhere, may have had an inkling that something bad was going to happen to certainly those airlines stocks."[12]

The *9/11 Commission Report* scantly covers the stock options issue. On page 499, footnote #130, the 9/11 Commission reports that, "some unusual trading did in fact occur, but such trade proved to have an innocuous explanation.... A single U.S. based institutional investor with no conceivable ties to al-Qa'eda purchased 95 percent of the UAL puts on September 6 as part of a trading strategy that also included buying 115,000 shares of American on September 10." This explanation only addresses the UAL and American put-options, ignores trades in other companies, and fails to identify the purchaser, thereby leaving even more unanswered questions.

This issue cannot be discounted, overlooked, or debunked as a conspiracy theory. The questions remain: who put in the calls for these options, and are the calls tied to Krongard, the CIA, the alleged terrorists, or others?

NOTES

1. http://www.themodernreligion.com/terror/wtc-unusualtrading.html.
2. http://www.themodernreligion.com/terror/wtc-unusualtrading.html.
3. http://www.sfgate.com/cgi-bin/article.cgi?file=/chronicle/archive/2001/09/29/MN186128.
4. http://66.159.17.51/cooperativeresearch/www/wot/sept11/suspicioustradingact.html.
5. http://www.sfgate.com/cgi-bin/article.cgi?file=/chronicle/archive/2001/09/29/MN186128.
6. http://www.cbsnews.com/stories/2001/09/19/eveningnews/printable311834.shtml.
7. scoop.co.nz/stories/HL0207/S00119.htm.
8. scoop.co.nz/stories/HL0207/S00119.htm.
9. http://www.signonsandiego.com/uniontrib/20050105/news_1b5elgindy.html.
10. http://www.portal.telegraph.co.uk/news/main/jhtml?xml=/news/2001/09/23/widen23.xml.
11. http://fromthewilderness.com/free/ww3/051602_liewontstand.html.
12. http://www.cbs.news.com/stories/2001/09/26/archive/printable 312663.shtml.

THE 9/11 WAR GAMES

BY REBEKAH COHEN

Among the many mysteries surrounding 9/11 is the emerging information that several government/military war games were taking place on the morning of September 11, 2001. The military war games on that day could have been a particularly interesting coincidence, or served the much greater purpose of confusing, distracting, and potentially even facilitating the September 11th terrorist attacks.

In May of 2001, Vice President Dick Cheney was nominated to oversee Domestic Counter Terrorism Efforts. According to Michael Ruppert's book, *Crossing the Rubicon* this position put domestic military control in the hands of Cheney, giving him the power to issue a scramble or a direct stand-down order in the unlikely case of a terrorist attack. Without Cheney's consent the military would not act. (Ruppert 2004).

Interestingly enough, several "live-fly" (as opposed to simulated) war games were taking place the week of 9/11. "I have an on-the-record statement from someone in NORAD that on the day of 9/11, the Joint Chief of Staff (Richard B. Myers) and NORAD were conducting a joint, live-fly, hijacked Field Training Exercised (FTX) which involved at least one (and almost certainly more) aircraft under U.S. control that was posing as a hijacked airliner," said Mike Ruppert (Kane 6/8/2004).

The confirmed war game taking place on 9/11 was 'Vigilant Guardian.' An annual drill in its second day, Vigilant Guardian was allegedly an exercise focusing on old Cold War threats and was conducted by NORAD. This "live-fly" war game was actually being used to test national air response systems—involving hijacking scenarios (Kane 6/8/2004).

Another drill taking place on 9/11 was titled 'Northern Vigilance.' This exercise was also conducted by NORAD once a year and involved deploying fighter jets to locations in Alaska and Northern Canada (Ruppert 2004). This drill succeeded in pulling military personnel and equipment north, away from the East Coast and away from the pending terrorist attacks. There is also evidence suggesting a war game, titled 'Vigilant Warrior,' was also being played on 9/11. This is a drill from the 1996 Persian Gulf. The name 'Vigilant' in both 'Vigilant Guardian' and 'Vigilant Warrior' suggests a possible connection between the two drills. The common first name suggests the possibility of the two games playing opposing forces (Ruppert 2004).

Another potential drill going on was hosted by the National Reconnaissance Office (NRO). They have claimed to have been "running a drill for the scenario of an errant aircraft crashing into its NRO headquarters (coincidentally, located only four blocks from Dulles airport in Washington D.C.)" (Kane 6/8/2004).

As early as 8:30 A.M., on the morning of September 11th, air force Major General Larry Arnold, involved with the Vigilant Guardian war game, questioned the validity of the calls in regards to possible terrorist activity. Upon hearing of the hijackings, he wondered if it was all a part of the exercise or the real thing. It was apparently around this time that the FAA, NORAD, and other agencies (FBI and CIA) were on an open line discussing the possibility of a hijacked plane. When the whereabouts of the taped conversation between these various agencies was questioned, it was revealed that FAA manager Kevin Delaney, destroyed the air traffic control tapes just months after 9/11. No reason was stated and the issue has gone un-pressed (*Haupt*, 5/30/2004).

Also taking place around 8:30 A.M., Colonel Deskins, Head of Northeast Air Defense Sector (NEADS) and mission crew chief for ongoing exercise Vigilant Guardian, was quoted as saying "uh, we have a hijacked aircraft and I need you to get some sort of fighters out here to help us out." Although, contrary to Colonel Deskins, Major General Eric Findley, who was in charge of NORAD on 9/11 in Colorado, claimed that no calls for help took place until 10:01 A.M. Another conflicting statement made by General Rick Findley claims that he commanded fighters into the air as early as 8:46 A.M (*Haupt*, 5/30/2004).

The controversial 2003 9/11 hearing revealed that their logs indicated 8:40 to be the first time the FAA reported a possible hijacking. Although, the "tower logs" were not physically present at the hearing and the fact was based on recollection only. Other reports claimed that NEADS was most likely aware of a potential hijacking as early as 8:20 A.M (*Haupt*, 5/30/2004).

There was never a direct mention of war games on 9/11 in the 9/11 Commission hearings. So the names of the possible war games and the people in charge of them on September 11th were not overtly specified or further subjected to mainstream criticism. However, when General Eberhart was questioned about the authority heads behind the war games, he replied with, "No comment." His unwillingness to divulge names of the people in charge is highly suspicious and warrants further explanation (Kane 1/18/2005).

Representative Cynthia McKinney (D-Altanta) attempted to bring some attention to the 9/11 war games during the House Hearing on FY06 Department of Defense Budget, on March 11th, 2005. She questioned Secretary of Defense, Donald Rumsfeld and Chairman of the Joint Chief of Staff, Richard Myers about the four war games that took place on September 11th. Myers responded to the question with very ambiguous explanations. He claimed that war gaming were being held by several different departments, and it was not NORAD's overall responsibility to respond to the attacks, but the FAA's. Nonetheless, he felt the gaming actually provided "an easy transition from an exercise into a real world situation" and contributed to a quick response. Myers failed to comment on McKinney's question of who was actually in charge of managing the war games on 9/11 (Kane 3/1/2005).

SOURCES:

Michael Kane, "Mr. Chairman, I have a Question: Representative Cynthia McKinney Rocks Rumsfeld on War Games" *http://www.fromthewilderness.com/free/ww3/030105_mckinney_question.shtml* , March 1, 2005

Michael Kane, "Crossing the Rubicon simplifying the case against Dick Cheney" *http://fromthewilderness.com/free/ww3/011805_simplify_case.shtml*, Jan. 18, 2005

Michael Kane, "9/11 War Games—No Coincidence" *http://inn.globalfreepress.com/modules/news/print.php?storyid=387*, June 8, 2004

Nico Haupt, "The lost war drill? (Chapter 9)" *http://inn.globalfreepress.com/modules/news/print.php?storyid=325*, May 30, 2004

Michael Ruppert, *Crossing the Rubicon: The decline of the American empire at the end of the age of oil* New Society Publishers, 2004.

ATTA AND THE $100,000

BY REBEKAH COHEN AND AMBROSIA PARDUE

General Mahmoud Ahmad, Chief of Pakistani Inter-Services Intelligence (ISI), secret service, is said to have had connections to the alleged terrorist "ring leader" and hijacker Mohammed Atta, as reported by the *Times of India* (October 9, 2001). [1] *Times of India* also reported that the $100 thousand wired to Atta six months prior to 9/11 from Pakistan by Ahmad Uhmar Sheikh was at the instance of General Ahmad.[2]

Michel Chossudovsky reported that General Mahmoud Ahmad was in the United States from September 4th until several days after 9/11. He had meetings at the State Department and with CIA and Pentagon officials during the week prior to September 11th. The nature of his visit has not been disclosed. There has been no evidence confirming his pre-September 11th consultations were routine, or if they were in any way related to his subsequent post-September 11th consultations pertaining to Pakistan's decision to cooperate with the White House.[3]

According to the Indian government intelligence report, the perpetrators of the September 11 attacks had links to Pakistan's ISI, which in turn has links to U.S. government agencies. This suggests that key individuals within the U.S. military intelligence establishment may well have known about the ISI contacts with the September 11 terrorist "ring-leader"

Mohammed Atta and failed to act.[4] The *Times of India* further reported the possibility of other ISI official's contacts with terrorists, suggesting that the attacks were not an act of "individual terrorism," but rather were part of a coordinated military intelligence operation stemming from the ISI.

Nicholas Levis of 911Truth.org raises the question about the reports that the ISI wired $100k to Mohammed Atta. Saying that the "ISI has often been credited as the creator of the Taliban, and its operatives have been linked to the bin Laden networks. ISI is also linked to CIA as a historically close ally."[5]

The *9/11 Commission Report* claims that "between $400,000 and $500,000 to plan and conduct the attack....was funded by al-Qa'eda..." (pg.172). There is no mention of the *Times of India* report.

Early October 2001, General Ahmad was dismissed from his position of Chief of ISI at the request of the FBI.[6]

Though one would think that this topic would cause a stir among journalists, it has barely been touched and has remained stagnate. The links are there, but unexamined. One can only speculate as to the connections between General Mahmoud Ahmad, Mohammed Atta, the $100k, and the United States government.

NOTES

1. http://www.globalresearch.ca/articles/CH0111A.html#c.
2. www.globalresearch.ca.
3. http://www.fromthewilderness.com/cgi-bin/MasterPFP.cgi?doc.
4. http://www.fromthewilderness.com/cgi-bin/MasterPFP.cgi?doc.
5. http://www.fromthewilderness.com/cgi-bin/MasterPFP.cgi?doc.
6. http://www.fromthewilderness.com/cgi-bin/MasterPFP.cgi?doc.

SOME 9/11 TERRORISTS STILL ALIVE? AND OTHER TROUBLING INACCURACIES

BY CHRIS KYLE

In the *9/11 Commission Report*, the original list of hijackers is repeated, and their pictures are presented. However, at least six of the named hijackers are confirmed to be alive. Waleed al-Shehri is reported to have been on American Airlines Flight 11, which hit the North Tower. Yet he was interviewed by a London based Arab-language daily, *Al-Quds al Arabi*, after September 11, 2001.

Among the named hijackers are Salem al-Hazmi, Saeed al-Ghamdi, Ahmed al-Nami, and Waleed al-Shehri. Al-Hazmi lives in Saudi Arabia and works for a petroleum/chemical plant in Yanbu. At the time of the events of 9/11, he had not left Saudi Arabia for two years. Al-Ghamdi is alive in Tunisia and had not left the country for ten months prior. He is learning to fly an airbus. Al-Nami, meanwhile, is an administrative supervisor for Saudi Arabian Airlines and lives in Riyadh. Both al-Ghamdi and al-Nami told David Harrison of the *Telegraph* (London 9/23/01) that they were quite shocked to hear that they had died in Pennsylvania, a place they had not heard of. Al-Shehri lives in Casablanca, Morocco, and was there during the attack. He is a pilot for Royal Air Marco.

Then there is the case of Mohammed Atta, the supposed ringleader of the attack. The Commission describes him as a devout Muslim. However, various accounts prove this not to be the case. Atta gambled, drank alcohol, and paid for lap dances. According to reporter Daniel Hopsicker, Atta at one time lived with a prostitute in Florida. While there, he drank heavily, used cocaine, and ate pork chops. None of these acts are those of a devout Muslim. (Griffin, 2005)

There is also the matter of Atta's bags. Two bags supposedly belonging to Mohammed Atta failed to get on Flight 11. In these bags were a copy of the Koran, Boeing flight simulation manuals, a religious cassette, a note to other hijackers regarding mental preparation, his personal will, passport, and international driver's license. The rest aside, who tries to bring their will aboard a plane they know is going to explode? This is a question the Commission could have looked into, but instead ignored. (Griffin, 2005)

Of course, this is not the only matter that the Commission ignored. There is also the matter of the flight manifests for the hijacked planes. The manifests that have been released have no Arab names listed. Efforts have been made by independent researchers to get the final flight manifests from these planes, but all such requests have been refused. (Griffin, 2005)

REFERENCES:
David Ray Griffin, *The 9/11 Commission Report: Omissions and Distortions*, Olive Branch Press, 2005.

THE DEMOCRATIC PARTY, LIKE THE REPUBLICAN PARTY AND THE MEDIA, COVERED UP THE DEEP COMPLICITY IN THE 9/11/01 ATTACK BY BUSH-CHENEY-RUMSFELD-MYERS

BY JOHN B. MASSEN, GUEST WRITER—SUMMARY ANALYSIS

On March 11, 2003, Congressman John Conyers, Ranking Member of the House Judiciary Committee, called an emergency meeting of 40 some top advisors, mostly lawyers, to discuss immediately initiating impeachment against Bush, Cheney, Rumsfeld, and Ashcroft, to head off the impending war against Iraq, which began eight days later. Also invited were Francis A. Boyle, professor of law at University of Illinois School of Law, and Ramsey Clark, former U.S. Attorney General, both of whom had drafted Bills of Impeachment, to argue the case for impeachment. The meeting ended with a second revised draft Bill of Impeachment, because eminent lawyers believed that Bush et al deserved impeachment for multiple violations of international treaties and laws. However, influential Democrats opposed impeachment on the ground that the effort would hurt their party's interest in gaining control of the federal government in the 2004 election.

On 9-13-01, the Senate Armed Services Committee, with a Democratic Chairman and majority membership, heard General Richard Myers testify that fighter aircraft responded to an apparently hijacked plane inbound to the U.S. and forced it to land in a remote base in Canada. Standard operating procedures were clearly in effect outside, but not inside, the U.S. on September, 11, 2001. If there had been no advance warning of the attack, fighter planes responding under standard operating procedures would have prevented all attacks inside the U.S. The Bush regime must have decided to permit the attack to succeed.

A comprehensive report was written, by myself, which cited Myers' testimony, the failure to prevent the 9/11 attacks, Bush's behavior at the Florida school, and evidence of planning long before 9/11, and aggression in Afghanistan and Iraq. The report was sent, by myself, to Conyers on November 17, 2003, to Rep. Barbara Lee on January 3, 2004, and to all 257 Democrats in the House and Senate plus DNC Chairman McAuliffe on January 26, 2004. The transmittal letters all strongly appealed for impeachment of the Bush regime for complicity in permitting the 9/11 attack to occur, and stressed that Democrats might receive, and should request, effective political support by a comprehensive political-educational campaign by MoveOn.Org and United For Peace and Justice that would assure a majority vote in the House and a 2/3 vote in the Senate. The Report was sent to MoveOn.Org and UFPJ, for use as they wished to inform and motivate their members.

David Ray Griffin's vital book, *The New Pearl Harbor: Disturbing Questions about the Bush Administration and 9/11*, was released in April 2004. It presented comprehensive evidence indicating deep complicity by the Bush regime in the 9/11 attack. The simplest "snapshot" of that evidence is this: (a) the North Tower (WTC-1) was struck at 8:46 AM, and collapsed 102 minutes later at 10:28 AM; (b) the South Tower (WTC-2) was struck at 9:03 AM and, with a much smaller fire, collapsed 56 minutes later (55 percent of WTC-1 time) at 9:59 AM; and (c) the 47-story WTC-7, which was two blocks away and not struck by a plane and had smaller interior fires, collapsed at 5:20 PM. (p.12) The collapse of WTC-2 before WTC-1 indicates the cause was not fires, but controlled demolition. (p.17)

Copies of Griffin's book were sent by myself to these Democrats: Dennis Kucinich on 3/27/04 with an impassioned plea; DNC Chair McAuliffe, Congresswomen Nancy Pelosi, and Senators Daschle, Feinstein and Boxer on 3/31/04; Congress members John Conyers, Elijah Cummings (Black Caucus Chair), Ciro Rodriquez (Hispanic Caucus Chair), Barbara Lee, Louise Slaughter (Co-chair of Women's Issues Caucus), and Tom Udall, between 4/05 and 4/28/04. All transmittal letters urged impeachment action, contending that such action and injecting the "complicity issue" into the 2004 presidential campaign was the only way to assure Bush's defeat; and repeated that Congressional Democrats might receive, and should request, effective political support from a comprehensive political-educational campaign waged by MoveOn.Org and UFPJ.

Of course, many Congressional Democrats received, from other persons, much information about the Bush regime complicity in addition to that reported above.

All Congressional Democrats and especially its leaders, and DNC Chair McAuliffe, were adequately informed of the Bush regime complicity and had staff and other resources to investigate further. Congressional Democrats had sworn to protect and uphold the constitution. They utterly failed in their obligations to the constitution and to their constituents to be an effective opposition party. The title of this essay is fully justified: the Democratic Party, like the Republican Party and the Media, covered up the deep complicity in the 9/11/01 attack by Bush-Cheney-Rumsfeld-Myers.

Why does the principal opposition party join the ruling party in covering up what are probably the worst presidential crimes in U.S. history? In response to my request for his evaluation of my report (cited above), Michael C. Ruppert, on 1/1/2004, provided an astute evaluation of how Congress operates:

"The flaw in your work is not in the legal foundation or in the way the evidence is presented, [but] in your basic assumption that the system functions and operates as you think it should or the way it is described in textbooks. History is replete with instances of impeachable or prosecutable conduct which are much better documented, more easily proven, and more glaring than what you have described."

"In Watergate, there was an abundance of evidence that Richard Nixon had committed offenses far greater than the one which brought him to the brink of impeachment—obstruction of justice. The issue was not what offense would be used to remove him, but (as far as Congress was concerned) finding an offense which could remove a sitting president without destroying the entire American system of government. The same question governs Congressional response to 9/11," Ruppert wrote.

Ruppert went on to write, "The entire system is corrupt. Those who participate in it rationalize—in order to protect their seat at a crap table—that when one player gets out of line the primary objective is to protect the crap game. (I thank Peter Dale Scott for this analogy.) I can guarantee you that many members of Congress are aware of every detail you have documented, and much, much more... To impeach Bush et al on the grounds you have delineated would open a can of worms that would call into question the legitimacy of the entire government. That will never be permitted.

"In the late 1990s I secured hard documents (much better evidence than you have presented from a legal standpoint) showing an active conspiracy to protect drug traffickers by the CIA that was sanctioned by the White House. An impeachment trial would have been open and shut. It never came about for the reasons I have stated above.

"In the case of the Clinton impeachment, while there were perhaps ten (or more) offenses upon which that president could have been removed and jailed, none of them were ever pursued. Why? Because they involved the simultaneous exposure of Republican corruption and/or demonstrated that the entire government was complicit in one degree or another. So what did they go after Clinton on? Extramarital sex and lying about it. It was the only charge available that did not bring down the whole system.

"I believe that (as it was with Watergate) Bush will likely be impeached after winning the 2004 election. On what charge? The forged Niger documents about alleged attempts by Saddam Hussein to reconstitute a nuclear weapons program and the malicious exposure of Valerie Plame (wife of Ambassador Joseph Wilson who was critical in exposing that lie) as a CIA case officer. That offense does not expose the whole crap game.

"There is no legal argument you can make that will make a broken system function the way that you want it to function."

Another valuable insight about the Democratic Party was provided on February 20, 2005 by Bruce Gagnon, Coordinator of the Global Network Against Weapons & Nuclear Power in Space. Gagnon writes:

"Hillary Clinton, who hopes to become president, is on the Sunday morning talk shows saying that our troops might be in Iraq for some time to come.

'We've been in Korea for 50 years,' she said. 'We are still in Okinawa,' she told the TV cameras.

"That is it. Pack up your bags, peace movement, and just go home. Hillary has made the pronouncement. She is in sync with George W. Bush, the neo-con crowd, Haliburton, Bechtel.... She wants to be president and she knows that the road to the White House has to pass through the gates of the military industrial complex... and the oil corporations... and the globalization crowd that intends to create a 'market economy' in Iraq (read privatization of everything there). Hillary has totally sold out.

"The war in Iraq, and the very long presence of U.S. troops there, will bleed America to the bone. The Democratic party, with few very noble exceptions, is on their knees in loyal complicity with the war machine. How can any self-respecting peace activist contemplate for a moment supporting such a party in the next election?"

Obviously, our nation is in very deep trouble. All citizens must unite and take back our nation from the corporate oligarchs!

John B. Massen finally retired at 90 in San Francisco this year. Massen's peace activism was principally in the United Nations Association of the USA, climaxed by his creation in 1980 and wide distribution of his highly acclaimed 16-poster exhibit on the Effects and Dangers of Nuclear War, co-sponsored by seven national organizations. E-mail: JackMassen@ aol.com

RECOMMENDED 9/11 RESOURCES:

Global Research—Michel Chossudovsky's site:
http://www.globalresearch.ca

Center for Cooperative Research—Paul Thompson's Timeline
www.cooperativeresearch.org

9-11 Review—Jim Hoffman's Site
http://www.911review.com

RICO—Rodriguez Versus Bush
http://www.911forthetruth.com

International Citizen's Inquiry into 9-11
http://www.911inquiry.org

From the Wilderness—Michael Ruppert's Site
http://www.fromthewilderness.com

Questioning the War on Terrorism—Carol Brouillet's Site
http://www.communitycurrency.org/9-11.html

9-11 Truth Alliance
http://www.911truth.org/

Crimes Against Humanity—Dave Ratcliffe's Site
http://www.ratical.org/ratville/CAH

Online Journal
http://www.onlinejournal.com

Justice for 9-11—Spitzer Complaint
http://www.justicefor911.org

The Great Conspiracy—Barrie Zwicker's site
http://www.greatconspiracy.ca

Global Outlook
http://www.globaloutlook.ca

Guerrilla News Network
http://www.gnn.tv/

Citizen's for Legitimate Government
http://legitgov.org/

Oil Empire
http://www.oilempire.us/

New York 9-11 Truth
http://www.ny911truth.org/

The Northern California 9-11 Truth Alliance
http://www.sf911truth.org

What Really Happened?
http://whatreallyhappened.com

9-11 Visibility Project
An activist oriented site...
http://www.septembereleventh.org

MUJCA-NET: Muslim-Jewish-Christian Alliance for 9/11 Truth
A new Interfaith group, based in Milwaukee
http://mujca.com

9-11 Citizen's Watch
http://www.911citizenswatch.org/

Propaganda Matrix
http://www.propagandamatrix.com/archiveprior_knowledge.html

THIS MODERN WORLD

by TOM TOMORROW

Panel 1:
WELCOME BACK TO OUR ONGOING *RONALD REAGAN COVERAGE!* IF YOU'RE JUST JOINING US, WE'VE BEEN DISCUSSING PRESIDENT REAGAN'S *BOUNDLESS OPTIMISM!*

BOY, HAVE WE *EVER!* FOR ABOUT A *WEEK,* NOW!

Panel 2:

WELL, HE HAD A LOT OF OPTIMISM TO *DISCUSS!*

HE SURE *DID!* THROUGH *DEFICITS, SCANDALS,* AND *ILLEGAL WARS*--WHEN LIFE HANDED HIM *LEMONS*--

--HE ELIMINATED GOVERNMENT REGULATION OF *LEMONADE FACTORIES!*

Panel 3:

TAKE THE *AIDS EPIDEMIC!* WITH TENS OF THOUSANDS DYING FROM A *MYSTERIOUS PLAGUE,* A LESSER MAN MIGHT HAVE SUCCUMBED TO *WORRY*--OR AT LEAST *MILD CONCERN!*

BUT NOT *RONALD REAGAN!* WHY, IT TOOK HIM *YEARS* TO EVEN *MENTION* AIDS!

Panel 4:

AND IT DIDN'T MATTER *HOW* MANY MEMBERS OF HIS ADMINISTRATION WERE FACING CRIMINAL INDICTMENT--OR *HOW* MANY MILLIONS WERE WASTED ON THE FANTASY OF A SPACE-BASED MISSILE DEFENSE SYSTEM--

--HE ALWAYS LET A *SMILE* BE *HIS* SPACE UMBRELLA!

Panel 5:

YES, FROM ARMS SALES TO *IRAN* TO DEATH SQUADS IN *CENTRAL AMERICA*--FOR HIM, THE KETCHUP BOTTLE WAS ALWAYS *HALF FULL*--

--AND THE *KETCHUP* WAS A *VEGETABLE!*

Panel 6:

COMING UP NEXT--A SINGLE WORD THAT *DEFINES* THE REAGAN LEGACY--AT LEAST AS FAR AS *WE'RE* CONCERNED!

WE'LL GIVE YOU A *HINT*--IT STARTS WITH "OP"--AND ENDS WITH "TIMISM"!

FIRST THESE MESSAGES.

TOM TOMORROW©2004 ... www.thismodernworld.com

CHAPTER 5

Junk Food News and News Abuse

By Mark Thompson, Sean Arlt, Brittny Roeland, Tricia Boreta, and Kate Sims

As an aside to our annual research, Project Censored shifts focus from important news stories that aren't being covered properly, to frivolous stories that are covered excessively over long periods of time. Dr. Carl Jensen, founder of Project Censored, coined the name Junk Food News.

In order to understand how issues of great importance are sidelined or censored, it is interesting to identify what is replacing them and why. Junk Food News stories generally deal with celebrities and brings in great ratings. Yet, though there are plenty of outlets for this sort of inconsequential entertainment, we repeatedly endure what is essentially gossip in place of meaningful news coverage.

Meanwhile, the lack of global exposure, local significance, or educational value is raising concern and dissatisfaction among many. To exemplify the waste of our precious airwaves, the Project Censored community casts its votes to determine the top ten most over-reported, empty-calorie news stories of the year. We point a finger at these sensations and encourage the world to ask the fundamental question: "Why should we care?"

The common response to this question is as frustrating as the problem itself. People don't like to hear bad news, and media organizations are becoming less fond of covering it. The original intent behind television and radio news was to keep people informed of politics and events that affect their lives. As time rolls forward we observe a shift in focus from education to entertainment, from service to ratings. People who support this kind of programming may want to avoid feelings of guilt, depression, or responsibility. The problem is that, when all is said and done, we can't hide behind Tom Cruise's latest love affair. We are responsible to one another for our decisions and our actions. By sacrificing news for useless gossip, we are hiding from real and inescapable issues that can only get worse.

Another explanation for the wide acceptance of this sort of media coverage may be that our expectation of news has been deliberately reconstructed by the media to advance ratings and corporate profit, rather than to advance the well-being of the general public and environment.

That being said, here are the top ten Junk Food News stories of the year. Enter the world of the superficial:

1. Brad Pitt and Jennifer Aniston breakup
2. The media obsession with Paris Hilton
3. Mary-Kate and Ashley Olson (business and personal lives)
4. Ashton and Demi Moore love affair
5. "Newlyweds" Nick and Jessica Simpson
6. Reality TV stars' lives
7. Britney Spears' pregnancy with Federline and upcoming reality TV show "Chaotic"
8. Barry Bonds and other baseball players on steroids
9. Kobe Bryant trial and confrontations with Shaquille O'Neal
10. Martha Stewart prison journals

Martha Stewart is a figure who is loved by some and loathed by others. But recently she has felt particularly unloved by our judicial system. Brought down on charges of fraud in a personal stock sale, Martha struggled to continue her business pursuits behind bars, and journalists jumped at the chance to call her a liar and a criminal. But, as it turns out, we can look forward to a bigger Martha news blowout in the future as her house arrest term ends and the CBS TV movie *Martha: Behind Bars* (starring Cybill Shepherd) goes on the air.

Los Angeles Lakers guard Kobe Bryant's sexual offense case was an obvious media target; his tremendous talent and popularity in the NBA made for a textbook contemporary cover story. If the TV-viewing audience loves anything, it's to see one of their nation's most popular role models transform into a monster. Though charges have been dropped, Kobe will inevitably struggle to regain his reputation.

And where would our chapter be without the belligerent blubbering of some of baseball's finest? With the publication of Jose Canseco's over-hyped autobiography, *Juiced*, Barry Bonds and several ball-playing behemoths were implicated in the use of illegal supplements during their stellar careers. The corporate media, of course, focused their attention on big hitters and their personal steroid issues, while the use of performance enhancing drugs in high school and college sports programs continues to go largely unnoticed. Ignoring a golden opportunity to address a serious health concern for many current and future professional athletes, corporate news chose to prey on the sob stories of baseball legends like Jose Canseco and Barry Bonds. America watched as Mark McGwire cried and reached for his water at the congressional hearing, denying any use of steroids. But it is unlikely that Jose's or Mark's performance will do anything to resolve the enhancement drug invasion that continues to plague serious athletes around the world.

Watching Britney Spears, the long time sex symbol, get married and pregnant is inspiring to her fans and annoying to everyone else, but for the corporate media it's nothing but marvelous. Her wedding, impregnation, and upcoming reality TV show promotions have all taken place in the same year, meaning that both Britney—and news coverage of her—will soon swell like never before.

Reality TV has clawed its way into reality through the mass media; the personal lives of reality stars have been highlighted to no end. The American public seems to have an endless appetite for Reality TV programming, and their options are growing like corn in Nebraska. Channel surfing tomorrow will undoubtedly mean sifting through an abundance of new and old reality shows as more and more get the "green light" from hand-rubbing studio execs.

The problem, however, is that when reality TV invades our news broadcasts it takes away people's rights to abstain from the growing craze. It seduces people into accepting these characters as important in their lives. The distinction between Reality TV and actual reality is being breached by this persistent programming; the more these shows and "celebrities" appear in our news, the more real they become to the viewers. The dramatic and childish behavior seen in numerous reality TV shows is not realistic nor is it acceptable, and the excessive news coverage of such shows does nothing but encourage people to think otherwise.

Number five on the list are the ever-popular Newlyweds Nick and Jessica. With careers in music and reality TV, both Jessica and Nick can't be avoided, but need they appear so often in our news? It seems the endless commercials weren't enough; broadcasters found it necessary to plug *Newlyweds* as if it were a political debate. The significance of these figures extends no further than entertainment; and they should be presented accordingly. Granted, the couple looks good in a photo, but their story belongs in *Star Magazine*, not on CNN.

Once again Ashton and Demi have worked their way into the lineup. The couple's fifteen-year age gap has been a huge deal to the press, not to mention the fact that again we are dealing with two sex symbols. Corporate news can't seem to keep its hormones under control. *Punk'd* creator and movie star Ashton Kutcher is only beginning his career, while long-time heartthrob Demi Moore has been on dorm room walls for decades. The fact is, these figures belong on dorm room walls, not on news studio teleprompters.

Coming in third this year are Mary-Kate and Ashley Olsen. The infamous countdown to their 18th birthday on June 13, 2004, marked a new low in useless information, and journalists were more than ready to take the dive. Hype about Mary-Kate using cocaine erupted into news broadcasts as the world took pride in overexposing and tormenting a young woman with anorexia. The intense media focus on these young women has an unhealthy impact, not only on the twins, but also on the world at large. One can't help wonder what effects such obsessive and critical coverage can have on the mental and physical health of the countless young women who idolize the duo. Coming in second (by only one vote) is heiress Paris. Her reality TV show (an international embarrassment) was a very lucrative success, and her new movie *House of Wax* hasn't done too badly either. But what about Paris Hilton so fascinates the corporate news media? Basically, she's hot—oh yeah, and an heiress. Either way you can't avoid her. Meanwhile, the sex footage that Rick Salomon took of Hilton certainly hasn't harmed her "career" and reporters are still salivating over the income that even the mention of her sex life brings.

Coming in first this year is America's favorite couple to gossip about, Brat Pitt and Jennifer Aniston. Their epic breakup came as a sad surprise to many, but it was a pot of gold to a corporate journalist. Speculations immediately filled the airwaves about Brat Pitt getting friendly with Angelina Jolie on the set of *Mr. and Mrs. Smith*. The real reason behind the split between Brad and Jennifer isn't known for sure, but evidently all theories have a place in the corporate news.

News Abuse

Sometimes news coverage begins with good intentions, only to fail under the weight of redundancy and a predilection for scandal. As a story unfolds and news stations across the country give it coverage, their message is received by millions of viewers. Each moment of coverage is a vital (and very expensive)[1] privilege. It is important that the people making these decisions take that privilege seriously.

When these precious moments are misused, it generates a condition we refer to as News Abuse. These are stories that have merit and some importance, at least initially. But when these stories become the target of salacious hype and an obsession with petty minutiae, it diminishes not only the credibility of the organization covering it, but the importance of the story itself. The audience begins to forget the humanity, and even the elements of the story, as it becomes buried beneath the circus of coverage.

What follows is our list of some of the most abused and over used stories of '04 and '05. They were voted on and ranked by our students listserve members at Project Censored:

1. The Michael Jackson trial
2. The Peterson trial
3. The Terri Schiavo tragedy
4. The perennial Terror alerts
5. The Kerry coverage (Vietnam/botox/flip-flopping)
6. Howard Dean's scream
7. Dan Rather's Bush-Service-Record report (his retraction and demotion)
8. Bush's Thanksgiving surprise for the troops
9. Discussion (ad nauseum) of the Swift Boat ads
10. Condoleezza Rice (her promotion, her brain, and her clothes)

Often a single event will occur that unleashes a number of follow up stories. From this, news programs will manufacture a series of "cliff hangers" that leave the audience eager for the next update. The latest Michael Jackson trial has provided just such an opportunity. From January 15, 2005 through the end of May the *New York Times* alone turned out more than 60 articles pertaining to Jackson. If a mouth opens about Michael Jackson during his trial there will be reports on it. If he dances on the hood of a car or shows up late to court,[2] it's on our doorstep the next morning. It is not clear that audiences actually prefer details that are insignificant to the real importance of the story. But under the current "cutting edge is dangerous" paradigm, networks seem disinclined to explore the deeper issues.[3]

The conviction of Scott Peterson brought closure to a tragic ordeal this year, and it also marked the end of an immense media fixation. The fact that Laci Peterson was pregnant at the time of her disappearance made the story uniquely devastating and reporters knew its shock value would make it take off instantly. Meanwhile a mother and father had lost their daughter, their life, as they knew it, their grandson-to-be, along with their privacy.

The Peterson trial received such a sustained barrage of coverage that some relevant information did actually emerge, such as the fact that, in the United States, the leading cause of death for pregnant women is no longer childbirth, but as the victims of murder by their male partner.[4] Yet this startling statistic received the same perfunctory analysis as any other tidbit of the trial, giving it the same news "weight" as (for example) the fact that Scott's extramarital affair was with a massage therapist.[5]

The Terri Schiavo tragedy, at number three this year, began as a sad family struggle and evolved into a political battle of epic proportion. A number of important social debates emerged from this story initially, but they soon became so encumbered by partisan rhetoric that any attempt at honest debate was quickly lost in the political melee.

At number four this year are the ubiquitous and strangely unsettling terror alerts. It's difficult to imagine where the world would be if it weren't for the television news media infatuation with terror alerts. There's nothing like curling up in front of the TV and watching the color-coordinated Parcheesi-board-like grid that invites one to assess the rising and falling degrees of terror in the daily forecast. It's one thing to be aware, but repeatedly threatening the population with terror alerts is not helpful or educational, it's annoying. No one has, as yet, clearly defined the purpose of the alerts. And then there's that strange, but well-established, correlation between falling presidential ratings and increased terror alert levels[6]...hmmm.

And what would an election year be without a bunch of over-blown, so-much-flash-so-little-substance stories about the candidates that do next to nothing to reveal, in any manner, who would actually make the best president? Was Kerry a hero? Was he a coward? Is he a flip-flopper? Did Bush show up for the National Guard? How much does he like golf? Is he stupid and inarticulate or crafty and ambitious? Between Bush's posturing, Kerry's dullness, and Dean's out and out weirdness, there was little room for honest critique or analysis:

The Dean Scream was unleashed in Iowa, marking the end of Howard Dean's presidential campaign and according to ABC12.com the media covered it almost 700 times in just a few days. Granted, political leaders don't normally produce the sound of a boar being skinned, but news organizations didn't hesitate to squeeze it for all it was worth.

As John Kerry's presidential campaign unraveled, none of the veterans that were with him on March 13, 1969 had any idea that their accounts of Kerry's actions that day might determine America's next president. The Swift Boat Veterans for Truth organization launched a series of claims against Kerry and the media slurped it up, broadcasting every detail from every interview. To this day it is unclear whether or not Kerry was the hero he claimed to be, but the tremendous news coverage of the dispute did nothing to illuminate how it would impact his ability to be a better or worse president than the incumbent.

When Bush, playing the hero, surprised the troops in Iraq, the media nipped again, just like a good lap dog. Bush's handlers had constructed the perfect plan for the 2004 Thanksgiving holiday. Bush's "disappearing act" was such a great topic for idle gossip that the mainstream just couldn't resist—and the turkey presentation (plastic or not) was a deliciously heartwarming camera-ready conclusion.

By far, the most truly nauseating event of the 2004 campaign was the Dan Rather Bush-service-record "fiasco." In the scramble to chastise Rather, *60 Minutes II*, CBS (and anyone else who happened to be in the room) for the false service records, the U.S. media managed to ignore the fact the story was—actually—true. The veracity of the assertion, and the content, of the story had been established many years before, by a number of different journalists.[7] (See chapter 15) But the mainstream has never let the facts stand in the way of a good story and "Memogate" has been called everything from the event that proves network media's "liberal bias"[8] to an example of the "crisis of credibility" that plagues modern journalism.[9]

And finally, at number 10, is Secretary of State and former National Security Advisor Dr. Condoleezza Rice. Her education, her humble beginnings, and her recent promotion have stirred up a tremendous amount of publicity. Her incredible scholastic achievements gained her a legendary reputation at Stanford and the mainstream media seem quite taken by her attractiveness and her understated, yet elegant, sense of style.

But what about her career and her previous associations? Didn't she used to work for an oil company? What about her role leading up to 9/11? Her evasive statements in interviews leave many analysts wondering about her veracity and how far she will to go to protect her cohorts. Her responses to interviews surrounding 9/11 have been questioned from the start. Many believe that she has lied or deliberately left out information on several accounts to preserve faith in the Bush Administration. About the briefing sent to the president that clearly stated an attack could involve airplanes, Condoleezza offered evasive statements like "I don't think anybody could have predicted that they would try to use an airplane as a missile, a hijacked airplane as a missile."[10] (See chapter 4.)

The alleged abuse of children by a powerful individual, the need to know and understand our candidates and public officials, the plight and condition of our troops overseas—all are profound and valid issues for news coverage.

So why, when it comes to telling a story, does the mainstream news so often fixate on a couple of the trees and miss the forest entirely? Are they really so terrified of losing a little market share? Vision and a little courage have been known to attract viewers in the past (Laugh In, The Donahue Show, and All In The Family come to mind). A bit of a shake up at a network can be a good thing from time to time.

NOTES
1. Ron Kaufman "Advertising: Past, Present and Future," http://www.turnoffyourtv.com/ programsratings/advertising2004.html.
2. Andrew Gumbel "Courtroom Thriller as Fans Flock to the Michael Jackson Show," *The Independent* (London), January 17, 2004, http://news.independent.co.uk/world/americas/story.jsp?story=482022.
3. Tom Rosenstiel, Carl Gottlieb, and Lee Ann Brady, "Quality Sells, But Commitment—and Viewership—Continue to Erode," Journalism.org—Reports and Surveys, 2000, http://www.journalism.org/resources/research/reports/localTV/2000/peril.asp.
4. Isabelle L. Horon, Ph.D.; Diana Cheng, M.D., "Enhanced Surveillance for Pregnancy-Associated Mortality—Maryland, 1993–1998" *JAMA.* Vol. 285:1455-1459. No. 11, March 21, 2001, http://jama.ama-assn.org/cgi/content/abstract/285/11/1455.
5. George Rush and Joanna Molloy With Suzanne Rozdeba and Ben Widdicombe "Enquirer Bares Witness in Calif. Case," *New York Daily News*, Friday, February 7th, 2003 http://www.nydailynews.com/news/gossip/v-pfriendly/story/57927p-54257c.html.
6. http://img70.exs.cx/my.php?loc=img70&image=aproval_vs_alert_chart_NEW.gif.
7. Greg Palast, "CBS' Cowardice and Conflicts Behind Purge," CommonDreams.org, January 16, 2005, http://www.gregpalast.com/printerfriendly.cfm?artid=407 Documentation: http://www.gregpalast.com/ulf/documents/draftdodgeblanked.jpg
8. Peter Johnson, "Rather's 'Memogate': We told you so, conservatives say" *USA TODAY*, September 27, 2004.
9. *St. Petersburg Times* (Florida) editorial, "Crisis of credibility," January 12, 2005.
10. James P. Pinkerton, "A rough day lies ahead for Rice," *Star Tribune* (Minneapolis, MN), April 4, 2004.

CHAPTER 6

Corporate Media Is Corporate America

BIG MEDIA INTERLOCKS WITH CORPORATE AMERICA AND BROADCAST NEWS MEDIA OWNERSHIP EMPIRES

By Bridget Thornton, Britt Walters, and Lori Rouse

The Project Censored team researched the board members of 10 major media organizations from newspaper to television to radio. Of these ten organizations, we found there are 118 people who sit on 288 different U.S. and international corporate boards proving a close on-going interlock between big media and corporate America. We found media directors who also were former Senators or Representatives in the House such as Sam Nunn (Disney) and William Cohen (Viacom). Board members served at the FCC such as William Kennard (*New York Times*) and Dennis FitzSimmons (Tribune Company) showing revolving door relationships with big media and U.S. government officials.

These ten big media organizations are the main source of news for most people living in the U.S. Their corporate ties require us to continually scrutinize the quality of our news for bias. Disney owns ABC so we wonder how the board of Disney reacts to negative news about their board of directors' friends such as Halliburton or Boeing. We see board members with connections to Ford, Kraft, and Kimberly-Clark who employ tens of thousands of U.S. residents. Is it possible that theU.S. workforce receives only the corporate news private companies want them to hear? Do we collectively realize that working people in the U.S. have longer hours, lower pay and fewer benefits than their foreign counterparts? If these companies control the media, they control the dissemination of news, turning the First Amendment on its head by protecting corporate interests over people

Another trend we found was the connections to higher education around the country. There are board members associated with USC (the *Washington Post*), Columbia (Gannett), Georgetown (Disney), NYU (the *Washington Post*), and Wharton (Knight-Ridder) to name a few. With the decreasing state and federal funding to universities, will we see our higher learning institutions tie themselves more to corporations than the government for their funding? Will higher education become increasingly elite and consumer-oriented? Will the universities eventually focus education around the production of workers or thinkers?

As the Roman Empire declined, Feudalism took the place of the government. The feudal lord was one of the few sources of jobs in the fourth and fifth centuries. These lords owned most of the land and resources. Today, we replace feudalism with corporatism. The mass population has few choices for their news, information and education. As corporate media applauds an ownership society, we must realize who gets to own. In corporate-dominated capitalism wealth concentration is the goal and the corporate media are the cheerleaders.

MAJOR MEDIA COMPANIES AND THEIR BOARDS OF DIRECTORS

MEDIA COMPANY	BOARD OF DIRECTORS
Gannett	Douglas H. McCorkindale, Louis D. Boccardi, James A. Johnson, Duncan M. McFarland, Stephen P. Munn, Donna E. Shalala, Solomon D. Trujillo, Karen Hastie Williams
New York Times	John F. Akers, Brenda C. Barnes, Raul E. Cesan, Lynn G. Dolnick, Michael Golden, William E. Kennard, David E. Liddle, Ellen R. Marram, Thomas Middelhoff, Janet L. Robinson, Henry B. Schacht, Arthur Sulzberger, Jr., Cathy J. Sulzberger, Doreen A. Toben

Washington Post	Donald E. Graham, Warren E. Buffett, Barry Diller, John L. Dotson Jr., Melinda French Gates, George J. Gillespie III, Ronald L. Olson, Alice M. Rivlin, Richard D. Simmons, George W. Wilson
Knight-Ridder	Mark Earnest, Kathleen Feldstein, Thomas Gerrity, Ronald McRay, Pat Mitchell, Kenneth Oshman, Vasat Prabhu, Anthony Ridder, Gonzalo Valdes-Fauli, John E. Warnock
The Tribune Company	Dennis J. FitzSimons, Jeffrey Chandler, Roger Goodan, Enrique Hernandez, Jr., Betsy D. Holden, Robert S. Morrison, William A. Osborn, J. Christopher Reyes, William Stinehart, Jr., Dudley S. Taft, Kathryn C. Turner
News Corp.	K. Rupert Murdoch, Chase Carey, Peter Chernin, Kenneth E. Cowley, David F. DeVoe, Viet Din, Rod Eddington, Andrew S.B. Knight, Lachlan Murdoch, Thomas J. Perkins, Stanley S. Shuman, Arthur M. Siskind, John L. Thornton
AOL/Time Warner	Richard D. Parsons, James L. Barksdale, Carla A. Hills, Stephen F. Bollenbach, Reuben Mark, Stephen M. Case, Michael A. Miles, Frank J. Caufield, Kenneth J. Novack, Robert C. Clark, R.E. Turner, Miles R. Gilburne, Francis T. Vincent, Jr.
General Electric	Jeffrey R. Immelt, James I. Cash, Jr., William Castell LVO, Dennis D. Dammerman, Ann M. Fudge, Claudio X. Gonzalez, Andrea Jung, A.G. Lafley, Rochelle B. Lazarus, Sam Nunn, Roger S. Penske, Robert J. Swieringa, Douglas A. Warner III, Robert C. Wright

Walt Disney   John E. Bryson, John S. Chen, Mr. Eisner,
Judith L. Estrin, Robert A. Iger,
Fred H. Langhammer, Aylwin B. Lewis,
Monica C. Lozano, Robert W. Matschullat,
Senator George J. Mitchell,
Leo J. O'Donovan, Gary L. Wilson

Viacom   Sumner M. Redstone, George S. Abrams,
David R. Andelman, Joseph A. Califano, Jr.,
William S. Cohen, Philippe P. Dauman,
Alan C. Greenberg, Charles E. Phillips,
Shari Redstone, Frederic V. Salerno,
William Schwartz, Robert D. Walter

BIG MEDIA INTERLOCKS WITH CORPORATE AMERICA AND MAJOR INSTITUTIONS INU.S.

Gannett
Asia Pacific Fund, Inc.
Associated Press
Carlisle Companies, Inc.
The John F. Kennedy Center for
the Performing Arts
Chubb Corporation
Continental Airlines, Inc.
Electronic Data Systems
Corporation
Goldman Sachs Group, Inc.
Graduate School of Journalism,
Columbia University
KB Home Corporation
Lennar Corporation
Lockheed Martin Corporation
Orange S.A.
PepsiCo, Inc.
Prudential Mutual Funds
SunTrust Banks, Inc
Target Corporation
Temple-Inland Corporation

Trustee, Financial Accounting
Foundation
UnitedHealth Group
WGL Holdings, Inc.

New York Times
Alcoa (Aluminum Company of
America)
APCOA Parking AG, German
Augustana College
Bewerbungskomitee Leipzig 2012
Carlyle Group, 2001
Eli Lilly and Company.
KarstadtQuelle AG, German
Fitch Ratings, a U.S./UK
Flamel Technologies S.A
Ford Motor Company
Hallmark Cards, Inc.
International Herald Tribune
Johnson & Johnson
Lehman Brothers Holdings, Inc.
Staples, Inc.

Lucent Technologies Inc.
PepsiCo, Inc.
Polestar Corporation, a British
    company
Times Square Business
    Improvement District
LHIW Real Estate
    Development Partnership
U.S. Venture Partners
    North Castle Partners, LLC
W.R. Grace & Co.

Washington Post
Berkshire Hathaway Inc.
Bill & Melinda Gates Foundation
Brookings Institution
Cravath, Swaine & Moore LLP
Georgetown University
IAC/InterActiveCorp, USA
    Interactive
Munger, Tolles & Olson LLP
BrassRing, Inc
Pulitzer Prize Board,
District of Columbia College
    Access Program
Federal City Council in Washing-
    ton, DC.
Summit Fund of Washington
Coca-Cola Company
Gillette Company
Life Trustee
Urban Institute Member
American Academy of Arts and
    Sciences
IAC/InterActiveCorp
Coca-Cola Company
New York University
Medical Sciences at UCLA
Conservation International
Channel 13/WNET

School of Cinema-Television, USC
University of North Carolina at
    Chapel Hill
Robert C. Maynard Institute for
    Journalism Education
drugstore.com
White Mountains Insurance
    Group, Inc.
Madison Square Boys and Girls
    Club
Pinkerton Foundation
Life Director and Chairman
    Emeritus, National Multiple
    Sclerosis Society
John M. Olin Foundation
William S. Paley Foundation
Arthur Ross Foundation
Museum of Television and Radio
The Jackson Laboratory
RAND Corporation
USC Annenberg School for
    Communication
Southern California Public Radio
Berkshire Hathaway
Edison International
City National Corporation
Dun & Bradstreet Corporation
Moody's Investors Service
J.P. Morgan & Co. Inc.
Morgan Guaranty Trust Company
    of New York
Union Pacific Corporation
Yankee Publishing Inc.
General Electric Investments
Advisory Board of Directorship
White Burkett Miller Center of
    Public Affairs, University of
    Virginia
Protestant Episcopal Cathedral
    Foundation

Newspapers of New England, Inc.
Bakersfield (California)
    Californian
Associated Press

Knight-Ridder
Adobe Systems, Inc.
Echelon Corporation
Economics Studies, Inc
H&R Block, Inc
Kimberly-Clark Corporation
Public Broadcasting Service
Starwood Hotels and Resorts
Wharton School of the University
    of Pennsylvania

The Tribune Company
3M Company
Allstate Corporation
Aon Corporation
Big Shoulders Fund
Boys and Girls Clubs
Business Council
Carpenter Technology Corporation
Caterpillar Inc.,
Nicor Inc.
Chandler Ranch Co
Chandler Trusts
Chicago Council on Foreign
    Relations,
Chicago Horticultural Society
Chicago Symphony Orchestra
Chicago Urban League
Children's Hospice International
Children's Memorial Foundation
Children's Memorial Medical
    Center
Cincinnati Association for the
    Performing Arts
CINergy Corp.

Commercial Club of Chicago
ConocoPhillips
Control Data Corporation
Economic Club of Chicago
ElderPort
Evanston Northwestern Healthcare
Executives' Club of Chicago
Federal Reserve Bank of Chicago
Fortune Brands, Inc.
General Electric Information Ser-
    vices.
Gibson, Dunn & Crutcher LLP
Grocery Manufacturers of America
Harvey and Mildred Mudd Foun-
    dation
Hydril Company
Illinois Tool Works Inc.
Inter-Con Security Systems Inc.
Inter-Con Security Systems, Inc.
    Kraft Foods, Inc.
Interspan Communications,
Junior Achievement of Chicago
Kellogg Graduate School of
    Management, Northwestern
Lake Forest Academy Board of
    Trustees
Lake Forest Bank and Trust
Lake Forest College
Louise Taft Semple Foundation
Lyric Opera of Chicago
McCormick Tribune Foundation
McDonald's Corporation
Media Security and Reliability
    Council, FCC
Museum of Science and Industry,
    Northwestern University
Boy Scouts of America
Newspaper Association of America
Nordstrom Inc.
Northern Trust Corporation

Northwestern Memorial Foundation
Northwestern Memorial Health-
Care
Partner, Gibson, Dunn & Crutcher
LLP
PepsiCo Inc,
Quaker Oats Company
Reyes Holdings LLC
Ronald McDonald House Charities
Rush-Presbyterian-St. Luke's
Medical Center
Schering-Plough Corporation
Schlumberger Limited
Secretary of Defense to the
Defense Policy Advisory
Committee on Trade (DPACT)
Southern Star Group and Fifth
Third Bancorp
Standard Technology, Inc.
Taft Broadcasting Comp
The Union Central Life Insurance
Company
Tupperware Corporation
United Way of Metropolitan
Chicago Inc.
University of Notre Dame Board of
Trustees
Wells Fargo & Company
Wintrust Financial Corporation
World Business Chicago
YMCA of Metropolitan Chicago

News Corp.
Allen & Company LLC
Arthur M. Siskind
British Airways
Georgetown University
Independent Newspapers Limited
Partner Kleiner, Perkins, Caulfield
& Byers

Rothschild Investment Trust C.P.
Tsinghua University of Beijing

AOL/Time Warner
Apollo Theatre Foundation
Citigroup
Estee Lauder
Colonial Williamsburg Foundation
Museum of Modern Art
Howard University
Committee to Encourage Corporate
Philanthropy
Barksdale Management Corporation
Colgate-Palmolive Company
Harvard University
Hills & Company
Hilton Hotels Corporation
ZG Ventures, L.L.C.

General Electric
America Movil
American Accounting Association
American Film Institute
American Museum of Natural
History
Anheuser-Busch Companies, Inc.
Ann Taylor Stores
Avon, U.S.
Babson College
Bechtel Group, Inc.
Boston Museum of Science.
Boys & Girls Clubs of America.
ChevronTexaco Corporation
Chubb Corporation
Coca-Cola Company
Columbia Business School.
Cosmetic, Toiletry and Fragrance
Association.
Dell Inc.
Douglas A. Warner III

GE Capital Services
General Electric Company
General Motors Corporation
Grupo ALFA
Grupo Carso
Grupo Mexico
Grupo Televisa
Hamilton College and Xavier
    University
Home Depot, Inc.
Internet Security Systems, Inc.
Investment Co. of America.
J.P. Morgan Chase & Co.
Kellogg Company
Kimberly-Clark de Mexico, S.A.
Lauder Institute Board of
    Governors (Wharton School
    of Arts & Sciences)
Mexico Fund, Inc.
Microsoft Corporation
Motorola, Inc.
Museum of Television and Radio
    Motion Picture and Television
    Fund Corporation
NBC Universal
New York Presbyterian Hospital
Nuclear Threat Initiative
Ogilvy & Mather North America
    CEO, chairman
Partners Healthcare
Penske Corporation
Procter & Gamble.
Scientific-Atlanta, Inc.
Simmons College
United Auto Group, Inc.
United States Senate *Ret.*
Universal Technical Institute, Inc.
World Wildlife Fund

Walt Disney
Boeing Company
California Health Care Foundation
CB Richard Ellis, Inc.
Northwest Airlines Corporation
Clorox
DLA Piper Rudnick Gray Cary
    LLP
Duke University
Estée Lauder Companies Inc.
FedEx Corporation
Georgetown University
Gillette Company
Halliburton Co.
ImpreMedia, LLC
Inditex S.A.
International Air Transport Associ-
    ation.
KMart Holding Corporation
Lincoln Center for the Performing
    Arts in New York City.
McKesson Corporation.
Preti, Flaherty, Beliveau &
    Pachios
Siemens Pyramid
Staples Inc.
SunAmerica Asset Management
    Corp.
Sybase, Inc.
Tenet Healthcare Corporation.
The Keck School of Medicine at
    the University of Southern Cali-
    fornia
United States Senator from 1980 to
    1995
University of California
University of Southern California
Western Asset
Yahoo!, Inc

Viacom

Akamai Technologies, Inc.
American Express Co.
American International Group, Inc.
Automatic Data Processing, Inc.
Bear Stearns Companies Inc.
    Boston University Law School
Brandeis University
Cadwalader, Wickersham & Taft
Cardinal Health, Inc.
CineBridge Ventures, Inc.
Cohen Group
Combined Jewish Philanthropies
National Association of Theatre
    Owners,
Consolidated Edison, Inc.
Dana Farber Cancer Institute
DND Capital Partners, L.L.C
European Fine Arts Foundation
Gabelli Asset Management

Head N.V.
John F. Kennedy Library Foundation
Lafarge North America Inc.
Lourie & Cutler
Midway Games Inc.
MovieTickets.com, Inc
Museum of Fine Arts in Boston
National Amusements, Inc.
National College of Probate Judges
Oracle Corporation
Popular Inc.
Rising Star Media
Sonesta International Hotels Corporation.
Lourie & Cutler, P.C.
United States House of Representatives 1973–1979
Willis Group Holdings Limited
Winer and Abrams

Broadcast News Media Ownership Empires

NEWS CORPORATION

TELEVISION

Fox Broadcasting Company: Atlanta, GA: WAGA; Austin, TX: KTBC; Baltimore, MD: WUTB; Birmingham, AL: WBRC; Boston, MA: WFXT; Chicago, IL: WFLD and WPWR; Cleveland, OH: WJW; Dallas, TX: KDFI and KDFW; Denver, CO: KDVR; Detroit, MI: WJBK; Greensboro, NC: WGHP; Houston, TX: KRIV and KTXH; Kansas City, MO: KDAF; Los Angeles, CA: KCOP and KTTV; Memphis, TN: WHBQ; Milwaukee, WI: WITI; Minneapolis–St. Paul, MN: KMSP and WFTC; New York, NY: WNYW and WWOR; Ocala, : WOGX; Orlando, FL: WOFL and WRBW; Philadelphia, PA: WTXF; Phoenix, AZ: KSAZ and KUTP; Salt Lake City, UT: KSTU; St. Louis, MO: KTVI; Tampa, FL: WTVT; and Washington, DC: WTTG.

BSkyB-FOXTEL, Fox Movie Channel, Fox News Channel, Fox Sports Arizona, Fox Sports Bay Area (with Rainbow Media Holdings), Fox Sports Chicago (with Rainbow Media Holdings), Fox Sports Detroit, Fox Sports Intermountain West, Fox Sports Midwest, Fox Sports Net, Fox Sports New England (with Rainbow Media), Fox Sports New York (with Rainbow Media), Fox Sports Northwest, Fox Sports Ohio (with Rainbow Media), Fox Sports Pittsburgh, Fox Sports Rocky Mountain, Fox Sports South, Fox Sports Southeast, Fox Sports West, Fox Sports West #2, FX, National Geographic Channel, SKYPerfecTV, SPEED Channel, STAR, and Stream.

FILM

20th Century Fox, Fox Searchlight Pictures, and Fox Television Studios.

MAGAZINES

donna hay, InsideOut, SmartSource, TV Guide, and *The Weekly Standard.*

BOOKS

HarperCollins Publishers: Access Travel, Amistad Press, Avon, Branded Books Program, Cliff Street Books, The Ecco Press, Eos, HarperAudio, HarperBusiness, HarperCollins, HarperCollins General Book Group, HarperEntertainment, HarperInformation, HarperResource, HarperSanFrancisco, HarperTorch, Morrow/Avon, Perennial, Regan Books, Quill, William Morrow, William Morrow Cookbooks, and Zondervan. **HarperCollins Children's Book Group**: Greenwillow Books, HarperFestival, HarperTrophy, Joanna Cotler Books, and Laura Geringer Books.

NEWSPAPERS

United States: *New York Post.* **United Kingdom**: *News of the World, News International, Sun, Sunday Times,* and *The Times.* **Australia**: *Advertiser, Australian,*

Courier-Mail, Daily Telegraph, Fiji Times, Gold Coast BAdvertiser, Australian, Courier-Mail, Daily Telegraph, Fiji Times, Gold Coast Bulletin, Herald Sun, Mercury, Newsphotos, Newspix, Newstext, NT News, PostCourier, Sunday Herald Sun, Sunday Mail, Sunday Tasmanian, Sunday Telegraph, Sunday Territorian,ulletin, Herald Sun, Mercury, Newsphotos, Newspix, Newstext, NT News, PostCourier, Sunday Herald Sun, Sunday Mail, Sunday Tasmanian, Sunday Telegraph, Sunday Territorian, Sunday Times, and Weekly Times.

TIME WARNER INC.

TELEVISION

Cartoon Network, Cartoon Network in Europe, Cartoon Network in Latin America, Entertainment Networks, TBS Superstation, TNT & Cartoon Network in Asia/Pacific, Turner Classic Movies, Turner Entertainment, Turner Network Television (TNT), and Turner South.

CABLE

CNN, CNN Airport Network, CNN en Español, CNN fn, CNN Headline News, CNN Interactive, CNN International, CNN Radio, Court TV (with Liberty Media), HBO, Kablevision (cable television in Hungary—53.75 percent), New York 1 News (24-hour news channel devoted only to NYC), Road Runner, and Time Warner Cable.

FILM

Film Production: Fine Line Features, New Line Cinema, and Turner Original Productions.

FILM & TV PRODUCTION/DISTRIBUTION

Castle Rock Entertainment, Warner Brothers, Warner Brothers Domestic Pay TV, Warner Brothers Domestic Television Distribution, Warner Brothers International Television Distribution, Warner Brothers International Theaters (owns/operates multiplex theaters in over 12 countries), Warner Brothers Studios, Warner Brothers Television (production), Warner Brothers Television Animation, The Warner Channel (Latin America, Asia Pacific, Australia, and Germany), Warner Home Video, The WB Television Network, HannaBarbera Cartoons, Telepictures Production, and Witt Thomas Productions.

MAGAZINES

All You, Asiaweek (Asian news weekly), *Business 2.0, Dancyu* (Japanese cooking), *Entertainment Weekly, EW Metro, Field & Stream, Fortune, Freeze, Golf Magazine, Inside Stuff, In Style, Life, Money, Outdoor Life, People, People en Español, Popular Science, President* (Japanese business monthly), *Progressive Farmer, Real Simple, Ride BMX, Salt Water Sportsman, SI for Kids, Ski, Skiing Magazine, Skiing Trade News, SNAP, Snowboard Life, Southern Accents, Southern Living, Sports Illustrated, Sports Illustrated International, Sunset, Sunset Garden Guide, Teen People, This Old House, The Ticket, Time, Time Asia, Time Atlantic, Time Canada, Time for Kids, Time Latin*

America, Time Money, Time South Pacific, Today's Homeowner, TransWorld Skateboarding, TransWorld Snowboarding, Verge, Wallpaper (UK), *Warp, Weight Watchers, Who Weekly, Yachting Magazine,* and *Your Future.* **American Express Publishing Corporation** (partial ownership/management): *Departures, Food & Wine, SkyGuide, Travel & Leisure,* and *Your Company.* **The Health Publishing Group**: *Health, Hippocrates, Coastal Living,* and *Cooking Light.* **The Parent Group**: *Parenting, Baby on the Way,* and *Baby Talk.* **Magazines listed under Warner Brothers label**: *DC Comics, Mad Magazine, Milestone, Paradox,* and *Vertigo.*

MUSIC

Recording Labels: American Recordings, Asylum, Atlantic Classics, The Atlantic Group, Atlantic Jazz, Atlantic Nashville, Atlantic Theater, Big Beat, Blackground, Breaking, CGD East West, China, Coalition, Continental, DRO East West, East-West, East West ZTT, Elektra, Elektra Entertainment Group, Elektra/Sire, Erato, Fazer, Finlandia, Giant, Igloo, Lava, Magneoton, Maverick, MCM, Mesa/Bluemoon, Modern, Nonesuch, 1 43, Qwest, Reprise, Reprise Nashville, Revolution, Rhino Records, Teldec, Warner Alliance, Warner Brothers, Warner Brothers Records, Warner Music International, Warner Nashville, Warner Resound, Warner Sunset, and WEA Telegram. **Other Recording Interests**: Ivy Hill Corporation (printing and packaging), Warner/Chappell Music (publishing company), Warner Special Products, and WEA, Inc. (sales, distribution, and manufacturing). **Joint Ventures**: Channel V (with Sony, EMI, Bertelsmann, and News Corp.), Columbia House, Heartland Music (direct order of country and gospel music—50 percent), Music Choice and Music Choice Europe (with Sony, EMI, and General Instrument), MusicNet (with RealNetworks, EMI, and BMG), Music Sound Exchange (direct marketing—with Sony), and Viva (German music video channel—with Sony, Polygram, and EMI).

SPORTS

Atlanta Braves, Atlanta Hawks, Atlanta Thrashers, Good Will Games, Philips Arena, and Turner Sports.

BOOKS

Back Bay Books; BookoftheMonth Club, Bulfinch Press, Children's BookoftheMonth Club, Crafter's Choice, History Book Club, HomeStyle Books, Leisure Arts, Little, Brown and Company, Little Brown and Company (UK), Money Book Club, The Mysterious Press, One Spirit, Oxmoor House (subsidiary of Southern Progress Corporation), Paperback Book Club, Sunset Books, Time Life AudioBooks, Time Life Books, Time Life Education, Time Life International, Time Life Music, TW Kids, Warner Aspect, Warner Books, Warner Treasures, and Warner Vision.

OTHER OPERATIONS

Amazon.com (partial), AOL MovieFone, CNN Newsroom (daily news program for classrooms), iAmaze, Netscape Communications, Netscape Netcenter portal, Quack.com, Streetmail (partial), Switchboard (6 percent), Turner Adventure Learning (electronic field trips for schools), Turner Home Satellite, Turner Learning, and Turner Network Sales.

ONLINE SERVICES

AOL.com portal, AOL Europe, AOL Instant Messenger, CompuServe Interactive Services, Digital City, DrKoop.com, ICQ, The Knot, Inc. (wedding content—8 percent with QVC 36 percent and Hummer), WinbladFunds, MapQuest.com (pending regulatory approval), Spinner.com, Winamp, and Legend (Internet service in China—49 percent). **Online/Other Publishing**: Africana.com, American Family Publishers (50 percent), Pathfinder, Road Runner, and Warner Publisher Time Distribution Services.

THEME PARKS

Warner Brothers Recreation Enterprises (owns/operates international theme parks).

MERCHANDISE/RETAIL

Warner Bros. Consumer Products.

VIACOM

TELEVISION

CBS Stations: Austin, TX: KEYE; Baltimore, MD: WJZ; Boston, MA: WBZ; Chicago, IL: WBBM; Dallas–Fort Worth, TX: KTVT; Denver, CO: KCNC, Detroit, MI: WWJ; Green Bay, WI: WFRV; Los Angeles, CA: KCBS; Miami–Ft. Lauderdale, FL: WFOR; Minneapolis, MN: WCCO; New York, NY: WCBS; Philadelphia, PA: KYW; Pittsburgh, PA: KDKA; Salt Lake City, UT: KUTV; and San Francisco, CA: KPIX. **UPN Stations**: Atlanta, GA: WUPA; Boston, MA: WSBK; Columbus, OH: WWHO; Dallas, TX: KTXA; Detroit, MI: WKBD, Indianapolis, IN: WNDY; Miami, FL: WBFS; New Orleans, LA: WUPL; Norfolk, VA: WGNT; Oklahoma City, OK: KAUT; Philadelphia, PA: WPSG; Pittsburgh, PA: WNPA; Providence, RI: WLWC; Sacramento, CA: KMAX; San Francisco, CA: KBHK; Seattle, WA: KSTW; Tampa, FL: WTOG; and West Palm Beach, FL: WTVX. **Others**: Alexandria, MN: KCCO; Escanaba, WI: WJMN; Los Angeles, CA: KCAL; Walker, MN: KCCW; and Washington, UT: KUSG.

CABLE

MTV, MTV2, Nickelodeon, BET, Nick at Nite, TV Land, NOGGIN, VH1, Spike TV, CMT, Comedy Central Showtime, The Movie Channel, Flix, and Sundance Channel. **Television Production and Distribution**: Spelling Television, Big Ticket Television, and King World Productions.

FILM

Paramount Home Entertainment and Paramount Pictures.

PUBLISHING

Simon & Schuster, Pocket Books, Scribner, Free Press, Fireside, Touchstone, Washington Square Press, Archway, Minstrel, and Pocket Pulse.

OTHER

Blockbuster, Paramount Parks, Famous Players theater chain, United Cinemas International (50 percent), and Famous Music.

RADIO

Infinity Broadcasting: Atlanta, GA: WAOK, WVEE, and WZGC; Austin, TX: KAMX, KJCE, KKMJ, and KQBT; Baltimore, MD: WBGR, WBMD, WJFK, WLIF, WQSR, WWMX, and WXYV; Boston, MA: WBCN, WBMX, WBZ, WODS, and WZLX; Buffalo, NY: WBLK, WBUF, WECK, WJYE, and WYRK; Charlotte, NC: WBAV, WFNZ, WGIV, WNKS, WPEG, WSOC, and WSSS; Chicago, IL: WBBM, WCKG, WJMK, WSCR, WUSN, and WXRT; Cincinnati, OH: WAQZ, WGRR, WKRQ, and WUBE; Cleveland, OH: WDOK, WNCX, WQAL, and WXTM; Columbus, OH: WAZU, WHOK, and WLVQ; Dallas, TX: KLUV, KOAI, KRBV, KRLD, KVIL, and KYNG; Denver, CO: KDJM, KIMN, and KXKL; Detroit, MI: WKRK, WOMC, WVMV, WWJ, WXYT, and WYCD; Fresno, CA: KMGV, KMJ, KOOR, KOQO, KRNC, KSKS, and KVSR; Greensboro/Winston-Salem, NC: WMFR, WSJS, and WSML; Hartford, CT: WRCH, WTIC, and WZMX; Houston, TX: KIKK and KILT; Kansas City, MO: KBEQ, KFKF, KMXV, and KSRC; Las Vegas, NV: KLUC, KMXB, KMZQ, KSFN, KXNT, and KXTE; Los Angeles, CA: KCBS, KEZN, KFWB, KLSX, KNX, KROQ, KRTH, and KTWV; Memphis, TN: WMC and WMFS; Minneapolis–St. Paul, MN: KDOW, WCCO, WLTE, and WXPT; Orlando, FL: WJHM, WOCL, and WOMX; New York, NY: WCBS, WFAN, WINS, WNEW, and WXRK; Philadelphia, PA: KYW, WIP, WOGL, WPHT, and WYSP; Phoenix, AZ: KMLE, KOOL, and KZON; Pittsburgh, PA: KDKA, WBZZ, WDSY, and WZPT; Portland, OR: KINK, KLTH, KUFO, KUPL, and KVM; Riverside, CA: KFRG, KVFG, KVVQ, and KXFG; Rochester, NY: WCMF, WPXY, WRMM, and WZNE; Sacramento, CA: KHTK, KNCI, KSFM, KXOA, KYMX, and KZZO; St. Louis, MO: KEZK, KMOX, and KYKY; San Antonio, TX: KTFM and KTSA; San Diego, CA: KPLN and KYXY; San Francisco,CA: KCBS, KFRC, KITS, KKWV, KLLC, and KYCY; San Jose, CA: KBAY and KEZR; Seattle, WA: KBKS, KMPS, KYCW, KYPT, and KZOK; Tampa, FL: WLLD, WQYK, WRBQ, WSJT, and WYUU; Washington, DC: WARW, WHFS, WJFK, and WPGC; and West Palm Beach, FL: WEAT, WIRK, WJBW, WMBX, and WPBZ.

VIVENDI UNIVERSAL

FILM AND TELEVISION

Universal Studios, Universal Pictures, October Films (majority interest), Universal Studios Home Video, United International Pictures (international distribution—33 percent), and Cinema International BV (video distribution—49 percent). **Television Production and Distribution**: CANAL+ (European payTV provider—51 percent), Universal Television Group (production and distribution), BrillsteinGrey Entertainment (50 percent) production, Multimedia Entertainment, USA Networks Inc. (43 percent), and Universal Pay Television (international distribution). **Partial ownership**: HBO Asia Telecine (Brazil), Cinecanal (Latin America), Showtime (Australia), Star Channel (Japan), and Telepiu (Italian pay television).

PUBLISHING

Rolling Stone, Larousse, Nathan, Anaya, Coktel, Atica, Scipione, Bordas, Retz, Robert Laffont, PlonPerrin, Les Presses—Solar Belfond, La Decouverte & Syros, Les Presses de la Renaissance, Pocket Jeuness 10/18, Fleuve Noir, Sierra, and Blizzard Entertainment.

INTERACTIVE

Universal Studios New Media Group, Universal Studios Online, Universal.com, Universal Interactive Studios (software and video games), Universal Digital Arts, Interplay (video game producer—majority ownership), GetMusic (online music retailer), Vizzavi (European multiaccess portal), Education.com, Flipside.com, @viso (50 percent with Softbank), AlloCiné, Bonjour.fr, Ad2One, Atmedica, Scoot, EMusic.com, Duet (with Sony), and MP3.com.

MUSIC

Universal Music Group: All Nations Catalog, Decca Records, Deutsche Grammophon, Geffen/DGC Records, GRP Recording Company, HipO Records, Interscope Music Publishing, Interscope Records, MCA Music Publishing, MCA Records, MCA Records Nashville, Motown, Polygram, Rising Tide, Universal Concerts (concert promotion), Universal Music and Video Distribution, Universal Music International, and Universal Records.

OTHER

Cinema International Corporation (international theaters—49 percent), Cineplex Odeon Corporation (theaters—42 percent), Duet (musicsubscription service with Yahoo! and Sony), United Cinemas International (international theaters—49 percent), Vivendi Environnement (the world's #1 water distributor), Vivendi Universal (owns 26.8 million shares in Time Warner), and Viventures (venture capital fund).

THEME PARKS/RECREATION/RETAIL

Universal Studios Hollywood: CityWalk. **Universal Orlando Resort**: CityWalk, Hard Rock Hotel, Portofino Bay Hotel, Royal Pacific Resort, Universal's Islands of Adventure Theme Park, Universal Studios Theme Park, CityWalk, Hotel Port Aventura, Universal Mediterranea (Spain), Universal Mediterranea Theme Park, Universal Studios Japan, and WetnWild Orlando.

TELECOMMUNICATION

Vivendi Telecom International, and Cegetel.

RETAIL

Spencer Gifts.

WALT DISNEY COMPANY

BROADCASTING
(INCLUDES THE CAPITAL CITY/ABC SUBSIDIARY)

Television: ABC Television Network. **Owned and Operated Television Stations**: Chicago, IL: WLS; Flint, MI: WJRT; Fresno, CA: KFSN; Houston, TX: KTRK; Los Angeles, CA: KABC; New York, NY: WABC; Philadelphia, PA: WPVI; Raleigh-Durham, NC: WTVD; San Francisco, CA: KGO; and Toledo, OH: WTVG. **Radio Stations**: ESPN Radio (syndicated programming); Albany, NY: WPPY; Atlanta, GA: WDWD, WKHX, and WYAY; Boston, MA: WMKI; Charlotte, NC: WGFY; Chicago, IL: WLS, WMVP, WRDZ, and WZZN; Cleveland, OH: WWMK; Dallas, TX: KESN, KMEO, KMKI, KSCS, and WBAP; Damascus, MD: WDMV; Denver, CO: KADZ and KDDZ; Detroit, MI: WDRQ, WDVD, and WJR; Flint, MI: WFDF; Fremont, OH: WFRO; Hartford, CT: WDZK; Houston, TX: KMIC; Jacksonville, FL: WBML; Kansas City, MO: KPHN; Los Angeles, CA: KABC, KDIS, KLOS, and KSPN; Louisville, KY: WDRD; Miami, FL: WMYM; Minneapolis–St. Paul, MN: KDIZ, KQRS, KXXR, WGVX, WGVY, and WGVZ; Mobile, AL: WQUA; New York, NY: WABC, WEVD, WPLJ, and WQEW; Norfolk, VA: WHKT; Oakland, CA: KMKY; Orlando, FL: WDYZ; Philadelphia, PA: WWJZ; Phoenix, AZ: KMIX; Pittsburgh, PA: WEAE; Providence, RI: WDDZ; Radio Disney; Richmond, VA: WDZY; Sacramento, CA: KIID; San Francisco, CA: KGO and KSFO; Seattle, WA: KKDZ; St. Louis, MO: WSDZ; Tampa, FL: WWMI; Washington; DC: WJZW, WMAL, and WRQX; West Palm Beach, FL: WMNE; and Wichita, KS: KQAM.

CABLE

A&E Television (37.5 percent with Hearst and GE); ABC Family; The Disney Channel; E! Entertainment (with Comcast and Liberty Media); ESPN, Inc., which includes Classic Sports Network, ESPN, ESPN2, ESPN News, ESPN Now, and ESPN Extreme (80 percent; Hearst Corporation owns the remaining 20 percent); SoapNet; Toon Disney; The History Channel (with Hearst and GE); Lifetime Movie Network (50 percent with Hearst); and Lifetime Television (50 percent with Hearst). **International Broadcast**: The Disney Channel Australia; The Disney Channel France; The Disney Channel Italy; The Disney Channel Malaysia; The Disney Channel Middle East; The Disney Channel Spain; The Disney Channel Taiwan; The Disney Channel UK; ESPN, Inc., International Ventures; ESPN Brazil (50 percent); ESPN STAR (sports programming throughout Asia—50 percent); Net STAR (33 percent), owners of The Sports Network of Canada; and Sportsvision of Australia (25 percent).

BOOKS

Hyperion Books, Miramax Books, and Walt Disney Company Book Publishing.

MAGAZINES

Magazine Subsidiary Groups: ABC Publishing Group; Disney Publishing, Inc.;

Diversified Publications Group; Financial Services and Medical Group; Miller Publishing Company. **Magazines:** *Automotive Industries, Biography* (with GE and Hearst), *Discover, Disney Adventures, Disney Magazine, ECN News, ESPN Magazine* (distributed by Hearst), *Family Fun, Institutional Investor, JCK, Kodin, Quality, Top Famille* (French family magazine), *Us Weekly* (50 percent), and *Video Business.*

MULTIMEDIA

Walt Disney Internet Group: ABC.com, ABC Internet Group, ABCNEWS.com, Disney.com, Disney Interactive (develops/markets computer software video games, and CDROMs), Disney Online (Web sites and content), Disney's Daily Blast, ESPN Internet Group, ESPN.sportzone.com, Family.com, Go Network, Mr. Showbiz, NASCAR.com, NBA.com, Oscar.com, Skillgames, Soccernet.com (60 percent), Toysmart.com (educational toys—majority stake), and Wall of Sound.

THEME PARKS & RESORTS

Disney Cruise Line, The Disney Institute, Disneyland (Anaheim, CA), Disneyland Paris, Disneyland Resort, Disney MGM Studios, Disney Regional Entertainment (entertainment end theme dining in metro areas), Disney's Animal Kingdom, Disney Vacation Club, Epcot, Magic Kingdom, Tokyo Disneyland (partial ownership), Walt Disney World (Orlando, FL), and Walt Disney World Sports Complex (golf course, auto racing track, and baseball complex).

FILM PRODUCTION AND DISTRIBUTION

Buena Vista Home Entertainment, Buena Vista Home Video, Buena Vista International, Caravan Pictures, Hollywood Pictures, Miramax Films, Touchstone Pictures, and Walt Disney Pictures.

FINANCIAL AND RETAIL

Financial: Sid R. Bass (crude petroleum and natural gas production—partial interest). **Retail:** The Disney Store.

MUSIC

Buena Vista Music Group, Hollywood Records (popular music and soundtracks for motion pictures), Lyric Street Records (Nashville-based country music label), Mammoth Records (popular and alternative music label), and Walt Disney Records.

THEATER AND SPORTS

Theatrical Productions: Walt Disney Theatrical Productions (productions include stage versions of *The Lion King, Beauty and the Beast,* and *King David*). **Professional Sports Franchises:** Anaheim Sports, Inc. and Mighty Ducks of Anaheim (National Hockey League).

OTHER INTERNATIONAL VENTURES

Hamster Productions (French television production), Japan Sports Channel, RTL2 (German television production and distribution), Scandinavian Broadcasting System, TeleMunchen (German television production and distribution), Tesauro of

Spain, and TV Sport of France. **Television Production and Distribution**: Buena Vista Television, Touchstone Television, Walt Disney Television, Walt Disney Television Animation (has three wholly owned production facilities outside the United States—Japan, Australia, and Canada).

SOURCES: U.S. Securities and Exchange Commission, <sec.gov/edgar/search edgar/webusers.htm> and *Columbia Journalism Review,* <www.cjr.org/tools/owners>.

CHAPTER 7

Media Democracy in Action

**MEDIA REFORM CONFERENCE 2005 AND UPDATES
ON INDEPENDENT MEDIA GROUPS INCLUDING: COMMON
DREAMS.ORG, BUZZFLASH.COM, CENTER FOR DIGITAL
DEMOCRACY, A-INFOS.CA, THE AUSTRALIAN GREENS:
WWW.GREENS.ORG.AU**

By Project Censored Interns: Sandy Brown, Joni Wallent, Kristine Snyder, Luke Judd, Christopher Cox, Jacob Rich, Lori Rouse, Mark Thompson, Sean Arlt, Brittny Roeland, and Britt Walters

Activism and Optimism: The National Conference for Media Reform 2005 St Louis

BY SANDY BROWN

On a beautiful May afternoon, four Project Censored intern-activists took flight en route to St. Louis, Missouri, with two others following close behind. We were some of the several thousands of concerned citizens converging on *The Gateway to the West* to participate in the National Conference for Media Reform May 13-15, 2005. We were filled with a sense of excitement, anticipating the four days of exploration, discourse and activism. All six of us had been working with Project Censored for some time, some of us two years or more, and hungered for the opportunity to place names with faces, to shake the hands of those journalists, educators and activists who had so profoundly affected the course of our educations. Bob McChesney,

Amy Goodman, George Lakoff, and Bill Moyers are heroes to some of us and an inspiration to all. The four days that followed blurred together into a collage of catch phrases and mental snap shots. Each night we would return to our rooms and marvel over the powerful messages we had consumed and struggle with how we might share this enthusiasm and momentum with those who could not be with us. Our subjective experiences at the end of this marvelous journey were married on the plane trip and car ride home. We are inspired to carry this message of hope and change into our lives, our school, our communities. Some of us will write, some produce documentaries, and some will sing poetry. We have all returned to work, to stand on the front lines of this movement that has the potential to rescue our failing democracy.

Directly Gathering Solutions and Momentum for Action: Spoken Words

BY JONI WALLENT—Student/Intern/Activist
To: St. Louis, Missouri, for the 2nd National Conference for Media Reform.

And what's going to happen next for the average person who doesn't accept what the media decides the news will be, controlling what eyeballs see? I am in looking out the airplane window, gathering momentum representing one organization, one student, one concerned and energetic individual. The following is a selection of the jewels I gathered through mind-bending, plug-yourself-in conversations taken home in the notes furiously scribbled on the open pages of my yellow three ring binder. Armed with pen in hand I listened as discussions twisted and challenged the collective minds of attendees around solutions.

"All we have to do is organize and we will win."—Robert McChesney.

The National Conference for Media Reform served as a strengthening of network and support for the freedom-of-information effort—reminding us we have the choice, if we don't like what's given, to turn off that which we don't like, and take the next step: ACTION. The conference lecture rooms and corridors resonated in a three-day solution-oriented vibe that noted our unique powers of direct action. Empowering panel discussions encouraged the direct calling of legislative and corporate representatives—as our voices need to be heard—the need to write letters to magazine and newspaper editors, addressing concerns inside envelopes, and to take to the information highways and the streets, as both blogger and protestor communicate and meet. Our media is political. It is a public space we use to discuss all other issues, serving a politically universal audience. At the National Conference our gathering of momentum was for productive media reform—not to criticize the corporate-control of private interest exercised over our media, but rather to focus on solutions that reclaim it. Attendees came together to support, network, and take positive steps forward in this discussion of our media.

To make change, to reclaim, Mark Cooper reminds us, "We need bottom-up heat—as consumers realize they are also producers, and each listener is also a speaker." Salim Muwakkil adds, "Whoever controls the media controls our destiny," encouraging the need for participation from all.

So what are the weaknesses of the left, what are the strengths of the right, and aren't the issues of free of speech and open media concerns that unite? Let's become our own media makers, creating info structures and networks of distribution. Be involved—respond and contribute—facing challenges not as red or blue, but collective purple states. And for the average people who don't accept the pre-spun lies news anchors read, let's be the traveling packs of journalists pulling out notepads from back pockets, because if each person acts like a tower with a signal we can reclaim the vacuums of our media as this conference reaffirmed the Call for solution-oriented Action.

Frequencies of Change
BY LUKE JUDD—Project Censored Intern/Activist/Film Maker

Over two thousand people gathered inside the Millennium Hotel in St. Louis for the 2005 National Media Reform Conference on May 13th, 14th, and 15th. Assumingly, the site was selected for geographic centrality. But being in the shadow of the arch and across the bridge from East St. Louis (AKA Monsanto town), held much greater symbolism than intended.

The Gateway arch, which is commonly referred to as the 'gateway to the west', reminds visitors by its design that everything that goes up must come down, and that all lines on a globe are round. And that was really the theme of the conference, that of hope. The whole weekend was filled with inspiring and empowering speeches. For me, one of the most powerful quotes came from author Norman Solomon during a Friday session entitled "News, Information and Corporate Media." After eloquent speeches by author Naomi Klein and journalist Juan Gonzalez, Solomon urged the over-capacity audience to, "Save pessimism for better times."

Solomon's attitude seemed to permeate the conference and the weekend.

There was not the Bush-bashing that one might expect to hear, but rather people networking, brainstorming and sharing solution-based ideas. The motto of the conference was "Gathering Momentum." That is exactly what one glorious weekend in St. Louis accomplished. Now we have to keep the momentum.

Though the media reform movement is up against the most powerful propaganda machine this planet has ever seen, it helps to remember that no government or border has withstood the eternal test of time. And as much as some of us may feel the course of this nation is a runaway train, the tracks are just smoke and mirrors. It's our job now, in the Media Reform Movement, to spoil the trick for those who still believe in magic.

I See a Future and It Is Bright

BY SANDY BROWN—Student/Intern/Activist/Documentary Film Maker

As the plane ascended and the customary hush fell over our fellow travelers, I found myself utterly energized, no doubt alienating all those around me with my incessant chatter. "Do you think we will get to interview Amy Goodman... I heard Phil Donahue was speaking... I wonder if there will be a lot of other students attending... Do you think we can find some good Blues... I've heard great things about the soul food in St. Louis." My voice was faltering as the plane touched down and my compatriots and I stepped out into the sultry evening air. Peter Phillips, Director of Project Censored, our professor and mentor, smiled and directed us to our van. A short while later, weary from the trip, we arrived at our accommodations... The luxury suites, i.e. those with running hot water, at the Budget Inn, nestled most intimately next to Dirt Cheap Cigarettes and Dirt Cheap Gas and Beer. The ambiance was all I had come to expect as a student intern and I dropped gratefully onto my perfectly broken-in mattress. None of us slept very well. My roommate Joni and I giggled and chatted well into the early morning, much too excited to sleep. It was all I could do to stay in bed. I was going to be interviewing people who had been making change, real change in the world and I was a part of that. I felt I was the luckiest girl in the world.

FRIDAY MAY 13, 2005: Seven o'clock arrived much earlier than usual and Joni and I were thankful for the abundant supply of reasonably hot water. Bleary-eyed and a little shaky, we all filed into the van after a brief 'shot gun' battle for the coveted front seat. St. Louis sparkled in the early morning light and our eyes searched the horizon for the landmark we all knew was just beyond our sight. My heart skipped when I first glimpsed The Arch.

It seemed unreasonable, much, much too big and to me and a little unwieldy, maybe even oddly representative of *The Mass Media Monster* I had imagined we had journeyed to engage in battle. I committed myself to an adventure in the belly of the beast later that day.

The Millennium Hotel, home to the conference and many attendees was situated Downtown directly across from The Arch. As we entered the convention area my eyes darted about seeking out that familiar face. I knew they were there, or would be shortly, and I waited with bated breath for our first encounter. What followed were three full days of back to back interviews, rushed meals and abbreviated phone calls. The environment was charged with kinetic energy and it was contagious. No sooner had we finished with one mind-blowing encounter, than Joni, my producer and public relations Diva, would lead me to the next. My mind reels in reflection on the conversations witnessed by me and my camera.

George Lakoff, in his endearing and enthusiastic manner reminded me to never forget the power of language and the interpretation of meaning. "We all have a metaphor for the nation as 'family.' We have founding fathers. We send our sons and daughters to war. So I worked out the details of that metaphor and when I did, I realized that if we have two different understandings of the nation, we have two different understandings of the family." It clicked. Suddenly I realized why blue collar America would vote for an administration that so obviously does not have its best interest at heart. One does not question an authoritarian father. You simply do as you're told and trust that all will be well. The media, having been so successful in feeding the public this perverted American portrait, has become more than complicit, it is culpable.

Amy Goodman, a long time role model of mine, articulated beautifully her hopes for the future of the media. Her understanding of the public's perspective and need for truth is illustrated by *Democracy Now!'s* massive syndication, now 300 stations strong. "We have to get more mainstream voices in the media. The media is not mainstream at all, but extreme. It does not represent most people." This struck me as profound, the concept of an 'extreme' media. This theme was expressed by many of the attendees and was the topic of several discussions.

Bill Moyers is, in fact, so disgusted by the current media climate and its lack of journalistic integrity that he is threatening to retire his rocking chair and return to the airwaves, no doubt to the chagrin of the folks at the Corporation for Public Broadcasting.

Even Bob McChesney, the conference facilitator, made time to speak with us. "To have an effective democracy, you can't have too much inequality. The United States has seen a stunning growth in inequality in the last 20 to 25 years and that's cancerous to democracy where everyone is supposed to be a political equal if not an economic equal. And that is a media problem. We have to ask, does our media system discourage inequality or encourage it? I think, regrettably, the evidence is very strong that our media system, by undercovering labor issues, by never covering this issue [media reform], by constantly hyping the issues of advertisers and corporations, encourages inequality and therefore, just on that level, is a significantly anti-democratic force."

Medea Benjamin, Danny Schechter, and Andy Messner are some of the many who spoke and contributed at the conference and took a moment to reflect on the media with us. The common denominator; "This is a time of coalition building and real progress. The movement has gained such momentum that change is inevitable."

As the editing process begins and I delve deeply into many hours of digital footage, I count my blessings slowly and carefully. I am a cog in this wheel of change. I feel the old ways grinding beneath the weight of it and bear the burden of this work with a light heart.

Media Reform Conference: We are the Mainstream!

BY KRISTINE SNYDER—Student/Intern/Activist

By far, the most exhilarating concept I brought home from the 2005 Media Reform Conference is the idea that this current reform movement is celebrating a parallel media. This is not an "alternative media" as I had become accustomed to calling the news from independent sources. This reformed media is not an alternative to corporate media. It is parallel and equal to corporate media. This movement celebrates the media being brought back to the public. It is the rebirth of our own media.

Real political change almost always begins with grass roots movements. Over and over people at the local level rather than at the center of major political activity have taken stands toward positive reform. The conference in St. Louis was a splendid celebration of yet another movement begun on a grass roots level. The question as to whether the movement will be a success was never a topic at hand. The high spirits of all attendees was a pleasure I did not expect. The seriousness of the terrible state of our current corporate media was not up for discussion, nor was it even a question to contemplate. The purpose of the reform convention was to discuss solution. This resounding attitude created a level of hope for all that attended; a level of hope we all brought back to our own local communities.

A huge solution buzzing at the conference was digital technology. The internet is an excellent example of this. Digital technology has been revolutionary and has radically altered the media landscape in terms of policy. The economic models that were in place have been demolished with this movement. Businesses are trying to make money and neither the FCC nor Congress knows what to do. Changes are happening too fast and their default is to protect existing players. Congress is pushing for only digital everywhere, which is of course driven by the current budget deficit. Huge conglomerates hold semi-permanent licenses on the public airways.

Today, only 40 percent of Americans have high speed internet. Pushing for community internet is the key. It is important to let localities have control of what is being set up! Congress is so busy protecting their existing players that they have forgotten to look at anyone else. Our up-and-coming parallel media is taking over…and with grand excitement!

This movement becomes a social justice issue when we look at the customers being targeted in the current digital market. People making over $75, 000 annually are 95 percent of the internet customers today. People making less than that make up only 5 percent of the current customer base. When there is no competition, there is no regulation, and equality, fairness, and representation issues always exist. Money and people are what move things. We are up against money but we have power with the people. Uniting with pride to make powerful change is not only stimulating but also motivating.

We have all suffered from inaccurate and untrue forms of history through all different forms of media. I arrived home realizing that community media need to support one another! People own the airwaves and we should be able to negotiate the value and use of those airwaves. Local communities should gain and retain control. I arrived home from St. Louis realizing what a special and momentious occasion had occurred. Let the celebration continue until we all meet again next year.

The Media Reform Movement Comes Alive in St. Louis

BY CHRISTOPHER ROBIN COX—Student/Activist/ Project Censored Intern

2,500 people took over the Millennium Hotel in downtown St. Louis, Missouri May 13-15 to collectively demonstrate how serious they are about mobilizing to fix the problems of our media. The Conference was a universal call to action for media activists. Speaker after speaker made it patently clear that media is an issue that affects us all, regardless of political ideology. Nearly fifty different panels were attended by people from 50 states and 10 countries. Danny Schechter, author of *Weapons of Mass Deception*, called it "the Million Word March."

Joni Wallent, Kristine Snyder, Britt Walters, Luke Judd, Sandy Brown, Peter Phillips and I represented Project Censored at the conference and were joined by organizations nationwide including: Free Speech Radio News and Television, Media Alliance, Adbusters, Center for Public Integrity, Indymedia, *The Nation*, *The Progressive*, *In These Times*, *Democracy Now!*, and the Pacifica Radio network.

Social theorist Lewis Gottschalk describes a "revolutionary event" as, "the event which demonstrates clearly that the conservative forces are no longer able to resist the revolutionary tide." If it were possible to label a single event as the moment when a social movement became revolutionary, the St. Louis Media Reform conference would be it.

Friday, May 13, was the first full day of action, and from the very first moment there was fresh electricity in the air. Exhibits were being set up in the Media Democracy Showcase—a vast room that contained tables filled with literature from every organization conceivable—while rooms all over the hotel were prepared for what would turn out to be a constant array of pertinent panel discussions, workshops, caucuses, and film showings.

Well-known media activists such as Amy Goodman, Jim Hightower, Al Franken, Norman Solomon, Phil Donohue, Naomi Klein and FCC commissioners Michael Copps and Jonathan Adelstein intermixed with the thousands of us focusing on solution-based approaches to media reform in the United States. Project Censored taped interviews with numerous participants including Medea Benjamin, Danny Schechter, George Lakoff, Amy Goodman, Robert W. McChesney, and Phil Donahue.

Bill Moyers described what he saw as the problem with corporate media today. "Judith Miller of the *New York Times*, among others, relied on the credibility of official but unnamed sources when she served essentially as the government stenographer for claims that Iraq possessed weapons of mass destruction. These 'rules of the game' permit Washington officials to set the agenda for journalism, leaving the press all too often simply to recount what officials say instead of subjecting their words and deeds to critical scrutiny. Instead of acting as filters for readers and viewers, sifting the truth from the propaganda, reporters and anchors attentively transcribe both sides of the spin, invariably failing to provide context, background or any sense of which claims hold up and which are misleading," Moyers said. "I decided long ago that this wasn't healthy for democracy."

Pete Tridish of the *Prometheus Radio Project* and Sascha Meinrath of the *Champaign-Urbana Community Wireless Network* (CUWiN) reported on the reality of wireless Internet communities. CUWiN is truly grassroots in their effort to bring Internet access to the world at large, one community at a time. The concept is simple: "A free wireless networking system that any municipality, company, or group of neighbors could easily set up themselves" (http://www.cuwireless.net). Sascha Meinrath spoke at length about this revolutionary grassroots technology. He lectured about a "mesh network" that is established with the use of nearby "nodes" on rooftops and the like. This makes it possible to establish Internet connectivity simply by installing the CUWiN network software. Perhaps the most grassroots element in this technology is the ability to disrupt, and indeed take over, the city center-based profit structure that Internet users are stuck with today.

Low-power radio is another technological frontier that was well represented at the conference. Pete Tridish was inspirational in his telling of the story of the beginnings of *Prometheus Radio Project* (PRP). Tridish spoke about "radio barn raising" events in which an entire radio station is built "from the microphone to the antennae." For more on PRP visit www.prometheusradio.org.

"For those of us who have been participating in the media reform movement for a decade or more, St. Louis was a point where a light at the end of the tunnel seems possible. Nowhere have I seen such enthusiasm for reform and the real prospect of success as was evident at this conference," said Peter Phillips, Director of Project Censored. "We are at a new point in the movement where the distrust of corporate news has opened the space for new sources of news for all Americans," Phillips added.

In an ideal world, there would be a conference like this every few months, so that all of people who are intensely unsatisfied with the media—70 percent according to Danny Schechter—could learn what Project Censored participants learned: that the media reform movement is exploding, and that the battle against corporate hegemony is winnable. In the words of FCC commissioner Michael Copps: "Winnable? I've got a two-word answer to that. Damn right!"

Media Reform: A Social Movement for the People

BY BRITT WALTERS—Project Censored Intern/Public Speaking Team

This years National Conference for Media Reform could quite possibly be considered the greatest mobilization of media activists to date and was undoubtedly unlike anything I have ever experienced. Although my work with Project Censored had previously initiated my intense interest surrounding the current state of corporate media, and consequently a passion for exposing its downfalls, there was no way I could be prepared for all the conference had to offer.

The extremely valuable and seemingly endless whirlwind of information touched base on a multitude of issues including: Media Ownership and Consolidation, Globalizing the Media Reform Movement, Media Policy, The FCC Past and Present, Online Tools for Media Reform Activism, and so much more.

In addition to the numerous seminars guaranteed to spark the flare of curiosity, Project Censored interns were also able to partake in the experience hands-on via instigating and conducting interviews and exchanging ideas with other organizations and projects around the country. Such components of the trip were absolutely amazing; nevertheless, it was the overall aura and underlying message of the conference as a whole that I found to be both most important and truly unforgettable.

The second I reached the conference registration desk at the Millennium Hotel in St. Louis, my feelings of great anticipation were bombarded with the externally strong wave of energy that was pulsating throughout the room. Often times, working for Project Censored, even though it is a rather large organization, the fight for media reform and the struggle to educate individuals about the problems with our current media structure can seem rather hopeless. There are those individuals who prefer to adopt an "ignorance is bliss" mentality by choosing to overlook the conflicts of interest existing between policy makers and corporate media. Furthermore, there are those who recognize the tribulations of the situation, yet feel there is no way to counteract it—or are too fearful to attempt to do so. However, no matter the topic at hand, the main essence throughout the sold-out conference was that change is both a necessity and a possibility. This massively large group of diverse attendees came together for the sole purpose of discussing the problems of the media and the ways in which everyone can work together to organize and create solutions. It was a blatant reminder that this is a battle certainly worth fighting and more importantly, a battle we are capable of winning.

In fact, this movement will without a doubt become one of the greatest and most important movements of our time. Creating parallel media and establishing a news media system *for* the people is essential to every individual regardless of race, gender, age, occupation or political association. It is not, therefore, surprising that so many individuals from a variety of locations, backgrounds and organizations have become involved in this movement. For no matter who you are, it is important that the news you receive about the world around you is not junk or entertainment disguised as news, but the vital information needed to promote a healthy democracy. Real news is necessary to all of us in order to make important decisions regarding the issues that directly affect our lives. Everyone, from environmentalist to educator, policymaker to party coordinator, artist to activist, media producer to media user, and all in between are directly affected by the media they consume, and are hence becoming actively involved in the movement at hand.

No one is alone in this struggle for change. In order to affect the full power of the people, we must all work together and pool our resources to perpetuate an increasing momentum. Overall, it is up to us as individuals to actively seek out the information we need—and it is up to us as a collective whole to work together to disseminate such information and rise up against the injustices of our current media system. In the end, it was the trip to St. Louis that really opened my eyes to the true power of working together. The conference exposed me to a multitude of new issues, new information and most importantly a new hope for the future of not only our media, but of our democratic way of life.

For reviews and program material on the Media Reform conference visit www.freepress.net.

UPDATES ON INDEPENDENT MEDIA

CommonDreams.Org
BY BRITTNY ROELAND

Common Dreams is a national non-profit citizens' organization working to bring progressive Americans together to promote progressive visions for America's future. Founded in 1997, Common Dreams is committed to being on the cutting-edge of using the internet as a political organizing tool, and creating new models for internet activism. Common Dreams is funded exclusively by members and supporters, therefore there is no corporate control, no advertising, and no hidden agendas involved in their views. With a small staff and a network of volunteers, the organization is proud of what is accomplished on a shoestring budget.

Common Dreams posts an eclectic mix of politics, issues and breaking news with an emphasis on progressive perspectives that are increasingly hard to find in the corporate-dominated media.

The news center's roots go back to the early '90s when Common Dreams Editor Craig Brown was the chief-of-staff to former Congressman Tom Andrews. With access to an incredible supply of daily newspapers, magazines, journals and briefing papers, members of Congress are deluged with information, but have very little time to scan through it, much less read it. Brown created a daily "newsclips" operation for the congressman and the staff. Early every morning interns and staff would scan dozens of designated publications looking for new articles or open editorials from a list of issues that were of greatest interest to the congressman and staff. By 9 a.m., all staff had a photocopied and collated copy of the "Daily Clips" to carry with them all day and read in between the chaos.

The magic of the internet has made it possible to create a "Daily Clips" for everyone. The Common Dreams News Center is updated daily, and provides people with easy access to articles throughout the media.

Every day activists are making news and speaking out on the issues of our time. But far too often the filter of the corporate-media ignores these voices. Progressive NewsWire brings the press releases and the statements of America's progressive community directly to you, no filters, no editing, and it is done in "real time." Progressive NewsWire started in June of 1998, and has archived news releases ever since.

BuzzFlash.com
BY JACOB RICH

Mark Karlin, who started BuzzFlash.com in May 2000, calls BuzzFlash's website "the internet democracy bulletin board of these times." It is easy to see how this may be true when the site daily posts more than 190 headlines that lead to articles from a huge variety of sources. On the average day, BuzzFlash connects readers to articles from news sources such American mainstays as the *New York Times*, the *Washington Post*, smaller papers like Ashland, Wisconsin's the *Daily Press*, international media like the *UK*

Guardian, the *Gulf Daily News*, and to blogs like the *Gadflyer* or *Thinkprogress.com*.

Not only does BuzzFlash offer one click access to an enlightening amount of information; it also does it with a sense of humor. For example, the headline on Buzzflash leading to a *New York Times* article, originally titled "In DeLay's Home District, Rumblings of Discontent Surface," is changed to "Tom DeLay's fan base erodes as home district Republicans call him an 'embarrassment.'" BuzzFlash has said "Remember, the White House wants him out because he distracts from Bush's Orwellian message points. There is only one Mafia King in the GOP."

If you think the mainstream media can be too partial and sanitize the significance of some news, BuzzFlash may be the place that resuscitates the news to new life. BuzzFlash may at times take its satire too far, but satire can sometimes do the truth justice. An article headline that BuzzFlash altered went from "Bush's attempt to play mortality card upsets African-Americans," to "African-Americans offended by Bush's 'Why do you want Social Security, you die early' sales pitch."

Mark Karlin started BuzzFlash.com in May 2000 with 34 readers, a number that is now up to about 150,000 a day, while during the Fall election of 2004 the website was getting 5,000,000 visitors a month. BuzzFlash also e-mails alerts of its stories every day to those who sign up for free subscriptions. Most media avoid reporting critically about their advertisers or the massive conglomerate that owns them. Just recently, General Motors pulled some of its advertising money from *The Los Angeles Times* after the *Times* published articles that were critical of General Motors. Buzzflash doesn't take any money from advertisers, and it is independently run, so it doesn't have to pull its punches.

BuzzFlash is supported by contributions from its readers and customers buying progressive merchandise such as books, videos, and cds. The right wing so-called 'echo chamber' plays up books that support their ideas, and sometimes this attention helps get these books on the *New York Times* bestseller list. BuzzFlash tries to do the same for leftist ideas by promoting and selling books, which also raises funds for BuzzFlash.

Of the more than 190 articles posted on Buzz Flash's website daily, about 80 percent come from other sources. Another 20 percent is original work written for BuzzFlash by contributing columnists and staff. BuzzFlash receives e-mails from its readers sending tips on articles that lead to stories coming from a wide variety of sources—creating a "quiltwork of commentary." Many articles are from local press that don't receive the attention they deserve. BuzzFlash helps give them national notice. For example, recently a reader sent in a tip on an article in a small North Dakota newspaper that revealed that there was a do-not-admit list for George Bush's social security meeting, even though it was a publicly funded event. This news gained national attention as a result of BuzzFlash exposure.

BuzzFlash puts special effort into exposing the hypocrisy of the right wing. They post a page called "the GOP Hypocrite of the Week" that calls attention to a new Republican every week. Currently the hypocrite of the week is actually a couple, Arthur Finkelstein and the man he just married in Massachusetts. Buzz Flash reports "The hypocrisy challenge for Mr. and Mr. Finkelstein is to explain how come Arthur makes his money supporting right wing demagogues who rally the GOP faithful by opposing just such rights for gays?" According to BuzzFlash, Arthur Finkelstein, "made his professional mark helping Jesse Helms rise to his perch of infamous and destructive power." BuzzFlash also adds, "The least he can do is devote his brain to science. There is much to be learned about how so many GOP leaders can be in denial about their 'values gap.'"

BuzzFlash operates out of Chicago, outside of the beltway where many reporters live and report and cozy up to the government. This may be part of the reason BuzzFlash can report on issues like the Iraq war, the budget crisis, and Tom DeLay threatening judges, while mainstream media gives more attention to the music George Bush is listening to on his I-pod.

According to Karlin the success of BuzzFlash is similar to Moveon.org; they both found people passionate about being informed on current affairs, and passionate about affecting the world with progressive change. BuzzFlash is working on expanding to more affiliate sites and is also planning to do some radio programming.

Center for Digital Democracy
BY SEAN ARLT

The communication revolution of 21st century has brought about unparalleled access to information while simultaneously connecting and stimulating the organization of many online communities. The Center for Digital Democracy (CDD), www.democraticmedia.org—a web based media group, was established to protect the openness and diversity of the internet. CDD is looking to amend the use of digital communications to enhance the democratic process through the development and encouragement of noncommercial, public interest programming.

The CDD's main instrument for pursuing these goals is the distribution of educational information to develop public understanding of the changing dimensions of theU.S. digital media system. The CDD offers a myriad of resources regarding digital television and cable TV's monopolistic ownership patterns. These resources include educational guides, news articles and press releases relating to the state of democracy in digital media.

On April 9th, 2005 Jeffrey Chester, executive director of the CDD, reported on the right wing coup that has begun to transform the Corporation for Public Broadcasting (CBP) into a conservative propaganda machine. Ken Ferree, the now active president of the CPB is a former key aide to Federal Communications Commission's (FCC's) Chairman, Michael Powell. During his time as an aide to Powell, Ken Ferree helped to compose the FCC's 2003 rules on media ownership—designed to almost completely eliminate the regulations on the media conglomerates. Mr. Chester reported that Ken Ferree and his right wing supporters were attempting to dismantle "liberal" programming on PBS and NPR.

On April 27, 2005, CDD discovered that the CBP majority directors were attempting to hide a national public opinion survey. The survey appeared in an annual report to Congress, but was never released to the public. The survey showed that the overwhelming majority of the U.S. public is happy with PBS and NPR's programming and that there was no public support for altering the stations. The Terrance Group's survey was conducted between June and July 2003, and surveyed 1,008 adults. The survey found that 80 percent of the sampling gave public broadcasting a favorable rating and only 10 percent indicated an unfavorable opinion of NPR and PBS. Furthermore, over 50 percent of those surveyed believed that PBS news was more "trustworthy" than the new shows on networks, including ABC, CBS, FOX, and CNN. Obviously unsatisfied with the results of the survey Ken Ferree and the other directors of the CPB chose not to publish the information.

The Center for Digital Democracy is also covering the potential take over of cable provider Adelphia Communications, who currently has over 5 million subscribers. The first and second largest media conglomerates, Comcast and Time Warner, are attempting to buy out Adelphia in what would be one of the largest media mergers of the 21st century. Comcast and Time Warner already control over 70 percent of the cable subscriptions in the top 20 U.S. markets and have almost total control over the programming on their subsequent stations.

The Center for Digital Democracy is an excellent example of the democratic power that new media can bring. Information about the state of the media is freely available to people all over America. Chester warns, however, that we are at a critical time in media reform, and without a tremendous effort on the side of grassroots organizations and independent media groups, the freedom of the internet as we know it could be swallowed up by corporate America.

A-Infos.ca

BY BRITTNY ROELAND

In February 1990, German anarchists invited to a European conference on the requirements and perspectives of international co-operation, in the Netherland town of Venlo, ascertained that there had been little continuous cooperation between the anarchist movements of the various countries. Everyone involved in the conference agreed that one of the main causes for this striking lack of international co-operation between anarchists was the isolation of the individual movements.

This was further amplified by the fact that most anarchists had to mainly rely on media under private or state control as a source of international information. This often resulted in an enormous informational deficit and a distorted view of the cultural, economical, political and social conditions in other countries. It was agreed that continuous problems and threats such as the internationalization of capital power was more important than ever. Therefore, the groups agreed on a loose but reliable international co-operation to help establish and support anarchist contacts, as well as improved flow of information among the different anarchist movements. Thus the A-Infos Network was created.

While this network was originally a co-operation of European groups, positive international responses quickly helped expand it to a network of anarchist individuals and groups world-wide, whose members meet every year to discuss the development of their work and make decisions that concern the whole network. Meanwhile groups and individuals from Canada, England, France, Germany, Greece, Italy, the Netherlands, Portugal, Russia, Sweden, Spain and Uruguay participate in the A-Infos network.

An international collective of revolutionary anti-authoritarian, anti-capitalist activists, involved in class/social struggle, coordinates the A-Infos Project. This is a group who consider themselves as revolutionary, class-struggling social anarchists, or anarcho-communists, or libertarian communists, or syndicalists, or hold similar opinions but use other labels. A-Infos is organized by people who hold the social theory that revolution is necessary to bring about the new classless social order, and that this revolution can only come about through the participation of the vast majority of working people.

In the struggle for a free society, A-Infos distributes news and articles in several languages, covering a wide range of areas, including workplace and environmental struggles as well as the fight against racism, sexism and homophobia. A-Infos also distributes news on indigenous people's anti-colonialist fight against settlers, occupation and marginalization, as well as anti-nationalist and anti-regional separatist activities. A-Infos is a specialized press agency, in the service of the movement of revolutionary anti-capitalist activists.

A-Infos is not an open "liberal" service that distributes anything they are sympathetic to. It is not Indymedia. It is first of all a free distribution tool for information from and about collectives of anarchists (and other anti-authoritarian revolutionaries) involved in the struggle.

A-Infos is run by the A-Infos Collective which makes all decisions through its direct-democratic decision-making process and discussion on the collective's e-mail list: a-infos-org. It is, however, not necessary to join the A-Infos Collective in order to contribute to its work. You can help, for example, by translating posts from one language to another. Another way to contribute is to send news articles for distribution.

For more information please visit www.A-Infos.ca.

The Australian Greens:
www.greens.org.au
BY MARK THOMPSON

In 1984, Petra Kelly, a key parliamentarian member of the West German Greens, made her second visit to Australia. She spoke out to various green party affiliates and encouraged them to band together and develop a national identity. Soon after her visit, 50 Greens activists, who had already wanted to gain recognition, came together in Tasmania and put together a national conference. In 1992, Green representatives from across the nation gathered in North Sydney and agreed to form the Australian Greens. The Australian Greens became part of the Global Greens network, with around 70 Green parties established worldwide. Greens have been elected to public office in 23 nations, and in European countries such as Germany, Latvia, and France, Green parties are part of governing coalitions.

Today the Australian Greens concentrate their energy for the purpose of providing information to the public about environmental and political concerns. It is their goal "to increase opportunities for public participation in political, social, and economic decision making, and to break down inequalities of wealth and power that inhibit participatory democracy." They try to achieve their political goals by publishing a magazine three times a year, filming campaigns which are showcased online, producing a variety of television and radio announcements, and managing a website with a plethora of weekly news stories.

Greens are found across Australia and throughout the world with Global Greens speaking in public to promote peace and encourage broad public involvement in their movement.

The Green website is loaded with daily articles and information that involves the many ecosystems and societies of Australia, as well as environmental issues that span the whole earth. The Greens aim to encourage the development of a consciousness that respects the value of all life.

The Greens are working to turn Australia into a model country that encourages social justice, ecologically sustainable economies, meaningful work programs, and universal cultural appreciation.

Clockwise from top left: intern Joni Wallant with journalist Joel Bleifuss of *In These Times*; intern Christopher Robin Cox interviewing Mediachannel.org founder Danny Schechter; Air America Radio host Al Franken addressing the convention; intern Sandy Brown interviewing author George Lakoff; Project Censored director Peter Phillips with *Democracy Now!* host Amy Goodman; Sandy Brown interviewing media reform leader Robert W. McChesney.

CHAPTER 8

Pulling Back the Curtain: The Best of PR Watch

BY LAURA MILLER

1. FAKE NEWS ON THE FRONT PAGE

If you were looking for public relations and spin in 2004, the presidential election and the continued U.S. military involvement in Iraq were obvious places to start. The year, however, saw one of the most common and overlooked tools of "perception management" become a front-page story. Fake news, and video news releases in particular, finally made it into the pubic eye.

A video news release, or VNR, is a simulated TV news story. Video clips paid for by corporations, government agencies, and non-governmental organizations are commonly passed off as legitimate news segments on local newscasts throughout the United States. VNRs are designed to be indistinguishable from traditional TV news and are often aired without the original producers and sponsors being identified, and sometimes without any local editing.

When a VNR touting the controversial Medicare reform law ended with "In Washington, I'm Karen Ryan, reporting," Senate Democrats, still smarting from the so-called reform's passage in late 2003, called foul. The VNR, which aired on 40 stations between January 22 and February 12, 2004, was paid for by the U.S. Department of Health and Human Services. Ryan, the "reporter," was in fact employed by a production company contracted by the Ketchum PR firm to create the VNR for HHS. An investigation by the U.S. General Accounting Office concluded that the VNR had violated a ban on government funded "publicity and propaganda." According to *The Hill*, a newspaper based in Washington, D.C., "VNRs are standard practice in the public-relations industry and local news reports often rely on them.... However, the Government Accountability Office said in its decision, 'our analysis of the proper use of appropriated funds is not based upon the norms in the public relations and media industry.'"

Karen Ryan was literally back in the news in October 2004, when the liberal-leaning People for the American Way identified another Ryan VNR. This time Ryan "reported" on the Bush Administration's No Child Left Behind law. A Freedom of Information Act investigation revealed that the U.S. Education Department paid $700,000 to the Ketchum firm to produce two VNRs as well as to rate newspaper coverage according to how favorably reporters described No Child Left Behind. "A number of local stations ran the VNR as is, and added a local twist by simply having their own reporter read the script," reported CampaignDesk.org, a journalist watchdog website (now CJRdaily.org). "The stations that took the time to have their own reporters record the script of the No Child Left Behind VNR had to have been fully aware of what they were doing: knowingly deceiving their viewers about the origins of the story—not to mention committing plagiarism—by passing off as their own original reporting words actually written by a PR company hired by the Bush Administration."

Most VNRs are created by firms specializing in production, but the U.S. Department of Agriculture's Broadcast Media & Technology Center (BMTC) is responsible for the production of 90 VNRs a year and "over 2,000 radio news stories," or audio news releases (ANRs), for the USDA and other federal agencies. With its $2.8 million annual budget, BMTC is "one of the most effective public relations operations inside the federal government," the *New York Times* concluded in its March 2005 exposé on government VNRs. BMTC's stories are frequently aired throughout the United States without their production being credited to the USDA.

A survey by *PR Watch* of USDA reports discovered that VNRs and ANRs produced by BMTC regularly supported Bush Administration issues on international trade, promoted USDA "accomplishments," and ignored opposition to USDA policies and White House proposals. For example, from October 2004 to April 2005 BMTC produced five VNRs and 29 ANRs on mad cow disease, a deadly neurological disease found in cows that can be transmitted to humans.

Overall the pieces ignored or glossed over safety concerns raised by the December 2003 discovery of mad cow disease in the United States. A March 2005 radio segment features University of Maryland Extension Livestock Specialist Scott Bareo, who said, "The BSE situation in the United States has been nothing but media hype. We have a food safety system in this country second to none." In an October 2004 piece, USDA Undersecretary J.B. Penn explained why U.S. beef is safe, "without having to test all animals."

"Listeners and viewers are entitled to know who seeks to persuade them," the Federal Communications Commission noted in an April 13, 2005 Public Notice on VNRs. Existing but rarely enforced federal laws and FCC rules already forbid government propaganda and set strong disclosure requirements for "political material and program matter dealing with controversial issues."

In early January 2005, another kind of fake news came to light: so-called pundit payola. Conservative commentators Armstrong Williams, Maggie Gallagher and Michael McManus were outed for taking money under the table to endorse Bush Administration programs. Williams had been paid $240,000 by Ketchum as a subcontractor on a Department of Education contract to promote No Child Left Behind. According to *USA Today*, Williams was hired "to promote the law on his nationally syndicated television show and to urge other black journalists to do the same." As part of the agreement, Williams was required "to regularly comment on NCLB during the course of his broadcasts," and to interview Education Secretary Rod Paige for TV and radio spots that aired during the show in 2004.

By the end of January, the *Washington Post* reported that Gallagher, a prominent advocate for marriage-promotion programs and a staunch opponent of same sex marriage, had accepted a $21,500 contract from the U.S. Department of Health and Human Services to promote President Bush's marriage-promotion initiatives. The next day, *Salon* reported that McManus, a syndicated columnist, had received $10,000 as a Department of Health and Human Services subcontractor with the Lewin Group, a health care consultancy. The HHS contract was to provide presentations and trainings in support of the Bush Administration's Community Healthy Marriage Initiative. "McManus provided training during two-day conferences in Chattanooga, Tenn., and also made presentations at HHS-sponsored conferences."

While there are differences between these cases, as far as journalistic ethics are concerned, all three pundits had crossed a line. They took money from someone whose interests they were plugging, while not disclosing the payments to their audience. The code of ethics of the Society of Professional Journalists is very clear that this is unacceptable. It states that journalists should: "Avoid conflicts of interest, real or perceived. Remain free of associations and activities that may compromise integrity or damage credibility. Refuse gifts, favors, fees, free travel and special treatment, and shun secondary employment, political involvement, public office and service in community organizations if they compromise journalistic integrity. Disclose unavoidable conflicts.... Deny favored treatment to advertisers and special interests and resist their pressure to influence news coverage."

It is important to keep in mind that corporations, seeking to sell their products, services and agendas, are the source of the majority of fake news. And in the business world, no one has relied on and benefited from prepackaged news more than healthcare companies. According to a 2002 survey by DS Simon Productions (a leading VNR producer), 88 percent of TV stations use VNRs from medical, pharmaceutical and biotech corporations in their newscasts. The company's head, Doug Simon, claimed during a teleconference hosted by *O'Dwyer's PR Services* that at least 90 percent of their VNRs are aired without disclosure. While attention has focused on federally funded fake news, corporations should not be let off the hook.

At the May 2005 National Conference on Media Reform, the Federal Communications Commission's Jonathan Adelstein said that the increasing commercialization of media is one of media consolidation's "most pernicious symptoms." Adelstein listed as examples "thinly disguised payola" and "video news releases, masquerading as news." Also guilty of commercializing media are "PR agents pushing political and commercial agendas, squeezing out real news coverage and local community concerns" and product placements, which are "turning news and entertainment shows alike into undisclosed commercials for an unwitting public," he said. The commissioner challenged the conference attendees to monitor the news for undisclosed VNRs and product promotions. "We're going to shut down this fraud that is being perpetrated on the American people by the media," he said.

2. DESPARATELY SEEKING DISCLOSURE

In some ways, Armstrong Williams got a bad rap. The conservative commentator, who was paid by the U.S. Department of Education to advertise and advocate for the controversial No Child Left Behind law, lost his syndicated newspaper column and was pilloried for not disclosing the payment. Williams did betray the public trust, but he was a small fry—a subcontractor receiving a $240,000 piece of a $1 million deal between the Education Department and Ketchum, one of the world's largest public relations firms.

That deal, it turns out, was just the tip of the iceberg.

Ketchum is the number one recipient of recent U.S. government PR spending, with contracts totaling more than $100 million. Since 1997, nine PR firms have received at least $1 million in public funds in a single year. The Bush Administration doubled federal PR spending over its first term, relative to the last term of the Clinton Administration, to $250 million.

That's according to an early 2005 report by the House Committee on Government Reform, which examined federal procurement records going back eight years, looking for contracts with major PR firms. The Committee launched its investigation following January's three "pundit payola" revelations and rulings by the Government Accountability Office. Congress' nonpartisan investigative arm found that fake television news segments, or video news releases, produced for two government agencies were illegal "covert propaganda."

Yet there is little information about how these millions of dollars were— or are—spent. Despite evidence that public funds have been misused, the details of government contracts with PR firms remain hidden.

The ethics code of the Public Relations Society of America (PRSA), the largest PR trade organization, includes admonitions "to build trust with the public by revealing all information needed for responsible decision making," to "be honest and accurate," to "reveal the sponsors for causes and interests represented," and to "avoid deceptive practices." When *PR Watch* asked the nine PR firms in the million-dollar league for information on their government work, responses ranged from cautious answers to deafening silence. None of the firms was willing to share any information not already publicly available—including contract agreements or "deliverables" like studies, brochures and VNRs—to clarify what they did with taxpayers' money.

Ketchum's government work is by no means unusual. It had contracts with the Education Department; Internal Revenue Service; U.S. Army, to "reconnect the Army with the American people" and boost recruiting around its 225th birthday; and the Health and Human Services Department, to "change the face of Medicare," promote long-term health care planning, encourage preventative care and present home care information. Large contract increases for Ketchum since 2003 mirror the Centers for Medicare and Medicaid Services' PR spending boost, suggesting that Ketchum's Medicare work may be more extensive than is currently known.

Another global PR giant, Fleishman-Hillard was the second largest recipient of federal funds, totaling $77 million. The contracts include work for the Social Security Administration; Library of Congress; Environmental Protection Agency; and Defense Department, to introduce "managed care" to employees, due to "rising medical costs" and "decreasing resources." While Fleishman-Hillard also did not return phone calls, its application for PRSA's prestigious Silver Anvil Award noted that the main challenge of its Defense contract was "the anger and frustration of the retired military community who were now required to pay an annual fee for guaranteed access to health care they said was promised them by their recruiter as a free lifetime benefit."

The firm has also worked for the White House Office of National Drug Control Policy (ONDCP), to "debunk the misconception that marijuana was harmless." For this contract, Fleishman-Hillard produced VNRs later ruled to be covert propaganda, because ONDCP "did not identify itself to the viewing audience as the producer and distributor of these prepackaged news stories."

3. WAR STILL SELLS

Throughout 2004 and into the spring of 2005 reports trickled out about the extent to which intelligence in support of the March 2003 Iraq invasion was engineered by the White House and Pentagon. The September 2004 report by the CIA-sponsored Iraq Survey Group said the United States would not find the weapons of mass destruction initially claimed by Bush as the reason to go to war. In May 2005, "The question of prewar intelligence [was] thrust back into the public eye with the disclosure of a secret British memo showing that, eight months before the March 2003 start of the war, a senior British intelligence official reported to Prime Minister Tony Blair that U.S. intelligence was being shaped to support a policy of invading Iraq," the *Washington Post*'s Walter Pincus wrote.

These revelations, however, seemed lost on the American corporate media, who have consistently failed to hold the Bush Administration accountable for the untold suffering being experienced by Iraqis, and also by U.S. servicemen and women and their families. Instead the major media remained mostly uncritical, enabling the Bush Administration to continue to distort reality and hide the unfortunate truths about the country's military engagements.

At home, photographs of American war casualties were rare in newspapers. The *Los Angeles Times* surveyed six major newspapers during a six-month period and discovered not a single picture of a dead U.S. soldier had been published by any of the papers. Americans, in general, saw a very sanitized version of war on major news outlets. Several different factors could be said to be responsible for the relatively bloodless view of the war in Afghanistan and Iraq. Regardless of the cause, the effect is a warped view of American foreign policy and military actions. And the distance between the perceptions of the United States held by media viewers outside the country, who are seeing much more graphic images of war, and Americans' perceptions of themselves has grown.

In May 2005, *Newsweek* magazine inadvertently stepped on a minefield when it reported on the desecration of the Koran at the U.S.'s Guantanamo Bay detention camp. The magazine retracted the story after reported pressure from the Pentagon. The incident illustrated how willing the Bush Administration was to bully a news publication for a small piece of reporting that may or may not have been entirely accurate, yet which reflected poorly on the Administration. The story, however, was close enough to other reports of U.S. disrespect of the Koran and Islam that White House scolds could not focus too much on whether or not the story was actually credible. Once *Newsweek* retracted the story, administration statements focused on the fact that *Newsweek* said it was wrong and on how damaging the report had been.

"This report, which *Newsweek* has now retracted and said was wrong, has had serious consequences," White House Press Secretary Scott McClellan said during a press briefing. "People did lose their lives. The image of the United States abroad has been damaged; there is lasting damage to our image because of this report. And we would encourage *Newsweek* to do all that they can to help repair the damage that has been done, particularly in the region."

"We have done a number of things, in terms of trying to address this *Newsweek* article, which *Newsweek* has now retracted," said State Department spokesman Richard Boucher. "Nonetheless, it has very sad and regrettable implications overseas—shocking, to some extent, to see that an article be published so—well, an article like this would be published, and one that can involve potential violence and deaths overseas as this one did."

From administration comments, one gets the sense that further diminishing world opinion of the United States is an equal sin to misreporting a story. The Associated Press reported in May, "'One of the military's new wartime challenges is dealing with global media that can instantly spread around the world information that may be false or damaging to U.S. interests,' Defense Secretary Donald Rumsfeld said."

4. A BILLION DOLLARS FOR YOUR VOTE

The U.S. 2004 Presidential election was so mired in controversies and spin that had it taken place in another country, U.S. cable news pundits might easily have labeled it as corrupt. From questions of the veracity of computerized voting to preemptive arrests of protesters outside the Republican National Convention to Republican strategist Frank Luntz's advice to campaigners that "No speech about homeland security or Iraq should begin without a reference to 9/11," a citizen's ability to confidently participate in the democratic election process was certainly hampered.

Over a billion dollars was spent to sway voters one way or the other in the Presidential race. In the three weeks leading up to the November 2, 2004 election, the Republican 527 group Progress for America (PFA) Voter Fund outspent the Democratic 527 group Media Fund three-to-one on political ads. (Overall, though, the Media Fund spent $54.5 million during 2004 to defeat Bush. The PFA Voter Fund spent $35.6 million in the President's support.) Progress for America's last minute advertising blitz—the largest single ad buy of the election at $14.2 million—was for "Ashley's Story."

"[The ad] shows Bush comforting 16-year-old Ashley Faulkner, whose mother died on 9/11. As it happens, the spot was made by Larry McCarthy, who produced the infamous Willie Horton ad that helped the first President Bush bury Michael Dukakis under charges that he was soft on crime. If that is the iconic attack ad, this is the ultimate embrace—to remind voters of the protectiveness they cherished in the President after 9/11. The ad has been ready since July, but sponsors waited until the end to unveil it," *Time* magazine reported. According to *USA Today*, the ad was supported by a Web site, www.ashleysstory.com, as well as "e-mails, automated phone calls, and 2.3 million brochures" mailed to voters.

"Ashley's Story" made *Advertising Age* columnist Bob Garfield's list of top 10 "Ads I Loved" for 2004. Garfield writes, "We said, 'It might come down to one commercial,' and it may well have. A retelling of candidate Bush's encounter with an Ohio Teenager answered undecideds' doubts. The president wasn't a dry-well-drilling gambler, moron and fool... he's a fearless leader who will hug us."

5. THE FIX BEHIND FIXING SOCIAL SECURITY

While Bush won the November 2004 election, many key Republican strategists scarcely had time to catch their breath before launching the next Bush campaign: the so-called reform of the U.S. Social Security program. By February 2005, Bush Administration ventriloquists were out in full force, breathlessly hyping "voluntary personal retirement accounts" as a way to save Social Security (by destroying it). Deputy White House chief of staff

Karl Rove, National Economics Council director Al Hubbard, and Barry Jackson, a special assistant to the president who handles Social Security reform, met with administration-friendly lobbyists for a "rah-rah" cheerleading session on Social Security privatization. According to *The Hill*, representatives from the Coalition for the Modernization and Protection of America's Social Security (COMPASS), a group formed by the Business Roundtable and the National Association of Manufacturers, as well as the conservative 60 Plus Association, America's Community Bankers, the National Retail Federation, the Mortgage Bankers Association and the Business Roundtable heard the trio reiterate George W. Bush's commitment to "reform" Social Security.

"The White House is running this as if it's a political campaign," Free Enterprise Fund president Stephan Moore told *Bloomberg News*. "There are regular meetings the White House has with all the groups to make sure everyone is singing from the same hymnal." To finance the campaign, business and trade association lobbyists are pressing their corporate members to fill the privatization collection plate. The *New York Times'* Glen Justice reports that although "most groups are still raising money, and the spending figures they quote are still often just targets, the lobbying could amount to more than $100 million."

Fresh off the Bush victory, Progress for America announced that it would spend $20 million on its Social Security reform campaign, featuring ads and promoting media appearances by trusted spokesmen. PFA recruited Texas A&M University economics professor and U.S. Social Security Administration trustee Thomas R. Saving as an advisor and pro-privatization spokesman. Nine-year-old Texan Noah McCullough, whose "encyclopedic command of presidential history" had earned him five appearances on Jay Leno's "Tonight" show, also got in on the Social Security privatization act, traveling to several states ahead of the President on his 60-day "personal retirement accounts" promotion tour and doing radio interviews where he answered trivia questions and pitched privatization.

The so-called Social Security crisis itself is an invention of ideological think tanks and corporate-funded groups. The liberal-leaning Center for Economic and Policy Research writes, "Social Security is more financially sound today than it has been throughout most of its 69-year history." The real crisis for Americans is how the lobbyist-driven campaign to privatize Social Security marginalizes and renders irrelevant actual democratic discussion on Social Security and its future solvency.

6. NUCLEAR ENERGY'S GREEN GLOW

"Several of the nation's most prominent environmentalists have gone public with the message that nuclear power, long taboo among environmental advocates, should be reconsidered as a remedy for global warming," the *New York Times* reported in May 2005. And while environmentalists who support nuclear power as a supposedly "emission-free" alternative to fossil fuels are not representative of the larger movement, the buzz about them had mushroomed.

Make no mistake—nuclear power has not become any safer or cleaner. Nuclear plants still pose a huge threat to the communities in which they are located and highly radioactive spent fuel has yet to be dealt with adequately. "It's not that something new and important and good has happened with the nuclear industry, it's that something new and important and bad has happened with climate change," Stewart Brand, a founder of the *Whole Earth Catalog* and a new devotee of nuclear energy, told the *Times.*

In fact, the only thing that the nuclear power industry has been working to clean up is its image. Over the past several years, *PR Watch* has seen a marked increase in industry efforts to change the public's perception of nuclear power, using public relations to quell safety concerns and undermine grassroots efforts to shut down nuclear plants.

The industry funded Nuclear Energy Institute (NEI) for several years now has promoted nuclear power as a "clean, green energy source." This message directly defies a 1998 ruling by the National Advertising Division (NAD) of the Council of Better Business Bureaus, which stated that the Nuclear Energy Institute should "discontinue" its "inaccurate" advertisements that claim nuclear power is clean. The NAD called on NEI to terminate its advertisements to "avoid any potential for consumer confusion and that broad, unqualified claims that nuclear energy is 'Environmentally Clean' or produces electricity 'without polluting the environment' be discontinued."

With lingering memories of the Three Mile Island and Chernobyl catastrophes, along with very real fears of nuclear terrorism post-9/11, the difficulty of selling nuclear power is not lost on the PR industry. Corporate Watch reported that "regaining public acceptance of nuclear power will be one of the PR world's biggest challenges, according to PR guru Dejan Vercic. Speaking at a 2004 meeting of the UK's Institute of Public Relations, he said that within five to ten years public relations agencies would have to win back the nuclear industry's ... 'license to operate.'"

7. TSUNAMI WASHES AWAY HUMAN RIGHTS IN INDONESIA

Indonesia is no stranger to the world of PR. Over the years, a litany of well-documented human rights violations increasingly isolated the Indonesian military on the world stage. To help clean up its image, the Indonesian government has turned to U.S.-based PR and lobbying firms. Hill & Knowlton and White & Case contributed to Indonesia's lobbying bill for mid-1991 through 1992, which totaled $6.8 million. Following the Indonesian military's 1991 massacre of hundreds of peaceful protesters in East Timor, the government paid Burson-Marsteller $5 million "to help improve the country's human rights and environmental image," according to the *Far Eastern Economic Review*. In 1996, Indonesia signed another $5 million contract with Burson-Marsteller. In early 2001, Indonesia's Sekar Mahoni Sakti Foundation hired Advantage Associates, "to create a positive view of Indonesia with the U.S. Congress, Administration, and Department of Defense," according to U.S. Foreign Agents Registration Act filings. One goal was "to lift an embargo on spare parts for the C-130 military aircraft."

Following the September 11 attacks, the war on terror has been Indonesia's PR theme. The government retained APCO Worldwide in 2003 to pitch its importance as a "front-line state in the war on terrorism." In 2004, Alston & Bird contracted with an Indonesian logging magnate to "position" the country "as a solid ally in President Bush's war on terror and one that is committed to democracy and human rights." In addition to policymakers and reporters, Alston & Bird was directed to sway other U.S. "opinion-shapers," including "think tanks and academia." *National Journal's CongressDaily* reported that former U.S. Senator Bob Dole, working for Alston & Bird, would be lobbying for "the restoration of a program to train Indonesian military officers in the United States." In December 2004, six U.S. Pacific Command officers led a three-day discussion for Indonesian Army, Navy and Air Force members, on "how to present information and news to the press," according to the *Jakarta Post*. Yet the payoff was slow in coming. A ban on U.S. military assistance for Indonesia, enacted after the military's post-referendum devastation of East Timor in 1999, remained mostly intact for five years.

Then came the December 2004 tsunami. While the Indonesian military's involvement in humanitarian efforts was necessary and normal, local and international observers complained of aid obstruction and continued military operations against supposed rebels in the Indonesian province of Aceh, "ground zero" for the tsunami. Riding a wave of compassion, the U.S. government resumed a prestigious military training program and "non-lethal" equipment sales for Indonesia in early 2005. The tragic deaths of more than 100,000 Acehnese provided the PR cover to resume U.S. support to one of the world's most brutal militaries.

8. FOOD INDUSTRY FOXES GUARD THE FDA HEN HOUSE

Food industry lobbyists met repeatedly and privately with Bush Administration officials while the Administration was drafting rules to protect the nation's food supply from bioterrorism throughout 2004. "The resulting regulations don't fully protect the public interest," stated the Center for Science in the Public Interest. The Grocery Manufacturers of America (GMA), Altria Group (formerly Philip Morris) and others lobbied to weaken proposed regulations requiring importers to notify the Food and Drug Administration before food shipments arrive from overseas. One GMA lobbyist explained, "We all want regulations to protect against bioterrorism, but in a way to achieve the goals and allow the business to operate in an efficient manner." The Bush Administration's Secretary of Health and Human Services, Tommy Thompson had nothing to say about the problem until after the 2004 presidential election, when he announced his resignation plans. In his departure speech in December, Thompson warned of possible health-related terrorist attacks. "For the life of me, I cannot understand why the terrorists have not attacked our food supply because it is so easy to do," he said.

9. SHELL GAME WITH HUMAN RIGHTS

Corporate lobby groups such as the International Chamber of Commerce (ICC) launched a fierce counter-campaign against the proposed Norms on Business and Human Rights, which were developed by a subcommission of the United Nations Commission on Human Rights. The Norms require businesses internationally to refrain from activities that violate human rights, constraints that have been vigorously opposed by the ICC and a the Royal Dutch/Shell oil company, a self-proclaimed leader in the corporate social responsibility (CSR) movement. "Is this not the kind of campaign one could expect only from companies lagging behind and from free-riders refusing to adapt to social and environmental concerns?" asked the Corporate Europe Observatory (CEO). The motive behind Shell's opposition, CEO suggested, is that "the company generally gets away easily with its inflated claims concerning its social responsibility record." A 2004 report by Christian Aid documented that Shell's operations in the Niger Delta in Nigeria are still causing serious problems for local communities. The report also found that most of the community development projects presented in various glossy Shell reports on CSR are in fact failing. "Hospitals, schools and water supply systems are built but never start working, and roads are mainly used to boost oil production," reported CEO. "But beyond the debate about the extent to which Shell's CSR claims are actually greenwash and poor-wash, it is clear that the company is determined to prevent the emergence of international mechanisms through which communities could hold it accountable to its pledges."

10. WAL-MART GETS PR HELP FROM HILL & KNOWLTON

"Wal-Mart is working with Hill & Knowlton on a PR campaign designed to rehabilitate the much-maligned company's reputation in California and pave the way for 40 new Wal-Mart Supercenters in the state in the next few years," *PR Week* reported in October 2004. The world's largest retailer published an "open letter to California residents" in 15 California newspapers on September 23. "As the company has grown, we've become a target for negative comments from certain elected officials, competitors and powerful special interest groups," Wal-Mart wrote. *PR Week* reported that several of H&K's California offices had been working with Wal-Mart for several months on the PR effort, "primarily handling media relations tasks." Wal-Mart has announced plans to increase retail space by 8 percent. The company, which is also facing a class action suit for sex discrimination, had a record year in sales and earnings for 2004.

Laura Miller is the editor of *PR Watch*, a quarterly publication of the Center for Media and Democracy. CMD senior researcher Diane Farsetta contributed to this article. For more information on these stories, visit CMD's websites: PRWatch.org and SourceWatch.org.

CHAPTER 9

FAIR's Fifth Annual "Fear & Favor" Report—2004

HOW POWER SHAPES THE NEWS

By Peter Hart and Julie Hollar

"We can get five reporters a month to do news stories about your product. If you want to be interviewed by 10 to 20 reporters per month, we can arrange that, too.... Media Relations, Inc. has placed tens of thousands of news stories on behalf of more than 1,000 clients." —Media Relations, Inc. solicitation

The PR agency's promises are a stark reminder that the news is, in many ways, a collision of different interests. The traditional tenets of journalism are challenged and undermined by other factors: Advertisers demand "friendly copy," while other commercial interests work to place news items that serve the same function as advertising. Media owners exert pressure to promote the parent company's self-interest. Powerful local and national interests demand softball treatment. And government power is exerted to craft stories, influence content—and even to make up phony "news" that can be passed off as the real thing.

Journalists, on the whole, understand these pressures all too well. A survey of media workers by four industry labor unions (*Media Professionals and Their Industry*, 7/20/04) found respondents concerned about "pressure from advertisers trying to shape coverage" as well as "outside control of editorial policy." In May, the Pew Research Center for the People & the

Press released a survey of media professionals that found reporters concerned about how bottom-line pressures were affecting news quality and integrity. In their summary of the report, Bill Kovach, Tom Rosensteil and Amy Mitchell wrote that journalists "report more cases of advertisers and owners breaching the independence of the newsroom."

The Fear & Favor report is an attempt to illustrate this growing encroachment on journalism with real examples that have been made public—not an exhaustive list by any means, but a reminder that such pressures exist, and that reporters serve the best interests of citizens and the journalistic profession by coming forward with their own accounts.

IN ADVERTISERS WE TRUST

USA Today (5/18/04) served notice that corporate advertisers have a remarkable influence over what we see on the TV screen. As the paper noted, in the media world "there is worry that the flood of grisly images flowing into living rooms from Iraq and elsewhere will discourage advertisers."

A General Motors spokesperson explained that her company "would not advertise on a TV program [just] about atrocities in Iraq," while an ad exec explained that "you don't want to run a humorous commercial next to horrific images and stories." A Ford representative said the company keeps a close eye on news images that accompany its ads, saying, "We're monitoring the content and will make decisions based on the nature of the content. But we don't have a lot of control."

But they do, of course. Commercial media wouldn't exist without, well, the commercials. And in order to keep the revenue flowing, media outlets increasingly blur the lines between their advertising and editorial divisions.

When a super-sized corporation comes to town, it brings along an ad budget to match, and newspapers sometimes seem more than willing to suspend the rules of critical journalism to ingratiate themselves with the wealthy new arrival. When furniture giant Ikea opened a new store in New Haven, Connecticut, the *New Haven Register* cranked out 12 Ikea stories in eight straight days—accompanied by at least 17 photographs and a sidebar on product information—with headlines such as "Ikea's Focus on Child Labor Issues Reflects Ethic of Social Responsibility" (7/25/04) and "Ikea Employees Take Pride in Level of Responsibility Company Affords Them" (7/27/04). The *Register*'s Ikea reporter was even sent to Sweden to visit the company's headquarters—on Ikea's dime, according to *Columbia Journalism Review* (11–12/04), a little detail the Register failed to disclose.

The back-scratching reached its apex the day of the grand opening, when the *Register* (7/28/04) heralded the arrival of Ikea and fellow super-store Wal-Mart, and remarked upon Ikea's "astonishingly low prices—a coffee table for $99, a flowing watering can for $1.99, a woven rocking chair, $59." Sound like an ad? It was the *Register*'s lead *editorial*.

While *Register* readers could have mistaken the paper's news for advertising, *Boston Herald* readers on January 7 could easily have mistaken the paper's front-page ad for news. When discount airline JetBlue launched several new flight services out of Boston's Logan Airport, Bostonians who picked up a free promotional *Herald* that day found that every item on the front page was devoted exclusively to the airline, including the lead headline, "JetBlue Arrives, Promises a Free TV to All Who Fly," and teasers like "Flight Attendant Gives Passenger Entire Can of Soda." After the front page, the paper resumed its actual news content—but nowhere did the *Herald* indicate that its front page was in fact a paid advertisement, and the 20,000 recipients of the promo paper missed out on the actual front-page news of the day (BostonPhoenix.com, 1/7/04).

When asked about the stunt, a *Herald* spokesperson said the paper had produced the "mock" front page "to commemorate JetBlue's launch into the Boston market" (WBUR.org, 1/9/04). She did acknowledge that "We probably should have said something... that indicated it wasn't our real front page," but wouldn't rule out future front-page promos.

When Kirksville, Missouri's KTVO-TV ran a news report that quoted a company that didn't advertise on the station rather than a competitor that did, the angry advertiser pulled its ads from the station. KTVO vice president and general manager Crystal Amini-Rad quickly apologized to the sales staff in a memo that also required news reporters to "have access to an active advertiser list... of sources which you can tap into" for expert opinion and industry comment—and told reporters that they "should always go" to station advertisers first on any story (*Columbia Journalism Review*, 9–10/04).

When Silver City, New Mexico's KNFT brought on progressive host Kyle Johnson as an alternative to the seven hours of Rush Limbaugh, Michael Savage and Bill O'Reilly the station aired every weekday, KNFT's advertisers boycotted the show. The station made Johnson raise the cash to pay for his airtime, and his listeners anted up. But the advertisers threatened to boycott the entire station if Johnson stayed on; faced with the prospect of a nearly $10,000-a-month loss, the station manager reluctantly gave the progressive host the boot (*Silver City Sun-News*, 7/21/04).

POWERFUL PLAYERS & PR

It's not just advertisers who have the clout to bend the rules of journalism. People in powerful positions have long pulled strings to influence news coverage, with journalists sometimes acting as witting accomplices.

When a journalist at *Bloomberg News* filed a report about a civil suit against Deutsche Bank (12/5/04), it didn't seem like a particularly remarkable story; a former female employee was accusing the company of firing her for complaining about, among other things, sexual harassment by Damian Kissane, a former Deutsche Bank exec. But to the surprise of the newsroom staff, editor-in-chief Matthew Winkler had it purged from the Bloomberg website and replaced six days later with a bowdlerized version that deleted the names of all parties involved. Shortly afterwards, he issued a memo to the staff, admonishing that *Bloomberg News* "must never be a mouthpiece for litigants who want to publish court filings to embarrass or gain an advantage over their opponents."

Winkler claimed the story "lacked context" and a sense of "why do we care about this" (*Washington Post*, 1/5/05). The *New York Post* (12/24/04) reported that Kissane, now Chief Operating Officer of the financial markets branch of the Royal Bank of Scotland, was said to have complained to Winkler. *Bloomberg* insiders cited by the *New York Post* suggested that Winkler rewrote the story in response to Kissane's complaint—perhaps unsurprisingly, since *Bloomberg*'s main business is selling market information to the financial industry.

When St. Paul, Minnesota's KSTP-TV needed a new lead anchor, it picked someone with years of experience—in PR. Cyndy Brucato had started at KSTP in the early '80s, but then moved on to communications work for Republican politicians, and for the previous eight years ran a PR firm, Halliday & Brucato, with her husband. There her clients ranged from the Minnesota House Republican Caucus to big pharmaceutical and tobacco companies. Brucato also held a state government position on the Minnesota Board on Judicial Standards, which she didn't give up when she started her journalism job.

Brucato argued that she had quit seeing clients at the firm and said she would disclose any conflicts of interest as they arose. Of course, ceasing to see clients hardly removes the financial interest involved; the firm is still run by her husband, and she noted that it "is something I have some equity in" (*City Pages*, 8/4/04).

Courts have consistently ruled that university administrations have to keep their noses out of college papers' business, but that didn't deter Arizona State University president Michael Crow. When ASU's *State Press* (10/7/04) ran a picture of a female breast with a pierced nipple on the cover of its weekly magazine supplement, Ira Fulton, who had given ASU $58 million in the previous year and a half, called Crow's office to complain. Crow immediately dispatched the student affairs president to warn the paper that "funding will be suspended ASAP if not corrected."

Virgil Renzulli, ASU's vice president for public affairs, claimed the real issue was that the *State Press* didn't have a clearly defined content policy; to the students' response that they follow the Society for Professional Journalists' code of ethics, he replied, "We think that there may be guidelines more appropriate for student journalists than the ones for other news organizations" (AP, 11/26/04).

Though the Administration insisted Fulton's complaint had nothing to do with the crackdown, Crow wrote him an October 16 letter assuring him that "the Office of Student Affairs will be monitoring the newspaper's forthcoming editorial decisions very closely and working with its management to ensure that the University's standards are clearly understood. I appreciate your direct engagement on this matter" (*Phoenix New Times*, 11/18/04).

As Crow told the *Arizona Republic* (11/20/04), "I don't think we want [the *State Press*] off campus. I think as an investor in the business, we want some say in how it's run." Now there's an education in how the media *really* works.

THE BOSS'S BUSINESS

When conservatives complained that CBS was promoting Bush critic Richard Clarke on *60 Minutes* without disclosing that his book *Against All Enemies* was published by Free Press, another Viacom subsidiary, CBS responded (*Hollywood Reporter*, 3/23/04) by saying that the show "has interviewed authors from virtually all the book publishing companies over its 36 seasons and is beholden to none of them. Publishers seek out *60 Minutes* because it is television's no. 1 news magazine." But the question is not whether authors wouldn't want to get on *60 Minutes* if they didn't work for the same company; the question is, are we really supposed to believe they don't get preferential consideration when they do?

As a report in the *American Journalism Review* noted (11–12/04), comments filed with the FCC regarding its ownership regulations provided some concrete examples that such mutual back-scratching does go on. AJR quoted a newspaper reporter whose bosses also owned a TV station:

"When the Nielsen TV ratings come out, I know I am expected to write a big story if the co-owned station's ratings are good and to bury the story if the co-owned station's ratings are down. Or another example: A few years ago, I ran a survey asking readers what they thought of local television news programs. My general manager told me the next time I do something that might affect our sister station, I better check with him first. I got the message. I haven't done a similar project since then."

The violation of the boundary between news and entertainment is perhaps nowhere as flagrant as on network "newsmagazine" shows. As a May 14 *Los Angeles Times* story explained, the NBC News program *Dateline* found plenty of news value in the entertainment offerings of NBC. "Despite criticism that NBC's news programs have been turned into brazen marketing tools for several of the network's prime-time series finales," the *Times* reported, "the management of the combined company seems delighted with the promotional firepower of its enterprise." The *Times* cited, among other things, the two-hour *Dateline* (5/5/04) devoted to the final episode of the sitcom *Friends*, as well as generous coverage of the NBC sitcom *Frasier* and the Donald Trump "reality" show *The Apprentice.*

Thanks to NBC's recent acquisition of Universal, network news president Neal Shapiro looks forward to NBC news programs getting first crack at interviewing movie stars affiliated with Universal films. He dismissed criticisms of this blurring of the lines between news and entertainment as "asinine" (*L.A. Times*, 5/14/04).

NBC Today anchor Katie Couric, interviewing Trump, remarked that he seems to "be the fifth member of the show these days... I have confidence you're going to be here a lot in the fall." To which Trump replied, "Jeff Zucker will not allow it to be any other way, will he?" Zucker is, as *Newsday*'s Verne Gay noted (4/21/04), "president of NBC's Entertainment, News and Cable Group and a leading proponent of a practice known in TV parlance as 'cross-promotion.'"

During the May "sweeps" period (when advertising rates are set based on audience share), *TV Guide* (6/11/04) counted over 117 minutes of NBC promotions on the Today show. CBS's *Early Show*, which runs an hour less than *Today*, finished second with just over 107 minutes. ABC's *Good Morning America* came in last with just under 36 minutes of self-promotion. Former *Morning Show* producer Steve Friedman told the magazine that "it's inevitable that a morning show or a magazine show will do these segments," adding: "You'd be a fool not to do it. It's a business."

Washington Post TV reporter Lisa de Moraes (8/6/04) catalogued the self-promotion she found in just that day's listings. ABC's *20/20* profiled reality TV star Victoria Gotti, whose *Growing Up Gotti* program just happened to be airing on the A&E cable channel—owned by ABC parent Disney. Over at CBS, the *48 Hours* newsmagazine profiled Yoanna House, who lost 60 pounds to try out for *America's Next Top Model*, a reality show airing on the UPN network—which, like CBS, is owned by Viacom. De Moraes pointedly remarked: "Remember how the broadcast networks explained that they would cover only three hours of each of the four-day Democratic and Republican conventions because they are nothing more than infomercials out of which no real news comes?"

The network that pays for the rights to broadcast the Olympic Games always happens to find the Olympics far more newsworthy than its network competitors. In 2004, according to the Tyndall Report's tally of network newscast coverage (8/28/04), *NBC Nightly News* devoted 106 minutes of news time to the Athens events; by comparison, ABC dedicated 34 minutes of news time, and CBS only 15. NBC executive producer Tom Touchet, who works on the *Today Show*, felt no conflict, telling the *Atlanta Journal-Constitution* (8/14/04) that his bosses haven't asked him to do anything he wasn't comfortable with.

On July 9, ABC's *20/20* presented a segment on the legend of King Arthur. While that might be an odd topic for a newsmagazine show, even more unusual was one of the guest "experts" chosen to share his views on the subject: Hollywood bigwig Jerry Bruckheimer, whose "expertise" consisted in being the producer of the new Disney film *King Arthur*. As the *Christian Science Monitor* (8/27/04) noted, "If the weakness of Bruckheimer's grasp of Arthurian lore was obvious, the connection between his movie and ABC television wasn't. Only at the end of the segment did the reporter mention that Disney owns ABC."

As the *Monitor* explained, Disney/ABC felt no need to even conjure up a good explanation for the decision: "The movie producer was included in the show for business reasons, not because he was the most knowledgeable source, acknowledges David Westin, president of ABC News. 'It made good sense for us, frankly,' he says, 'to take advantage of all the marketing and publicity for the movie.'"

GOVERNMENT AND OTHER "OFFICIAL" PRESSURE

The relationship between the press and government should, in theory, be a somewhat confrontational one. When stories surface that local governments are refusing to speak to certain reporters or media outlets, one can only hope that in some way this means the media in question are doing their job, and politicians are angry about it.

Government officials also know that applying a little pressure to the media can go a long way. It's worth remembering that these same media companies are often engaged in high-stakes lobbying, trying to extract favors from federal or state regulators they're also obligated to cover—so even if they don't cave in to pressure, they're not often eager to embarrass the officials who apply it.

Occasionally, though, some examples of government pressure attempts are made public. When celebrity reporter Kitty Kelley was promoting her critical book about the Bush family, a White House official called NBC News president Neal Shapiro to discourage the network from doing interviews with her (*New York Times*, 9/9/04).

Even some of the most celebrated journalism is affected by government pressure: CBS's April 28 investigation of the abuse and torture at Abu Ghraib prison in Iraq, for example, was held for two weeks at the request of the Pentagon.

It's not just that press-state relations are often uncontentious; sometimes they're downright cozy. When California Gov. Arnold Schwarzenegger traveled to New York for the Republican National Convention, the tab wasn't picked up by the GOP, or even the state he serves; instead, a handful of the largest media companies in the country—including Fox, NBC Universal, TimeWarner, Disney and Viacom—paid the bill (*New York Times*, 8/26/04).

At the *Austin American-Statesman*, editorial page editor Arnold Garcia Jr. got what other reporters might have considered a scoop: Local business Temple-Inland Inc. was planning a major—and potentially controversial—expansion of its corporate headquarters. But instead of reporting the news, he suppressed it.

Garcia got the tip while playing golf with Austin Mayor Will Wynn. Later, when Garcia e-mailed Wynn for more information, the mayor told the editor that he'd rather the information not appear in print, since he wanted time to line up political support for the company's decision, which was likely to encounter stiff environmental opposition.

News of the company's plans leaked out two months after Garcia first learned of them, thanks to an investigation by a local environmental group. Their digging yielded more bad news. As Garcia explained in a column to the paper's readers (1/29/04): "Worse, in an incredible lapse of judgment, I offered to send a draft [to Wynn] of whatever editorial resulted."

New Mexico Governor Bill Richardson no doubt appreciated the effusive speech that welcomed him to the Border Governors Conference.

Richardson, attendees learned, "has done more for New Mexico in two legislative sessions than any previous governor accomplished in decades." No small praise, especially considering the source: Monica Armenta, an anchor at New Mexico TV station KOB. To make matters worse, Armenta didn't even write the words herself—that was left to the governor's staff. Armenta told the *American Journalism Review* (10–11/04) that she'd learned her lesson, though she added, "I've done hundreds of these over the years, and so have many other people in this market."

Upsetting the political applecart is part of a journalist's job—but it might cost them that job.

Rep. Nick Smith's (R.-Mich.) intention to vote against George W. Bush's 2003 Medicare drug plan didn't sit well with powerful GOP lawmakers, who Smith said made him an offer: If he changed his vote, his son Brad, who wanted to run for his father's congressional seat, would receive $100,000 in campaign support. Smith not only stuck to his "no" vote, he told people about the alleged bribe, with the story eventually making its way into the news, including a Robert Novak syndicated column (11/27/03).

Soon afterward, Smith tried to revise his tale, issuing a press release (12/4/03) that denied the $100,000 offer. But reporter Kevin Vandenbroek of radio station WKZO (12/1/03) came forward with evidence that made Smith's new denial hard to swallow: a tape of an interview where Smith discussed the "$100,000-plus" offered to his son's campaign.

Vandenbroek's scoop, however, didn't please everyone at his station; according to Slate (3/24/04), while some station officials were proud of his work, "there were others that might have been uncomfortable that it was focusing on a member of the Republican Party." A few weeks later, Vandenbroek reported that George W. Bush made several dubious claims in an interview with NBC, which prompted a phone call to the station from local Republican officials. Vandenbroek told Slate that after that incident, "I got called in and told to stay away from politics." The station eventually dismissed Vandenbroek for violating company e-mail policy following an exchange with a far-right author who refused to appear on the station.

As Slate's Timothy Noah put it, "Vandenbroek's prominence in reporting a major political story ought to make WKZO proud. Instead, it apparently made the Kalamazoo radio station nervous."

OP-ED'S ODD ETHICS

The *St. Louis Post-Dispatch* had some regrets after running an op-ed (5/18/04) by syndicated columnist James Glassman, in which Glassman slammed the new documentary *Super Size Me*, which takes a critical look at McDonald's. The paper identified Glassman, who called the film an "outrageously dishonest and dangerous piece of self-promotion," as a fellow at the conservative American Enterprise Institute and as the host of a website called TechCentralStation.com. But as a May 20 editor's note acknowledged, had the *Post-Dispatch* actually looked at TechCentralStation.com, it would have discovered that McDonald's is prominently listed as a sponsor, and perhaps also noticed "the lavish spinoff website that TechCentralStation.com has devoted solely to discrediting *Super Size Me*." Readers, the paper noted, likely would have appreciated knowing of this affiliation.

Less than a month later, Glassman struck again: In a June 6 Los Angeles Times op-ed co-authored by a TCS colleague, he attacked "left-wing activists" for trying to force Abbott Laboratories to give up its patent on Norvir, an important AIDS drug, after the company jacked the drug's price up by 400 percent. But once again, left unmentioned was the connection between TCS and the company it was defending: Abbott is a member of PhRMA, the pharmaceutical trade association, which, like McDonald's, is a TCS funder (Center for American Progress, 6/10/04).

Glassman's particularly popular in the *Washington Times*: Three times in as many months, the paper published op-eds by Glassman that pushed views and policies that would directly favor TCS sponsors. Glassman praised Bush policies that have been a financial boon to tech companies like TCS backers Intel, Microsoft and Qualcomm (10/27/04); blasted the use of generic anti-AIDS drugs in developing countries, another threat to PhRMA (11/17/04); and trashed global warming science and the Kyoto Protocol (12/16/04), which are both anathema to TCS sponsor ExxonMobil. Not once was his TCS affiliation or relationship to the sponsors disclosed.

When the *Austin Chronicle*'s William M. Adler read a pro-nuclear-industry op-ed in the *Austin American-Statesman* by University of Texas professor Sheldon Landsberger (3/4/04), he thought it sounded strangely familiar. After some enterprising digging, Adler confirmed his hunch: Landsberger's piece contained phrases nearly identical to those in an op-ed by another academic, both of whom had agreed to sign their names to pro-industry columns written entirely by nuclear industry propagandists.

Landsberger's column argued that the public was being burned by the federal government because the feds were failing to provide sufficient funds for developing the Yucca Mountain nuclear waste dump in Nevada. In the op-ed, the nuclear industry lobbyist who actually wrote the column remarked: "This is stealing money from taxpayers who were required to support the waste management project."

According to the *Chronicle* (4/16/04), Landsberger, a nuclear engineering professor, admits that he's been allowing his name and university position to be used like this by the nuclear industry two or three times a year for the past four or five years. And as Adler documents, the industry has been placing ghost-written columns for decades under various names.

The *Statesman* ran a letter of apology from Landsberger in its letters to the editor section on April 14. While that's a welcome correction, it's hardly a solution to the problem. As Bill Perkins, a founding partner of the PR firm responsible for Landsberger's op-eds, said (*Washington Post*, 4/25/04): "I doubt that there is a public affairs campaign by any advocacy group in the country that doesn't have some version of this.... This is fairly conventional."—*J.H.*

SIDEBAR:
PBS: BOWING UNDER PRESSURE

Public broadcasters have a more explicit reliance on government than commercial broadcasters: They survive in part on federal and state funding. With that relationship comes the danger that public broadcasters, who have an explicit obligation to present divergent and underrepresented views, will bow to political pressure.

After South Carolina Educational Television aired a documentary on gays in the South, a state lawmaker threatened to cut the agency's funding. Though the program in question was not funded by SCETV, state Rep. John Graham Altman was incensed that the "militant homosexual agenda" found a home on public TV (Associated Press, 11/28/04). AP noted that the agency's funding had already declined as of late—from $20.3 million to $12.7 million in the past four years. No action has been taken as of early 2005.

But consider the rightward drift of PBS, and you see how political pressure works. In 2004, PBS scaled back *Now With Bill Moyers* from one hour to 30 minutes—even as Moyers retired and was replaced by a less political host—and added two shows from a distinctly conservative perspective: *Tucker Carlson Unfiltered* and the *Wall Street Journal Editorial Report*.

According to reports in the public broadcasting newspaper *Current*

(1/19/04, 6/7/04) and the *New Yorker* (6/7/04), conservative lawmakers' complaints about the alleged liberal bias of *Now* led PBS officials to strive to "balance" their lineup. At the center of this controversy is the Corporation for Public Broadcasting (CPB), the organization through which federal funding is distributed to public broadcasting.

During confirmation hearings for CPB appointee Cheryl Halpern, Sen. Trent Lott (R.-Miss.) criticized a commentary by Moyers as "the most blatantly partisan, irresponsible thing I've ever heard in my life," adding that "the CPB has not seemed to be willing to deal with Bill Moyers and that type of programming." Halpern responded: "The fact of the matter is, I agree," though she said at the time there was little the CPB could do about it.

But there was something the CPB could do. According to Ken Auletta's investigation in the New Yorker, PBS president Pat Mitchell was meeting with Lynne Cheney and conservative television producer Michael Pack to discuss a possible series about Cheney's children's books. And after former House Speaker Newt Gingrich told Mitchell that there weren't enough conservatives on PBS, the *New Yorker* reported that Mitchell "proposed to Gingrich that he co-host a PBS town-hall program," an idea that was frustrated by Gingrich's contract with Fox News Channel.

When the committee reconvened in late July, Lott "noted progress" on the subject of liberal bias (*Public Broadcasting Report*, 7/23/04). That senators like Lott hold public broadcasting's purse strings tells you all you need to know about PBS's public affairs programming.—*P.H.*

Reprinted with Permission from *Extra!* March/April 2005

CHAPTER 10

Index on Censorship: Annual Report

By Rohan Jayasekera

It's an old and familiar graffiti joke. Next to the slogan *"Jesus Is Coming,"* some wit has painted the words *"...And Boy Is He Pissed!"*

Offended? Increasingly, more people seemed to be more willing to complain about bad language, indecency and blasphemy in 2004. And many more of the complaints came from members of religious traditionalist groups.

Christian groups in the U.S., Muslim organizations, Christian organizations in Europe and the Middle East, and Hindu and Buddhist organizations in Asia took a high profile lead in campaigning against obscenity on TV and other media.

For them a return to traditional moral values seemed like the best defense against the wave of indecency and irreligious behavior that tempts their children and, as they see it, undermines decent standards. And sooner or later they eventually end up fingering the media and entertainment industries as the prime offenders.

There's nothing new about religious groups targeting the media and the arts. What is new is the scale of support they are now able to rally through the Internet, and their determination to not only stop the smut, but see the smut-peddlers fired and their corporate employers punished with huge fines.

Many such groups not only believe Jesus is coming, but they also believe they know what's pissing him off. And in 2004 they got better organized to do something about it. Or, as one group typically put it, to get "mobilized to combat and eliminate the destructive influence of pornography, obscenity and indecency… [and] promote the Biblical ethic of decency and Judeo-Christian values."

The current stampede in the U.S. was triggered, of course, by the now-famous Janet Jackson "wardrobe malfunction," in which she briefly exposed a breast during the live broadcast of the 2004 Superbowl football game. The U.S. Federal Communications Commission (FCC) decision to fine CBS $550,000 for the infraction, plus its reluctance to clarify the indecency rules, has resulted in self-censorship by broadcasters confused by what constitutes indecency by FCC standards.

So they err on the side of caution. Some 66 ABC network affiliates chose not to run the patriotic war film *Saving Private Ryan* in November 2004 because of fears that the FCC might later rule the film's rough soldierly language indecent and fine accordingly (it didn't), or worse, deny them their new licenses come renewal time.

Political leaders are falling in behind them, some even overtaking them in the race to make someone pay for the sins on TV. Wisconsin lawmaker James Sensenbrenner recently advocated jail sentences for the worst offending broadcasters.

The phenomena were not limited to the U.S. Across the rest of the world religious groups took offence at films and TV broadcast and then turned to the government and their regulators for action.

The difference was that many got violent as well.

In Russia a gang of Orthodox Christian activists vandalized an art exhibition entitled *Caution, Religion!* that featured several works challenging the role of religion in Russian society. The vandals went free; it was the gallery director and the curator of the exhibition that ended up in court.

In Egypt the state bowed to religious groups and axed the TV miniseries *A Girl from Shubra*, about the relationship between a Christian woman and a Muslim man during the 1940s. The program was ruled to "deal with relations between Christians and Muslims in a way that undermines national unity."

In India supporters of the Hindu hard-line Shiv Sena party vandalized movie theatres to protest against the Bollywood film *Girlfriend*, about a love affair between two women. Indian Roman Catholic groups demanded the banning of a film, *Sins*, which depicted a priest having an affair with a girl half his age.

The steamroller was at work in Britain as well. Regulators got more calls as they simplified their procedures: UK Advertising Standards Authority chairman Lord Borrie said it had "never been easier to complain."

The BBC's director of television Jana Bennett was forced to robustly defend the right to screen controversial shows like the satirical musical *Jerry Springer—The Opera* in the face of outrage from religious groups.

Based on the real Springer's own lurid show, the musical represents a head-on collision between high art and trash culture, according to the BBC itself. Set during a typical Jerry Springer program, the show features a generic line-up of unfortunates whose bizarre fixations and sexual fetishes are eagerly devoured by a baying studio audience.

The rambunctious satire has been performed around the world and won several top awards. Michael Reid, founder of Britain's Christian Congress for Traditional Values was not impressed: "A claim of artistic value is the customary defense for using the most odious and hateful material, deliberately chosen by the admission of BBC executives to challenge traditional values—in this case the sacred image of Jesus Christ," he said. "It is the height of intellectual pretension to claim metaphor, satire and artistic dream sequences justify obscene mockery of Christ as a sexual deviant. That is an argument for no restraint at all in the name of art."

"Broadcasters are having to withstand more pressure than at any time since the 1980s," said the BBC's Bennett. *Jerry Springer—The Opera* drew a record 49,000 complaints. It was, she said, "easy for relatively small numbers of protesters to organize what may appear to be mass protests." A FCC estimate obtained by *Mediaweek* magazine revealed that nearly all indecency complaints in 2003—99.8 per cent—were filed by the Parents Television Council, a single U.S. activist group.

But there was a nasty twist in the tale. The BBC had to call in security guards for its executives after another evangelical Christian group opposed to the Jerry Springer broadcast posted their addresses and telephone numbers on its website. Some received threats.

Significantly, the group said they got their inspiration from British members of the Sikh faith, who had shortly before organized successfully—then violently—to secure the closure of a supposedly "offensive" play written by one of their own faith.

The play, called *Behzti (Dishonor)*, was closed down after gangs of Sikhs attacked the Birmingham Repertory Theatre where it was being performed. The playwright was physically threatened and verbally abused, her family harassed.

The most shocking act of violence came in the Netherlands in November 2004 with the murder of Dutch filmmaker Theo van Gogh, a writer and director who had made a professional career out of giving offence. But an alleged radical Islamist killed him after he directed a film called *Submission*, written by a Somali-born woman member of the Dutch parliament, which highlighted violence against women in Muslim societies.

"Overall, the debate touches on a central question about how we live now," noted *Index on Censorship*'s editor-in-chief Ursula Owen. "Should people in a diverse, multicultural society be protected from offence and insult simply because they demand it in the name of religion, curtailing free speech where necessary?"

"The answer from *Index on Censorship* has to be a resounding no. Most of our contemporary ideas about freedom of speech and imagination come from the Enlightenment. The battle for the Enlightenment was fought over the church's desire to place limits on thoughts and words. We may have thought we'd won the battle forever, but we may not have."

INDEX

Index is a regularly updated online and print chronicle of free expression violations logged by *Index on Censorship*. Here are selections from just some of the entries for the more than 90 countries we tracked in 2004.

AFGHANISTAN: Some 150 new publications opened after the Taliban's 2001 ouster, but Fazil Rahman Orya of the daily *Mashal Democracy* warned that regional warlords still threaten editors who criticize them in print. Sebghatullah Sanger, publisher of the weekly *Jumhori Ghag* admitted that self-censorship was 'visibly high' as a result. (IWPR)

ALGERIA: Journalist Hafnaoui Ghoul was freed on 24 November seven months into a nine month jail sentence for defamation brought over his investigation into the deaths of 13 newborns in a hospital in the town of Djelfa and other reports of local corruption. He was freed early without explanation. (RSF)

AUSTRALIA: Australian officials ordered members of U.S. rap act *D12* to attend a briefing on 'appropriate standards of behaviour' when in Australia, their next destination on a 2004 world tour. A spokeswoman said such lectures were 'common practice.' Any artist could be assessed 'to make sure their act met community standards.' (Scoop.nz)

AZERBAIJAN: Rauf Arifoglu, opposition figure and editor of the daily *Yeni Musavat*, was sentenced by a Baku court on 20 October to five years in jail for 'disturbing public order' and 'refusal to comply.' He had already spent nearly a year in detention, accused of fomenting riots after the country's disputed presidential elections in October 2003. (RSF)

BAHRAIN: On 21 April Nada Haffadh, a member of Bahrain's upper house of parliament, was appointed as Bahrain's first woman minister, taking the health portfolio. She is the first woman to head a health ministry in an Arab state. (BBC)

BANGLADESH: Syed Abul Maksud, deputy chief news editor of the state *Bangladesh Sangbad Sangstha*, resigned on 3 March after official criticism of an article describing the 27 February stabbing of academic Dr Humayun Azad as 'a naked display of fascism.' Azad had written a controversial novel about Bangladesh religious groups who collaborated with the Pakistani army during the 1971 war of independence. (*Daily Star*)

BELARUS: On 17 October Belarus held national parliamentary elections and a referendum on lifting a two-term limit in favor of incumbent president Aleksandr Lukashenka. Independent media endured closures, fines and print bans before the vote, even Russian and U.S. media were targeted. On 18 October the Central Election Committee announced that 78% had voted for the constitutional change. (ishr.org, charter97.org)

BRAZIL: In May, *New York Times'* Brazil correspondent Larry Rother had his visa revoked by the Brazilian Ministry of Justice, after writing an article about the drinking habits of Brazilian President Luiz Inácio Lula da Silva. (CPJ, IAPA, BBC)

BULGARIA: On 16 November Romanian journalist George Buhnici was arrested by Bulgarian authorities on suspicion of espionage. Buhnici had used a hidden camera while making a documentary about cigarette smugglers. He was later charged with 'using tools of espionage to acquire secret information.' (mediaonline.ba, EJC)

BURMA: On 12 May, sports journalist Zaw Thet Htwe had a death sentence for treason commuted to three years' imprisonment. Htwe and three others were accused of plotting to kill junta leaders. Others allege that his real 'crime' had been to accuse junta members of misappropriating foreign funds meant for Burmese football. (RSF, BMA)

CANADA: On 22 September Holocaust denier Ernst Zundel was sentenced to a further six months in prison. He had been jailed on 21 January after Canadian security services reported him as a threat to national security.

The 65-year-old Canadian citizen had been deported from the U.S. in February 2003. (Canadian Free Speech)

CHINA: Officials placed several human rights activists under house arrest in the run up to the 15th anniversary of the Tiananmen Square massacre on 4 June among them Hu Jia, who had highlighted official failures to tackle the AIDS crisis in China and Ding Zilin, leader of 'The Mothers of Tiananmen,' whose children died in the 1989 massacre. (RSF)

COLOMBIA: Staff at the weekly *Semana* were threatened after investigating secret talks between the government and right-wing paramilitaries in July. The talks raised fears that paramilitary leaders might be offered immunity from prosecution in return for disarming. 'In the heat of the conflict the independent media have become a nuisance to the warlords. Critical judgment is perceived as a threat and the truth is turned into a military target,' the magazine commented. (*Semana*, Crisisweb.org)

CONGO DRC: Journalist Mbuyi Tshibwabwa, also known as Mbote ya Kabambi, was arrested, beaten and hospitalized in August after being charged with 'military indiscipline.' He had refused to accompany the Eighth Military District Commander General Obedi Rwibasira on a mission in North Kivu. (JED)

COTE D'IVOIRE: On 7 November, Ivorian journalist Antoine Masse was killed in Dekoue by French forces as he was covering a demonstration against their intervention. The day before, cameraman Lazare Ahua was wounded as he filmed a French retaliatory attack triggered by a raid by Ivorian aircraft in Bouake. (UNJCI)

CUBA: On 26 April, Carlos Brizuela Yera of the independent Cooperativa de Periodistas Independientes de Camagüey news agency was jailed for three years. Journalist Lester Téllez Castro and eight rights activists got sentences ranging from three years house arrest to seven years jail for 'public disorder' and 'resistance to authority' at a demonstration in March 2002. (RSF, WIPC, HRW).

ECUADOR: Patricio Orduoez Maico, a gay rights activist who had filed a complaint against police officers who assaulted him, survived a murder attempt on 12 March, just a week after he detailed the case at an international human rights meeting in Quito. (AI)

EGYPT: Abdel Halim Qandil, editor of the weekly al-Arabi and one of the country's most outspoken opposition journalists, was beaten up in Cairo on

2 November. His assailants repeatedly told him to 'stop talking about people in high places.' His paper opposed an extended mandate for President Hosni Mubarak. (RSF)

ERITREA: The last remaining foreign correspondent in the country, Jonah Fisher of Reuters and the BBC, was expelled by the government on 9 September. No reason was given for the decision but three weeks earlier the Information Minister Ali Abdu Ahmed had accused him of 'racist negative reporting.' (CPJ)

GAMBIA: Reporters sans Frontières correspondent Deyda Hydara was murdered on the night of 16 to 17 December, shot three times in the head as he left his Banjul office. Hydara, 58, was the managing editor and co-owner of the private weekly *The Point*, and had been the local correspondent for Agence France-Presse since 1974. (RSF)

GHANA: Ghana's inspector general of police met with media representatives to discuss coverage of the December election. He urged the media not to provoke violent clashes as election campaigns progress. He was particularly concerned by phone-in programs, which he believed fostered political attacks. (allafrica.com)

INDIA: An international group of investors has come to the rescue of persecuted news website *Tehelka*, famous for its exposés of corruption in India's political and defense establishment. A judicial commission eventually cleared *Tehelka* of a string of counter-allegations from the state but not before the website was forced to close. (*The Age*)

INDONESIA: Indonesia's most famous human rights activist, Munir Said Thalib died of arsenic poisoning on a Garuda Indonesia flight to Amsterdam on 6 September. Munir had dared to expose the security forces' brutality in Aceh and Papua. More recently, Munir campaigned against extended powers for the country's intelligence service. (BBC)

IRAQ: On 24 March the head of the U.S. Coalition Provisional Authority (CPA), Paul Bremer, signed an order setting up the Iraqi Communications and Media Commission (ICMC). The body has been allocated a budget of $6 million and will be based on Western models such as the UK regulator Ofcom and the U.S. Federal Communications Commission. (BBC)

IRAN: A film satirizing the Iranian religious establishment, *Marmoulak* (*The Lizard*), was withdrawn on 15 May following pressure from religious authorities. In the film a criminal disguises himself as a mullah and then revels in the privileges and power his clerical robes bring him. It had grossed over $1 million in Tehran in three weeks. (BBC)

ISRAEL: Mordechai Vanunu, jailed for 18 years for leaking Israeli nuclear secrets was elected rector of Glasgow University in December. Students said they voted for him to show their support for human rights and opposition to nuclear weapons. Previous incumbents include Winnie Mandela and Benjamin Disraeli. (BBC)

ITALY: Reporter Fabrizio Gatti of the daily *Corriere della Sera* was given a 20-day suspended jail sentence on 5 May for giving a false identity to a policeman. He had posed as an illegal Romanian immigrant named 'Roman Ladu' to investigate conditions at a refugee center. His reports won him a top journalism prize. (RSF)

JAPAN: The Japanese comic *Shueisha* self-censored a storyline in September following protests at its *manga* depiction of the 1930s Rape of Nanking in which up to 300,000 Chinese citizens were killed by invading Japanese forces. Right-wingers, extreme nationalists and militarists deny that the massacres took place. (*Telegraph*)

LEBANON: France ordered the banning of TV broadcasts by Lebanon's militant Hezbollah group for broadcasting 'hate speech' and 'threatening public order.' Paris-based satellite operator Eutelsat to stop broadcasting *al-Manar* TV in December or pay fines of more than $8,100 a day in penalty thereafter. (*Al-Jazeera*)

NEPAL: Maoist rebel leader Krishna Bahadur Mahara apologized for the murder a month earlier of journalist Dekendra Raj Thapa in an 11 September letter to the Federation of Nepalese Journalists. But a few weeks later another rebel leader, Kshetra Bahadur Regmi, alias Kisaan, threatened to kill three other journalists after they reported the abduction of seven teenagers by Maoists from two schools in Parbat district. (RSF, AFP)

NETHERLANDS: Theo Van Gogh, a controversial filmmaker, writer and columnist known for his provocative views was murdered on 2 November in Amsterdam. Van Gogh had received death threats after his film *Submission*, which criticizes the oppression of women in Islam, was screened on Dutch television at the end of August 2004. The suspected murderer, a 26-year-old man with dual Dutch and Moroccan nationality who is known to have links to radical Islamist groups, was arrested the same day. (IFJ, RSF)

NIGERIA: Protesters at an anti-government demonstration in Lagos were tear gassed and arrested, among them Nobel laureate Wole Soyinka, human rights lawyer Gani Fawehinmi and leading human rights activist Beko Ransome-Kuti. All were later freed without charge. The police said the marchers did not have a permit for the protest. (IRIN)

MALAYSIA: The government warned local media on 15 April to cut back on news related to the alleged affair of Malaysian-born model Sarah Marbeck and England football captain David Beckham, saying that she tarnished the country's moral image. (*The Age*)

MEXICO: Roberto Javier Mora García, editorial director of *El Mañana* newspaper, was assassinated on 19 March, stabbed 26 times outside his house in Nuevo Laredo. He was known for his exposé of drug trafficking and murder in the region. On 28 March Mario Medina Vázquez, a U.S. citizen, was jailed for the killing, though he claimed his confession had been extracted by torture. On 13 May Vázquez was himself killed by another prisoner in Tamaulipas state prison. (RSF,PSF)

MOROCCO: Anas Guennoun, director of the weekly *al-Ahali*, was jailed for 10 months on 2 April for criminal defamation. Guennoun, who still faces other separate defamation charges, was the first journalist to be jailed in Morocco since 7 January and a statement by the government that committed the country to 'fast track' democratization. (RSF)

PERU: Journalist Alberto Rivera Fernandez was assassinated in his office in Pucallpa, eastern Peru on 21 April. The host of the program *Transparencia* on Frecuencia Oriental radio, a former member of parliament and president of the Ucayali Journalists' Federation, he had recently criticized local authorities for profiteering from the sale of land occupied by squatters. (IPYS, CPJ)

PALESTINE: Khalil al-Zaben, a prominent Palestinian journalist and human rights adviser to Yasser Arafat, was killed by unknown gunmen outside his Gaza office on 2 March. He died after being struck by a dozen bullets. (APFW)

PAKISTAN: From mid to late March the authorities barred foreign and local reporters from entering Wana, regional capital of the western province of South Waziristan, during a bloody 12-day confrontation between government troops and Islamic militants. The Pakistan Federal Union of Journalists protested against the 'undeclared ban' on covering the military operation. (CPJ, PPF, *New York Times*)

PHILIPPINES: On 28 November 2004, the body of Stephen Omaois, a reporter for the biweekly newspaper *Guru Press* in remote Kalinga province was found in a garbage can on the outskirts of the northern city of Tabuk. Omaois, 24, was the 13th journalist killed in the Philippines in 2004. (IFJ)

POLAND: Beata Korzeniewska of the daily newspaper *Gazeta Pomorska* was jailed for a month after an appeal court reversed her earlier acquittal on charges that she had libeled Torun city judge Zbigniew Wielkanowski. (IPI)

RUSSIA: On 6 September Raf Shakirov was forced to resign as editor of *Izvestia* in a dispute with officials over his newspaper's coverage of the Beslan crisis—deemed too 'emotional' and graphic—and for criticism of the government's handling of the siege. *Izvestia* is a privately owned newspaper that strives to keep in line with the Kremlin as part of owner Vladimir Potanin's attempts to appease the government. (novayagazeta.ru, *Moscow Times*)

RWANDA: In the first criminal case against a newspaper since Paul Kagame came to power in 1994, Charles Kabonero, editor of *Umuseso*, was acquitted on 23 November of 'ethnic divisionism' but convicted of defamation. This followed an article in August accusing parliamentary vice president Denis Polisi of abuses of power. Kabonero was ordered to pay a fine of 8,000 Rwandan francs (US$15) and a symbolic one franc in damages to Polisi. (Amnesty)

SAUDI ARABIA: Academic Said bin Zair was arrested on 15 April after appearing on Qatar-based *al-Jazeera* TV to discuss a tape attributed to al-Qa'eda leader Osama Bin Laden, in which he condoned suicide bombings. On 11 May his son Mubarak bin-Zair was arrested for 'false allegations' after he appeared on *al-Jazeera* and denounced his father's detention. The month before lawyer Abderrahman al-Lahem was jailed for appearing on the station to criticize the 17 March arrest of intellectual critics of the state, following pro-reform protests in Riyadh. (BBC, APFW)

SERBIA & MONTENEGRO: The editor of Montenegrin daily *Dan*, Dusko Jovanovic, was murdered in a drive-by shooting on 28 May in Podgorica. Jovanovic was considered close to the conservative opposition in Montenegro and critical of prime minister Milo Djukanovic. (CNN)

SOMALIA: Radio reporter Abdiqani Sheik Mohamed was physically attacked and banned from the Middle Shabelle region by militiamen loyal to clan chief Mohamed Omar Habeb on 26 September. He had reported that the elders of the Jowhar community had asked the committee of a local mosque to resign. (RSF, sojonsomalia. com)

SOUTH KOREA: A 12 March amendment to the electoral law gives the National Election Commission increased powers over the internet, including the ability to force service providers to reveal names and addresses of users. On 23 March, a 21 year-old student known as Kwon was arrested and charged with 'disseminating false information.' He had posted more than 70 satirical images of prominent politicians on various websites. (RSF)

SRI LANKA: In December the country's Buddhist clergy campaigned against a concert by Bollywood star Shahrukh Khan, complaining that the event coincided with the anniversary of the death of conservative monk Gangodawila Soma Thera. On the day of the show, attended by more than 20,000 people, a bomb attack killed two people including Lal Jayasundara, a 20-year-old photojournalist. (PTI, FMM)

SUDAN: On 10 April Islam Salih, *al-Jazeera's* bureau chief in Sudan, was convicted of spreading false news and sentenced to one month's imprisonment and a fine of one million Sudanese pounds ($3,800). He was charged following *al-Jazeera's* coverage of fierce fighting between rebels and government troops in Darfur. (RSF)

TANZANIA: In March journalist Jenerali Twaha Ulimwengu was given back the Tanzanian citizenship stripped from him in 2001 for allegedly failing to prove his parents' nationality. At the time the order was seen as a way of punishing him for repeated criticism of the government in his articles and broadcasts. (MISA)

THAILAND: Reporters from foreign news agencies were barred in May from entering military controlled areas in southern Thailand after reports of clashes between Muslim militants in Yala, Pattani and Songkhla provinces on 28 April angered prime minister Thaksin Shinawatra. A military spokesman also asked local media to 'sympathize with us and report news for the benefit of our country.' (*Bangkok Post*)

TONGA: Democracy activist Alani Taione was released on bail on 4 March, given back his passport and allowed to return to New Zealand, where he has lived since 1987. Taione, who is accused of importing a banned publication into Tonga, is due to appear before the Supreme Court on 24 March. (RSF)

TUNISIA: The International Federation of Journalists provisionally expelled the Association des Journalistes Tunisiens (AJT) on 8 March after a decision by the AJT to award its Plume D'Or award for press freedom to President Ben Ali in late 2003. (IFJ)

TURKEY: In March, an appeals court overturned *Atilim* journalist Asiye Zeybek Guzel's 12-and-a-half year sentence for 'membership of an illegal organization'. Guzel has said she was raped at the anti-terrorism unit's Istanbul center and denied the charges. She was released in 2002, fled to Sweden and was re-sentenced in absentia. (BIA, Info-Turk)

TURKMENISTAN: Mukhamed Berdiyev, a Moscow-based correspondent for Radio Free Europe's Turkmen service, was beaten by three men and left for dead in his home on 30 April. They also destroyed his computer. An official at the Turkmen embassy in Moscow dismissed the report as attention seeking by a reporter 'constantly addressing the so-called issue of human rights in Turkmenistan.' FE/RL)

UNITED KINGDOM: A production of the play *Corpus Christi* by Terrence McNally, which portrays a gay Jesus Christ-like character, was described as a 'blasphemous, hate-filled mockery' by conservative group Christian Voice. Scots parliamentarian Iain Smith called on people to see the production before rushing to condemn it. A center director, Roy McLachlan, later resigned because he said he could not 'square his beliefs with the play.' (*Scotsman*)

UNITED STATES: On 16 March a federal judge imposed a running fine of $1,000 a day on journalist Jim Taricani of WJAR TV in Providence, Rhode Island for refusing to reveal the source of a film showing a local official accepting a bribe from a FBI informant. Providence Mayor Vincent Cianci Jr has since been sentenced to five years of jail. (RSF)

UZBEKISTAN: British ambassador to Uzbekistan Craig Murray criticized both the government for its censorship and Uzbek journalists for not trying harder. Murray said: 'Uzbek journalists are rather parasitical people who do not publish any truth, don't seek the truth, don't try to publish it and really they are a disgrace to their profession.' (IWPR)

VIETNAM: The government tightened 'management of internet operations' on 12 May as announced by *An Ninh The Gioi*, mouthpiece of the Public Security ministry. Decision No 71 ruled that taking advantage of the Web to disrupt 'social order and safety' or breach the nation's 'fine customs and traditions' was 'strictly forbidden.' (RSF)

YEMEN: On 6 December the corpses of Mohammed Salem al-Sagheer and his wife were found in the capital Sana'a. Al-Sagheer was the editor-in-chief of the newspaper *al-Waseet* and a businessman. He had supported private sector and opposition newspapers by providing printing facilities at affordable prices. (IFJ)

ZIMBABWE: A Harare magistrate's court acquitted four directors of the banned *Daily News* and cleared them of charges of illegally publishing the paper on 20 September. The newspaper, banned in October 2003, briefly resumed publishing in January 2004 after having won a court case against the government's closing order. It had to stop the presses again on 5 February, when Zimbabwe's Supreme Court upheld the draconian Information and Protection of Privacy Act. (MISA)

Rohan Jayasekera is an associate editor at *Index on Censorship*. He directed the magazine's international free expression support programs in Iraq during 2004.

THIS MODERN WORLD

by TOM TOMORROW

CHAPTER 11

Non-embedded Reporting from Iraq

By Dahr Jamail

"Any dictator would admire the uniformity and obedience of the U.S. media."—Noam Chomsky

"In a time of universal deceit—telling the truth is a revolutionary act."
—George Orwell

The struggle to maintain personal safety while working in Iraq as an independent, non-embedded journalist nearly matches the struggle to combat the corporate media "coverage" of the horrific situation on the ground. Growing a beard, dressing local, using different cars, exiting the hotel at different times to avoid kidnapping are all part of the deal; yet the risk of working independently in occupied Iraq is necessary if we are to get the real story. Yet by assuming these risks, trust is immediately earned from people I wish to interview; and in this way, an independent journalist is able to report stories that a reporter accompanied by U.S. soldiers never could.

One of the myriad of stories failing to be reported by corporate media is the strength, dignity and generosity of the Iraqi people. When I am working on a story, inevitably I am asked by Iraqis to join them for lunch, or even to spend the night at their home inside embattled Fallujah. If time doesn't allow for a meal, then to not at least share tea with someone would be an insult. The constant outpouring of warmth and generosity from a people who have suffered through two wars, decades of dictatorship, 13 years of brutal economic sanctions, and now a bloody occupation dragging on with no end in sight is overwhelming.

My hope is that the spirit of the Iraqi people as well as the horrific circumstances they are enduring under the illegal, U.S.-led occupation of their country are brought forth to the reader in the following web logs.

Media Held Guilty of Deception

BY DAHR JAMAIL, INTER PRESS SERVICE

ROME, Feb 14/05 (IPS)—A people's tribunal has held much of Western media guilty of inciting violence and deceiving people in its reporting of Iraq. The World Tribunal on Iraq (WTI), an international peoples initiative seeking the truth about the war and occupation in Iraq made its pronouncement Sunday after a three-day meeting. The tribunal heard testimony from independent journalists, media professors, activists, and member of the European Parliament, Michele Santoro.

The Rome session of the WTI followed others in Brussels, London, Mumbai, New York, Hiroshima-Tokyo, Copenhagen, Stockholm and Lisbon. The Rome meeting focused on the media role.

The informal panel of WTI judges accused the governments of the United States and Britian of impeding journalists in performing their task, and intentionally producing lies and misinformation.

The panel accused western corporate media of filtering and suppressing information, and of marginalizing and endangering independent journalists. More journalists were killed in a 14-month period in Iraq than in the entire Vietnam War.

The tribunal said mainstream media reportage on Iraq also violated article six of the Nuremberg Tribunal (set up to try Nazi crimes) which states: "Leaders, organizers, instigators, and accomplices participating in the formulation or execution of a common plan or conspiracy to commit any of the foregoing crimes (crimes against peace, war crimes, and crimes against humanity) are responsible for all acts performed by any persons in execution of such a plan."

The panel that heard testimonies included Francois Houtart, director of the Tricontinental Centre in Belgium that has backed several peoples' movements in Latin America, and Dr. Samir Amin, director of the Third World Forum in Dakar, Senegal. Dr. Haleh Afshar, who teaches politics and women's studies at the University of York in Britain, and Italian author and newspaper editor Ernesto Pallotta witnessed the proceedings.

"This is not simply an exercise to denounce the mainstream media for their bias and incompetence," said Dr. Tony Alessandrini, a human rights activist who has published several articles on the U.S. colonization of Iraq. "These denunciations have been going on for months. Here in Rome, we must go further."

Alessandrini, who helped organize the WTI added, "What we are being asked to consider is not simply media bias, but rather the active complicity of media in crimes that have been committed, and are being committed, on a daily basis against the people in Iraq."

Several experts gave strong testimony. Dr. Peter Phillips, director of Project Censored at Sonoma State University in California where he teaches media censorship, provided taped testimony. He said that at no time since the 1930s has the United States been so close to "institutionalized totalitarianism," and added, "U.S. society has become the least informed, best entertained society in the world."

The WTI Rome session also heard testimony from Dr. David Miller from Scotland, author of *Tell Me Lies: Propaganda and Media Distortion in the Attack on Iraq.* "This is about condemning journalistic complicity of war crimes," said Dr. Miller who is also co-editor of Spinwatch, a group that monitors public relations and propaganda. Miller said the Pentagon "does not recognize the concept of independent journalists, who are seen as providers of unfriendly information." He further notes that mainstream media in the United States and in Britain are "complicit in the selling of the invasion and ongoing occupation. All studies conducted on mainstream media show dominance by government policies, and wartime coverage by TV news in the UK is generally sympathetic to the government's case."

Fernando Suarez, who lost his son Jesus Suarez during the invasion of Iraq when he is said to have stepped on an illegal U.S. cluster bomb, also testified at the tribunal. Suarez testified that he was first told by the Pentagon that his son died from a gunshot to the head, then that he died in an accident, and then that he had died in 'friendly fire.' On inspecting his son's body Suarez said he discovered that his son had died from stepping on a cluster bomb. "I never had the truth from them," Suarez added. "I found the truth, and the truth was very simple. On March 26 the Army dropped 20,000 cluster bombs in Iraq, but only about 20 percent exploded. The other 80 percent are in the cities and the schools and acting as mines." Suarez said: "Bush said he sent my son because Iraq had illegal weapons, and my son died from an illegal American weapon, and nobody has spoken about this. The media will not talk about the illegal American weapons."

Several witnesses testified about media disinformation regarding the siege of Fallujah. They were presented copies of the award winning documentary *Weapons of Mass Deception* by journalist and filmmaker Danny Schechter, who is also executive editor of Mediachannel.org, an online media issues network.

Alessandrini said evidence of active complicity of the mainstream media in wrongs committed against the people of Iraq, and the wrongs of deception and incitement, was now overwhelming. "We work from the understanding that history will recall the crimes committed against the people of Iraq by the U.S.," he said. "It is our responsibility to record these crimes in order to ensure these crimes are never again repeated."

Iraqi Women Paying the Price
BY DAHR JAMAIL, ISLAM ONLINE
January 24, 2005

Kidnapping has become the crime of choice amongst Iraqi criminal gangs. With 70 percent unemployment in "liberated" Iraq, crime is running rampant, with organized crime enjoying a free hand amidst the terrible security situation.

The families of the kidnapped are at times forced to pay up to several million dollars ransom unless they want to receive pieces of their loved ones, or even their dead bodies. While media attention has focused heavily on the kidnapping of Westerners, the kidnapping of Iraqis, in particular Iraqi women, is much more common. As far back as July 2003, Human Rights Watch (HRW) reported that "the poor security situation in Baghdad and other Iraqi cities is causing women and girls to severely restrict their movements for fear of rape and abduction." HRW blames the huge increase in kidnappings and sexual assaults on the collapse of the security forces of ex-dictator Saddam Hussein and the U.S. occupation's slow reorganization of Iraq's police force. Within three months of the fall of Baghdad, HRW had documented 70 cases of rape and abduction of Iraqi women. As brutal as the regime of Saddam Hussein was, violent crime against women averaged only one case every three months under Hussein's rule, whereas in July 2003, there were several per week. And the situation is far, far worse today.

On December 4, 2004, Inji, a 29-year-old veterinarian, was in her clinic near Kirkuk. She and Mohamed, her assistant, were asked to accompany a man who needed help inoculating some cattle. They drove down a small dirt road to where the man said the cattle would be located. "I didn't expect anything bad to happen," she says wearily. "The roads to the nearby villages are all unpaved and deserted. Then another car stopped. It had three passengers, people I presumed to be his relatives or friends, but that wasn't the case. One of the passengers walked up and hit me on the head with his gun," she said, still processing the horrible events, "I saw them hit Mohamed when they pulled me into the car. After 15 minutes I tried to speak and they hit me again." They drove along dirt roads for two hours. Then Inji was dragged out of the car, while other men pulled Mohamed from a second car. "The men ordered me to take off my jewelry, then beat me so much I could no longer feel pain," she says quietly. The kidnappers then used her mobile phone to call her husband, Turhan. He was told that his wife was kidnapped, and that he had 24 hours to pay $20,000 in ransom. Otherwise, he was told, she would be sold. "I was kept in a dark room on a bare floor with a dirty blanket," she explained. "They made me call my husband and tell him to prepare the money, and I swore to them that my family could not afford this money." One of the kidnappers responded, "Let the democracy that you call for collect the money for you." "I called my husband and begged him to save me," she said, "but then the man grabbed my phone and told my husband not to call the police or they would kill me." "I thought the only people being kidnapped were those who were dealing with the Americans or were rich," she explained, her hands held up in confusion. Inji has no affiliation with the occupiers or with any political party, nor does she work for the government. Miraculously, her husband managed to raise the money and ransom Inji. But it does not always end well for the victims and their families.

Abdulla Hamid, a 50-year-old Baghdad resident, related how his neighbor's son was kidnapped. The family managed to raise and pay the $15,000 ransom. They were then contacted by the kidnappers, who told them to pick their son up at the morgue.

Or, take for example Seif, a student at the Baghdad Medical School. After he was abducted, his family, incapable of producing the $40,000 demanded by his captors, made the mistake of contacting the police, who tracked down the kidnappers. Seif was killed during the exchange of gunfire between the police and his captors.

While Iraqi government officials continue to blame the kidnappings on various Iraqi resistance groups, the groups themselves deny any involvement. With Iraq's borders left virtually wide open during the first 6 months of the occupation, terrorist groups and criminal gangs alike flowed into the lawless country. Not all criminal gangs were satisfied with ransom money. Twenty-three-year-old Sajidah and her 17-year-old sister-in-law Hanan were kidnapped just weeks after Sajidah's wedding. The two women were taken to Yemen, where they found 130 other Iraqi women who had been kidnapped and forced into prostitution by their captors. Miraculously, they were able to contact family members who managed to make their way to Yemen and free the two women.

Fakhriyah is around 20 years old, but she doesn't know for sure. In fact, she can no longer recall her father's name, as she is now a drug addict. "I was living in an orphanage and was kidnapped the day Baghdad fell," said Fakhriyah. She described how an American tank was stationed near the orphanage due to its proximity to an airport, and how the U.S. troops allowed the orphanage to be looted. "The kidnappers took turns raping me, and I don't remember how long they kept me until they threw me out on the street," she said, dazed and high on glue, trying to blot out her miserable existence. She uses any drug she can get her hands on, "so I don't feel what's going on around me or who is raping me again."

As horrific as the regime of former dictator Saddam Hussein was Iraqis now long for the security it provided. Rape was uncommon then. Now, kidnapping and rape are everyday occurrences. Just three weeks ago the Al-Zaman newspaper reported that 11 children had been abducted in Baghdad in a single day. These stories are commonplace, and they have caused widespread fear in Baghdad and other cities, scaring many women and girls off the streets. Women now go out only when necessary, and are generally accompanied by male relatives.

"I don't go anywhere at night, and only go to school and places close to my home," said Intisar, a 21-year-old physics student at Baghdad University, citing her fear of being kidnapped.

Layla, a 52-year-old pharmacist in the al-Adhamiya district of Baghdad said that she lives in constant fear of being kidnapped, or having one of her children kidnapped. "We are all afraid and I cannot go alone anywhere," she said. "Even my older daughters, I fear for them. This is not a normal life we are living anymore."

Who bears the responsibility for this state of affairs? Aside from those directly committing these crimes, the responsibility lies with the occupiers. According to international humanitarian law, the occupying power has the duty to restore and maintain public order and safety, and to respect the fundamental rights of the occupied territory's inhabitants. Despite the facade of an independent "interim Iraqi government," the U.S. occupation effectively controls

Iraq to this day. The occupiers set up the "laws" which are currently in effect in Iraq, and thus are primarily responsible for the atrocious security situation that has allowed crimes of this kind to become commonplace in Iraq today.

Additionally, the Fourth Geneva Convention states that "women shall be especially protected against any attack on their honor, in particular against rape, enforced prostitution, or any form of indecent assault." This is yet another example of the occupation forces violating international law. As usual, it is the people of Iraq, and particularly women, in this case, who are paying the heaviest price.

U.S. Military Resorting To Collective Punishment

BY DAHR JAMAIL, INTER PRESS SERVICE

BAGHDAD, Jan 18/05 (IPS)—The U.S. military is resorting to collective punishment tactics in Iraq similar to those used by Israeli troops in the occupied territories of Palestine, residents say. Military bulldozers have mown down palm groves in the rural al-Dora farming area on the outskirts of Baghdad, residents say. Electricity has been cut, the local fuel station destroyed and the access road blocked.

The U.S. action comes after resistance fighters attacked soldiers from this area several weeks back. "The Americans were attacked from this field, then they returned and started cutting down all the trees," says Kareem, a local mechanic, pointing to a pile of burnt date palms in a bulldozed field. "None of us knows any fighters. We all know they are coming here from other areas to attack the Americans, but we are the people who suffer from this."

Military action followed a similar round of attacks and retaliation earlier this month when U.S. Army Brigadier-General Mark Kimmit told reporters that the military had launched Operation Iron Grip in the area to send "a very clear message to anybody who thinks that they can run around Baghdad without worrying about the consequences of firing rocket propelled grenades(RPGs)." Gen. Kimmit said, "There is a capability in the air that can quickly respond against anybody who would want to harm Iraqi citizens or coalition forces."

Then as now, local people denied any knowledge of harboring resistance fighters. And now, as then, they say they have to pay the price. "They destroyed our fences, and now there are wolves attacking our animals," said Mohammed, a schoolboy. "They destroyed much of our farming equipment, and the worst is they cut our electricity. They come by here every night and fire their weapons to frighten us." People need electricity to run pumps to irrigate the farms, he said. "Now we are carrying water in buckets from the river, and this is very difficult for us," Mohammed said. "They say they are going to make things better for us, but they are worse."

Going into fields after U.S. retaliation has become hazardous, as they are littered with unexploded mortar shells. A farmer who called himself Sharkr said, "We asked them the first time and they said, 'Okay, we'll come and take care of it.' But they never came."

Other residents say soldiers beat them up during random home raids. "I was beaten by the Americans," said Ihsan, a 17-year-old secondary school student. "They asked me who attacked them, but I do not know. My home was raided, our furniture destroyed, and one of my uncles was arrested."

People in Abu Hishma, a village in the area, spoke of similar experiences. After U.S. soldiers were attacked, the entire village was encircled with razor wire. Residents were forced to acquire identity badges and enter through a military controlled checkpoint. The main farm road was blocked by four large concrete slabs after attacks several weeks ago. Residents used tractors to remove the blocks, but last week they say the military installed four larger blocks. "They humiliate us when we talk to them," said Hamoud Abid, a 50-year-old farmer. "They would not tell us when they will remove these blocks, so we are all walking now."

A military spokesperson in Baghdad declined to comment on the statements by the people in al-Dora, and declined a request for his name. But he said there were ongoing security operations in al-Dora.

Fallujah Refugees Tell of Life and Death in the Kill Zone
BY DAHR JAMAIL, THE NEW STANDARD

December 03, 2004—Men now seeking refuge in the Baghdad area are telling horrific stories of indiscriminate killings by U.S. forces during the peak of fighting last month in the largely annihilated city of Fallujah.

In an interview with *The New Standard*, Burhan Fasaía, an Iraqi journalist who works for the popular Lebanese satellite TV station, LBC, said he witnessed U.S. crimes up close. Fasaía, who was in Fallujah for nine days during the most intense combat, said Americans grew easily frustrated with Iraqis who could not speak English. "Americans did not have interpreters with them," Fasaía said, "so they entered houses and killed people because they didn't speak English. They entered the house where I was with 26 people, and [they] shot people because [the people] didn't obey [the soldiers'] orders, even just because the people couldn't understand a word of English."

A man named Khalil, who asked *The New Standard* not to use his last name for fear of reprisals, said he had witnessed the shooting of civilians who were waving white flags while they tried to escape the city. Fasaía further speculated, "Soldiers thought the people were rejecting their orders, so they shot them. But the people just couldn't understand them." Fasaía says American troops detained him. They interrogated him specifically about working for the Arab media, he said, and held him for three days. Fasaía and other prisoners slept on the ground with no blankets. He said prisoners were made to go to the bathroom in handcuffs, using one toilet in the middle of the camp. "During the nine days I was in Fallujah, all of the wounded women, kids and old people, none of them were evacuated," Fasaía said. "They either suffered to death, or somehow survived."

Many refugees tell stories of having witnessed U.S. troops killing already injured people, former fighters and noncombatants alike. "I watched them roll over wounded people in the street with tanks," said Kassem Mohammed Ahmed, a resident of Fallujah. "This happened so many times."

Other refugees recount similar stories. "I saw so many civilians killed there, and I saw several tanks roll over the wounded in the streets," said 27-year-old Aziz Abdulla, who fled the fighting last month.

Another resident, Abu Aziz, said he also witnessed American armored vehicles crushing people he believes were alive. Abdul Razaq Ismail, another resident who fled Fallujah, said, "I saw dead bodies on the ground and nobody could bury them because of the American snipers. The Americans were dropping some of the bodies into the Euphrates near Fallujah."

A man called Abu Hammad said he witnessed U.S. troops throwing Iraqi bodies into the Euphrates River. Others nodded in agreement. Abu Hammed and others also said they saw Americans shooting unarmed Iraqis who waved white flags. Believing that American and Iraqi forces were bent on killing anyone who stayed in Fallujah, Hammad said he watched people attempt to swim across the Euphrates to escape the siege. "Even then, the Americans shot them with rifles from the shore," he said. "Even if some of them were holding a white flag or white clothes over their heads to show they are not fighters, they were all shot."

Associated Press photographer Bilal Hussein reported witnessing similar events. After running out of basic necessities and deciding to flee the city at the height of the U.S.-led assault, Hussein ran to the Euphrates. "I decided to swim," Hussein told colleagues at the AP, who wrote up the photographer's harrowing story, "but I changed my mind after seeing U.S. helicopters firing on and killing people who tried to cross the river." Hussein said he saw soldiers kill a family of five as they tried to traverse the Euphrates, before he buried a man by the riverbank with his bare hands. "I kept walking along the river for two hours and I could still see some U.S. snipers ready to shoot anyone who might swim," Hussein recounted. "I quit the idea of crossing the river and walked for about five hours through orchards."

U.S. military commanders reported at least two incidents during which they said Iraqi resistance fighters used white flags to lure Marines into dangerous situations, including a well-orchestrated ambush. Proponents of relaxed rules of engagement for U.S. troops engaged in "counter-insurgency" warfare have cited such incidents from last month's experience in Fallujah as arguments for more permissive combat regulations. Some have said U.S. forces should establish what used to be called "free-fire zones," wherein any human being encountered is assumed to be hostile, and thus a legitimate target, relieving American infantrymen of their obligation to distinguish and protect civilians. But if the stories Fallujan witnesses have shared with TNS are accurate, it appears the policy might have preceded the argument in this case.

U.S. and Iraqi officials have called the "pacification" of Fallujah a success and said that the action was necessary to stabilize Iraq in preparation for the country's planned "transition to democracy." The military continues to deny U.S.-led forces killed significant numbers of civilians during November's nearly constant fighting and bombardment.

Weapons Used in Fallujah
BY DAHR JAMAIL

BAGHDAD, Nov 26/04 (IPS)—The U.S. military has used poison gas and other non-conventional weapons against civilians in Fallujah, eyewitnesses report. "Poisonous gases have been used in Fallujah," 35-year-old trader from Fallujah Abu Hammad told IPS. "They used everything—tanks, artillery, infantry, poison gas. Fallujah has been bombed to the ground." Hammad is from the Julan district of Fallujah, where some of the heaviest fighting occurred.

Other residents of that area also report the use of illegal weapons. "They used these weird bombs that put up smoke like a mushroom cloud," Abu Sabah, another Fallujah refugee from the Julan area, told IPS. "Then small pieces fall from the air with long tails of smoke behind them." He said pieces of these bombs exploded into large fires that burnt the skin even when water was thrown on the burns. Phosphorous weapons as well as napalm are known to cause such effects. "People suffered so much from these," he said.

Macabre accounts of killing of civilians are emerging through the cordon U.S. forces are still maintaining around Fallujah. "Doctors in Fallujah are reporting to me that there are patients in the hospital there who were forced out by the Americans," said Mehdi Abdulla, a 33-year-old ambulance driver at a hospital in Baghdad. "Some doctors there told me they had a major operation going, but the soldiers took the doctors away and left the patient to die."

Kassem Mohammed Ahmed, who escaped from Fallujah a little over a week ago, told IPS he witnessed many atrocities committed by U.S. soldiers in the city. "I watched them roll over wounded people in the street with tanks," he said. "This happened so many times."

Abdul Razaq Ismail, who escaped from Fallujah two weeks back, said soldiers had used tanks to pull bodies to the soccer stadium to be buried. "I saw dead bodies on the ground and nobody could bury them because of the American snipers," he said. "The Americans were dropping some of the bodies into the Euphrates near Fallujah."

Abu Hammad said he saw people attempt to swim across the Euphrates to escape the siege. "The Americans shot them with rifles from the shore," he said. "Even if some of them were holding a white flag or white clothes over their heads to show they are not fighters, they were all shot." Hammad said he had seen elderly women carrying white flags shot by U.S. soldiers. "Even the wounded people were killed. The Americans made announcements for people to come to one mosque if they wanted to leave Fallujah, and even the people who went there carrying white flags were killed."

Another Fallujah resident, Khalil, 40, told IPS he saw civilians shot as they held up makeshift white flags. "They shot women and old men in the streets," he said. "Then they shot anyone who tried to get their bodies...Fallujah is suffering too much, it is almost gone now." Refugees have moved to another kind of misery now, he said. "It's a disaster living here at this camp," Khalil said. "We are living like dogs and the kids do not have enough clothes."

Spokesman for the Iraqi *Red Crescent* in Baghdad Abdel Hamid Salim told IPS that none of their relief teams had been allowed into Fallujah, and that the military had said it would be at least two more weeks before any refugees would be allowed back into the city. "There is still heavy fighting in Fallujah," said Salim. "And the Americans won't let us in so we can help people." In many camps around Fallujah and throughout Baghdad, refugees are living without enough food, clothing and shelter. Relief groups estimate there are at least 15,000 refugee families in temporary shelters outside Fallujah.

As U.S. Forces Raided a Mosque

BY DAHR JAMAIL

BAGHDAD, Nov 19/04 (IPS)—An eyewitness commentary to IPS through a U.S. raid on a Baghdad mosque Friday gives a vivid picture of what a 'successful raid' can be like. U.S. soldiers raided the Abu Hanifa mosque in Baghdad during Friday prayers, killing at least four and wounding up to 20 worshippers. At 12:30 p.m. local time, just after Imam Shaikh Muayid al-Adhami concluded his talk, about 50 U.S. soldiers with 20 Iraqi National Guardsmen (ING) entered the mosque, a witness reported. "Everyone was there for Friday prayers, when five Humvees and several trucks carrying INGs entered," Abu Talat told IPS on phone from within the mosque while the raid was in progress. "Everyone starting yelling 'Allahu Akbar' (God is the greatest) because they were frightened. Then the soldiers started shooting the people praying." Talat said he was among a crowd of worshippers being held back at gunpoint by U.S. soldiers. Loud chanting of "Allahu Akbar" could be heard in the background during his call. Women and children were sobbing, he said. "They have just shot and killed at least four of the people praying," he said in a panicked voice. "At least 10 other people are wounded now. We are on our bellies and in a very bad situation." Talat gave his account over short phone calls. He said he was witnessing a horrific scene. "We were here praying and now there are 50 here with their guns on us," he said. "They are holding our heads to the ground, and everyone is in chaos. This is the worst situation possible. They cannot see me talking to you. They are roughing up a blind man now." He then evidently could talk no further.

The soldiers later released women and children along with men who were related to them. Abu Talat was released because a boy told him to pretend to be his father. Other witnesses gave similar accounts outside the mosque. "People were praying and the Americans invaded the mosque," Abdulla Ra'ad Aziz from the al-Adhamiya district of Baghdad told IPS. He had been released along with his wife and children. "Why are they killing people for praying?" He said that after the forces entered "they went to the back doors and we heard so many bullets of the guns—it was a gun bigger than a Kalashnikov. There were wounded and dead, I saw them myself."

Some of the people who had been at prayer were ordered by soldiers to carry the dead and wounded out of the mosque, he said. "One Iraqi National Guardsmen held his gun on people and yelled, 'I will kill you if you don't shut up'," said Rana Aziz, a mother who had been trapped in the mosque. "So they made everyone lie down, then people got quiet, and they took the women and children out." She said someone asked the soldiers if they would be made hostages. A soldier used foul language and asked everyone to shut up, she said. Suddenly, she laughed amid her tears. "The Americans have learnt how to say shut up in Arabic, *Inchev*'."

Soldiers denied Iraqi Red Crescent ambulances and medical teams access to the mosque. As doctors negotiated with U.S. soldiers outside, more gunfire was heard from inside. About 30 men were led out with hoods over their heads and their hands tied behind them. Soldiers loaded them into a military vehicle and took them away around 3.15 p.m.

A doctor with the Iraqi Red Crescent confirmed four dead and nine wounded worshippers. Pieces of brain were splattered on one of the walls inside the mosque while large bloodstains covered carpets at several places. A U.S. military spokesperson in Baghdad did not respond to requests for information on the raid.

Media Repression in a 'Liberated' Land
BY DAHR JAMAIL

BAGHDAD, Nov 18/04 (IPS)—Journalists are increasingly being detained and threatened by the U.S.-installed interim government in Iraq. Media have been stopped particularly from covering recent horrific events in Fallujah. The "100 Orders" penned by former U.S. administrator in Iraq, L. Paul Bremer, include Order 65, passed March 20, to establish an Iraqi communications and media commission. This commission has powers to control the media because it has complete control over licensing and regulating telecommunications, broadcasting, information services and all other media establishments.

On June 28, when the United States handed over power to a 'sovereign' Iraqi interim government, Bremer simply passed on the authority to Ayad Allawi, the U.S.-installed interim prime minister who has had longstanding ties with the British intelligence service MI6 and the CIA.

A glaring instance is the curbs placed on the Qatar-based TV channel al-Jazeera. Within days of the'"handover" of power to an interim Iraqi government last summer, the Baghdad office of al-Jazeera was raided and closed by security forces from the interim government. The network was accused of inaccurate reporting and banned initially for one month from reporting out of Iraq. The ban was then extended "indefinitely."

On Tuesday this week the interim government announced that any al-Jazeera journalist found reporting in Iraq would be detained. The al-Jazeera office in Baghdad was bombed by a U.S. warplane during the invasion of March last year. The TV channel had given its exact coordinates to the Pentagon to avoid such an occurrence. One of their journalists was killed in the bombing. Al-Jazeera now broadcasts a daily apology "because we cannot cover Iraq news well since our offices have been closed for over three months by orders from the interim government."

Other instances of political repression abound. The media commission sent out an order recently asking news organizations to "stick to the government line on the U.S.-led offensive in Fallujah or face legal action." The warning was sent on the letterhead of Allawi. The letter also asked media to "set aside space in your news coverage to make the position of the Iraqi government, which expresses the aspirations of most Iraqis, clear."

Last week a journalist for the al-Arabiya network was detained by U.S. forces outside Fallujah when he attempted to enter the besieged city. Citing another al-Arabiya correspondent as its source, the U.S.-based Committee to Protect Journalists (CPJ) said the Arabic satellite station had lost contact with Abdel Kader Saadi, a reporter and photographer living and working in the Sunni Muslim city, on Nov. 11.

French freelance photographer Corentin Fleury was detained by the U.S. military with his interpreter, 28-year-old Bahktiyar Abdulla Hadad when they were leaving Fallujah just before the siege of the city began. They had worked in the city for nine days leading up to the siege, and were held for five days in a military detention facility outside the city. "They were very nervous and they asked us what we saw, and looked over all my photos, asking me questions about them," Fleury told IPS. "They asked where the weapons were, what the neighborhoods were like, all of this." Fleury said he had photographed homes destroyed by U.S. warplanes, and life in the city leading up to the siege. "They wanted information from me regarding the situation in Fallujah, but they have yet to release my translator," he said. "I made a silly photo of him holding a sniper rifle, and I think this is why they are holding him. I've been trying to get information for the last five days on him, and the French embassy has been trying to get him out, different journalists he's worked with are sending letters, but there has been no luck so far."

U.S. Military Obstructing Medical Care

BY DAHR JAMAIL, INTER PRESS SERVICE

BAGHDAD, Dec 13/04 (IPS)—The U.S. military has been preventing delivery of medical care in several instances, medical staff say. Iraqi doctors at many hospitals have reported raids by coalition forces. Some of the more recent raids have been in Amiriyat al-Fallujah, about 10 km to the east of Fallujah, the town to which U.S. forces have laid bloody siege.

Amiriyat al-Fallujah has been the source of several reported resistance attacks on U.S. forces. The main hospital in Amiriyat al-Fallujah was raided twice recently by U.S. soldiers and members of the Iraqi National Guard, doctors say. "The first time was November 29 at 5:40 a.m., and the second time was the following day," said a doctor at the hospital who did not want to give his real name for fear of U.S. reprisals. In the first raid about 150 U.S. soldiers and at least 40 members of the Iraqi National Guard stormed the small hospital, he said. "They were yelling loudly at everyone, both doctors and patients alike," the young doctor said. "They divided into groups and were all over the hospital. They broke the gates outside, they broke the doors of the garage, and they raided our supply room where our food and supplies are. They broke all the interior doors of the hospital, as well as every exterior door." He was then interrogated about resistance fighters, he said. "The Americans threatened to do here what they did in Fallujah if I didn't cooperate with them," he said.

Another doctor, speaking on condition of anonymity, said that all of the doors of the clinics inside the hospital were kicked in. All of the doctors, along with the security guard, were handcuffed and interrogated for several hours, he said. The two doctors pointed to an ambulance with a shattered back window. "When the Americans raided our hospital again last Tuesday at 7 p.m., they smashed one of our ambulances," the first doctor said. His colleague pointed to other bullet-riddled ambulances. "The Americans have snipers all along the road between here and Fallujah," he said. "They are shooting our ambulances if they try to go to Fallujah."

In nearby Saqlawiyah, Dr. Abdulla Aziz told IPS that occupation forces had blocked any medical supplies from entering or leaving the city. "They won't let any of our ambulances go to help Fallujah," he said. "We are out of supplies and they won't let anyone bring us more."

The pattern of military interference in medical work has apparently persisted for many months. During the April siege of Fallujah, doctors there reported similar difficulties. "The marines have said they didn't close the hospital, but essentially they did," said Dr. Abdul Jabbar, orthopedic surgeon at Fallujah General Hospital. "They closed the bridge which connects us to the city, and closed our road. The area in front of our hospital was full of their soldiers and vehicles." This prevented medical care from reaching countless patients in desperate need, he said. "Who knows how many of them died that we could have saved." He too said the military had fired on civilian ambulances. They also fired at the clinic he had been working in since April, he said. "Some days we couldn't leave, or even go near the door because of the snipers. They were shooting at the front door of the clinic." Dr. Jabbar said U.S. snipers shot and killed one of the ambulance drivers of the clinic where he worked during the fighting. "We were tied up and beaten despite being unarmed and having only our medical instruments."

Asma Khamis al-Muhannadi, a doctor who was present during the U.S. and Iraqi National Guard raid on Fallujah General Hospital, told reporters that troops dragged patients from their beds and pushed them against the wall. "I was with a woman in labor, the umbilical cord had not yet been cut," she said. "At that time, a U.S. soldier shouted at one of the (Iraqi) national guards to arrest me and tie my hands while I was helping the mother to deliver."

Other doctors spoke of their experience of the raid. "The Americans shot out the lights in the front of our hospital, they prevented doctors from reaching the emergency unit at the hospital, and we quickly began to run out of supplies and much needed medication," said Dr. Ahmed, who gave only a first name. U.S. troops prevented doctors from entering the hospital on several occasions, he said.

Targeting hospitals or ambulances is in direct contravention of the Fourth Geneva Convention, which strictly forbids attacks on emergency vehicles and the impeding of medical operations during war. In several places doctors said U.S. troops had demanded information from medical staff about resistance fighters. "They are always coming here and asking us if we have injured fighters," a doctor at a hospital said.

A U.S. military spokesman in Baghdad told IPS that routine searches of hospitals are carried out to look for insurgents. He said it has never been the policy of coalition forces to impede medical services in Iraq.

"During times of universal deceit, telling the truth becomes a revolutionary act."—George Orwell

CHAPTER 12

Political Economy of Mass Media

FCC OWNERSHIP REVIEW—THE DEBATES

BY ANN STRAHM

The media blackout of the Federal Communications Commission's recent attempt to consolidate media ownership is very important to the debates around (de)regulation—especially since the proponents of deregulation include all the national network broadcasters and newspapers. According to recent research, 72 percent of the American public knew "nothing at all" about the proposed changes.[1] The study further looked at attitudes of citizens and found that the remaining 23 percent who had heard "a little," and the 4 percent who had heard "a lot," tended to view the proposed changes negatively;[2] thus allowing an inference to be made that if Americans are not aware, they do not exhibit negative attitudes towards the FCC's regulatory changes. However, if they are aware of the changes, they tend to view them in a negative light. Thus, those who would argue against further deregulation of mass media because of the clear threat it poses to the public good have their criticism buttressed by the exceptional lack of transparency on the part of deregulation proponents regarding the FCC's ownership rules review.

The media regulatory system is set up (like the rest of the economy) in such a way that economic interests are the only interests taken into account. All other interests must be framed in terms of the cost benefits to those who are providing information in the public interest. As Marilyn Waring's research into the United Nations System of National Accounts indicates, economic profit and exchange is the only value to be achieved. Anything external to the concerns of profit and exchange are valueless. In this case, caps on ownership are debated, not in terms of how they help democracy, but in how they hinder economic development. Free speech is argued in terms of access to consumers through targeting audiences, not in terms of substantive democracy—information dispersal.

The current incarnation of the FCC started rather dubiously. Through the mid-1920s, most radio broadcasters were college and university-associated non-profit stations. The few for-profit stations were used to advertise and promote their owner's primary business. In 1927, the Radio Act was quietly and hurriedly passed following a federal judicial ruling that the Department of Commerce's licensing scheme was unconstitutional. Concerned that the airwaves needed an arbiter of control, the Radio Act of 1927 established the Federal Radio Commission (FRC), whose only instruction was to determine "which applicants would get preference for the scarce channels." To do this, the FRC "should favor those station applicants that best served the "public interest, convenience or necessity."[3]

The meaning of "public interest, convenience or necessity" has been debated by activists, lobbyists, policy makers, politicians, and intellectuals since it was first conceptualized and put on paper. According to Robert McChesney, the FRC was to serve listeners over users. What this meant was that the FRC was to favor those broadcasters who "seemed the most inclined toward serving the public and who were the least inclined toward promoting their own 'private or selfish interests,'" except for commercial advertising because even though it was a selfish interest, without "advertising, broadcasting would not exist," argued the FRC. Additionally, the FRC's conceptualization of the "public interest" was the broadcaster's provision of "a well rounded program" that served the "entire listening public within the listening area of the station."[4]

The reason for congressional inclusion of "public interest, convenience, or necessity," into the bill was to ensure its constitutionality and to insure that the FRC was not given a free hand to act as it saw fit. Even so, when congress reviewed the impact of the bill over the following two years, representatives were astounded at the incredible rise in network-owned broadcasting, while a rapid decline had simultaneously taken place in the non-profit broadcasting sector. This corporate manifestation led a shocked Senator C.C. Dill (who also helped author the Radio Act of 1927) to comment, the "great feeling about radio in this country ... is that it will be monopolized by the few wealthy interests."[5] In an effort to stop this effective corporate monopoly of the public airwaves, Congress passed the Davis Amendment in 1928, requiring the FRC to essentially undo its previous decisions and democratically reallocate the spectrum—focusing its efforts on regions that did not have a strong system of radio broadcasting. Of the five FRC representatives appointed, three were involved in the corporate broadcast industry. As such, to assist its reallocation decisions, the FRC met with representatives of corporate broadcasting and its trade association, the National Association of Broadcasters. Not surprisingly, these meetings were not publicized, nor was input from representatives from non-profit and consumer groups invited;[6] thus, the only realized outcome of this reallocation was that the FRC's "General Order 40" increased consolidation of broadcast spectrum into the hands of corporate broadcasting. This has remained the effective modus operandi of the various incarnations of the FRC and FCC to this day.

As the percentage of advertising-funded, corporate-owned stations rose, the non-profit stations declined to less than 2 percent of all broadcasting.[7] The FRC, in its *Third Annual Report*, argued that capitalist stations were serving the public interest because they were motivated by the market—thus, they received the lion's share of broadcast spectrum—while non-profit stations were "propaganda" stations because they promoted one viewpoint rather than "satisfying audience needs." This led to a rise in the level of social activism on the part of progressives to stop the hemorrhaging caused by the FRC.

The broadcast reform movement believed that regulation would not solve what had become a cozy relationship between the FRC and the broadcast industry. Instead, the reformists argued, a percentage of the broadcast spectrum should be allocated to non-profit broadcasters, using funding schemes like those found in Britain and Canada. One idea bandied about was government subsidized stations, bankrolled through taxes and/or license fees. However, many in the movement thought the idea of a government subsidy would mean government control. An advertiser-subsidized model was also discussed and abandoned due to the recognition that advertising-driven programming was part of the problem. Additional barriers stood in the way of the reform movement. Besides internal movement disagreements on tactics and planning, the movement faced a deep-pocketed corporate lobbying machine. The broadcast industry was well aware of the reform movement and did everything in its power to subvert reform efforts. The commercial broadcasters engaged in public relations campaigns and formed "advisory councils," which were little more than facades. Another hurdle facing the progressive movement was the lack of media coverage regarding the issue. When there was coverage, it was biased in favor of corporate media.

Between 1930 and 1933, the struggle over broadcast restructuring took place. A significant percentage of the American population was dissatisfied with the current structure of U.S. broadcasting. But, even with tremendous public outcry and well over three-fourths of the House and Senate supporting the reinstitution of non-profit broadcast set-asides, legislation failed in 1930.

The reasons for this failure were twofold. The first was that the country was in the midst of the Great Depression and Congress was focused on economic recovery. The second reason for this failure was that congressional support for reform "tended to wane the less theoretical the issue became and the more the commercial broadcasters directed their fire against it."[8] Additionally, as Billy Tauzin and Dennis Hastert have done, Senator C.C. Dill continuously blocked all legislation until January 1932, (when the public outcry could no longer be ignored) when he authorized an FRC study of the broadcast industry. The report, *Commercial Radio Advertising*, unsurprisingly, was uncritical of the current commercial broadcast makeup. Surprisingly, the report undercut and diffused the reform movement's criticism of corporate broadcasting.[9]

The decisive period for the structure of public broadcasting came during the months between March, 1933 and the signing of the Communications Act of 1934. During this time, media reformists, believing that the newly-elected President Roosevelt would be sympathetic to their case, were undermined by Roosevelt, who publicly sided with the reformists, but who had his aides quietly working with the industry to increase their control over the broadcast airwaves. The broadcast industry wanted to have permanent legislation enacted, but did not want a public debate (which would be required if Congress was to attempt passage of such a bill). Thus, the Roper Committee was created to construct legislation. The Roper Committee, like the construction of the 1996 Telecommunications Act, operated secretly, effectively subverting any opportunity for media reformists or public-interest input. The Roper Committee recommended no change in the current broadcast allocation, but did recommend all regulation be done by a single government agency—much to the delight of the broadcast industry. Dill and his House counterpart, Representative Sam Rayburn, pushed the legislation through committee, bringing it to the floor for a vote in little time.

Media progressives, knowing they had been duped and undermined, found an ally in "Father" John B. Harney, who submitted an amendment to Dill's bill that would have insured at least 25 percent of the radio spectrum was reserved for non-profit and public interest. The Harney proposal was voted down in committee, but found additional support in Senators Robert Wagner and Henry Hatfield, who introduced the amendment on the Senate floor. When it became apparent that the (Harney) Wagner-Hatfield Amendment might have a chance, Dill inserted a clause in the bill, section 307(c), which required the FCC to hold hearings on the possibility of reserving 25 percent of the airwaves for non-profits—effectively undermining the Wagner-Hatfield Amendment. On June 18, 1934 President Roosevelt signed the Communications Act of 1934 into law amidst a flurry of New Deal acts. This act effectively destroyed the media reform movement, leaving us with an FCC whose principal actors, with few exceptions, behave as high-paid hustlers for the major media conglomerates.

Former FCC Chair Michael Powell and Commissioner Kathleen Abernathy (both Republicans) are proponents of the ideological philosophy of deregulation, while former Commissioner and current Chair Kevin Martin seems more concerned with how market forces affect consumers (for example, he forced Powell to make some side deals in order to agree to the proposed changes in ownership caps). On the Democrat side, neither Commissioners Copps nor Adelstein are antideregulation, they (like, to some degree, Martin) appear more concerned with the permanence of FCC decisions and whether or not the decisions are being made with a satisfactory level of research.

While Powell was Chair of the FCC, he made multiple statements indicating his loyalties to the corporate class. For example, he stated "public interest" is like an "empty vessel," and that his only god is the "free market." Additionally, he consistently referred to "consumer welfare," rather than the "public good" when discussing the FCC's obligations to the public interest. One telling example of Powell's ideological bent towards deregulation is his statement in the 1998 Biennial Review Order where he argued, "... I start with the proposition that the rules are no longer necessary and demand that the Commission justify their continued validity."

Many arguing against the relaxation of the FCC's ownership caps are concerned with the conceptual transformation of what "information" is (it's meaning and value), as well as of the very nature of information itself. The concern here is that rather than creating news, public affairs information, and entertainment for public consumption, media corporations are creating "copyright-protected" goods that can be repackaged for other uses. For example, executives refer to the Tribune Company as a "content company" because its *Chicago Tribune*, they say, is a "content factory" for the company's online sites, broadcast stations, and cable news outlets. In sum, information is being transformed from what has been nominally considered a public good (that is, available to all), to something that can be privatized and treated as a commodity. What is important, critics argue, is that there is an ever-widening chasm developing between the needs of the public's access to information, and the market's orientation to producing goods (i.e. content) for profit. Critics contend that large media conglomerates only create content that they can repurpose for use on multiple formats under their ownership, creating value-added commodities.

Additionally, while there are positive outcomes of the professionalization of the field of journalism, an important negative consequence has been an increase in the homogenization of content. Much of the homogeneity, critics have argued, can be laid at the feet of concentration. While concepts of objectivity and neutrality, use of facts without analysis, and reliance on officials and experts have led to more professional presentations of news, it also has led to a model of "journalism that describes events with little analysis, relies upon polls and statistics to show social trends but without providing historical context, and provides no vehicle of expression of ordinary people at the grassroots level." (Shah, n.p.) This "serves the interests of the owners ... because it avoids asking deeper questions about the exercise of power, the dispensation of social justice, and the prospects for cultural survival." (Shah, n.p.) Thus, we are left with scandal, celebrity, disaster, politics as horse race, etc. (what Bagdikian terms "soft entertainment"), which leaves us with little useful information to help us make sense out of our lives.

Ultimately, this allows corporate media conglomerates to hold down production costs, increase profitability, and ensure hegemonic status through the ownership of multi-platform, continuous streaming content. While some may point out the few exceptions to this (for example, Michael Moore's books and films, or the television series *The Simpson's*), these serve to reinforce abstract social critique as acceptable if it leads to increased profits for the publisher or network that distributes the product. However, explicit critique is not acceptable even if it is popular with the audience (for example, Michael Moore's *TV Nation* and Phil Donahue's MSNBC show, both of which were quite popular with the viewing audience, but not with advertisers or owners).

An important part of the above discussion revolves around the effect it will have on the public good. According to economists Besen and O'Brien, the term "public good" means something that costs additional user(s) nothing after content in the intellectual property realm has been created and provided to the original user(s). Therefore, the public good is an article of intellectual property that can be repackaged and sold to additional users at no further cost to the producers. This notion of "public good" is extended through the idea that information produced in one medium can be used in another, i.e. information produced for a newspaper can be modified into a story to be used in a broadcasting medium. The incentive? Additional money with no additional costs—profit.

Another element in the attempts to eliminate or undermine the public interest regulatory scheme, Robert Corn-Revere, a partner in the law firm Davis Wright Tremaine, argued before the Senate Commerce Committee that any notion of the "public interest," is a regulation of "broadcast content" that would "necessarily implicate the First Amendment, and reviewing courts would not be required to defer to the policymakers findings." He added that set-asides for educational or information programming are also "content-based," and thus violate media's First Amendment rights to freedom of speech.[10] It would appear then, that ideas about what constitutes the "public interest," has been reinterpreted by corporate media to suit their own purposes—which is to say that any regulation requiring corporate media to air programming that serves the public is government regulation of content, and therefore in violation of the Constitution.[11] It is also interesting that deregulation proponents like Corn-Revere ignore the other First Amendment right—the right to a free press. This tells us that the debate over what is in the public interest would most likely take a dramatically different tone if we were to examine the media through the lens of free press instead of free speech.[12] Related to this issue of media content, recent studies have examined what happens when media ignores a story.

Research by the Project for Excellence in Journalism shows that when corporate media does not cover an issue, citizens do not substitute alternative news sources in an effort to obtain the information because they do not have access to alternative news sources (or know how to obtain them). The importance of this lies in the fact that, if an issue or event is ignored by mainstream media, citizens most likely are not even aware of the issue and would thus preclude even attempting to search out, from alternative sources, answers and additional information. Using this issue as a starting point, we begin to develop an understanding as to why issues of media ownership are so important and so vigorously fought over.

Deregulation proponents claim broadcast networks are experiencing the negative effects of a weak economy as well as increased competition from newer media sources and need to make large investments in the digital expansion of television broadcasting. Critics, however, point out that a great number of the new media outlets are owned and operated by the same media monopolies that own most traditional media outlets. Research findings show, for example, that two companies control the cable going into 40 percent of all households that purchase cable television (of which five broadcasting networks dominate those channels) and two companies control the direct-broadcast satellite market. Thus, it would seem that arguments of deregulation proponents do not fit the reality of the media market.

One of the most important arguments for proponents of deregulation involves the Internet. They promote the Internet as revolutionary. As a revolutionary tool, they claim, it has many benefits such as easy access to ideas, the potential to foster interpersonal communications, the immediacy and availability of updated information, and its fuction as a tool for media enhancement, not to mention its usefulness as a venue for bringing together different types of media. However, this "revolutionary" fervor ignores fundamental issues. For example, large media conglomerates own the most popular sites, which are popular because of the name-recognition value, and not necessarily because they provide better information. Additionally, deregulation proponents ignore the fact that over one-half of the American public does not have access to the Internet. It is telling that they ignore this group, given that those without Internet access tend to represent the same demographics as those who are least targeted for marketing, i.e. the older, the poorer, and people of color.

As part of the "Internet as a revolutionary tool" argument, proponents of deregulation contend that the very essence of the Internet, providing text, still photographs, and streaming audio and visual, makes it perfect for newspaper/broadcast efficiencies. It is for this reason, they argue, that the "efficiencies" of newspaper/broadcast cross-ownership are so valuable because these co-owned entities can use the Internet as a hybrid between the two genres, passing information back and forth, as well as uploading articles and live streams, etc.

The Supreme Court, in its 1978 decision to uphold the newspaper/television cross-ownership ban said, "it is unrealistic to expect true diversity from a commonly-owned station-newspaper combination. The divergence of their viewpoints cannot be expected to be the same as if they were antagonistically run."[13] The rationale behind this argument is that the inherent quality of newspapers allows them to provide in-depth news, information, and analysis—the focus is on news rather than entertainment. Broadcast television, on the other hand, provides immediate information and allows for the viewing of visual images, as well as dominating the fields of political news and advertising. Although cable television was in its infancy and neither the Internet nor direct broadcasting satellite (DBS) were available in 1978, critics of deregulation contend their advent and expansion does not change the veracity of the Court's argument when it comes to news and public affairs information. Additionally, critics argue that, since most communities have only one or two newspapers, and national broadcasters own the few television stations, the diversity of viewpoint is already dangerously limited, allowing the merger of these two genres will put what diversity there is in further jeopardy.

Beyond dealing with issues of viewpoint, diversity and quality of news,[14] the effects of repackaging content for other outlets speaks to the issues of labor. Virtually all monopolization allows industry to reduce its labor costs; once companies merge into one, employees are viewed as redundancies (two or more workers performing the same tasks). The whole point of mergers is to create efficiencies and economies of scale—thus, the "dead-weight" of redundant workers is eliminated and labor costs are reduced. Corporate media is no different in this regard (see Braverman's *Labor and Monopoly Capital*). One example of this can be found in radio. Since the 1996 Telecommunications Act, radio executives estimate over 10,000 radio industry jobs have been lost.

Virtually all deregulation critics point out that the most important problem of media monopoly is the transformation in how news and public affairs programming is viewed. Increasingly, such programming is viewed less as a service to the community, and more as programming that (like all other programming) must be justified by high profit levels. The concern here is the effects that transformation has on the type of information being made available to the public. As discussed elsewhere in this paper, the concern is that the only news and public affairs information being produced is that which can be repurposed for other media outlets, thus increasing competitiveness and profitability with no concern for citizens' rights to access information. Additionally, smaller media outlets that own limited genres of media, being unable to offer a multitude of platforms (i.e. broad customer reach) to advertisers, will purchase news content from their competitors (synergies) rather than investing in bettering their own, thus appealing to the synergistic tendencies of advertisers.

Synergies, which which allow smaller media outlets to participate in joint ventures with their competitors in an effort to raise their own profitability, minimize the diversity of content available to readers, viewers, listeners, and Internet surfers. The search for advertising revenue means that the media will continue to abandon the population that do not interest advertisers (those without money), in favor of programs that appeal to those with disposable incomes. W. Baker agrees, pointing out that when "the main objective behind every minute of airtime is to maximize profits, standards take a back seat to better margins. Trawling for eyeballs becomes commonplace," leading to homogenization of programming. Additionally, critics of deregulation contend that monopolization has led to corporate owners' unhealthy control over local broadcast programming decisions—through financial penalties—for preempting network programming with programming of local interest.

Advocates of deregulation question the validity of the FCC's current regulatory scheme on localism. They argue that, since many broadcast television stations are not owned locally, but rather are owned by corporate groups with headquarters elsewhere, these local stations, whether owned by a broadcast network or by a broadcast network affiliate, have contractual obligations to air national network programming. Additionally, they argue, most local television stations carry some level of local news reporting. Thus, they say, the FCC's concern around the issue of localism is inappropriate. Further, deregulation proponents contend that, given the costs of producing local content, many independent broadcast stations eliminate most of their local news and information infrastructure in favor of syndicated and/or national programming, especially as many of the most important local stories are covered nationally.

Deregulation proponents also contend that consumers have a variety of non-broadcast media available to them, so while they may not be provided with local news and information broadcasts, the information is "comprehensively addressed by an abundance of national as well as local media outlets which consumers use interchangeably" (Fox et al, 50). Finally, they argue that the national broadcast audience continues to shrink and only a small proportion of the consumers watch free over-the-air television. They say that the problems are not just advertising revenue, but audiences who are abandoning broadcast television, the increase in production cost, the costs associated with the transition to digital broadcasting, and the decline in advertising revenues.

Critics point out that the argument of media substitutability in any given market assumes that different types of media outlets serve similar purposes in the same market; however, the evidence shows this not to be the case. For example, people who primarily watch broadcast news frequently supplement that news with the addition of print media, but if the broadcast news were no longer available, people would not substitute print media as their primary source of news. Furthermore, critics stress that just because the number of over-the-air viewers is declining, that doesn't mean that the viewers aren't watching those broadcast programs on cable. In fact, one only needs to glance at the financial statements of the media giants who say they are in danger of financial collapse because of these FCC rules and regulations to understand they are only crying wolf.[15]

Deregulation proponents argue that the FCC's focus on information in the public interest (through news and public affairs programming) as a measure of viewpoint diversity is unfair because it ignores the contributions that entertainment programming makes to the marketplace of ideas. They provide examples of their prime-time programs to argue that public affairs information is dispersed via entertainment as well as news. Television shows such as *Will & Grace* and *Ellen* are cited as examples of how entertainment discusses sexual orientation, while shows such as *All in the Family* and *The Cosby Show* have provided a challenge to racial stereotypes. Also, *The O'Reilly Factor* and *Donahue*, they argue, provide contrasting perspectives for the viewing public. Additionally, they argue, the fact that the FCC uses news and public affairs programming as its measure of viewpoint diversity should be considered an examination of content and thus a violation of media's First Amendment rights. Deregulation proponents also add that diversity of viewpoint should be viewed in the context of the number of choices available to media consumers. In this view, the FCC is unable to meet the burden of proof necessitated by the Telecommunications Act of 1996.

Deregulation critics, however, point out that there is something more important at stake. They contend that ownership creates an unnoticed shift in "editorial viewpoints and news coverage," especially important given the media's function as gatekeeper in the "marketplace of ideas." Through their efforts to achieve higher and higher levels of profit, there is a tendency in large media conglomerates to homogenize news and public affairs.

Through the control [of] the marketplace of ideas, the public interest takes a back seat to the goal of making large profits. In order to turn those big revenues, parent companies engage in self-censorship, news coverage reduction, and news content manipulation. As a substitute, the media allows a barrage of mindless celebrity 'news,' sensationalism, 'follow-up' stories related to network programming, and the ubiquitous water-skiing squirrel story. (Simon, n.p.)

For instance, a Pew Research Center for People and the Press (PEW)/Columbia Journalism Review (CJR) study showed that 41 percent of the 300 reporters surveyed acknowledged that they intentionally avoided, or softened the tenor of, newsworthy stories in an effort to benefit the interests of the parent corporation (Kohut, 42; Lieberman, 44; PEW, n.p.). Thus, as the critics assert, a multiplicity of channels does not translate into a multiplicity of viewpoints being presented on the airwaves and in print.

According to Simone Murray, large media conglomerates that are horizontally, vertically, and/or diagonally integrated create a clear tension between "journalistic ethics and shareholder profit," leading to problems in the context of viewpoint diversity. She argues that such integrative ownership, along with the voluminous number of corporate media joint-ventures, destroys the "Chinese walls" separating journalism from corporate owners. This means that economic constraints (i.e. corporate concerns over content repurposeablity) run roughshod over journalistic norms. In sum, homogenized content that can be rebroadcast, reprinted, and restreamed ("cultural synergy"[16]) to the largest number of consumers, takes precedence over information that is useful to a limited number of citizens in a given locale. Further, given the foray of advertisers into control over publication and broadcast content they advertise through, even more content homogeneity can be expected, all of which place downward pressure on viewpoint diversity, which is the "lifeblood of American democracy and culture."[17] Also, virtually all the owners of these media corporations are staunchly conservative, and that means that views falling outside of that paradigm are off limits. The extent of these problems is well illustrated by Fox affiliate David Boylan's comment: "We paid $3 billion for these television stations. We decide what the news is. The news is what we tell you it is."[18]

In sum, proponents of deregulation argue that the ownership cap should be relaxed or eliminated because of the "(i) the financial health of the networks and the future of free, over-the-air television are at stake; (ii) the world of television has changed in recent years and the rules are unnecessary and antiquated; (iii) national ownership rules do not promote localism or diversity; and (iv) the ownership cap is unconstitutional" (Frank, 5). Additionally, deregulation advocates contend that all new forms of media can be considered competition, which have greatly diminished their market share and reduced profits dramatically. Also, they argue, the FCC is at fault for not allowing media conglomerates to take the natural course of buying up more newspapers and/or more broadcast stations. As such, regulatory regimes are burdensome and are standing in the way of accumulation, which ultimately affects the consumer negatively. Critics of deregulation argue that all forms of information should be considered a public good that is accessible to all citizens so they have the knowledge necessary for decision-making and active participation in their democracy. Media monopoly, they argue, serves to reduce localism, competition, and diversity, as well as allowing a small number of people and corporations to decide what citizens will see and hear. Additionally, critics contend, as the search for profits increases, the media content becomes homogenized.

It should be noted that deregulation proponents had promoted themselves at the FCC En Banc hearing as being completely committed to the FCC-regulated "public interest" as defined by the Telecommunications Acts of 1934 and 1996 (localism, diversity, and competition). At the same time, however, they were arguing in often closed-door sessions before the FCC and the U.S. Senate that such government concern is a fetter on business. They offer rather simplistic, often erroneous, discussion, arguing that FCC regulations are a cost to doing business—to achieving higher profits and obtaining larger conglomeration—rather than a means to ensure the public good. In fact, the argument they present is one that conflates the public good and democracy with their own desires for increased profits. Additionally, those advocating deregulation do not appear to base their argument on sound premises, instead, choosing to focus on a narrow economic discussion. Also, those advocating for FCC ownership cap relaxation or elimination seem to rely less on attempting change through public discussion—i.e. democratic mechanisms—and instead, attempt change through lobbying and the placement of personnel, who are conducive to those changes, in government positions. These tactics are implemented to achieve ownership cap relaxation, without creating any kind of persuasive argument to achieve their goals. Thus, it appears that large media use government policy mechanisms to address their needs and wants, while those against deregulation have no choice but to go, hat in hand, to those same mechanisms in an attempt to argue against the most harmful effects of potential outcomes.

The history of the FRC/FCC has been repeated over the years in contemporary America. There has remained an effective lobbying and co-opting of the American legislative system by a deep-pocketed, very powerful media industry. Originally, Senator Dill, like our current Senator Hollings, had helped to author a bill that was to ensure equal access to the public airwaves. Instead, these bills (Radio Act of 1927 and Telecommunications Act of 1996), crafted in secrecy, ultimately served to codify the consolidation of the broadcast system into the hands of a corporate broadcast media that is becoming increasingly concentrated into fewer hands. However, we see both bills bring forth an ever-growing movement of American citizens, unhappy with what is coming to them across the broadcast spectrum, becoming more vocal about their distaste—demanding changes in the allocation of the spectrum. While we know the outcome of the historical media reform movement, what remains to be seen is the effectiveness of the current media reform movement. One hopes for a dissimilar outcome, effectively stopping the repeats of history.

The recent debates in the FCC have been significant. The proverbial veil was lifted and the machinations brought out into the open, allowing citizens to see what really goes on behind the curtain. Copps (then Adelstein) effectively eliminated the secrecy that has cloaked the wielding of power over our airwaves. The Copps/Adelstein self-proclaimed "Magical Mystery Tour" has galvanized a nationwide movement that has not slowed—even with the recent Congressional undermining (reducing the ownership caps from 45 percent to 39 percent, satisfying Fox and Viacom).[19] In some ways, each step the current Congressional and Executive bodies take to undermine the movement, it simply gets louder, and even more irate citizens join in.

What is the same is, of course, a powerful corporate system that has effectively blacked-out the ability of Americans to obtain information about the issue at hand through mainstream media sources. What is different is a modern-media pipeline that is still new enough that it has not been completely and effectively taken over by the corporate media system—the Internet.[20] During the "Tour," Copps continued to express amazement at the incredible numbers of citizens who come to his town hall meetings. By the time the FCC made its decision and Congress began its (public outcry induced) examination of the FCC's decision, over "2.3 million comments registering opposition to media concentration were made to either the FCC or Congress."[21]

Bringing the FCC's decision-making process out into the light, through an unprecedented open and public debate (between Copps and Powell in particular), has permanently changed how Washington makes policy, particularly in matters related to corporate media. Those doors will not be closed soon (there are too many people crowding the entrance), and discussion and debate dealing with media issues have taken on a much more democratic tone. Back-room wheeling and dealing Washington-style has been effectively exposed. How American citizens are able to use this to their advantage and fight to bring more democratic structure to the media system (broadcasting in particular) remains to be seen.[22]

Ann Strahm is a doctoral candidate in sociology at the University of Oregon. She is co-host of *LeftOut!*, a progressive talk-radio show in Eugene, Oregon.

BIBLIOGRAPHY

Abernathy, Kathleen Q. "Opening Remarks." Federal Communications Commission Broadcast Ownership En Banc. Richmond, VA, February 27, 2003.

Bagdikian, Ben. Interview. *Frontline: Smoke in the Eye*, 1999, available: http://www.pbs.org/wgbh/pages/frontline/smoke/interviews/bagdikian.html.

Baker, William F. "Statement," *United States Senate Committee on Commerce, Science & Transportation*. Washington, D.C.: July 17, 2001.

Besen, Stanley M. and O'Brien, Daniel P. "An Economic Analysis of the Efficiency Benefits From Newspaper-Broadcast Station Cross-Ownership," *Charles River Associates Incorporated*. July 21, 1998; in *Comments of Gannett Co., Inc.* U.S. Federal Communications Commission 2002 Biennial Regulatory Review. January 2, 2003.

Copps, Michael (FCC Commissioner). Interview. *NOW With Bill Moyers*. Public Broadcasting System. 25 October 2002. Available: http://www.pbs.org/now/transcript/transcript_bmjfcc.html.

Copps, FCC Commissioner Michael J. *USC Media Consolidation Forum.* Los Angeles 28 April 2003.

Copps, Michael J. "Remarks." Federal Communications Commission Broadcast Ownership En Banc, Richmond, VA, February 27, 2003.

Frank, Alan. "Statement," *United States Senate Committee on Commerce, Science & Transportation*, Washington, D.C.: 17 July 2001.

Kohut, Andrew. "Self-Censorship: Counting the Ways," *Columbia Journalism Review*, May/June 2000: 42-43.

Lieberman, Trudy. "You Can't Report What You Don't Pursue." *Columbia Journalism Review*, May/June 2000: 44-49.

Martin, Kevin J. "Opening Remarks." Federal Communications Commission Broadcast, Ownership En Banc, Richmond, VA, February 27, 2003.

McChesney, Robert, *Rich Media Poor Democracy: Communication Politics in Dubious Times.* Urbana, IL: University of Illinois Press, 1999.

Murray, Simone. "Media Convergence's Third Wave: Content Streaming." PR2K: Public Right to Know Conference. Australian Centre for Independent Journalism, University of Technology Sydney. Sidney (Australia), October 27, 2001.

Pew Research Center, The. "Self Censorship: How Often and Why: Journalists Avoiding the News." With the *Columbia Journalism Review*. April 30, 2000. Available: http://people-press.org/reports/display.php3?ReportID=39.

Powell, Michael. Interview. *NOW with Bill Moyers*. Public Broadcasting System. April 4, 2003. Available: http://www.pbs.org/now/transcript/transcript_powell.html.

Powell, Michael K. "Markets and Consumer Welfare: Bunking the Myth." *Federal Communications Bar Association.* Washington DC,: June 21, 2001.

Powell, Michael. "Statement." Federal Communications Commission Broadcast Ownership En Banc. Richmond, VA: February 27, 2003.

Project For Excellence In Journalism. "New Federal Rules for Media Ownership: How Much Does the Public Know?" Washington, DC: February 27, 2003.

Shah, Hemant. "Journalism in an Age of Mass Media Globalization." *International Development Studies Network*. Canada: Canadian Consortium of University Programs in International Development Studies, n.d., Available at: http://www.idsnet.org/Papers/Communications/HEMANT_SHAH.htm.

Simon, Donald R. "Annotating the News: Journalism, Big Media & Antitrust Law." *Media Reform Network* n.d. Available: http://www.mediareform.org/news.php?id=319

Waring, Marilyn. *Counting For Nothing: What Men Value and What Women Are Worth.* Second Edition. Toronto: University of Toronto Press, 1999.

NOTES

1. Project for Excellence in Journalism Study, "New Federal Rules for Media Ownership."
2. Project for Excellence in Journalism Study, "New Federal Rules for Media Ownership."
3. Robert W McChesney, "Conflict, Not Consensus: The Debate over Broadcast Communication Policy, 1930–1935," in William S. Solomon and Robert W. McChesney, eds., *Ruthless Criticism: New Perspectives in U.S. Communication History.* (Minneapolis: University of Minnesota Press, 1993), p. 225.
4. Robert W. McChesney, *Telecommunications, Mass Media, and Democracy: The Battle for the Control of U.S. Broadcasting, 1928–1935,* (New York: Oxford University Press, 1994), p. 27. FRC 1929, p.32.
5. U.S. Senate, 70th Congress, 2nd Session. *Hearings Before the Committee on Interstate Commerce on S.4937.* Washington, DC: U.S. Government Printing Office. 4 February 1929.
6. *Congressional Record* 78. 15 May 1934, pp. 8830-34.
7. *Congressional Record* 78. 15 May 1934, pp. 8830-34.
8. Robert W. McChesney, "Conflict, Not Consensus: The Debate over Broadcast Communication Policy, 1930–1935" in *Ruthless Criticism: New Perspectives in U.S. Communication History.* William S. Solomon and Robert W. McChesney, eds. (Minneapolis: University of Minnesota Press, 1993), p. 240.
9. See Robert W. McChesney, *Telecommunications, Mass Media, and Democracy: The Battle for the Control of U.S. Broadcasting, 1928–1935.* (New York: Oxford University Press, 1994), pp. 121-187.
10. Robert Corn-Revere, "Testimony." *Senate Commerce, Science and Transportation Committee.* Washington, D.C. 23 July 2003.
11. This argument is based on an 1886 Supreme Court decision, *Santa Clara County v. Southern Pacific Railroad,* where a clerk, ignoring the court's decision, wrote that corporations are legal individuals who are accorded the same rights and liberties as human citizens. Subsequent decisions reinforced this argument. This is important because it allows the corporate media to argue that any form of economic regulation violates corporate First Amendment Rights.
12. If a freedom of the press argument was made by advocates of regulation most likely corporate deregulation advocates would again argue that private ownership equals freedom – again, using the 1886 Santa Clara County decision.
13. *FCC v. National Citizens Committee for Broadcasting,* 436 U.S. 775, 779 (1978).
14. This so concerns the academic journalism community that the heads of major schools of journalism have begun meeting to discuss how to combat this trend.
15. According to the 10K forms provided to the Securities and Exchange Commission, News Corporation Ltd. Had net profits of $1.808 billion pounds (or, approx. $1.3 billion U.S. dollars) in 2003. NBC's revenues were up 24% in 2002 to $7.1 billion, giving it $1.7 billion in profits. Disney had a net profit of $1,236 billion in 2002, and Viacom showed net profits of $725.7 million for the same year. Additionally, a cursory review of these corporate 10K's over the past three years show all maintain a steady increase in earnings and profits.

16. Janet Wasko; *Hollywood in the Information Age: Beyond the Silver Screen*. Cambridge, UK: Polity, 1994; "The Magical-Market of Disney"; *Monthly Review*, Vol. 52, No. 11, pp. 56-71; and *Understanding Disney: The Manufacture of Fantasy*; Cambridge, UK: Polity Press, 2001, especially pages 70-83.
17. American Federation of Television and Radio Artists (AFTRA) and the Writers Guild of America, East (WGAE), pg. 7.
18. Davide Boylan of Fox affiliate WTVT in Tampa FL. Cited in: *Extra!* Update, June 1998; Jim Hightower, *Thieves In High Places*. New York: Viking, 2003, p. 137.
19. Bill McConnell, "New Ownership Cap Fits Fox, CBS Perfectly." *Broadcasting & Cable* 26 January 2004.
20. The author, having followed this on a personal, and then research, level over the last 18 months, has seen the power that this new media offered the media reform movement, allowing word-of-mouth passing of information about the FCC's further erosion of ownership caps to be enhanced.
21. Jonathan Adelstein quoted in, Robert W. McChesney, "The Escalating War Against Corporate Media," *Monthly Review* (March 2004), p. 26.
22. Currently a coalition ranging from civil rights and labor to religious and advocacy groups (such as the NRA) have continued the fight in the courtroom. Currently, a federal court is hearing the case that these groups hope will stop the FCC media ownership cap increases.

CHAPTER 13

U.S. Military and the Media

By Robin Andersen, Norman Solomon, David L. Altheide, Jennifer N. Grime, Lisa Parks

The Military Entertainment News Complex: War as Video Game
BY ROBIN ANDERSEN

After 9/11, especially during the build-up to war in Iraq, critical media watchers noted the highly positive coverage of the move toward war. Concerned voices were all but silenced, as were the demands for peace that were taking place in the streets of cities across the globe. Instead of a spectrum of voices, military officials and a bevy of "consultants" (former generals) dominated TV screens "explaining" the strategies, logistics, preparations and weapons of war. It is now irrefutable that at the same time the public was being deliberately lied to about the justifications for war in Iraq, TV networks and cable channels were sponsoring the military enterprise through patriotic graphics and promotional bumpers that adopted the military's terms of engagement. Much has been written to date in the corporate press about the failure of intelligence, and more comprehensive evaluations of the manipulation of intelligence by the executive branch have been published and produced by the alternative/independent media. These are the first drafts of what will be understood historically as the folly that began the 21st Century. As this folly continues, it is essential to understand the role played by the media industries, not in recording an accurate account of the history of war, but in helping to make that history. In the waning decades of the 20th Century, the merger that was forged during World War II between the military and the media took on increasingly significant proportions. Indeed we might say that without the media industry as a major partner, the military could not have become the cultural and political force able to define and execute the military interventions that began the 21st Century.

TV CELEBRATIONS OF THE WEAPONS OF WAR

Contemporary news coverage of conflict and of the military can best be understood as part of a new geography of war, one defined and dominated by the merger between the media and the military. This merger is driven by the highly profitable economic development of computer based digital technologies shared by the entertainment and weapons industries. Computer-based digital technologies are core components of high-tech weapons systems—they can also be seen on TV screens as the graphic depictions of the war on terror. To illustrate this point, consider an example of war reporting: During the build up to the Iraq war, the local Fox station in New York City, broadcast a news story about the weapons of war. PLAN OF ATTACK is lettered over a digitalized pulsing graphic of layers of red targeting cross hairs. The announcer intones over ominous music:

> Well the U.S. wants to take on the so-called Butcher from Baghdad, but this plan of attack will require some serious weapons. Fox 5 got a look at some of these weapons and you better believe they're a lot more advanced than what we used the first time around. They're mean, Saddam-fighting machines. Linda Schmidt gets an up close and personal look...

As the reporter speaks, viewers are shown a grainy, monochromatic field with squares and rectangles transforming into white blurs. We hear, "The U.S. Air Force in Afghanistan zeroing in and firing at buildings, trucks and terrorists." Under the coarse satellite field the framed station banner reads WAR GAMES. Linda tells us, "Watch closely and you can see a person running on the ground." We are told to look for "a white dot moving across the center of your screen; they're firing at him, and then, they nail him!" The white dots blurs just as the squares did moments before. Cut to a picture of a large artillery weapon: "It made its debut in Afghanistan, in the war on terror, being fired out of an Air Force gun ship." We see more satellite footage supplied by the Air Force; this time a weapon is fired out of a plane. "The military will also use it in Iraq, if we go to war, to take out what they call soft targets: In other words, Iraqi soldiers." Cut to a factory setting now. A man with a ponytail says proudly, "The Air Force soldiers call it the Meat Grinder." Linda nods with a knowing smile, "The Meat Grinder." The man with the ponytail responds, "Yes Ma'am." Linda goes on to marvel at how light and easy the 16 pound weapon is to use as she holds it on her shoulder and aims.

Though the footage supplied by the military depicted actual weapons in real war footage, it was labeled WAR GAMES and looked strikingly similar to first-person shooter video games. Satellite photography offers the blurred images of buildings and human targets as they are destroyed. In addition, by handling and aiming the weapon, or we might say, "playing with it," Linda moves the viewer into the zone of gaming and the participatory mode central to a player's experience of an interactive video. This is the new visual rhetoric of war—call it the digital spectacular. As news reporting looks and feels more like entertainment, that entertainment has a particular type of sensibility. News reports resemble video games. Media celebrates war and its weaponry, not only for ratings and patriotic fervor, or even because of pressure from White House public relations teams; Positive reporting on high-tech war has become fundamental to an industry highly invested in creating and profiting from the very same technologies used in weapons—the computer-based digital simulations at the core of video games. Such simulations are now seen across the media spectrum and have become fundamental to news representations of war.

THE MILITARY ENTERTAINMENT COMPLEX

The highly positive, stylized imagery of high-tech war celebrated on TV news is only the most visible display of a fundamental merger that continues to take place between the military and the media industries. During the 1990s, the military and the media industries worked together on the research and development of digital, computer-based technologies. Over the course of that decade designers, artist, and executives from the entertainment industry met with analysts and engineers from the Department of Defense at numerous institutes and conferences to share expertise in pursuit of the 3D virtual worlds constructed for the fields of entertainment, news, film, video games and warfare. Computer games, most notably *America's Army*, have become key training and recruiting tools for the military. The characters that inhabit virtual game worlds, locked in endless battles between good and evil, double as "warfighters" and "kill targets" for military training. On TV news they are terrorists running across a satellite field and the next target of a high-tech weapon systems.

The graphic style and video game sensibility so prevalent on TV news depictions of war should be understood as part of a trans-industrial complex that has transformed the media and aligned the industry's economic interests with those of the military. The National Research Council published the findings of a conference held in Irvine, California in 1996. The report articulates the mutual interests of the Department of Defense (DOD) and the media industry:

> Modeling and simulation technology has become increasingly important to both the entertainment industry and the U.S. Department of Defense (DOD). In the entertainment industry, such technology lies at the heart of video games, theme park attractions and entertainment centers, and special effects for film production. For DOD, modeling and simulation technology provides a low-cost means of conducting joint training exercises, evaluating new doctrine and tactics, and studying the effectiveness of new weapons systems… These common interests suggest that the entertainment industry and DOD may be able to more efficiently achieve their individual goals by working together to advance the technology base for modeling and simulation.[1]

And work together they have. At Irvine, members from DOD's Defense Modeling and Simulations Office (DMSO), and from the Defense Advanced Research Projects Agency (DARPA), together with Navy and Air Force representatives met with representatives from Pixar, Disney, Paramount, and George Lucas' Industrial Light and Magic. Joining this group were other computer researchers from industry and academia. Their purpose was to investigate the mutual interests and benefits of collaboration in creating "the technical advances upon which future entertainment and defense systems will be built."[2]

ARTIFICIAL INTELLIGENCE

Taking a look at some of the history of development of the digital spectacular helps illustrate the media/military merger. The military has long dreamed of electronic machines able to simulate human activities and skills. Realizing this goal would require computer generation and Artificial Intelligence (AI). In the early 1980s, the military pioneered the first wave of research into AI. In 1983, DARPA's Strategic Computing Program outlined a 5-year, $600,000,000 plan for a new generation of computer applications that would be needed for the creation of "intelligent" machines, including autonomous land, sea, and air vehicles. "These vehicles would have human abilities, such as sight, speech, human understanding, natural language, and automated reasoning," and be capable of reconnaissance as well as attack missions.[3]

In addition to intelligent machines, synthesized human skills and responses are necessary for convincingly rendered computer-generated characters (CGCs), key components of simulated training exercises and video games. The media and the military have found common ground in their interest in CGC.

FLIGHT SIMULATION AND IMAGING

Another advanced computer technology essential to both video games and military training is flight simulation and imaging. The military took the lead in developing this technology as well, a technology that has become so much a part of the visual imaging of war across the media landscape. Computerized flight simulation is a crucial point in the history of computer generation and interactive electronic gaming. James Davis, writing in *Aerospace America* (1993), notes that the image generator component designed initially for military flight simulation modeling is at the heart of any computer -based visual system.[4]

For years the media industry excelled by turning the military's computer research into popular entertainment and handsome profits. However, by the 1990s, as it became clear that video games were bringing about an "entertainment revolution,"[5] the media industry picked up the pace of R&D[6] and took the next research steps in computer gaming with highly profitable results. The flow of networking and software innovations began to even out, and in some cases, even reversed direction. Important advances made by commercial researchers in the entertainment industry were then appropriated by the military.[7] Cyberlife Technology's *Creatures 2.0* offered the cutting edge in artificial life simulation and helped realize the dream of smart weapons systems such as pilotless fighter aircraft. Another essential technological advance useful to the military, particularly for recruitment and training, is interactive first-person shooter technology developed by id Software in 1994 with their game *Doom 1.9*. "The U.S. Marine Corps Modeling Simulation Management Office has adapted *Doom 1.9* for the purposes of tactical combat training exercises."[8] Positioning the warrior behind a gun, in a fighter jet, or looking from a weapon's eye view at a digitalized enemy is the same camera perspective often presented on television news. Viewers are invited to assume the position of warrior often through the use of footage and graphics from actual weapons systems being used in war and provided by the military.

The University of Southern California's Institute for Creative Technology is a research center with the stated mandate to "enlist the resources and talents of the entertainment and game development industries and to work collaboratively with computer scientists to advance the state of immersive training simulation"[9] In an interview with the *New York Times*, ICT's creative director James Korris explained the military's interest in collaborating with Hollywood when he said they wanted some "fairy dust."[10] They found it at ICT in L.A. working with such dream makers as Paul Debevec, creator of the "trailing bullet" in *The Matrix* who was charged with "improving the richness of the photorealistic detail in the computer-generated animations" used for military training. A number of producers, directors and writers of feature films specializing in special effects are also part of ICT's talent pool.[11] ICT's multistory office complex (designed by Herman Zimmerman, a *Star Trek* production designer) houses a staff of 45 including "a cadre of rumpled techies intent on constructing training scenarios that deliver a visceral wallop."[12] Military training without the fairy dust was dull; when soldiers were first placed in early models they kept getting bored. With ICT's Digital Walls, that doesn't happen anymore. Stimulating immersion training is created by converting "flats," a standard of Hollywood set design, into a "convincing 3-D effect of a rugged mountain landscape." In addition, Jacquelyn Morie, ICT's manager for creative development, explains that sound is also a key stimulus. The virtual battlefield now includes the "whup, whup" of a helicopter swooping across the ceiling as a rumble floor vibrates to approximate real combat. The long- awaited *Mission Rehearsal Exercise* (MRE), a curved-screen simulation that wraps around officers-in-training and presents a a variety of options for emergency action, allows trainees to interact with digital actors, who themselves "listen" and "respond" with instantly variable "emotions."[13] Likewise, when synthetic characters, becoming known as "synthespians," can act and react in realistic ways to numerous stimuli, they make video games more engaging.

This trans-sector reciprocity is currently a stable, on-going mutually beneficial industrial relationship. Hollywood has become a full partner in new weapons training and development. At the ICT the management skills of former media executives from NBC, Paramount and Disney can direct designers from Silicon Valley to help adapt the same digital effects used for movies, amusement parks and video games to military platforms.

CYBORG SOLDIERS ON A VIRTUAL BATTLEFIELD

Through the 1990s, military public relations material promoted high-tech war, complete with battlefields of the future that were digitalized and "net-ready." With complex communications systems, all aspects of war, from the foot soldiers on the ground to thundering tanks and pilotless aircraft overhead, would be networked to wireless computers mapping real-time movements over enemy terrain and providing information on exact locations of friends and foes.[14] The computerized helmets worn by soldiers would receive signals from the Global Positioning Satellite, and data from numerous sources would be networked and integrated into a central command system monitored by computers. Robot scouts would send surveillance imagery to commanders instantaneously.

Writer Der Derian witnessed a simulated battlefield of the first fully digitalized task force in California's Mojave Desert during the Army training exercise, Desert Hammer VI in 1994. The soldiers of the 194th brigade were "digitally enhanced, computer-accessorized, and budgetarily gold-plated from the bottom of their combat boots to the top of their kevlars."[15] They rode atop the latest M1A2 Abrams battle tanks and carried day and night vision scopes mounted on their M-16s. Real-time airborne and satellite surveillance and digitalized battlefield communication registered on helmet-mounted displays. Every warrior carried a computer in a rucksack with 1-inch LED screens for their video cameras, and helmets were connected by radio communication to a battle command vehicle coordinating the attack though a customized Windows program.

Such visions of futuristic virtual war are no doubt in the minds of those who plan and execute combat operations in foreign lands, but just as the TV coverage of war is often entertaining fiction, so too are futuristic battlefields. Just as one young soldier recounted in the film *Fahrenheit 9/11*, "It's not like a video game when real people die." The battlefields of virtual war games have little in common with invading and occupying real countries. It is a long perceptual leap from the gold-plated war games to Iraq, where soldiers have refused missions because their HUMVIES are not bullet-proofed. The media industries help create the virtual simulations of such weapons systems even as they portray real war through digitally entertaining formats; both technologies share the fictional sensibilities of games, not reality.

WAR AND ELECTRONICALLY MEDIATED NEWS

It should come as no surprise that the convergence between the media and the military, as both pursue mutually beneficial goals, would have some alarming consequences. We might ask, under these circumstances, how the media could possibly adopt an independent stance toward an enterprise they are so integrally connected to. Mapping the media landscape of the digital spectacular, we see from press reports to TV coverage, and from movies to video games, a profound alignment between the executive branch, the military, and media coordinates. These confabulations have created a new audiovisual milieu as they have transformed the look and feel of news coverage. On television, war becomes virtual, an empowering game where high-tech weapons provide all the solutions to global problems as evil enemies disappear in puffs of smoke.

There are considerable consequences to the new military/entertainment complex outlined here. As we have seen, the boundaries between war and peace begin to lose distinction in an age when so many resources, technologies, creative talents and cultural practices are devoted to the anticipation, preparation, planning and imaginings of warfare. As Paul Virilio argues in his concept of "pure" war, the spatial, temporal and logistical distinctions that once separated war from peace have lost their defining power.[16] The "logistics" of war, the broad nexus of military planning in preparation for armed conflict, including transportation and training, flow into, and become integral to civilian society. The role of media takes a new path, one that augments and promotes the weapons created by the new economic conglomerations, instead of informing the public of what war is really like. With such economic, technological and cultural interdependence with war, the media are now incapable of the independence needed to fulfill the First Amendment requirements for democracy. In an age of pure war, peace is not part of an imagined future.

CONCLUSION

The public is invited to sit in awe of fantastical displays of high-tech weaponry characteristic of TV's coverage of war. The interconnections between the military, news reporting and entertainment technologies are part of the merger between digital information systems and the new technology of war. The highly profitable economic arrangements that have coalesced between the media and the military have resulted in war reporting that shares the graphic styles and sensibilities of video games.

Merging war reporting with the creation and promotion of high-tech war technologies ignores and hides the extraordinary and unpleasant realities of war, such as death, destruction and suffering. It is the nature of virtual experience itself to deliver high-tech thrills with no consequences. We vanquish so many enemies and then the game is over. This is experience in which empathy, compassion and responsibility have been thoroughly expurgated. As part of a military/entertainment complex, the corporate media can no longer be considered a legitimate source for objective information capable of nurturing a knowledgeable or humanitarian polity.

Robin Andersen is Associate Professor and Chair of the Department of Communications Studies at Fordham University.

NOTES
1. Cited in Burston (2003). "War and the Entertainment Industries: New Research Priorities in an Era of Cyber-Patriotism," in *War and the Media*, eds. Daya Kishan Thussu and Des Freedman (Thousand Oaks: Sage).
2. Burston (2003, 164).
3. Douglas Kellner (2003). "Postmodern Military and Permanent War," in *Masters of War: Militarism and Blowback in the Era of American Empire*, ed. Carl Boggs, (New York: Routledge) p. 229-244.
4. James Davis (1993). Virtual Systems: Generating a New Reality," *Aerospace America* 31 (August) p. 33.
5. See Poole (2000). "Trigger Happy: Video Games and the Entertainment Revolution," (New York: Arcade Publishing).
6. For production perspective, one of the biggest companies in this industry, Electronic Arts, makes one in every four videogames, and has "twice as many in-house game developers as Disney has animators" Burston 2003 p. 164).
7. Birgit Richard (1999). "Norm Attacks and Marine Doom," Ars Electronica: Facing the Future: A Survey of Two Decades, ed. Timothy Druckrey ((Cambridge, MA: MIT Press).
8. Patrick Crogan (2003). "Gametime: History, Narrative, and Temporality in Combat Flight Simulator 2," in *The Videogame Theory Reader*, eds. Mark J.P. Wolf and Bernard Perron (New York: Routledge) p. 279.
9. From the ICT website. Cited in Burston (2003, 166).
10. Hugh Hart (2001). "Bringing Hollywood Pizazz to Military Training," *New York Times* (Nov. 15).
11. John Milius, scriptwriter for *Apocalypse Now* and Randal Kleiser who directed, *Honey, I Shrunk the Kids* have also worked with the team (Hart 2001). "Priorities in an Era of Cyber-Patriotism," in *War and the Media*, eds. Daya Kishan Thussu and Des Freedman (Thousand Oaks: Sage).
12. Hart (2001).
13. Burston (2003, 167).
14. See Kellner (2003).
15. James Der Derian (2001). *Virtuous War: Mapping the Military-Industrial Media-Entertainment Network*, (Boulder: Westview Press).
16. See Paul Virilio and Sylvere Lotringer (1997). *Pure War* (New York: Semiotext(e)).

News Media and "the Madness of Militarism"

BY NORMAN SOLOMON

Media activism has achieved a lot. Still, we cannot be satisfied—considering the present-day realities of corporate media and the warfare state.

War has become a constant of U.S. foreign policy, and media flackery for the war-makers in Washington is routine—boosting militarism that tilts the country in more authoritarian directions. The dominant news outlets provide an ongoing debate over how to fine-tune the machinery of war. What we need is a debate over how to dismantle the war machine.

When there are appreciable splits within or between the two major political parties, the mainstream news coverage is apt to include some divergent outlooks. But when elites in Washington close ranks for war, the major media are more inclined to shut down real discourse.

Here's an example: In late February 2003, three weeks before the U.S. invasion of Iraq began, management at MSNBC cancelled the nightly "Donahue" program. A leaked in-house report said Phil Donahue's show would present a "difficult public face for NBC in a time of war." The problem: "He seems to delight in presenting guests who are anti-war, anti-Bush, and skeptical of the Administration's motives." The danger—quickly averted by NBC—was that the show could become "a home for the liberal anti-war agenda at the same time that our competitors are waving the flag at every opportunity."

When the two parties close ranks, so do the big U.S. media. The silence of politicians and media must not be our silence.

In the last months of his life, Martin Luther King Jr. talked about the necessity of challenging the warfare state. In January 1968, he said: "I never intend to adjust myself to economic conditions that will take necessities from the many to give luxuries to the few. I never intend to adjust myself to the madness of militarism..." In March 1968, he said: "The bombs in Vietnam explode at home; they destroy the hopes and possibilities for a decent America."

In 2005, we can say: "The bombs in Iraq explode at home. They destroy the hopes and possibilities for a decent America." Soldiers return from their killing missions with terrible injuries to body and spirit. Suffering festers due to the tremendous waste of resources spent on war instead of helping to meet human needs. Meanwhile, corruption of language embraces death.

Factual information that undermines the patterns of wartime deception doesn't get much ink or airtime. But another kind of spiking takes place in psychological and emotional realms.

It's essential that we confront the falsehoods repeatedly greasing the path to war, as when *New York Times* front pages smoothed the way for the invasion of Iraq with deceptions about supposed weapons of mass destruction. At the same time, there is the crucial need to throw light on the human suffering that IS war. We need to do both—exposing the lies and the horrific results. Illuminating just one or the other is not enough.

In recent weeks, a lot of media attention has gone to the Bush Administration's flagrant efforts to manipulate public television. We're hearing about the need to defend PBS. That's understandable, given the right-wing assault on the network. If you're starving, you understandably want some crumbs back. But that doesn't mean that all you want is restoration of the crumbs. What we actually need, and should demand, is genuine public broadcasting.

There was no golden era of PBS. The crown jewel of the network's news programming—with the most viewership and influence—has long been the nightly *NewsHour With Jim Lehrer*. As with many other subjects, the program's coverage of war has relied heavily on official U.S. sources and perspectives in sync with them. The media watch group FAIR (where I'm an associate) has documented that during one war after another—such as the Gulf War in 1991, the bombing of Yugoslavia in 1999 and the invasion of Iraq two years ago—the *NewsHour*'s failure to provide independent coverage has been empirical and deplorable. Such failures are routine and long-standing for the show, as FAIR's research makes clear.

To accept such a baseline of journalistic standards—or, worse yet, to tout it as an admirable legacy for public broadcasting—is to swallow too much and demand too little. A military/media industrial complex has grown huge while sitting on the windpipe of the First Amendment. And a media siege is normalizing the murderous functions of the warfare state. We are encouraged to see it as normality, not madness.

Norman Solomon is a syndicated columnist and author of *Target Iraq: What the News Media Didn't Tell You* (Context Books, 2003) co-authored by Reese Erlich. His next book, *War Made Easy: How Presidents and Pundits Keep Spinning Us to Death*, will be published early summer, 2005, by Wiley. His columns and other writings can be found at www.normansolomon.com. He can be reached at: mediabeat@igc.org. This article was adapted from a presentation at the National Conference for Media Reform, held May 13-15 in St. Louis.

News Management and the Iraq War

BY DAVID L. ALTHEIDE & JENNIFER N. GRIME, ARIZONA STATE
UNIVERSITY

A British journalist, John Pilger (Pilger 2002), documented an early discussion about using the 9/11 attacks as a pretext for invading Iraq:

> On the morning of September 12 2001, without any evidence of who the hijackers were, Rumsfeld demanded that the U.S. attack Iraq. According to Woodward, Rumsfeld told a cabinet meeting that Iraq should be "a principal target of the first round in the war against terrorism." Iraq was temporarily spared only because U.S. Secretary of State Colin Powell persuaded Bush that "public opinion has to be prepared before a move against Iraq is possible. (Pilger 2002)

We examine how the military used the corporate media to prepare the public for the Iraq War and previous wars.

The corporate media helped prepare the country for the Iraq Invasion by what was reported, as well as what was not reported. Research reveals how the corporate media and a major think-tank, the Project for a New American Century (PNAC), provided misinformation and propaganda that fueled public passion, promoted fear (Altheide 2002), and stressed relying on strong central authority to enact major legal changes in order to protect the public (Altheide forthcoming). These efforts provided much of the legitimacy for the Iraq War. Yet there was something very familiar about the pattern of propaganda, distortion and discovery has been used in other wars (Altheide 1995). We propose that the current structure of policy and critique is now institutionalized and, essentially, connects criticism and challenge as part of a War Program.

Over three decades of distorted reporting about the Middle East—including the 1979 Iranian Hostage Crisis—as well as the coverage of the First Gulf War in 1991, helped shape public perceptions about Saddam Hussein in particular and "Arabs" in general (Adams 1981; Altheide 1981; Altheide 1982). Governments and the corporate media work side-by-side in most conflicts. Government news sources repeatedly claimed through the national press and several press conferences that Saddam Hussein was implicated in the 9/11 attacks on the United States, had not complied with UN weapons inspections, and still harbored numerous weapons of mass destruction (WMD) that he planned to use against the U. S. as well as deliver to terrorists. Subsequent reports would show that the White House claims about each of these points were wrong. Counter-claims by others, including U. S. senators, were dismissed by the White House, and received little press or broadcast attention. There was very little reporting by major news media about contrary views cautioning that this attack was not necessary at that time. (The search for WMD officially ended on January 12, 2005.) Nor was there much reporting about other claims that the aftermath of the war would be difficult, could cost billions of dollars and require the U. S. military presence for many years. Eighteen months after President Bush declared, "Mission Accomplished," a large percentage of the American people continued to accept the basic premises that President Bush outlined for going to war, although public opinion is somewhat less supportive of the U. S. position in Iraq (Kull 2004).

We suggest that the Iraq War was presented to U.S. and international audiences as a War Program, or a sequence of reports that blends imagery and language of the current conflict with previous wars, and incorporates critiques of war policy within the news frame about movement toward war. War Programming refers to the organization and structure of the discourse of recent reportage about wars, and not mere content. War Programming encompasses content as well as thematic emphases and dominate frames. There are several steps to War Programming:

WAR PROGRAMING:

1. Reportage and visual reports of the most recent war (or two);
2. Anticipation, planning and preparing the audiences for the impending war, including "demonizing" certain individual leaders, e.g., Noriega, Hussein;
3. Coverage of the sub-segments of the current war, using the best visuals available to capture the basic scenes and themes involving the battle lines, the home front, the media coverage, the international reaction, anticipation of the war's aftermath;
4. Following the war, journalists reaction and reflection on various governmental restriction, suggestions for the future (which are seldom implemented);
5. Journalists' and academics' diaries, biographies, exposes, critiques and studies about the war, and increasingly the media coverage;
6. Media reports about such studies, etc., which are often cast quite negatively and often lead to the widespread conclusion that perhaps the war was unnecessary, other options were available, and that the price was too high; all of this will be useful for the coverage of the next war.
7. For the next war, return to step 1.

Because the main frame involves the inevitability of war and the U. S. preparation for it, critiques that attempt to question the propaganda campaign propelling the country toward war were ignored. Mass media audiences in the United States tended to accept this War Program although foreign audiences, which did not share the ideologically embedded accounts of previously broadcast United States wars, interpreted the visuals and official narratives much differently (Kull 2004; Kull et al. 2002).

While the War Program frame emerged in news coverage of other conflicts, three considerations made it especially well suited to the Iraq War: 1. A very well-organized think-tank—the Project for a New American Century (PNAC)—whose members were government officials as well as publishers, guided news reports; 2. A compliant press that relied on access to key Administration officials and other institutional news sources, many of whom were affiliated with the PNAC; 3. A climate of support and mutual concerns by political leaders and journalists about the 9/11 attacks and broad definitions about working together to protect the United States. The PNAC received very little news media coverage prior to the invasion of Iraq even though it was part of the "public record" in government documents, and had been briefly mentioned in several newspaper and radio reports in the late 1990s. Only a few newspaper articles dealt with PNAC six months before the United States attacked Iraq on March 20. No reports about the PNAC appeared on the major TV networks regular evening newscast during this time.

THE PROPAGANDA CAMPAIGN

The propaganda campaign in the Iraq War consisted of numerous messages about Iraq's stockpile of WMD, Saddam Hussein's support for terrorists, and the likelihood that terrorists would use such weapons against the United States (Altheide 2004; Doob 1966; Kellner 2003; Kellner 2004; Lasswell et al. 1979; Speier 1969). The PNAC played a major role in leading the U. S. to war with Iraq as news sources, cabinet members, presidential advisors, journalists and publishers. The propaganda campaign was also aided by what was omitted from presentation to the public, and the way in which information was managed. These changes included an increasing commercialization and entertainment emphasis of news, as well as a closer relationship between journalists and the military commanders, particularly those who become reporters or consultants with major networks.

Much of the Gulf war coverage originated from the White House and the federal government, and most of it was incredibly positive and non-critical. Network news shows featured guests who supported the war. An analy-

sis by Fairness and Accuracy in Reporting (FAIR) of network news interviewees one week before and one week after Secretary of State Colin Powell addressed the United Nations about Iraq's alleged possession of Weapons
of Mass Destruction, found that two thirds of the guests were from the United
States, with 75 percent of these being current or former government or military officials, while only one—Senator Kennedy—expressed skepticism
or opposition to the impending war with Iraq (FAIR) 2003) . Other analyses indicated similar information control:

> Of the 574 stories about Iraq that aired on NBC, ABC, and CBS
> evening news broadcasts between September 12 (when Bush
> addressed the UN) and March 7 (a week and a half before the war
> began), only twelve dealt primarily with the potential aftermath. .
> .(Cunningham 2003, p. 24).

THE PROJECT FOR A NEW AMERICAN CENTURY

The Project for a New American Century (PNAC) began as a conservative think tank that was very influential in changing U. S. foreign policy as
well as promoting favorable news coverage about going to war with Iraq following the attacks of 9/11 (http://www.newamericancentury.org/). The Iraq
War was informed by these efforts and the resulting propaganda campaign
to convince the American people that attacking Iraq was tantamount to
attacking "terrorists" and others who threatened the United States (Armstrong 2002). Among the members who signed many of the proclamations
laying the foundation for a new American empire (Bacevich 2002; Kagan
2003; Kagan and Kristol 2000) were former and current governmental officials, including: Elliot Abrams, William Bennett, Jeb Bush, Dick Cheney,
Steve Forbes, Donald Kagan, Norman Podhoretz, Dan Quayle, Donald
Rumsfeld, Paul Wolfowitz. Many members of the PNAC joined the Bush
Administration and became credible claims-makers, who constructed the
frames for shaping subsequent news reports. The PNAC emphasized changing American foreign policy to become a hegemon and police its international interests as a new kind of benevolent American empire (Bacevich
2002; Barber 2003; Johnson 2004; Kaplan 2003; Mann 2003). This would
include expanding the military, withdrawing from major treaties as well as
engaging in preemptive strikes against those who would threaten U. S. interests. Those messages, in turn, were carried by the mass media for months
leading up to the invasion of Iraq. The United States was well on its way
to justify attacking Iraq in 1992 when Dick Cheney and others, who would
occupy positions in the Bush Administration eight years later, drafted the

Defense Planning Guidance document. An overview and analysis of the PNAC and its role in shaping U. S. foreign policy was the subject of David Armstrong's essay in *Harper's* in October 2002:

> The plan is for the United States to rule the world....It calls for dominion over friends and enemies alike. It says not that the United States must be more powerful, or most powerful, but that it must be absolutely powerful (Armstrong 2002, p. 76).

We argue that the PNAC, working with a compliant news media, developed, sold, enacted and justified a war with Iraq that has resulted—as of this writing (April 2005)—in more than 10,000 dead or wounded American soldiers, plus numerous contract workers (not including mercenaries), along with an estimated 100,000 dead or wounded Iraqis (BBC 2004; Cooney and Sinan 2004; Yousef 2004). The work of the PNAC in shaping U. S. policy toward Iraq received very little news attention.

CONCLUSION

The Iraq War was sold to the American people as legitimate and necessary by a combination of well-placed news sources (especially the PNAC) and news media reticence to oppose an administration that had provided false information about the 9/11 attacks and the impending threat of Weapons of Mass Destruction. Such managed news had consequences for public support. Opinion poll data show how public perceptions were informed by news reports. Public support of the Iraq War and trust in the Bush Administration followed the more critical news reports; as more information about the PNAC and the elusive WMD became available, public approval for the war declined, as did trust in President Bush (Morin and Wilbank 2004).

There has been very little news coverage of the PNAC's plan to direct the Iraq War and change foreign policy. The news production of the Iraq War was consistent with the framework of War Programming noted above. Within weeks after the war commenced, critiques began to emerge about policy, facts, motivations and interests. As War Programming suggests, news organizations began to reflect on "what went wrong" in their coverage of Iraq, including missing the PNAC influence. Curiously, essentially the same sequence has been followed in previous wars. We have seen that War Programming is now a package; propaganda is joined to the news process when journalists and news sources operate with media logic, share in the construction and emotional performance of events, and limit the public forums for discussion, and especially dissent. One observer noted:

Surely it is now time for a fundamental reappraisal of the way the press operated. Because, like it or not, the media were co-conspirators in America's rush into this illegal war. How badly we needed—before the war—solid reporting that explained how a kitchen cabinet of neoconservatives and their bellicose friends were cooking up a war that has brought so much bloodshed to Iraq and danger to the world (*Columbia Journalism Review* Staff 2004 p. 46-47).

A dominant discourse, War Programming, emerged and now essentially guides journalistic coverage of war in the United States. War Programming reflects the cooptation of news organs avowedly "objective" and impartial, but as we have seen repeatedly, the actual practice of news work and reporting sustains powerful institutional actors like the PNAC and other key claims makers. While other work suggests changes that could be made in news practices to challenge this discourse (Altheide and Grimes forthcoming), it is important to stress that the consequences of not challenging War Programming discourse are not comforting for a free society, including altering foreign policy and attacks on basic civil liberties. These issues were not relevant, until after the war, and then they would be taken up on schedule as part of overall War Programming.

REFERENCES

Adams, William C. 1981. *Television Coverage of the Middle East*. Norwood, N.J.: Ablex Pub. Corp.

Altheide, David. 1981. "Iran vs. U.S. TV News! The Hostage Story Out of Context." Pp. 128-158 in *TV Coverage of the Middle East*, edited by William C. Adams. Norwood, NJ: Ablex.

—. 1982. "Three-in-One News: Network Coverage of Iran." *Journalism Quarterly* Fall: 482-486.

—. forthcoming. *Terrorism and the Politics of Fear*. Walnut Creek, CA: AltaMira Press.

Altheide, David L. 1995. *An Ecology of Communication: Cultural Formats of Control*. Hawthorne, NY:: Aldine de Gruyter.

—. 1996. *Qualitative Media Analysis*. Newbury Park, CA: Sage.

—. 2002. *Creating Fear: News and the Construction of Crisis*. Hawthorne, NY: Aldine de Gruyter.

—. 2004. "Consuming Terrorism." *Symbolic Interaction* 27: 289-308.

Altheide, David L., and Jennifer N. Grimes. forthcoming. "War Programming: The Propaganda Project and the Iraq War." *The Sociological Quarterly*.

Armstrong, David. 2002. "Dick Cheney's Song of America: Drafting a Plan for Global Dominance." *Harper's Magazine* October 2002: 76-83.

Bacevich, A. J. 2002. *American Empire : the Realities and Consequences of U.S. Diplomacy*. Cambridge, Mass. ; London: Harvard University Press.

Barber, Benjamin R. 2003. *Fear's Empire : War, Terrorism, and Democracy*. New York ; London: W.W. Norton & Co.

BBC. 2004. "Iraq Death Toll 'Soared Post-War'." *BBC Newscast* October 29, 2004.

ColumbiaJournalismReviewStaff. 2004. "Brits vs Yanks: Who Does Journalism Right." *Columbia Journalism Review*: 44-49.

Cooney, Daniel, and Omar Sinan.2004. "More than 5,500 Iraqis Killed During 1 Year." *The Arizona Republic.* May 24, 2004. A.A4.http://www.azcentral.com/arizonarepublic/news/articles/0524iraq-violent24.html.

Cunningham, Brent. 2003. "Re-Thinking Objectivity." *Columbia Journalism Review* July/August 2003: 24-32.

Doob, Leonard. 1966. *Public Opinion and Propaganda.* Hamdon, CT: Archon Books.

(FAIR), Fairness and Accuracy in Reporting. 2003. "In Iraq Crisis, Networks are Megaphones for Official Views."

Johnson, Chalmers A. 2004. *The Sorrows of Empire : Militarism, Secrecy, and the End of the Republic.* New York: Metropolitan Books.

Kagan, Robert. 2003. *Of Paradise and Power : America and Europe in the New World Order.* New York: Alfred A. Knopf.

Kagan, Robert, and William Kristol. 2000. *Present Dangers : Crisis and Opportunity in American Foreign and Defense Policy.* San Francisco: Encounter Books.

Kaplan, Robert D. 2003. "Supremacy by Stealth: Ten Rules for Managing the World." *The Atlantic* July/August: 66-90.

Kellner, Douglas. 2003. *From 9/11 to Terror War : the Dangers of the Bush Legacy.* Lanham, Md. ; Oxford: Rowman & Littlefield.

—. 2004. "Media Propaganda and Spectacle in the War on Iraq: a Critique of U.S. Broadcasting Networks." *Cultural Studies <=>Critical Methodologies* 4: 329-338.

Kull, Steven. 2004. "U. S. Public Beliefs and Attitudes About Iraq August 20, 2004." Program on International Policy Attitudes.

Kull, Steven, Clay Ramsey, and Evan Lewis. 2002. "Misperceptions, the Media and the Iraq War." *Political Science Quarterly* 118: 569-598.

Lasswell, Harold Dwight, Hans Speier, and Daniel Lerner. 1979. *Propaganda and Communication in World History.* Honolulu: Published for the East-West Center by the University Press of Hawaii.

Mann, Michael. 2003. *Incoherent Empire.* London ; New York: Verso.

Morin, Richard, and Dana Wilbank.2004. "Most Think Truth Was Stretched to Justify Iraq War." *Washington Post.* February 13, 2004. A01.

Pilger, John.2002. "Axis of evil; John Pilger exposes the frightening agenda in Washington that is behind the United States threat to world peace." *Morning Star.* December 14, 2002. 19.

Speier, Hans. 1969. *Social order and the risks of war; papers in political sociology.* Cambridge, Mass.,: M.I.T. Press.

Yousef, Nancy A.2004. "U.S. Killing More Iraqis than Rebel Forces Are." *The Arizona Republic.* September 25, 2005. A. A26.

An Episodic Pattern: U.S./NATO Targets Media Infrastructures

BY LISA PARKS

This is a historical tale about the turning of Yugoslav radio and television facilities into ruins and the subsequent globalization of media industries in the region. This essay is part of a larger project in which I explore the restructuring of media industries in Slovenia and Croatia, but here I shall concentrate on the dismantling of Yugoslavia's communications infrastructure, which can be understood as part of a broader episodic pattern of U.S.-led warfare followed by media sector privatization that has occurred in Afghanistan and Iraq as well. Although these wars have distinct histories and players, they share similarity in the way the U.S. military (and its allies) eradicated old communications infrastructures only to replace them with new systems open to Western commercial investment. The conflicts in Yugoslavia, Afghanistan and Iraq, in other words, are not irrelevant to one another. As Michael Hardt and Antonio Negri remind us, "Each local war should not be viewed in isolation, but seen as part of a grand constellation, linked in varying degrees both to other war zones and to areas not presently at war."[1]

During the late 1990s U.S./NATO forces launched a campaign to destroy radio and TV transmitters throughout Bosnia and Serbia. These assaults on the Yugoslav media infrastructure enabled U.S./NATO forces to restructure a nation once integrated by its broadcast and telecommunication networks— networks that for more than 40 years worked to unite the people of Yugoslavia (which was no small feat after World War II). The communications infrastructure was juridically controlled by the federal government and the Yugoslavian National Army (JNA) in socialist Yugoslavia, but programming and day to day technical maintenance depended on the broadcasting organizations of federal republics, which implied political autonomy for the more developed Serbian radio and television (RTVS) stations in Belgrade, Zagreb and Ljubljana, yet much less in Kosovo and Montenegro. Media critic Milan Milosevic described Yugoslav TV programming as "strongly multinational," indicating, "Until 1974 studios in different parts of the country coordinated their programming to make room for one another's productions. Entertainment, cultural and news broadcasts of one TV center were regularly integrated into the programming of other centers."[2] Despite this early history of television in Yugoslavia, he continues, Belgrade TV effectively made the war thinkable during the three years prior to 1991 and thus "TV studios proved to be colossal laboratories of war engineering."[3]

Many writers have explored how media were used before and during the war in propagandistic ways to foster the nationalist sentiments and ethnic hatred that fueled the military conflicts of the 1990s.[4] Fewer, however, have understood or evaluated whether U.S./NATO's physical attack on the broadcast and telecommunication infrastructure was a legitimate response. The calculated destruction of a capital-intense national resource such as the broadcast infrastructure is particularly troubling given the enormous economic crisis that transpired in Yugoslavia throughout the 1980s due in part to meddling by the IMF and other Western financial institutions, which, among other things, set out to reduce the state's debt by eliminating its "loss-making" enterprises. This culminated in the elimination of thousands of factories and the layoff of millions of employees in Yugoslavia during the late 1980s and early 1990s.[5]

This financial intervention, in effect, reinforced a 1982 U.S. National Security directive that called for "expanded efforts to promote a 'quiet revolution' to overthrow Communist governments and parties and to integrate Eastern Europe into a market oriented economy."[6] It was this condition of widespread unemployment and financial crisis in Yugoslavia, economists argue, that catalyzed and fueled the animosities based on ethnic and religious difference and led to civil war. Nick Beams contends that the intervention by "NATO powers is nothing more than the continuation, by other—that is military—means, of the agenda carried out in the preceding period—the destruction of all the previous economic and social development in Yugoslavia, and the transformation of the entire region into a kind of semi-colony of the major capitalist powers."[7]

During the war in Yugoslavia, Serbian, Croatian, Bosnian and U.S./NATO forces all waged attacks on national infrastructures in an effort to disrupt communication and mobility during the war. Damage assessment reports and press releases regularly mentioned broadcast and telecommunications networks, bridges, and roads that were either damaged or destroyed.[8] U.S. and NATO policies titled Operation Joint Endeavor included a strategy of Offensive Counterinformation "designed to limit, degrade, disrupt or destroy adversary information capabilities and information systems."[9]

At NATO press conferences, military officials proudly detailed the destruction of various communications complexes. For instance, at a September 17, 1995 press conference Captain Doubleday presented several images captured by an unmanned aerial vehicle of bombed communications facilities allegedly being used for Serb air defense systems. They included the control building for the radio relay site in Gorazde, a Prnjavor radio relay site, and a radio relay site on Lisina Mountain near Banja Luka. As Doubleday presented each image to a news pool he stated, "a bad picture but hopefully you get the idea" implying the total annihilation of these facilities.[10]

The destruction of the Yugoslav communications networks was also documented by the post-conflict assessment teams of the United Nations Environment Programme, deployed after the war to determine the extent of environmental hazards throughout former Yugoslavia. While investigating sites struck by bombs containing depleted uranium, units also observed communications facilities in ruins and integrated these observations into reports as the dispersion of these heavy metals posed serious environmental risks.[11]

Certainly, the most high profile destruction of the Yugoslav communications infrastructure occurred in April 23, 1999 when NATO forces decisively bombed Radio Television Serbia (RTS) in the heart of Belgrade killing 16 civilian employees and wounding 19 others. In early April 1999 NATO requested that RTS air 6 hours of Western programming per day and RTS' refusal to do so, combined with Slobodan Milosevic's propagandistic appropriation of the network, led to a series of aerial assaults. The Serbian Ministry of Information reported that between March 24, 1999 and June 10, 1999, U.S./NATO bombs destroyed more than ten private radio and television stations, and 36 TV transmitters, so that the broadcast infrastructure for the entire territory of Serbia was severely damaged. The studios and transmitter located at the Business Center USCE, which housed TV stations BK TV, Pink, Kosava and SOS Channel, and several other radio stations, were bombed two times in six days. The transmitter of the TV station Palma was bombed and destroyed on April 28, and the satellite station "Yugoslavia" in the village of Prilike near Ivanjica was severely damaged.[12]

Human Rights Watch called the April 23 bombing of RTS one of "the worst incidents of civilian deaths, and certainly the worst in Belgrade," claiming, "the purpose of the attack again seems to have been more psychological harassment of the civilian population than to obtain direct military effect."[13] By the end of the three-month offensive, NATO aircraft had made a total of 37,465 sorties. Their bombs hit factories, kindergartens, oil refinery plants, private homes, hospitals, electricity and water supply systems and other public service facilities, such as trains, buses and motorways."[14]

Political leaders and journalists around the world condemned the NATO attack on RTS. Olli Kivinen, senior editor for the Finnish newspaper *Helsingin Sanomat* wrote, "The attack against TV offices in Belgrade was…clearly wrong and must not be accepted…NATO's bombing of transmitting facilities works against the free flow of information. The alliance does not realize that the harshest propaganda can easily turn against its perpetrators. Viewers can find ways to decipher the truth, even from TV reports glossed and edited by the state."[15]

In addition to its aerial assaults on the facilities, NATO pressured other international organizations to stop relations with RTS. In late 1999 NATO, at Germany's suggestion, pressured the satellite operating system Eutelsat's board of directors to discontinue transmitting the RTS signal via satellite, preventing it from being accessed by viewers in European countries. The Serbian Ministry of Information called this "a criminal decision" and accused NATO of "the destruction of RTS buildings in Belgrade, Novi Sad and Pristina, the brutal killing of journalists, the repeated destruction of radio-TV transmitters, and the jamming of RTS signals."[16]

The organization Reporters Without Borders condemned the Eutelsat decision claiming the "silencing of the Serb media," even when those in question are the "instruments of propaganda," "is not a good solution in view of the need for pluralist informing in Yugoslavia."[17] Some speculated that NATO had a public relations crisis, given that Western Europeans could watch Serbian TV news and view the extensive damage being wrought by an aggressive aerial campaign that they were helping to subsidize. Within a month of the Eutelsat decision, RTS negotiated a contract with the Israeli company Spacecom for the carriage of its signal on the Amos 1 satellite.[18]

The Yugoslav communication infrastructure may lie in ruins, but in some cases the former republics now share transponder space on the same satellite to distribute their signals internationally. This replacement of ground-based communication infrastructures with satellite distribution is a symptom of the Westernization of media infrastructures, given the fact that these new state and commercial broadcasters do not own satellites and therefore must lease time on them from the Western media companies that own and operate them. In addition, the handful of new national commercial television networks that have emerged in Croatia, Slovenia and Bosnia during the past ten years air syndicated television series from the U.S., Western Europe and South America, funneling their scarce financial resources into the pockets of foreign (in many cases U.S.) television producers. Just months after the U.S./NATO bombed RTS, Michael Parenti visited Belgrade and wrote, "the only TV one could see…were the private channels along with CNN, German television and various U.S. programs." He continued, "Yugoslavia's sin was not that it had a media monopoly but that the publicly owned portion of its media deviated from the western media monopoly that blankets most of the world, including Yugoslavia itself."[19] As of early 2005, RTS remains the most popular television station in Serbia, but TV

Pink, which airs telenovelas and American reruns such a *The O.C.*, is only slightly behind in the ratings.[20] In Slovenia, the new commercial networks Pop TV and Kanal A are owned by the U.S. company Central European Media Enterprises, as is Croatia's commercial network NOVA TV. In Bosnia commercial TV networks TV Hayat and Mreza Plus have been funded by USAID.

The destruction of the Yugoslav communication infrastructure can be read, on the one hand, as opening up the media markets in the region to a wider range of international programming, and, on the other hand, as paternalistically subsuming this once autonomous socialist state broadcast system into a U.S.-dominated global media economy. While the media sectors of other former communist states such as Poland, the Czech Republic, and Hungary underwent similar transformations during the early 1990s, the circumstances of Yugoslavia differ markedly since they resulted in part from a civil war. That is, this opening of the media sector occurred only after the violent destruction of an infrastructure that was collectively owned by the citizens of socialist Yugoslavia and had historically worked to integrate and unify them.

As Michael Parenti astutely observes, "When the productive social capital of any part of the world is obliterated, the potential value of private capital elsewhere is enhanced…And every television or radio station closed down by NATO troops or blown up by NATO bombs extends the monopolizing dominance of the western media cartels."[21] Indeed, American television reruns now fill television networks throughout the former Yugoslav republics, and new cable and satellite channels owned by Western media companies operate throughout the region. This same pattern has played out in Afghanistan and Iraq as well. Just as soon as the communications infrastructures of the Taliban and Saddam Hussein were pummeled (in addition to the al-Jazeera station in Kabul), U.S. aircraft flew over cities transmitting U.S. commercial TV news, and the spectrum in each country has since been privatized. It is impossible, then, to separate the discussion of media globalization from U.S. military intervention given the episodic pattern that has taken shape: aerial assaults on broadcast and telecomm infrastructures pave the way for U.S. multinational contracting and profiteering in the media sector.

Lisa Parks, PhD, is Associate Professor of Film and Media Studies at UC Santa Barbara. She is the author of *Cultures in Orbit: Satellites and the Televisual* (Duke UP, 2005) and co-editor of *Planet TV: A Global Television Reader* (NYU Press, 2003). She is working on a new book called *Mixed Signals: Media Technologies and Cultural Geography*.

NOTES

1. Michael Hardt and Antonio Negri, *Multitude: War and Democracy in the Age of Empire*, New York: Penguin Press, 2004, p. 4.
2. Milan Milosevic, "The Media Wars: 1987–1997," in *Burn This House: The Making and Unmaking of Yugoslavia*, Jasminka Udovicki and James Ridgeway, eds., Durham: Duke University Press, 1997, p. 108.
3. Ibid, 109.
4. See, for instance, James Gow, Richard Paterson and Alison Preston, eds., *Bosnia by Television*, London: British Film Institute, 1996; James Sadkovich, *The U.S. Media and Yugoslavia 1991–1995*, Praeger, 1998; Dubravka Ugresic, *The Culture of Lies: Antipolitical Essays*, London: Phoenix, 1996; Michael Ignatieff, *Virtual War: Kosovo and Beyond*, New York: Picador, 2001.
5. Nick Beams, "IMF Shock Therapy and the Recolonisation of the Balkans," *World Socialist Website*, April 17, 1999, available at http://www.wsws.org/articles/1999/apr1999/imf-a17.shtml, accessed March 10, 2005. Also see Nick Beams, "'Structural adjustment' and Dismemberment of Yugoslavia," *Financial Express*, April 28, 1999, available at http://www.hartford-hwp.com/archives/27c/493.html, accessed March 10, 2005.
6. Cited in Michel Chossudovsky, *The Globalisation of Poverty, Impacts of IMF and World Bank Reforms*, London: Zed Books, 1997, p. 244.
7. Beams, "IMF 'Shock Therapy' and the Recolonisation of the Balkans."
8. In some cases, facilities were destroyed simply because they had been occupied and commandeered by Serb forces. For instance, in Kosovo allied aircraft struck a telephone exchange in Pristina alleging that it was used by the Yugoslav Army for military communications. See "Battle Damage in Kosovo," *AFM* (Air Force Magazine), Jan. 2000, pp. 28-32, available at http://www.aeronautics.ru/nws001/afm114.htm, accessed Mar. 10, 2005.
9. Headquarters, Air Force Doctrine Center, *Information Operations*, Air Force Doctrine Document 2-5 (Maxwell AFB: AFDC, 5 August 1998), p. vii. Cited in Arthur N. Tulak, "Physical Attack Operations in Bosnia: Counterinformation Operations in a Peace Enforcement Environment."*Air and Space Power Chronicles – Chronicles Online Journal*, Mar. 15, 1999, available at http://www.airpower.maxwell.af.mil/airchronicles/cc/tulak.html, accessed Mar. 10, 2005.
10. News Briefing on Bosnia by Captain Doubleday, Office of Assistant Secretary of Defense (Public Affairs), Sept. 18, 1995, available at http://www.fas.org/irp/imint/bb950918.htm, accessed Mar. 10, 2005.
11. "1999 Post-Conflict Assessment in FR Yugoslavia,"UNEP Post Conflict Assessment Unit, 1999–2002, available at http://postconflict.unep.ch/photos/yugoslavia/pcassessment/frypcassessment.html, accessed Feb. 28, 2005.
12. Serbian Ministry of Information, *Charges for the Hague Against the NATO Leaders*, Serbia Info, serbia-info.com, June 29, 1999. Cited in Carol Holland, "Destruction of the Yugoslav Media," International Action Center (New York), available at http://www.iacenter.org/warcrime/10_media.htm, accessed Feb. 10, 2005. The US/NATO campaign against Yugoslavia led former U.S. Attorney General Ramsey Clark of the International Action Center to file a complaint with the International War Crimes Tribunal on July 30, 1999. See it at http://iacenter.org/warcrime/indictmt.htm, accessed on Feb. 20, 2005. Also see books published by the IAC including John Catalinotto and Laura Flouders, eds. *Hidden Agenda: NATO/US Takeover of Yugoslavia*, NY: Interna-

tional Action Center, 2004 and Ramsey Clark, ed, NATO and the Balkans, NY: International Action Center, 1998.

13. Cited in Julie Hyland, "Human Rights Watch says NATO killed over 500 civilians in air war against Yugoslavia," Feb. 14, 2000, World Socialist Website, available at http://www.wsws.org/articles/2000/feb2000/nato-f14.shtml, accessed March 20, 2005.

14. Ibid.

15. "Perspectives: IPI Members from Four Countries not involved in the fighting discuss NATO's bombing of the Chinese Embassy and Serbian TV," *IPI Global Journalist Online* (undated), http://www.globaljournalist.org/archive/Magazine/perspectives-19993q.html, accessed on Mar. 11, 2005.

16. Press release, Serbian Information Ministry, May 27, 1999, available at Voices Against the War in Kosovo website, posted May 31, 1999, http://www.softmakers.com/fry/rtssat.htm. Also see "Plug Pulled on Serb satellite TV," BBC News, May 27, 1999, available at http://news.bbc.co.uk/1/hi/world/monitoring/354430.stm, accessed Feb. 28, 2005.

17. Press release Serbian Information Ministry, May 27, 1999, available at Voices against the war in Kosovo website, posted May 31, 1999, http://www.softmakers.com/fry/rtssat.htm

18. "Serbian TV Back on Satellite," BBC News, June 23, 1999, available at http://news.bbc.co.uk/1/hi/world/monitoring/376682.stm, accessed Feb. 28, 2005.

19. Michael Parenti, "The Rational Destruction of Yugoslavia," Nov. 1999, Michael Parenti Political archive available at http://www.michaelparenti.org/yugoslavia.html, accessed Mar. 21, 2005. This is an excerpt from his book *To Kill A Nation: The Attack on Yugoslavia*, London: Verso, 2001.

20. "RTS and TV Pink Most Popular Stations in Serbia,"*Mediaonline.ba: Southeast European Media Journal*, Jan 19, 2005, available at http://www.mediaonline.ba/en/vijesti.asp?ID=984, accessed Feb. 28, 2005.

21. Parenti, "The Rational Destruction of Yugoslavia."

THIS MODERN WORLD

by TOM TOMORROW

Panel 1:
IT BEGINS WITH A STARTLING REVELATION.

CNN HAS OBTAINED VIDEO FOOTAGE AND SUBSTANTIATING DOCUMENTS WHICH PROVE BEYOND ANY DOUBT THAT SECRETARY OF STATE *CONDOLEEZA RICE*--

Panel 2:
--IS *ACTUALLY* A HIDEOUS MULTI-TENTACLED ALIEN BEING WHICH FEEDS ON A STEADY DIET OF *HUMAN BRAINS!*

MORE *BRAINS,* PLEASE!

WE JUST GOT A FRESH SHIPMENT IN FROM GITMO, MADAME SECRETARY!

Panel 3:
THE RIGHT-WING OBFUSCATION MACHINE QUICKLY SPRINGS INTO ACTION!

SECRETARY RICE'S DIETARY PREFERENCES ARE HER *OWN BUSINESS*--AND I FIND THIS INVASION OF HER PRIVACY *DEPLORABLE!*

THE ISSUE ISN'T *BRAIN EATING*--THE ISSUE IS *LIBERAL XENOPHOBIA!*

Panel 4:
AND WHILE LIBERALS DEBATE THE APPROPRIATE COURSE OF ACTION--

I THINK IT WOULD BE BEST TO POLITELY OVERLOOK THE MATTER-- LEST WE FIND OURSELVES SWEPT UP IN THE POLITICS OF *PERSONAL DESTRUCTION!*

THAT *WOULD* BE DISAGREEABLE!

Panel 5:
--*CONSERVATIVES* STAY ON THE *ATTACK!*

THE PURPORTED MEMO FROM SECRETARY RICE DEMANDING THAT BRAINS BE HARVESTED MORE "EFFICIENTLY" IS PRINTED ON A STRANGE, OTHERWORLDLY *METALLIC* SUBSTANCE--

--BUT EVERYONE *KNOWS* THAT *REAL* WHITE HOUSE MEMOS ARE ALWAYS PRINTED ON *PAPER!*

IT IS AN *OBVIOUS* FORGERY!

Panel 6:
AND AFTER WOLF BLITZER RESIGNS IN DISGRACE, THE WHOLE THING IS QUIETLY FORGOTTEN.

HEY, WASN'T CONDI SUPPOSED TO BE SOME KIND OF SPACE MONSTER OR SOMETHING?

NAH, DIDN'T YOU HEAR? THAT WAS ALL A BIG FRAUD! THE MEMO WAS A *FAKE!*

OH! WELL, *THAT'S* CERTAINLY A RELIEF!

TOM TOMORROW©2005 ... www.thismodernworld.com

CHAPTER 14

Junk Library Science

By Geoff Davidian and Project Censored Interns: Sean Arlt, Jacob Rich, Bridget Thornton, and Michele Salvail

Recommended reading for summer 2005*
Confessions of an Economic Hit Man by John Perkins

Intriguing autobiographical exposé of how Mr. Perkins assisted American intelligence agencies and multinational corporations persuade other nations to take action to benefit narrow U.S. foreign policy and commercial objectives. Praised by some (mostly liberals) as an honest look at dubious U.S. actions that contribute to anti-Americanism abroad, condemned by others (mostly conservatives) as the rantings of an egomaniac.

INTRODUCTION

The corporate media blending of news with entertainment—and its influence on how we see the world—has been a perennial concern of Project Censored. With the formation of media giants—and the consolidation of local newspaper and broadcast ownership—TV, radio, cable and newspapers are less reliable or interested in proving or disproving the matters at hand in a democracy.

The alternatives—universities, independent publishers and libraries—became bulwarks of relevance in a politicized, commercialized information world.

But as this year's Project Censored Investigative Report suggests, these institutions may not be adequately separating non-fiction from fancy. In our team investigation into John Perkins' best selling book, *Confessions of an Economic Hit Man*,[1] we found that none of the writer's claims that were not previously known could be independently verified.

If this were just another thriller, a simple memoir alleging nothing consequential, no one would care whether the claims were fact or fiction.

But Perkins' story goes to the heart of what America is; it paints presidents as economically tied to corporations, complicit in the subjugation of nations, and personally benefiting from their policies.

Nevertheless, from the Library of Congress to community bookshops, universities to best-seller lists, *Hit Man* is cataloged as a "non-fiction" source under headings such as "Imperialism—History—20th Century," and "Corporations, American—Foreign Countries."

While libraries do research themselves in some cases, for the most part they simply copy publishers' claims in terms of veracity of content, perpetuating the bias in what amounts to Junk Library Science.

THE ISSUE

That is what we EHMs do best: we build a global empire. We are an elite group of men and women who utilize international financial organizations to foment conditions that make other nations subservient to the corporatocracy running our biggest corporations, our government, and our banks. Like our counterparts in the Mafia, EHMs provide favors. These take the form of loans to develop infrastructure—electric generating plants, highways, ports, airports, or industrial parks. A condition of such loans is that engineering and construction companies from our own country must build all these projects. In essence, most of the money never leaves the United States; it is simply transferred from banking offices in Washington to engineering offices in New York, Houston, or San Francisco.

Despite the fact that the money is returned almost immediately to corporations that are members of the corporatocracy (the creditor), the recipient country is required to pay it all back, principal plus interest. If an EHM is completely successful, the loans are so large that the debtor is forced to default on its payments after a few years. When this happens, then like the Mafia we demand our pound of flesh. This often includes one or more of the following: control over United Nations votes, the installation of military bases, or access to precious resources such as oil or the Panama Canal. Of course, the debtor still owes us the money—and another country is added to our global empire.[2]

More than 100 years ago, philosopher William James asked us to consider a society in which millions were kept permanently happy on the one simple condition that a certain lost soul on the far-off edge of things should lead a life of lonely torture.[3]

> What except a specific and independent sort of emotion can it be which would make us immediately feel, even though an impulse arose within us to clutch at the happiness so offered, how hideous a thing would be its enjoyment when deliberately accepted as the fruit of such a bargain.

But John Perkins' treatise on post World War II America portrays a world where a few are kept permanently happy on the one simple condition that millions of souls lead lives of economic misery and exploitation, through a system in which religious groups, corporations, dictators and U.S. policy converge wherever poor nations have resources U.S. industry wants.

What makes Perkins' story more chilling yet is that it is listed as nonfiction in libraries, book stores and even the *New York Times*' best-seller list. That classification ironically gives Perkins, who made his living by lying, a cult following among groups most disgusted by his story—environmentalists, social justice advocates and progressives.

At a standing-room-only appearance at the University of Michigan in February 2005, Perkins received a standing ovation after he went point by point through events he says he participated in that explain why terrorists would want to hit the United States. He was put up during that Michigan visit at an official university residence and spent a day with students telling them how exciting their lives would be, facing the problems of their times—problems he claims to have caused in many ways.

From Colombia and Ecuador to Saudi Arabia and Malaysia, Perkins posits his own observations to connect well-known dots, revealing, he writes, a pattern of deceit and fraud resulting in U.S. "empire," which rewarded his ethical weakness with great wealth.

Perkins writes of his domestic involvement as well. He was paid as a consultant and expert witness to advance the fortunes of the Seabrook nuclear power plant in New Hampshire—an undertaking that fell into the same pattern of optimistic forecasts followed by economic disaster for those who bought into the sales pitch.

Perkins, 60, gives us a good insight into everything wrong with capitalism, and in doing so shows us an example of the kind of person who makes it all wrong.

From Iran in the 1950s to Iraq today, Perkins suggests that the United States has plundered countries and killed or removed leaders who balk at doing business at the end of a gun in an extension of global empire. In Panama, Manuel Noriega and Omar Torrijos both got in our way, says Perkins, so Torrijos was killed and Noriega arrested and imprisoned in the U.S. Meanwhile, Ecuador's President, Jaime Roldós, who stood up to American oil companies, died in a helicopter crash.

"And we wonder why terrorists attack us?" he writes.

The Project Censored team set out with the goal of proving that John Perkins was telling the truth by dividing up the countries and assignments to check the facts for ourselves.

If Perkins' story were true, if the U.S. government and corporations intentionally schemed to suck the marrow from the people of the world most in need of help, why weren't the governments of Ecuador and Colombia speaking out? Why weren't the folks in New Hampshire up in arms? Why isn't the New Hampshire attorney general investigating this billion-dollar boondoggle?

Many on the left applaud Perkins' work because it fits nicely into critical understandings of U.S. global empire. Yet, without documentation and verifiable content his book lacks the necessary prerequisites for academic scholarship and become just another tale of greed and corruption—muckraking without the muck.

And whether or not Perkins was lying—again making money off unwitting consumers—why were students, environmentalists and anti-nuclear groups rallying around him after the greed, drunkenness and ethical lapses he details?

Gary McCool, interim director of the Lamson Library at New Hampshire's Plymouth State University, told Project Censored that "everything that is not 'fiction' is not necessarily 'fact.'" For example, autobiographies and memoirs may be a writer's best recollection rather than an attempt to mislead.

Libraries don't want to impose regulation or judgment, he said. Categorizing is, however, the heart of what a librarian does, and has been since ancient Alexandria, built by the Greek architect Dinocrates in the 3rd century BC. The library there held 400,000 to 700,000 scrolls in its heyday.

Of course, McCool noted, libraries have not always classified by the categories now used. In fact, he said, some libraries maintained their collections based on the color of the covers. In some smaller libraries today, the staff may not have the type of collection that requires careful examination of every acquisition. But research libraries are different: their collections are not driven by popularity and the librarian does not decide on the quality of the content without having it in hand.

You would think McCool would be the perfect source for analyzing the historical value of *Hit Man*, having spent 10 of his 61 years fighting the Seabrook funding scheme that Perkins was paid to lie about. But he has not read the book and his library does not possess it.

Here is what a librarian, with a copy of the book in hand, would face when trying to determine whether to catalog it fiction or history:

SEABROOK

"My job was to justify, under oath, the economic feasibility of the highly controversial Seabrook nuclear power plant," Perkins writes.[4]

In a pattern not different from Perkins' explanation, the people of New Hampshire were stuck with a massive project that they neither wanted nor needed, based on false promises and a campaign of misinformation.

> Part of my job on the Seabrook case was to convince the New Hampshire Public Service Commission that nuclear power was the best and most economical choice for generating electricity in the state. Unfortunately, the longer I studied the issue, the more I began to doubt the validity of my own arguments. The literature was constantly changing at that time, reflecting a growth in research, and the evidence increasingly indicated that many alternative forms of energy were technically superior and more economical than nuclear power.
>
> The balance also was beginning to shift away from the old theory that nuclear power was safe. Serious questions were being raised about the integrity of backup systems, the training of operators, the human tendency to make mistakes, equipment fatigue, and the inadequacy of nuclear waste disposal. I per-

---

* From the Social Sciences/Economics Department Web site at University of Michigan— Dearborn

sonally became uncomfortable with the position I was expected to take—was paid to take—under oath in what amounted to a court of law.[5]

In 1981, the directors of the New Hampshire Electric Co-op agreed to buy a 25 megawatt share, or two-percent ownership, of the Seabrook project at a time when Public Service of New Hampshire was desperate for money.

Librarian Gary McCool along with other members sued the co-op to stop the deal.

"If things increased in cost, it would mean ever-increasing debt with only the members to pay," McCool said.

Arguing *pro se* before the state supreme court, McCool prevailed at five of eight oral arguments. But because so much had already been sunk into the project—$75 million or more—the court required that any alternative project to the twin nuclear plants planned for Seabrook include a savings of the existing outlay.

Meanwhile, the folks Perkins says paid him were putting out the message, "You will freeze in the dark if you don't build Seabrook. If you want to bathe and turn on lights, you need Seabrook."

After the Public Service Company of New Hampshire (PSNH) began building the Seabrook nuclear power plant, the New Hampshire legislature passed the "anti-CWIP" statute, which prohibited any recovery in rates for construction costs expended by a utility in construction of a plant until such plant was actually on line. When it became apparent that PSNH would not recover its investment, it created "a factual background which must be unique in the annals of public utility financing."

> Public Service Company of New Hampshire (PSNH or company) is the owner of an approximately 35% interest in the Seabrook Unit I nuclear generating station, which for practical purposes had its construction phase completed on or about October 31, 1986, at a cost to PSNH of $1.77 billion. The total project cost, we were told at argument, has, since the completion date, been increasing at the rate of $50 million per month. Because its final licensing proceeding is yet to be complete, the plant is producing neither electricity nor income, and the likelihood and timing of either event are matters of speculation and uncertainty.[6]

Of little consolation, McCool was right. Within a short time, both the co-op and the Public Service Company of New Hampshire were bankrupt.

"The bottom line is they built the plant," McCool said. It cost the members $185 million to buy in, and millions in legal fees and costs out of our pockets. "And New Hampshire was saddled with the highest electric rates in the nation for years to come."

Some of the costs were caused by anti-nuclear protestors who tied up the project, keeping the utility from gaining revenue through the production of electricity, McCool acknowledges, "but the definitive study of that has not been done, although that's a common discussion around here."

Whether Perkins is telling the truth could be an issue in the push to build a new generation of nuclear plants. If he is telling the truth, it is bad for the contractors and utilities. If he is lying, it is good for them.

"I never had faith in the bureaucratic process," says Paul Gunter, director of the Reactor Watchdog Project for the Nuclear Information and Resource Service. NIRS is the national information and networking center for citizens and environmental activists concerned about nuclear power, radioactive waste, radiation and sustainable energy issues, which initiates large-scale organizing and public education campaigns on specific issues.

"I was chaining myself to the gates by that time," said Gunter, who was part of the Clamshell Alliance, formed in 1976 to protest the construction of the nuclear reactor in Seabrook.

The Alliance consisted of a loosely-knit coalition of anti-nuclear groups, mostly from New England, organized around a central office which served to disseminate information between groups and to coordinate group activities. The Alliance organized a number of direct, non-violent actions at Seabrook to voice their concerns between 1976 and the late 1080s.[7]

But the Alliance was up against big guns: McCool, who was put on the co-op board after the bankruptcy, says rural co-ops were manipulated into participating in the nuclear "upgrade" by the offer of cheap loans from the Rural Electrification Agency. It was a sort of federal money laundering, he said.

One thing McCool and Gunter have in common: They were in the middle of the action, and they never heard of John Perkins.

What's a librarian to do?

SAUDI ARABIA

The United States' plan was to get Saudi Arabia to hire American engineering and construction companies with petrodollars to build infrastructure and to get the American and Saudi economies more intertwined. The results were used to convince other countries that, with loans, their countries could modernize.[8]

But Saudi Arabia didn't have the debts these other countries would end up with.

Saudi Arabia is different than other countries, and the World Bank and the IMF weren't involved.

The information that Perkins gives on Saudi Arabia does not reveal anything that can't be found through other research, and none of our research reveals Perkins' presence or involvement in these Saudi transactions.

For example, Perkins writes that engineering companies were awarded huge contracts—information that can be found with a simple Google search of "Bechtel" and "Saudi Arabia."

> Jubail Industrial City is the largest civil engineering project in the world today. It also is one of Bechtel's most remarkable achievements—a megaproject that has required vast resources and logistical planning on an unprecedented scale.
>
> Bechtel has managed the project since it began, and last year, the Royal Commission for Jubail and Yanbu asked the company to manage Jubail II, a $3.8 billion expansion of the city's industrial and residential areas.
>
> Before the early 1970s, Saudi natural gas deposits were considered more of a nuisance than an asset. Gas from oil wells was typically flared off. The challenge was to put this wasted energy to productive use by powering Saudi industrial development.[9]

Perkins' book is informative but he doesn't get into details, like the "extremely profitable contract" MAIN was awarded in Saudi Arabia; he doesn't specify what the project was. For example, in the notes Perkins credits Thomas W. Lippman among others.[10] In fact, Perkins repeatedly cites a Lippman book published in 2004, the year *Hit Man* was published.

Perkins writes about the United States-Saudi Arabian Joint Economic Commission, known as JECOR, and what does he say? "JECOR embodied an innovative concept that was the opposite of traditional foreign aid programs: it relied on Saudi money to hire American firms to build up Saudi Arabia"[11] This is basically the information that Lippman gives.

If Perkins is using his skills as a liar to put himself into the picture, he provides enough information to help his book sell, but nothing new.

What's a librarian to do?

PANAMA

The historical politics in the *Hit Man* are well documented and closely follow the economic theories of leftists and academia.

It seems, however, that the story of the man John Perkins could be almost entirely made up. Furthermore, why would a writer take the time to document well-know facts so well, yet manage to leave out any direct references to MAIN or his most important conversations and decisions? Without independent confirmation, Perkins is unable to substantiate these claims.

A big problem in verifying his story on Panama comes from the conversation between Omar Torrijos and Perkins.[12] Perkins gives neither a specific time (sometime in 1972) nor place (one of the Generals villas) and lists no witnesses. How is a librarian to determine this?

The off chance remained that imprisoned former Panamanian President Manuel Noriega, who was taken from his country by force and tried in the United States, could verify Perkins had met with Torrijos. We attempted to contact Noriega at the federal facility in Florida, where he is said to be held incommunicado.

But one month after Perkins' book was published, Noriega was said to have suffered a minor stroke.

Noriega's attorney's office referred Project Censored to the correctional facility where Noriega was held, but officials said he could only communicate through letters.

Noriega's lawyer, Frank Rubino, would not comment on anything to do with Noriega or Panama. And no, they would not speak to us about his medical status.

What's a librarian to do?

COLOMBIA

(For notes related to research see appendix.)
Perkins claims his job "was to present the case for exceedingly large loans.... I felt I had no choice but to develop inflated economic and electric load forecasts."[13]

The contracts were for "hydroelectric facilities and distribution systems to transport electricity from deep in the jungle to cities high in the mountains."[14]

Despite the vivid recollection and dialogue in the story,[15] we found no confirmation that Colombian rebels attacked the plant's engineer, Manuel Torres. However, from 1976–1983 there were several news stories reporting guerilla violence and wars between the state and indigenous communities in the jungles and mountains, according to the LexisNexis database.

After Perkins left in 1980, things went downhill for the South American nation.

The Colombian president, who was previously against foreign investment, did a quick turn around and became a big supporter of President Ronald Reagan. Again, this was three years after Perkins left Colombia and the same year he left Chas. T. Main, Inc. altogether. While he *may* have had a hand in the debt situation, there is no documentation of it. For one thing, there was little press coverage in the United States of Colombia in 1977.

Despite the size of Colombia's debt and its relations with the United States and the UN, there is no evidence that John Perkins or Chas. T. Main, Inc. had a direct influence on the economic situation in the country. Perkins does not present enough facts to substantiate his claim. Furthermore, Project Censored found no IMF, World Bank or Inter American Development Bank records of contracts awarded to Chas. T. Main, Inc., from 1976–1981.

What's a librarian to do?

CONCLUSION

"If Perkins truly cared about exposing these injustices, he would take a more academic approach to the book. He would craft it to withstand strong scrutiny. He would cite many sources and give precise illustrations. He would make his book appealing to those with the power to change it or amend it. Instead, he sensationalizes the content. He appeals to the leftist, as we all agree. He wrote a book that is so unbelievable that it cannot be used to incite serious, scholarly debate. Could it be that he wrote this book at the behest of 'the other side' to which he still may belong? He describes the entire system as too complex to penetrate, too difficult to topple.

"I felt from the beginning of the project that if he could be bribed as many times as he had, why not this time too?"

—Bridget Thornton, 2005 Project Censored Investigative team

Einar Greve, a former Chas. T. Main, Inc. vice-president who hired Perkins in 1971, is quoted in *The Business*: "The basic theory is wrong." Developing countries "were not purposely put into hock."[16]

Professors in ivory towers came up with the idea of doing a Marshall Plan for the underdeveloped world. But the Third World did not have the education and industrial background of Europe and the plan failed for decades.

"That these countries were saddled with big debts they couldn't pay definitely took place, but it was because of poor planning," he said. "There were also many projects that should never have been built, but it was largely because of incompetence, not by design."

In New Hampshire, Gary McCool says library databases make more information available than ever. For example, founded in 1967, OCLC Online Computer Library Center is a nonprofit, membership-based computer library service used by more than 53,548 libraries in 96 countries and territories to "locate, acquire, catalog, lend and preserve library materials," according to its website. "Researchers, students, faculty, scholars, professional librarians and other information seekers use OCLC services to obtain bibliographic, abstract and full-text information when and where they need it."

McCool said that in addition to what the publishers say about their products, online services provide access to other analyses of materials, including such sources as Amazon.com's reader review. But, he concedes, it is possible for a publisher to post its own reviews, all favorable to the work.

Ultimately, it is up to the reader to sift the facts.

And with consolidation of media ownership coupled with integrated production and marketing, that task is no less difficult for the reader than for the librarian.

Even with access to critical trade publications, the publisher's description trumps the professional reviewer.

For example, *Publisher's Weekly*[17] reviewed Perkins' work, but had no impact on the non-fiction classification at most libraries:

> The story as presented is implausible to say the least, offering so few details that Perkins often seems paranoid, and the simplistic political analysis doesn't enhance his credibility. Despite the claim that his work left him wracked with guilt, the artless prose is emotionally flat and generally comes across as a personal crisis of conscience blown up to monstrous proportions, casting Perkins as a victim not only of his own neuroses over class and money but of dark forces beyond his control. His claim to have assisted the House of Saud in strengthening its

ties to American power brokers may be timely enough to attract some attention, but the yarn he spins is ultimately unconvincing, except perhaps to conspiracy buffs.

Is it possible that the existing system of classification needs reform; that the fiction/non-fiction division should offer more gray area? Some additional classifications might include, "Memoir—Unsubstantiated," or "History—Documented."

And *Economic Hit Man*, who says it was his lies that ate up 10 years of McCool's life; his lies that brought nuclear power to New Hampshire over protestors who chained themselves to plant gates; his lies that led to the subjugation of millions in the Third World, might be a classification "Capitalism—Worst-case Scenario."

EPILOGUE

Following its success with *Hit Man*, Berrett-Koehler Publishers, Inc., has taken a bold step to market its stock to people who have bought its books. But don't consider this opportunity "an offer to sell, nor a solicitation of an offer to buy these securities."

> We are pleased to announce the first-ever Direct Public Offering of Berrett-Koehler stock. This is an Offering of 125,000 shares of Common Stock of The Berrett-Koehler Group, Inc. (which is the parent company of Berrett-Koehler Publishers, Inc.). The price of the shares is $8.00 per share. The minimum number of shares offered to any one investor is 100 shares. Thus, the minimum investment is $800.00. The shares are being sold on a first-come, first-served basis.
>
> This Direct Public Offering has been registered for offer and sale in California, District of Columbia, Illinois, Indiana, Minnesota, New Mexico, New York, and Wisconsin. Only persons residing in these states and district are eligible to purchase stock in this Offering, unless there is an applicable exemption from registration in a particular state or the prospective investor resides outside of the United States.
>
> This announcement is neither an offer to sell nor a solicitation of an offer to buy these securities. The offer is made only by means of the Direct Public Offering Circular. Copies of the Circular may be obtained only from The Berrett-Koehler Group, Inc.

Geoff Davidian is a veteran reporter who has covered government, politics, courts, congress, the president, war and the United Nations since 1978 for newspapers in Phoenix, Milwaukee, Houston and Portland, Maine. He publishes: www.putnampit.com and www.shorewoodvillage.com on the Internet.

APPENDIX ON COLOMBIA

1. MEDIA SEARCH:

LEXIS SEARCH:

Colombia and United States 1976–1980: Nothing pertaining to hydroelectric contracts using the following searches: "Colombia and United States," "Colombia and Hydroelectric contracts," "Colombia and foreign investment," "Colombia and Chas T. Main."

Most of the articles pertained to guerilla fighting, hijacked planes, kidnappings, drug trafficking, and the coffee industry.

FACTIVA:

No news with "Chas T. Main," 1976–1980. No news with "Hydroelectric Contracts," 1976–1980 No news about Colombia business contracts.

2. COLOMBIAN POLITICAL/ECONOMIC ENVIRONMENT (1960s TO 1987)

Source: U.S. Library of Congress http://countrystudies.us/colombia/28.htm

Colombia became one of the largest recipients of United States assistance in Latin America during the 1960s and early 1970s.

Many Colombian policy makers had become disenchanted with the Alliance for Progress—a program, conceived during the administration of President John F. Kennedy, which called for extensive United States financial assistance to Latin America as well as Latin American support for social change measures, such as agrarian reform—and with United States economic assistance in general. Many felt that Colombia's economic dependence on the United States had only increased.

Mid-to-late 1970s: U.S. aid under the Michelson and Turbay governments allied with Cuba joined Andean alliance in support of Sandinistas' Support for Panama and new canal treaty.

The Bilateral Extradition Treaty between Colombia and the United States, signed by both countries in 1979, and U.S. $26 million in United States aid helped to produce what Washington considered to be a model anti-narcotics program Betancur initially refused to extradite Colombians as a matter of principle.

1981: reversed alliance with Cuba and Sandinista support under the

Turbay government. Realigned with the U.S.: fervently denounced communism.

1982: Falklands War, the Turbay government, along with the United States, abstained on the key OAS vote to invoke the Inter-American Treaty of Reciprocal Assistance (Rio Treaty). After the war, Colombia remained one of the few Latin American countries still willing to participate with the United States in joint naval maneuvers in the Caribbean. Colombia also sent troops to the Sinai in 1982 as part of the UN Peacekeeping Force required by the 1979 Treaty of Peace Between Egypt and Israel.

1982: Betancur steered Colombia away from support of the Reagan Administration's Latin American policies and toward a nonaligned stance. Betancur reversed Turbay's anti-Argentine position on the South Atlantic War and called for greater solidarity between Latin America and the Third World. In 1983 Colombia, with the sponsorship of Cuba and Panama, joined the Nonaligned Movement, then headed by Castro.

1985: Betancur abandoned his nationalistic rhetoric on the debt and drug issues, promoted fiscal austerity policies to address Colombia's economic crisis, and cooperated with the United States in an anti-drug trafficking campaign. As a result, the United States supported Colombia's debt negotiations with the IMF and the World Bank.

May 1984: following the murder of Betancur, an opponent of the drug cartels, a "war without quarter" against the Medellin cartel ensued and Colombia extradited drug traffickers to the United States. During November 1984 to June 1987, Colombia extradited thirteen nationals—including cartel kingpin Carlos Lehder Rivas—and three foreigners to the United States

Under the National Front governments, Colombia enjoyed a windfall of international investment, including loans and grants from the IDB, IMF, United Nations Development Programme (UNDP), and International Labour Organisation (ILO). Colombia preferred to handle security and global matters through the international forums provided by the UN General Assembly and Security Council. Pursuing a somewhat independent course, Colombia became a respected voice in the General Assembly and other international arenas on matters of international law.

Enforcing Contracts 2004 (Source: World Bank, Snapshot of Business Environment—Colombia) The ease or difficulty of enforcing commercial contracts in Colombia is measured below, using three indicators: the number of procedures counted from the moment the plaintiff files a lawsuit until actual payment, the associated time, and the cost (in court and attorney fees), expressed as a percentage of debt value. In Colombia, the cost of enforcing contracts is 18.6, compared with the regional average of 23.3 and OECD average of 10.8.

NOTES

1. *Confessions of an Economic Hit Man*, (2004, San Francisco, Berrett-Koehler Publishers, 250 pp., $24.95).
2. Ibid, p. 154.
3. William James. "The Moral Philosopher and the Moral Life." An address to the Yale Philosophical Club, published in the *International Journal of Ethics*, April 1891. Online at http://www.philosophy.uncc.edu/mleldrid/American/mp&ml.htm
4. *Hit Man*, p. 154.
5. Ibid, p. 163.
6. Petition of Public Service Company of New Hampshire (New Hampshire Public Utilities Commission) No. 87-311 SUPREME COURT OF NEW HAMPSHIRE 130 N.H. 265; 539 A.2d 263; 1988 January 26, 1988
7. See the Clamshell Alliance Papers at http://www.izaak.unh.edu/specoll/mancoll/clamshell.htm
8. *Hit Man*, chapters 15-16, p. 81-98.
9. See Bechtel Web site, http://www.bechtel.com/spjubail.htm
10. *Hit Man*, p. 233
11. Ibid. p. 84.
12. Ibid. p.71 *et seq.*
13. *Hit Man*, p. 122.
14. Ibid.
15. Ibid. p. 124.
16. Joe Lauria, "Controversial book raises doubts over U.S. aid policy." *The Business*, March 13, 2005, online at http://thebusinessonline.com/33260/Read
17. *Publisher's Weekly* used the classification "Biography & Autobiography I Business; Political Science I Conspiracy & Scandal Investigations; Business & Economics I Government & Business" in a Nov. 8, 2004 review online at http://reviews.publishersweekly.com/bd.aspx?isbn=1576753018&pub=pw

THIS MODERN WORLD

by TOM TOMORROW

CHAPTER 15

Cowardice and Conflicts: The Lynching of Dan Rather

By Greg Palast

"Independent" my ass. On January 10, 2005, Dan Rather and four CBS television news producers were professionally lynched. The five journalists had exposed a rich kid whose powerful daddy got him out of the military draft during the war in Vietnam. The rich kid is the President; the daddy was another President, and the lynching rope was what CBS corporate executives laughably called an, "Independent Review Panel" whose job it was to pass judgment on Rather and his team's journalistic ethics.

The "panel" consisted of just two guys—together as qualified for the job as they are for landing the space shuttle: Dick Thornburgh and Louis Boccardi.

Remember Thornburgh? He was on the Bush Number One Administration's payroll. His grand accomplishment as Bush Sr.'s Attorney General was to whitewash the investigation of the Exxon Valdez oil spill. Thornburgh let the petroleum giant off the hook on paying out big damages. These days, Thornburgh pulls down the fat paychecks as counsel to Kirkpatrick & Lockhart, the Washington law-and-lobbying outfit hired by CBS to investigate Rather and company. Undoubtedly, Thornburgh owes this posh position to his former job as a Bush League *consigliere*.

What did Thornburgh discover for CBS? Surprise! He concluded that his former *padrone*, Bush Sr., did not put in the fix to get Bush Jr. out of the Vietnam draft.

Thornburgh's stinky conflict of interest hardly suggests "independent." Why not just appoint Karl Rove as CBS' grand inquisitor and be done with it?

Then there's Boccardi, not exactly a prince of journalism. This is the gent who, as CEO of the Associated Press, spiked his own wire service's exposure of Oliver North and his treasonous dealings with the Ayatollah Khomeini. Legendary AP investigative reporters Robert Parry and Brian Barger were hot on North's trail in 1986, but found their stories exposing the Iran-Contra scandal stopped by their bosses. The two AP reporters did not know that their superior, Boccardi, was on those very days deep in the midst of talks with North, participating in the conspiracy.

I spoke with Parry at his home in Virginia. He was sympathetic to Boccardi, who at the time was trying to spring AP reporter Terry Anderson then held hostage in Iran. But to do so, Boccardi joined, unwittingly, in a criminal conspiracy to trade guns for hostages. Boccardi then spiked his own news agency's investigation of it.

Some years later Parry discovered a 1986 e-mail from North to National Security Advisor John Poindexter in which the criminal colonel noted that Boccardi "is supportive of our terrorism (sic) policy" and wants to keep the story "quiet." Poindexter was indicted, then pardoned. Boccardi was not, and there is no indication he knew he was abetting a crime. But the AP demoted journalist Barger and forced him to quit for the offense of trying to report the biggest story of the decade.

And who are the journalists whom CBS has burned at the corporate stake? The first lined up for career execution is *60 Minutes* producer Mary Mapes. Besides the Bush draft dodge story, Mapes produced the exposé of the torture at Abu Ghraib when other networks had the same material and buried it.

DODGING THE DRAFT-DODGE STORY

And what was the crime committed by Mapes and Dan Rather that justified turning their careers to toast?

CBS said, "The Panel found that Mapes ignored information that cast doubt on the story she had set out to report—that President Bush had received special treatment 30 years ago, getting to the [Texas Air National] Guard ahead of many other applicants...."

Well, excuse me, but that story is stone cold solid, irrefutable, backed-up, sourced, proven to a fare-thee-well. I know, because I'm one of the reporters who broke that story way back in 1999, for Britain's *Guardian*. No one has challenged the *Guardian* report, or a follow-up by BBC Television, whatsoever, though we've begged the White House for a response.

CBS did not "break" this story of Chicken-Hawk George; it's just that Dan Rather, with Mapes' encouragement, found his journalistic soul and the *cojones*, finally, after 5 years delay, to report it.

Did our self-proclaimed "war president" receive special treatment in "getting to the Guard ahead of many other applicants"? Bush tested in the 25th percentile out of 100, yet, he leaped ahead of *thousands* of other Vietnam evaders because the then-Speaker of the Texas legislature, Ben Barnes, sent a message to General James Rose, head of the Guard, to give the privileged Little George a coveted pilot's post.

I have yet to see in America's media any report about two crucial documents supporting the BBC/CBS story. The first is Barnes' signed and sworn affidavit to a Texas Court, from 1999, in which he confesses, under oath, that he arranged the Air Guard fix. At the time, Texas Governor George W. Bush was given the opportunity to challenge Barnes' testimony. Bush dodged the question, suggesting investigators speak to his commander—who was dead.

And there is a second document splashed across TV screens a year before Rather's *60 Minutes* story, backing the Barnes confession. Our BBC investigative team got our hands on a whistleblower's note from the confidential files of the U.S. Justice Department. Written before Barnes' revelation, it confirmed the politician's maneuvers to get Bush Jr.'s wealthy bottom out of Vietnam and into the cushy pilot's seat at the behest of Bush Sr.

BBC also obtained a statement from the very man who made the call to the Air Guard general on behalf of Bush at Barnes' request. No one has come forward with evidence to exculpate the Bushes—*no one*.

Yet CBS President Leslie Moonves publicly castigated Rather for ignoring solid evidence that "cast doubt" on the mountain of information showing Bush Sr. helped his son evade the draft. (To provide an incentive for the network to divulge its evidence, I offered the CBS honcho $100,000 cash money if he could produce the goods. This was at the Sundance Film Festival where the BBC film on the draft-dodger-in-chief screened. Admittedly, for a network executive, that's mere pocket change. Still, it was easy money left untouched.)

THE MYSTERY MEMOS

Mapes and Rather did make a mistake, citing four memos which could not be authenticated. But let's get serious folks: these "Killian" memos had not a darn thing to do with the story-in-chief—the President's use of his daddy's connections to duck out of Vietnam.

The memos, ostensibly written by Bush's former commander Lt. Col. Jerry Killian, were a goofy little addition to the story not included in the *Guardian* or BBC reports. The memos referred to George Bush's attempt to dodge his unit's drills. Killian's secretary verified the commander's anger over special treatment for Bush though she would not verify the authenticity of these particular memos, as she did not type them. The memos may or may not be the real thing—but either way, they do not refer to, nor "cast doubt" on the overwhelming evidence that Bush Sr. called in chits to get his son out of the draft.

Yep, Rather should have said on air that two of three experts who opined on Killian's signature found it authentic and one dissented. However, CBS inquisitors took this minor error about memos and used it to discredit the entire story. And, crucial to the network's real agenda, this nonsensical distraction allowed the White House to resurrect the fake reputation of George Bush as Vietnam-era top gun.

This was a hatchet job. It appeared to be modeled on the a similar political axe-attack against BBC News issued some months earlier known as the "Hutton Report."

In that case, a used-up lordship named Hutton put his name on a viciously biased government "investigation" of BBC's ballsy uncovering of an official lie: that Saddam Hussein had weapons of mass destruction. Lord Hutton seized on a minor error by one reporter to attempt to discredit the entire BBC report of governmental mendacity.

But to the English elite's dismay, the British public stood with the "Beeb."

Yet, in my own country, the American press itself, notably the *New York Times*, joined in the lynch mob against Rather and his producer, repeating the allegations against the *60 Minutes* report without any independent verification of the charges whatsoever. (Given that the accusation is that Rather did not sufficiently verify allegations, the repetition of the unchecked libel against Rather confirmed the British suspicion that Americans are incapable of irony.)

I would note that neither CBS nor the *New York Times* punished a single reporter for passing on, as hard news, the Bush Administration's fibs and whoppers about Saddam Hussein's nuclear and biological weapons programs. Shameful repetitions of that propaganda produced no resignations—indeed, picked up an Emmy or two.

Yes, I believe heads should roll at CBS: those of the "news" chieftains who for five years ignored the screaming evidence about George Bush's slinking out of the draft during the war in Vietnam through the abuse of political connections.

REDSTONE'S SHADOW OVER BLACK ROCK

What on earth would motivate CBS to eat the flesh of its own employees? Why the rush to burnish the Bushes' reputations? The answers won't be found at Black Rock, CBS' headquarters.

On the top page of the network's craven and dead wrong apology to the President is an imprint of the cyclopsian CBS eyeball. But the CBS logo is just a cover. This vile spike-after-broadcast served only CBS' master, the network's owner, Viacom Corporation.

"From a Viacom standpoint, the election of a Republican administration is a better deal. Because the Republican administration has stood for many things we believe in, deregulation and so on…. I vote for Viacom. Viacom is my life, and I do believe that a Republican administration is better for media companies than a Democratic one."

That more-than-revealing statement, made weeks before the presidential election, by Sumner Redstone, billionaire honcho of CBS' parent company, wasn't reported on CBS. Why not? Someone should investigate.

Viacom needs the White House to bless its voracious and avaricious need to bust current ownership and trade rules to add to its global media monopoly. Placing the severed heads of reporters who would question the Bush mythology on the White House doorstep will certainly ease the way for Viacom's ambitions.

THE PRICE OF "ASKING QUESTIONS"

It's little known that Rather had three years earlier predicted his own career death. In June 2002, the CBS anchor appeared on the BBC. He looked old, defeated and made a confession he dare not speak on American TV. "*Fear keeps journalists from asking the toughest of the tough questions,*" the aging American journalist told the British television audience.

A deadly censorship—self-censorship—had seized U.S. newsrooms, Rather revealed. After the September 11 attack, news on the U.S. tube was bound and gagged. Any reporter who stepped out of line, he said, would be professionally lynched as un-American. "It's an obscene comparison," he said, "but there was a time in South Africa when people would put flaming tires around people's necks if they dissented. In some ways, the fear is that you will be necklaced here, you will have a flaming tire of lack of patriotism put around your neck." No U.S. reporter who values his neck or career will, Rather said, "bore in on the tough questions."

Dan poured out his heart to a British audience. However, back in the

USA, he smothered his professional conscience and told his TV audience, "George Bush is the President. He makes the decisions. He wants me to line up, just tell me where."

During the war in Vietnam, Rather's predecessor at CBS, Walter Cronkite, asked some pretty hard questions about Nixon's handling of the war in Vietnam. Today as then, our sons and daughters are dying in Bush family wars; but, unlike Cronkite, Dan could not, would not, ask the tough questions of George Bush, Top Gun Fighter Pilot, Our Maximum Beloved Leader in the war on terror. While BBC television was exposing documentation pointing to fabrication of evidence to seduce our nations into war, Dan and his U.S. colleagues kept their silence and spiked their own stories.

In that 2002 British broadcast, without his network minders snooping, you could see Dan seething and deeply unhappy with himself for playing the game. "What is going on," he said, "I'm sorry to say, is a belief that the public doesn't need to know, limiting access, limiting information to cover the backsides of those who are in charge of the war. It's extremely dangerous and cannot and should not be accepted, and I'm sorry to say that up to and including this moment of this interview, that overwhelmingly it has been accepted by the American people. And the current administration revels in that, they relish and take refuge in that." Rather resolved, on the UK broadcast, to become a real reporter again. That was his mistake.

NO QUESTIONS ASKED

This is not a story about Dan Rather. The white millionaire celebrity can defend himself without my help. This is really a story about fear, the fear that stops other reporters in the U.S. from following evidence about this Administration. American newsmen, practicing their smiles, adjusting their hairspray levels, bleaching their teeth and all the other activities that are the heart of U.S. TV journalism, will look to the treatment of Dan Rather and say, "Not me, babe."

They will ask no tough questions, as Dan predicted, lest they risk corporate "necklacing" in which their careers as news actors are burnt to death.

Greg Palast is the author of the New York Times bestseller, "The Best Democracy Money Can Buy" and a contributing editor to Harper's Magazine. His documentary for BBC Television "Bush Family Fortunes," including evidence of the President's dodging the Vietnam draft, won the 2005 George Orwell Prize for Courage in Journalism.

Censored 2006 Resource Guide

SOURCES OF THE TOP 25 CENSORED STORIES

For the complete *Project Censored Guide* (more than 1,000 independent media sources) go to: <www.projectcensored.org>

ASHEVILLE GLOBAL REPORT
P.O. Box 1504
Asheville, NC 28802
Tel: (828) 236-3103
E-mail: <editors@agrnews.org>
Web site: <www.agrnews.org>

AGR covers news underreported by mainstream media, believing that a free exchange of information is necessary to organize for social change.

BULLETIN OF THE ATOMIC
SCIENTISTS
6042 South Kimbark Ave.
Chicago, IL 60637
Phone: (773) 834-1800
Fax: (773) 702-0725
E-mail: <letters@thebulletin.org>
Web site: <www.thebulletin.org>

The mission of the *Bulletin* is to educate citizens about global security issues, especially the continuing dangers posed by nuclear and other weapons of mass destruction, and the appropriate roles of nuclear technology.

CANADIAN DIMENSION
2B-91 Albert Street
Winnipeg, Manitoba
Canada R3B 1G5
Phone: (204) 957-1519
Fax: (204) 943-4617
E-mail:
<info@canadiandimension.mb.ca>
Web site:
<www.canadiandimension.mb.ca >

Canadian Dimension is a magazine that shows there is an alternative to the corporate agenda and the dictates of the global market; that the dream of a better society is still alive. It provides a forum for debate, where red meets green, feminists take on socialists, socialists take on social democrats, whites hear from aboriginals, activists report from all corners of Canada, trade unionists report from the front lines, campaigns make connections, and the latest books, films, web sites, CDs, and videos are radically reviewed.

CAPITOL HILL BLUE
Web site:
<www.capitolhillblue.com

The Chronicle of Higher Education
1255 23rd St., NW, Suite 700
Washington, DC 20037
Fax: (202) 452-1033
E-mail: <letters@chronicle.com>
Web site: <http://chronicle.com>

The Chronicle of Higher Education is the No. 1 source of news, information, and jobs for college and university faculty members and administrators.

COMMON DREAMS
PO Box 443
Portland, ME 04112-0443
Tel: (207) 775-0488
Fax: (207) 775-0489
E-mail: <editor@commondreams.org>
Web site: <www.commondreams.org>

A national nonprofit, grassroots organization whose mission is to organize an open, honest and nonpartisan national discussion of current events.

CORP WATCH
1611 Telegraph Avenue #702
Oakland, CA 94612
Phone: (510) 271-8080
Web site: <www.corpwatch.org>

CorpWatch counters corporate-led globalization through education,

network-building and activism. We work to foster democratic control over corporations by building grassroots globalization a diverse movement for human rights and dignity, labor rights and environmental justice.

DEMOCRACY NOW!
PO Box 693
New York, NY 10013
Tel: (212) 431-9090
Fax: (212) 431-8858
E-mail:
<mail@democracynow.org>
Web site: <www.democracynow.org>

Democracy Now! is a national, daily, independent, award-winning news program airing on over 225 stations in North America. Pioneering the largest public media collaboration in the U.S., *Democracy Now!* is broadcast on Pacifica, community, and National Public Radio stations, public access cable television stations, satellite television (on Free Speech TV, channel 9415 of the DISH Network), short-wave radio and the internet.

DOLLARS AND SENSE
740 Cambridge Street
Cambridge, MA 02141, USA
E-mail: <dollars@dollarsandsense.org>
Web site: <www.dollarsandsense.org>

Continues to meet the need for "left perspectives on current economic affairs," as our masthead proclaims. We print articles by journalists, activists, and scholars on a broad range of topics with an economic theme: the economy, housing, labor, government regulation, unemployment, the environment, urban conflict, and activism.

EARTH FIRST! JOURNAL
P.O. Box 3023
Tucson, AZ 85702-6900
Tel: (520) 620-6900
Fax: (413) 254-0057
E-mail: <collective@earthfirstjournal.org>
Web site: <www.earthfirstjournal.org>

Reports on radical environmental movements. The journal publishes hard-to-find information about strategies to stop the destruction of the planet.

THE ECOLOGIST
Unit 18 Chelsea Wharf
15 Lots Road
London
SW10 0QJ
Tel: 44 (0) 20 7351 3578
Fax: 44 (0) 20 7351 3617
E-mail: <editorial@theecologist.org>
Web site: <www.theecologist.org>

Published in four continents, *The Ecologist* is a key player in major environmental campaigns against GM crops, rainforest destruction, climate change and the impact of globalization, *The Ecologist*'s early-warning signs have helped set environmental and political agendas across the world.

FREE PRESS
1240 Bryden Rd.
Columbus, OH 43205
Phone: (614) 253-2571

E-mail: <truth@freepress.org>
Web site: <www.freepress.org>

The Free Press now honors community activists annually, and believes that there's still a place for community-based journalism.

GLOBAL RESEARCH
CRG / CRM
101 Cardinal Leger,
C.P. 51004, Pincourt, QC,
J7V9T3, Canada
Telephone: (514) 425-3814
Fax: (514) 425-6224
E-mail: <crgeditor@yahoo.com>
Web site: <www.globalresearch.ca>

The Centre for Research on Globalization (CRG) is an independent research and media group of progressive writers, scholars and activists committed to curbing the tide of "globalization" and "disarming" the New World Order.

GRAIN
Girona 25, pral. E-08010
Barcelona, Spain
Phone: (34) 033011381
Fax: (34) 933011627
E-mail: <grain@grain.org>
Web site: <www.grain.org>

An international non-governmental organization promoting the sustainable management and use of agricultural biodiversity based on people's control over genetic resources and local knowledge.

THE GUARDIAN (London)
3-7 Ray Street
London EC IR 3DR UK
E-mail:<editor@
guardianlimited.co.uk>
Web site: <www.guardian.co.uk>

HARPER'S MAGAZINE
666 Broadway, 11th Floor
New York, NY 10012
Phone: (212) 420-5791
E-mail: <giulia@harpers.org>
Web site: <www.harpers.org>

Harper's Magazine aims to provide
readers with a unique perspective on
the world. *Harper's* editors sift through
the culture's vast output of information,
and searching for gleaming points of
significance.

THE INDEPENDENT (London)
Independent House
191 Marsh Wall
London E14 9RS
England
Tel: (020) 7005 2000
E-mail: <customerservices@
independent.co.uk>
Web site: <www.independent.co.uk>

An independent, daily London
newspaper.

INTER PRESS SERVICE (IPS)
E-mail: <online@ips.org>
Web site: <www.ips.org>

Inter Press Service, the world's leading
provider of information on global
issues, is backed by a network of
journalists in more than 100 countries,

with satellite communication links to
1,200 outlets. IPS focuses its news
coverage on the events and global
processes affecting the economic,
social and political development of
peoples and nations.

IN THESE TIMES
2040 North Milwaukee Avenue
Chicago, IL 60647
Tel: (773) 772-0100
Fax: (773) 772-4180
Web site: <www.inthesetimes.com>

In These Times is a national, biweekly
magazine of news and opinion
published in Chicago. For 27 years, *In
These Times* has provided
groundbreaking coverage of the labor
movement, environment, feminism,
grassroots politics, minority
communities and the media. *In These
Times* features award-winning
investigative reporting about corporate
malfeasance and government
wrongdoing, insightful analysis of
national and international affairs, and
sharp cultural criticism about events
and ideas that matter.

THE IRISH TIMES
10-16 D'Olier St
Dublin 2
Ireland
E-mail: <lettersed@irish-times.ie>
Web site: <www.ireland.com>

The Irish Times aims to present the
facts after we have established them,
having heard both sides of the story. It
also acts as the authoritative and

independent commentator and analyst on important events in the affairs of Ireland—North and South—Britain, the European Union, the United States and, where feasible, pivotal news spots in the world.

JANE'S DEFENSE WEEKLY
110 N. Royal Street, Suite 200
Alexandria, VA 22314
Phone: (703) 683-3700
and (800) 824-0768
Fax: (703) 836-0297
E-mail:
<customerservices.us@janes.com>
Web site: <http://defense.janes.com>

Jane's Information Group is a leading provider of intelligence and analysis on national and international defense, security and risk developments. Jane's is an independent organization with an unrivalled reputation of accuracy, authority and impartiality. Jane's delivers partners and clients a strategic advantage from intelligence acquired by a unique worldwide network of independent analysts. Governments, militaries, business leaders and academics in over 180 countries rely on Jane's providing timely and insightful information on threat and security issues.

THE LANCET
360 Park Ave. South
New York, NY 10010
Phone: (800) 462-6198
Fax: (800) 327-9021
E-mail: <USLancetCS@elsevier.com>
Web site: <www.thelancet.com>

An independent and authoritative voice in global medicine. We seek to publish high-quality clinical trials that will alter medical practice; our commitment to international health ensures that research and analysis from all regions of the world is widely covered.

THE LAW.COM
Web site: <www.law.com>

An online magazine covering legal issues

LEFT TURN MAGAZINE
P.O. Box 445
1463 E. Republican St. #25A
New York, NY 10159-0445
E-mail: <leftturn@leftturn.org>
Web site: <www.leftturn.org>

Left Turn magazine focuses on the issues and debates within the growing anti-capitalist movement.

LIP MAGAZINE
P.O. Box 1070
Dickson, ACT 2602
E-mail: <editor@lipmag.com>
Web site: <www.lipmag.com>

LiP takes creative aim at a culture machine that strips us our desires and sells them back as product and mediocracy. Brazen, audacious and presumptuous, *LiP* combines a biting aesthetic consciousness with a structural understanding of power. Refusing to be colonized by despair, cynicism or apathy, *LiP* gives voice to those working for a sustainable society rooted in cooperation and diversity. *LiP* confronts the miserabilist capitalist system with dangerous humor, liberated eroticism and informed revolt.

MOTHER JONES MAGAZINE
222 Sutter St. 6th Floor
San Francisco, CA 94108
Phone: (415) 321-1700
Fax: (415) 321-1701
E-mail: <backtalk@motherjones.com>
Web site: <www.motherjones.com>

Mother Jones is an independent nonprofit whose roots lie in a commitment to social justice implemented through first rate investigative reporting.

THE MOTLEY FOOL
Web site: <www.fool.com>

The Motley Fool, when it comes to matters of money, believes in transparency and accountability. Day in and day out, they dedicate ourselves to delivering responsible investing ideas and sound financial education.

NACLA REPORT ON THE AMERICAS
North American Congress on Latin America
38 Greene st. 4th fl., New York NY 10013
Phone: (646) 613-1440
Fax (646) 613-1443
E-mail: <teo@nacla.org>
Web site: <www.nacla.org>

NACLA provides policy makers, analysts, academics, organizers, journalists and religious and community groups with information on major trends in Latin America and its relations with the United States.

THE NATION
33 Irving Place
New York, NY 10003
Tel: (212) 209-5400
Fax: (212) 982-9000
E-mail: <info@thenation.com>
Web site: <www.thenation.com>

The Nation will not be the organ of any party, sect, or body. It will, on the contrary, make an earnest effort to bring to the discussion of political and social questions a really critical spirit, and to wage war upon the vices of violence, exaggeration, and misrepresentation by which so much of the political writing of the day is marred.

NATIONAL PUBLIC RADIO (NPR)
635 Massachusetts Ave., NW
Washington, D.C. 20001
Phone: (202) 513-2000
Fax: (202) 513-3329
Web site: <www.npr.org>

NPR is an internationally acclaimed producer and distributor of noncommercial news, talk, and entertainment programming. A privately supported, not-for-profit membership organization, NPR serves a growing audience of 26 million Americans each week in partnership with more than 780 independently operated, noncommercial public radio stations.

NATIVE AMERICAS: HEMISPHERE
JOURNAL OF INDIGENOUS ISSUES
Cornell University
American Indian Program
P.O. Box DH
Ithaca, NY 14851-9963
Phone: (800) 9-NATIVE
Fax: (607) 255-0185
Web site: <www.nativeamericas.com>

An academic journal covering
Indigenous issues based out of Cornell
University.

NEWS FROM INDIAN COUNTRY
3059 Seneca Turnpike
Canastota, NY 13032
Fax: (315) 829.8393
E-mail:
<ssharkey@indiancountry.com>
Web site:
<www.indiancountrynews.com>

Indian Country Communications, Inc.
is an independent, Indian-owned,
reservation based business. NFIC
contains national, cultural and regional
sections PLUS special interest articles,
features, entertainment, letters and the
most up-to-date pow-wow directory
throughout North America.

THE NEWSTANDARD
203 Bassett St.
Syracuse, NY 13210
Phone: (877) 262-1539
Office Fax: (202) INK-4805
E-mail: <ed-letters@
newstandardnews.net>
Web site: <www.newstandardnews.net>

The *NewStandard* presently provides

uncompromised investigative journalism
and 24-hour news coverage of current
events in three major topic areas: the
war in Iraq; civil liberties and security;
and U.S. business and economy, all
presented from a people's perspective.

OXFAM PRESS RELEASE
Oxfam House
274 Banbury Road
Oxford
OX2 7DZ
E-mail: <media.unit@oxfam.org.uk>
Fax number: 01865 312580

Oxfam works internationally as part of
a world-wide movement to build a just
and safer world. Oxfam is an
independent British organization,
registered as a charity, affiliated with
Oxfam International, and it has
partners, volunteers, supporters, and
staff of many nationalities.

THE PALM BEACH POST
P.O. Box 24700
West Palm Beach, FL 33416
Phone: (800) 926-POST
Web site: <www.palmbeachpost.com>

A local Palm Beach, Florida newspaper.

PEACE MAGAZINE
PO Box 248, Stn P
Toronto, ON M5S 2S7
Canada
Tel: (416) 588-8748
E-mail: <office@peacemagazine.org>
Web site: <www.peacemagazine.org>

Journalists, educators, and activists
keep up to date on the important work

of peacemaking by reading this popular
and respected magazine. Four times a
year we publish articles, news stories,
book and film reviews, letters, and a
Peace Crossword. We discuss
disarmament; conflict resolution;
nonviolent sanctions; peace institutions
(e.g. the United Nations and the World
Court); conflicts and crises around the
world; profiles of activists and
researchers; and controversies about
development, population, and
environmental protection.

PR NEWSWIRE
810 7th Ave., 35th floor
New York, NY 10019
Phone: (212) 596-1500 and (800) 832-
5522
E-mail:
<information@prnewswire.com>
Web site: <www.prnewswire.com>

Whether your news has to go around
the corner or around the globe, PR
Newswire serves all of your information
distribution needs. PR Newswire is the
world leader in the electronic delivery
of news releases and information
directly from companies, institutions
and agencies to the media, financial
community and consumers.

PRIMEZONE MEDIA NETWORK
5200 W. Century Blvd. Suite 470
Los Angeles, CA 90045
Phone: (800) 307-6627
(310) 642-6930
Fax: (800) 307-3567
(310) 642-6933
Web site: <www.primezone.com>

PrimeZone Media Network operates a
global newswire service, specializing in
the delivery of corporate financial news
and multimedia content to the media,
investment community, individual
investors and the general public.

SAN ANTONIO EXPRESS-NEWS
400 3rd St.
San Antonio, TX 78287-2171.
Phone: (210) 250-3000

A local San Antonio, Texas newspaper.

SEATTLE POST-INTELLIGENCER
P.O. Box 1909
Seattle, WA 98111-1909
Phone: (206) 448-8000
Web site:

A local independent Seattle
newspaper.

STOCKGATE TODAY
Web site:
<www.investigatethesec.com>

An online resource center dedicated to
analyzing the inner workings of the
SEC.

TOM PAINE.COM
Institution for America's Future
1025 Connecticut Ave., NW, Suite 205
Washington, DC 20036
Website: <www.tompaine.com>
E-mail: <editor@tompaine.com>

For people who want to keep in touch
with the progressive community but
don't have time to surf dozens of

websites. It's also for people who care about the progressive cause and are looking for an online home. Each day we scour the country—from Capitol Hill to newspapers to think tanks and activist groups—and highlight the news, ideas and actions that you need to stay fully informed. Because we're based in Washington, D.C., expect us to be obsessed with the workings of the nation's capitol.

TRUTH OUT
P.O. Box 55871
Sherman Oaks, CA 91413
Web site: <www.truthout.org>

A webzine and listserve that covers the issues of the day from a different perspective.

UK OBSERVER
119 Farringdon Rd.
London EC1R 3ER
United Kingdom
Phone: (020) 7278-2332
Web site:
<http://observer.guardian.co.uk>

An independent, London-based newspaper.

WASHINGTON FREE PRESS
PMB #178, 1463 E. Republican St.
Seattle, WA 98112
Phone: (206) 860-5290
E-mail: <editor@wafreepress.org>
Web site:
<www.washingtonfreepress.org>

This paper is what journalism should be: news in the public interest and opinion from the heart. This paper is a volunteer operation in which no one is making a profit or bowing to commercial pressures. It is not distributed in news stands for a profit, but is instead distributed by volunteers who want to get underreported news out to their neighborhoods. This paper is not aligned with any political party or other specific interest, and you'll probably find articles written by middle-of-the-road muckrakers, by Trotskyites and traditionalists, and by generally unclassifiable individuals, as long as they write accessibly and with a spirit of public and planetary betterment.

WORLD SOCIALIST
E-mail: <editor@wsws.org>
Web site: <www.wsws.org>

The *World Socialist* Web Site is the Internet center of the International Committee of the Fourth International (ICFI). It provides analysis of major world events, comments on political, cultural, historical and philosophical issues, and valuable documents and studies from the heritage of the socialist movement. The *WSWS* aims to meet the need, felt widely today, for an intelligent appraisal of the problems of contemporary society. It addresses itself to the masses of people who are dissatisfied with the present state of social life, as well as its cynical and reactionary treatment by the establishment media.

WORLD WAR 4 REPORT
89 Fifth Ave. #172
Brooklyn NY 11217
USA
E-mail: <feedback at ww4report.com>
Web site: <http://www.ww4report.com>

WW4 Report has been monitoring the global War on Terrorism and its implications for human rights, democracy and ecology since the immediate aftermath of 9/11. With an international network of contacts and correspondents, they scan the world press and Internet for important stories overlooked by the mass media, and examine the headlines with a critical eye for distortion, deceit and propaganda.

Z MAGAZINE
18 Millfield Street
Woods Hole, MA 02543.
Phone: (508) 548-9063
Fax: (508) 457-0626
E-mail: <zmag@zmag.org>
Web site: <www.zmag.org>

Z is an independent monthly magazine dedicated to resisting injustice, defending against repression, and creating liberty. It sees the racial, gender, class, and political dimensions of personal life as fundamental to understanding and improving contemporary circumstances; and it aims to assist activist efforts for a better future.

Index

!Paper, 179
2004 Presidential Election, 185, 281, 287, 292
48 Hours, 301
60 Minutes, 243, 299, 398-400
60 Plus Association, 289
9/11, 97, 123, 155, 160-161, 167, 203-235, 243, 288, 290, 355, 366, 368-370
9/11 Commission Report, 203-204, 208-210, 214-215, 224, 228
A-Infos.ca, 278-279
AAPS, *see* American Association of Physicians and Surgeons
ABA, *see* American Bar Association
Abbott Laboratories, 304
ABC News, 55, 57, 221, 301
Jabbar Abdul (Dr.), 336
Abdulla Aziz (Dr.), 335
Abernathy, Kathleen, 341, 351
Abraham, Herard, 144
Abrams, Elliot, 369
Abu Ghraib, 82-84, 119, 141-142, 190, 302, 398
Academic Freedom Bill of Rights, 89-90, 167
Accenture Ltd., 179
Adbusters, 270
Adelphia Communications, 277
Adelstein, Jonathan, 270, 284, 353
al-Adhami. Imam Shaikh Muayid, 332
Advantage Associates, 291
Advertising Age, 288
Advocacy News, 80
Aerospace America, 359, 363
Afghanistan, 57, 67, 82, 97, 129, 154-155, 157, 206, 209, 230, 286, 310, 356, 373, 377
Afshar, Haleh, 322

Agence France-Presse, 209, 313
Agency for International Development, 133, 143
Agency for Toxic Substances and Disease Registry (ATSDR), 153
Ahmad, Mahmoud, 227-228
Ahmed, Nafeez, 205
AIDS, 36, 79, 86, 101-102, 127, 304, 312
Akre, Jane, 164-165
Alessandrini, Tony, 323
Algeria, 310
Ali, Ben, 317
Alien Tort Claims Act (ATCA), 137, 150
aliens, 40
Allawi. Ayad, 333
Allianz Group, 213-214
Alshehhi, Marwan, 218
Alston & Bird, 291
Altman, John Graham, 305
Altria Group, 292
America's Army, 357
America's Next Top Model, 301
American Airlines, 26, 214-215, 222, 228
American Association of People with Disabilities, 184
American Association of Physicians and Surgeons (AAPS), 80
American Bar Association (ABA), 157
American Civil Liberties Union (ACLU), 176
American Health Care Association, 107
American Indian Trust Reform Act, 104
American Indians, 37, 103
American Prospect, 157
American Psychiatric Association (APA), 80-81
American's Community Bankers, 289
Amin, Samir, 322

Amiriyat al-Fallujah, 335
Amnesty International, 84, 145, 158
AMR Corporation, 222
Anderson, Terry, 398
Anderson Cooper Show, 216
Andrews, Tom, 274
Aniston, Jennifer, 238, 240
anorexia, 240
ANRs, *see* audio news releases
Anuaks, 116-119, 121-122
AOL/Time Warner, 247, 251
APA, *see* American Psychiatric Association
APCO Worldwide, 291
Arafat, Yasser, 315
Arbour, Louise, 43
Aristide, Jean Bertrand, 140, 144
Arizona Republic, 299, 372
Arizona State University, 366
Armed Forces of Haiti (FADH), 144
Armstrong, David, 370-371
Army Corps of Engineers, 76-77
Army Reserve, 141, 171
Arnold, Larry, 225
Arnwine, Barbara, 183
Artificial Intelligence, 358
Ash, Marc, 66
Ashcroft, John, 39, 150, 157
Asher, Hank, 54
Asheville Global Report, 46, 59-60, 78, 125, 403
Associated Press, 48, 64, 78, 108, 154, 207, 248, 250, 287, 305, 329, 398
Association des Journalistes Tunisiens, 317
ATCA, *see* Alien Tort Claims Act
ATSDR, *see* Agency for Toxic Substances and Disease Registry
Atta, Mohammed, 205, 209, 218-219, 227-229
audio news releases (ANR), 282
Auletta, Ken, 306
Austin American-Statesman, 302, 304
Australia, 18, 254-255, 259-260, 262, 279-280, 310, 351
Australian Greens, 16, 263, 279
Ayyoub, Tariq, 65
Azerbaijan, 310
Aziz, Abdulla, 329
AZT, 102

Baghdad University, 326
Bahrain, 311
Baker, James A., 183
Balaran, Alan, 103-104
Bangladesh, 311
Bank of Alex Brown, 223
Bank of America, 159
Barnes, Ben, 399
Barnes, Roy, 194
baseball, 238-239, 261
Baxley, Dennis, 167
BBC, 50, 52, 67, 70-71, 209, 218, 309, 311, 313-314, 316, 370, 372, 379, 398-402
Beams, Nick, 374, 378
Bechtel, 178, 232, 250, 388
Beckham, David, 315
Beer, David, 142
Belarus, 311
Benjamin, Medea, 268, 270
Bennett, Jana, 309
Bennett, William, 369
Berg, Phillip, 160
Bergen Record, 221
Bermuda, 179
Berthelsen, Christian, 222
Betancur, 393-394
BGH, *see* bovine growth hormone
Bi-National Planning Group, 91-92
Big Pharma, 80
bin Laden, Osama, 190, 205-206, 208, 316
Black Box voting, 174, 180
Black Power Movement, 195
Black Rock, 401
Bloomberg Business News, 223
BMJ story, 80-81
BMTC, *see* Broadcast Media & Technology Center
Boca Raton, 142, 144, 177
Boccardi, Louis, 246, 397-398
Boeing, 229, 245, 252
Bollywood, 308, 317
bombings, 316
Bonds, Barry, 238-239
Bosnia, 373, 376-378
Boston Herald, 297
Boucher, Richard, 287
bovine growth hormone (BGH), 164

Boxer, Barbara, 183, 231
Boyle, Francis A., 230
BPG, *see* Bi-National Planning Group
Bradley, Henry, 183
Brand, Stewart, 290
Branfield, Gary, 83
Brazil, 141, 259-260, 311
Bremer, Paul, 69-70, 313, 333
Bremer's Mandates, 36
BriarPatch, 431
Broadcast Media & Technology Center
   (BMTC), 282
Broward County (Fla.), 173, 176, 192
Brown, Craig, 274
Bruckheimer, Jerry, 301
Bryant, Kobe, 238
Brzezinski, Matthew, 122-123
Buckley Jr., William F., 88
Buddhism, 307, 317
Bulgaria, 311
Bulletin of the Atomic Scientists, 93, 403
Bureau of Indian Affairs, 104
Burma, 311
Burson-Marsteller, 291
Bush, George W., 48, 53, 79, 151, 157,
   162, 170, 233, 289, 303, 399
Bush, Jeb, 51, 186, 198, 369
Bush, George H. W., 79
Bush Administration, 36, 38-40, 59, 71,
   73-74, 77, 80, 93, 95, 104-105, 118,
   122, 126, 130, 133, 135, 138, 149-152,
   161, 163, 170, 187, 195, 200, 207-208,
   210, 212, 217, 230, 243, 282-283, 285-
   288, 292, 365, 369-370, 400
Business Center USCE, 375
Business Roundtable, 289
Business Week, 149
Buzzflash, 16, 52, 71, 147, 169, 263, 274-
   276
CACI, *see* California Analysis Center Incor-
   porated
caging list, 49
Cal OSHA, 128
Calabresi, Steven, 157
California Analysis Center Incorporated
   (CACI), 83
California Common Cause, 177

California Rural Legal Assistance (CRLA),
   128
Calipari, Nicola, 66
Callen, Pamela, 143
Caltech-MIT Voting Technology Project,
   174
CampaignDesk.org, 282
Campus Watch, 168
Canada, 18, 22, 36, 91-92, 129, 169, 175,
   180, 225, 230, 255, 260, 262, 278, 311,
   339, 351, 403, 405, 409
Canadian Polaris Institute, 180
cancer, 21, 130, 156, 164, 253
Canseco, Jose, 238-239
Capitol Hill Blue, 53, 404
Carlyle Group, 176, 248
Carter, Jimmy, 121, 183
Carter-Baker Commission on Federal Elec-
   tion Reform, 183
Caution, Religion, 308
CBS, 101, 193, 207, 209, 224, 238, 243-
   244, 257, 277, 299-302, 308, 353, 369,
   397-402
Center for Digital Democracy (CDD), 16,
   263, 276-277
Center for Economic and Policy Research,
   289
Center for International Policy, 97
Center for Public Integrity, 84, 270
Center for science in the Public Interest,
   292
Central Intelligence Agency (CIA), 10, 12,
   15, 83-84, 90, 95, 120, 123, 135, 206-
   209, 213, 219, 223-224, 226-228, 232,
   333
Chamblain, Louis Jodel, 145
Chambliss, Saxby, 194
Champaign-Urbana Community Wireless
   Network, 271
Chao, Elaine, 158
Charles, Leon, 140
Chas. T. Main, 390, 393
Chavez, Cesar, 108
Chavez, Hugo, 177
Chemical Security Act, 123
chemicals, 70, 122, 130
Cheney, Dick, 225, 227, 369, 371
Cheney, Lynne, 306

Chenoy, Anuradha, 59
Chernobyl, 290
Chester, Jeffrey, 277
Chicago Tribune, 30, 45
Chimere, 144
China, 58-59, 72-75, 118, 141, 149, 256-257, 312
Chomsky, Noam, 88, 321
Chossudovsky, Michel, 91, 134, 137, 205, 227, 233, 378
Chretien, Jean, 91
Christian Aid, 292
Christian Congress for Traditional Values, 309
Christian Legal Society (CLS), 137, 159-160
Chronicle of Higher Education, 44-45, 110, 404
Churchill, Ward, 90
CIA, *see* Central Intelligence Agency
Cianci Jr., Vincent, 318
Civil Assistance Plan, 92
Civil Rights Movement, 195
Civilian Death Toll, 36, 44
CJRdaily.org, 282
CJTF-HOA, 118
Clamshell Alliance, 387, 395
Clark, Ramsey, 230, 378-379
Clark, Richard, 207
Clarke, Richard, 299
Class Action Fairness Act, 87
Cleland, Max, 194
Clinton, Bill, 107
Clinton, Hillary, 232
CNN, 10, 12, 35, 44, 46, 66, 177, 187, 190, 193, 197, 208-209, 216-217, 240, 255-256, 277, 316, 376
Coalition for the Modernization and Protection of America's Social Security (COMPASS), 289
Coalition Provisional Authority, 69, 313
Cobell, Elouise, 103-104
Cobell v. Norton case, 104-105
Coca-cola, 131, 249, 251
cocaine, 175, 229, 240
Cohen, William, 245
Cohn, Marjorie, 43

Collective for the Defense of Women in Guatemala, 124
Colombia, 93-95, 130-131, 312, 383-384, 389-390, 393-394
Colombian Trade Union Federation, 131
Columbia Gannett, 246
Columbia Journalism Review, 262, 296-297, 347, 351, 371-372
Combined Joint Task Force-Horn of Africa, 118
Comcast, 260, 277
commercial media, 296
Committee to Protect Journalists (CPJ), 64, 67, 311, 313, 315, 334
Common Cause, 124, 177, 183
Common Dreams, 16, 38, 263, 273-274, 404, 431
Communism, 166-167, 394
Community Healthy Marriage Initiative, 283
COMPASS, *see* Coalition for the Modernization and Protection of America's Social Security
computerized voting, 172, 194
Confessions of an Economic Hit Man, 381-382, 395
Congo DRC, 312
Construction and Operating License, 163
Conyers, John, 193, 229, 231
Cooperative Research, 221, 223, 233
Copps, Michael, 270-271, 351
Corentin Fleury, 65, 334
Cornyn, John, 41
Cornyn-Leahy bill, 41
Corporate Europe Observatory (CEO), 292
Corporate Social Responsibility (CSR), 292-293
Corporate Watch, 290
Corporation for Public Broadcasting, 125, 267, 277, 306
Corpus Christi (play), 318
Council for National Policy (CNP), 126
Council of Better Business Bureaus, 290
Count Every Vote Act, 183
Counterpunch, 135, 431
Couric, Katie, 300
Courier Mail, 220
Coyle, Joseph T., 81

Côte d'Ivoire, 312
CPA, *see* Coalition Provisional Authority
CPJ, *see* Committee to Protect Journalists
Creatures 2.0, 359
Crispell, Tom, 223
CRLA, *see* California Rural Legal Assistance
Croatia, 373, 376-377
Cronkite, Walter, 402
Crossing the Rubicon, 216-217, 221, 225, 227
Crow, Michael, 299
Cuba, 82, 216, 312, 393-394
Cultural Survival Quarterly, 117
Cummings, Elijah, 231
Cuyahoga County (Ohio), 173, 187, 192, 196, 201
Cyberlife Technology, 359
Czech Republic, 377
D12, 310
da Silva, Lula, 311
dairy cows, 164
Daniel Guttman, 84
Darfur, 119-122, 317
DARPA, *see* Defense Advanced Research Projects Agency
Daschle, Tom, 231
Davidian, Geoff, 18, 381, 393
Davis, James, 359, 363
Davis, Thomas G., 178-179
Dawes Act, 103
DCI Israel Children's Rights Monitor, 114
DCI/PS, 114-115
De La Rue Company, 176
de Moraes, Lisa, 300
DEA, *see* Drug Enforcement Agency
Dean, Howard, 241-242
Dean, Jeffrey, 175
Death Squad, 137-138
Debevec, Paul, 360
Defense Advanced Research Projects Agency (DARPA), 54, 178, 358
Defense for Children International (DCI), 113
Defense Modeling and Simulations Office, 358
Defense Planning Guidance, 370
Delaney, Kevin, 226

DeLay, Tom, 275-276
Democracy Now!, 65-66, 68, 87, 101, 138, 172, 267, 270, 280, 404
Democratic Party, 51, 148, 193, 229, 231-233
Denver Election Commission, 177
Department of Defense, 53, 60, 83-84, 91-92, 96, 111, 120, 133, 156, 169, 180, 213, 226, 291, 357-358
Department of Fish and Wildlife, 152
depleted uranium (DU), 137, 155-157, 375
Deployment Health Support Directorate, 156
Depository Trust Commission (DTCC), 98, 100
Der Spiegel, 218
Derian, Der, 361, 363
Desert hammer VI, 361
Deutsche Presse-Agentur, 220
Deutsche Bank, 223, 298
Dewey, Thomas, 186
Dickenson, Jim, 184
Die Zeit, 218
Diebold Systems, 174, 181
Dietz, Leonard, 156
Dill, C.C., 338, 340
Disney, 245-246, 248, 252, 260-262, 301-302, 352-353, 358, 360, 363
Disraeli, Benjamin, 314
Dissident Voice, 155
Diversified Dynamics, 178-179
Djukanovic, Milo, 316
DNA, 128, 155
DOD, *see* Department of Defense
Doe v. Unocal, 150
Doggett, Lloyd, 171
Dole, Bob, 158, 291
Dollars and Sense, 86, 138, 404
Domenici, Peter, 161
Domestic Counter Terrorism Efforts, 225
Dominican Republic, 141, 146
Donahue, Phil, 266, 270, 342, 364
Doom, 359, 363
Draft (military), 169-172
Draheim, Andy, 177
Drug Enforcement Agency (DEA), 95, 218-221
DS Simon Productions, 284

DU, *see* depleted uranium
Dukakis, Michael, 288
Dylan, Bob, 195
DynCorp, 94
Early Show, 300
Earthfirst, 75
Easterbrook, Frank, 158
Eberhart, 226
Ecologist, 68-69, 133, 405
Ecosystem, 36, 75
Ecstasy, 218-220
Ecuador, 93-95, 312, 383-384
Edison Media Research, 48, 198-199
Edison-Mitofsky polling group, 190
Education Department, 282, 284-285
Egypt, 206, 209, 308, 312, 394
Einstein, Albert, 88
Elder, John, 175
Election Center, 181
Election.com, 180
Election Incident Reporting System, 173
Election Reform Committee, 183
Election Technology Council (ETC), 181
Elections Systems & Software (ES&S), 176-178, 181
Electoral Politics, 137, 172
Electronic Privacy Information Center, 57
Eli Lilly and Company, 248
embezzlement, 175
Energy Policy Act, 161
Engelhardt, Tom, 96
England, 125, 250, 254, 278, 315, 387, 406
Enlightenment, the, 310
Enron, 99, 179, 213
Environmental Protection Agency (EPA), 76, 122, 285
Eritrea, 121, 313
Eschberger, Tom, 176
Esperance, Pierre, 143
Essential Worker Immigration Coalition (EWIC), 107, 110
Ethiopia, 116-118, 120-121
Ethiopian Army, 116, 118
Ethiopian People's Revolutionary Defense Front (EPDRF), 116-118
Euphrates, 42, 329-331

Eutelsat, 314, 376
exit polls, 48-50, 181, 186-192, 194, 198-199
Exxon Mobil, 151
Exxon Valdez, 77, 397
FAA, *see* Federal Aviation Administration
FADH, *see* Armed Forces of Haiti
Fahrenheit 9/11, 361
FAIR (Fairness and Accuracy in Reporting), 16, 31, 44, 295, 365, 369
Fallujah, 5, 36, 41-43, 46-47, 65, 321, 324, 328-336
Family Steering Committee, 161, 217
Far Eastern Economic Review, 291
Farsetta, Diane, 293
Fasa'a, Burhan, 42
Faulkner, Ashley, 288
FBI, *see* Federal Bureau of Investigation
FCC, *see* Federal Communications Commission
FDA, *see* Food and Drug Administration
Fear & Favor Report, 295-306
Federal Aviation Administration (FAA), 207, 220, 226
Federal Bureau of Investigation (FBI), 53-54, 90, 95, 123, 132, 204, 206, 208, 213, 219-221, 223, 226, 228, 318
Federal Communications Commission (FCC), 16, 22, 164-165, 200, 245, 250, 269-272, 277, 283-284, 299, 308-309, 313, 337-339, 341, 346-353
Federal Emergency Management Agency (FEMA), 211-212
Federal Judiciary, 160
Federal Radio Commission (FRC), 338-340, 349, 352
Federal Voting Assistance Program (FVAP), 180
Federalist Society, 7, 137, 157-158, 160
Federalist Society for Law and Public Policy Studies, 157
Feeney, Tom, 186, 198
Feinstein, Dianne, 231
FEMA, *see* Federal Emergency Management Agency
Ferree, Ken, 277
Field Training Exercised (FTX), 225
Financial Wire, 98-99

Findley, Eric, 226
Finkelstein, Arthur, 276
First amendment, 18, 30, 159, 165, 246,
    343, 347, 352, 362, 365
Fish and Wildlife Service, 76, 152
Fisher, Jonah, 313
FitzSimmons, Dennis, 245
Flahavan, Richard, 170
Fleury, Jean Senat, 145
Flight 77, 203, 214-215
Flocco, Tom, 223
Flynn, Michael, 93-95
FOIA, *see* Freedom of Information Act
Foley, James B., 144
Food and Drug Administration (FDA), 87,
    152, 154, 292
Forbes, Steve, 369
Ford Motor Company, 245, 248, 296
Forward, 220-221
Fourth Geneva Convention, 327, 336
Fox Network, Fox News Network, 101, 137,
    164-166, 193, 207, 209, 218-219, 221,
    254, 302, 306, 346, 348, 350, 356
Fox, Vicente, 198
France, 133, 206, 260, 262, 278-279, 314
Franken, Al, 270, 280
Frasier, 300
FRC, *see* Federal Radio Commission
Free Enterprise Fund, 289
Free Speech Radio News and Television,
    270
Freedom of Information Act (FOIA), 38-39,
    41, 64, 131, 170, 282
Freepress.org, 48, 50, 198, 405
Friedman, Steve, 300
Friends, 300
Frist, Bill, 129
From the Wilderness, 223, 234
Front for the Advancement and Progress of
    Haiti, 145
Frontera, Michael, 177
Frontline, 122, 129, 351
Fulton, Ira, 299
Fund, John, 183
Gadflyer, 275
Gagnon, Bruce, 232
Gallagher, Maggie, 283
Gambia, 313

Gannett, 246, 248, 351
Garfield, Bob, 288
Garlasco, Marc E., 45
Garner, Jay, 70
Gelber, Dan, 167
GEMS, 175
General Electric, 32, 100, 247, 249-252
General Motors, 252, 275, 296
Genocide Watch, 116, 121
Georgetown, 246, 249, 251-252
Germany, 85, 129, 189, 206, 218, 255,
    278-279, 376
al-Ghamdi, Saeed, 228
Ghana, 313
GID, *see* Jordanian intelligence
Gingrich, Newt, 88, 306
Girlfriend, 308
Giuliani, Rudolph, 213
Glassman, James, 304
GlaxoSmithKline, 101-102
Global Greens network, 279
Global Network Against Weapons &
    Nuclear Power in Space, 232
Global Positioning Satellite, 361
Global Research, 134, 233, 405
global warming, 290, 304
Global Wealth Inequality, 7, 137
GMA, *see* Grocery Manufacturers of Amer-
    ica
Golden, Rena, 216
Goldstone, Richard, 83
Good Morning America, 300
Goodman, Amy, 66, 87, 138, 172, 264,
    266-267, 270, 280
Goodwin, Joseph R., 77
GOP, 180, 185-187, 189, 193-194, 198,
    200, 275-276, 302-303
Gordon, Joy, 60-62
Gore, Al, 189, 198
Gotti, Victoria, 301
Gottschalk, Lewis, 270
Gousse, Bernard, 145
Government Accountability Office, 40, 282,
    285
Gowing, Nik, 67
Grain, 68-70, 405
Graye, Michael K., 175
Greece, 278

Greenwire, 151, 154
Griffin, David Ray, 204, 210, 229-230
Grocery Manufacturers of America (GMA), 250, 292
Growing Up Gotti, 301
Guantanamo Bay, 287
Guardian, 50-52, 68, 112, 132, 134, 147, 149, 205-206, 225-226, 275, 398, 400, 406, 411
Guatemala, 96, 124
guerillas, 43
Gulf Daily News, 275
Gulf War, 44, 156-157, 365-366, 368
Gunter, Paul, 387
Ha'aretz, 218-221
Haass, Richard, 93
Hadad, Bahktiyar Abdulla, 65, 334
Hufschmid, Eric, 205
Hagel, Chuck, 200
Haig, Alexander, 120
Haiti, 16, 109, 137-147
Haitian National Police, 138-140, 142, 144
Halliburton, 118, 132-133, 180, 245, 252
Halliday & Brucato, 298
Halpern, Cheryl, 306
Hammad, Abu, 42, 329-331
Hanjour, Hani, 215
Hannon, William H., 184
Harper's, 52, 60, 70-71, 370-371, 402, 406
Harris, Katharine, 51
Hart Group, 83
HartInterCivic, 181
Hasen, Richard L., 184
Hatch, Orrin, 158
Hatfield, Henry, 341
Haupt, 226-227
HAVA, *see* Help America Vote Act
al-Hazmi, Salem, 228
Health and Human Services (HHS), 281-283, 285, 292
Health Care Personnel Delivery System (HCPDS), 170
Helmly, James, 171
Helms, Jesse, 276
Help America Vote Act (HAVA), 172, 180-182, 193-194
Helsingin Sanomat, 375

Hezbollah, 314
Hightower, Jim, 270, 353, 431
Hill & Knowlton, 291, 293
Hill, The, 282, 289
Hillman, Gracia, 183
Hilton, Paris, 238, 240
Hindu, 307-308
HIV, 101-102, 127
Hollywood, 120, 192, 218, 259, 261, 299, 301, 353, 360, 363
Homeland Security, 36, 56, 79, 92, 122-124, 162, 179, 203, 288
Homeland Unsecured, 162
Hopsicker, Daniel, 229
hormones, 23, 240
Horowitz, David, 89, 168
Horton, Willie, 288
Hotel Rwanda, 119-120
House Committee on Government Reform, 285
House Energy and Commerce Committee, 125
House of Wax, 240
Houtart, Francois, 322
HR-6, 161-162
Hubbard, Al, 289
Human Rights Watch (HRW), 45, 121, 150, 158, 312, 324, 375, 379
Hungary, 255, 377
Hunt, Ray L., 118
Hunt Oil Company, 118
Hussein, Bilal, 329
Hussein, Saddam, 60-61, 72, 133, 232, 324, 326, 366, 368, 377, 400
Hustler Magazine, 52
Hutton Report, 400
ICC, *see* International Chamber of Commerce
ICT, *see* Institute for Creative Technology
id software, 359
IFJ, *see* International Federation of Journalists
Ikea, 296-297
IMET, *see* International Military and Educational Training
IMF, *see* International Monetary Fund
immigration, 6, 37, 91, 106-110, 128, 221
Impact Press, 134

IMU, *see* Islamic Movement of Uzbekistan
In These Times, 21, 48, 172, 199, 270, 280, 406
Independent press, 35
Independent (UK), 406
Index on Censorship, 16, 307, 310, 319
India, 60, 204, 227-228, 308, 313
Indonesia, 58-60, 151, 291-292, 313
Industrial Light and Magic, 358
Industry Week, 149
Indymedia, 124, 270, 279
Information Awareness Office, 54, 57
Information Clearing House, 155
Information Management Journal, 52
Information Technology Association of America (ITAA), 180-181
ING, *see* Iraqi National Guardsmen
Institute of Public Relations, 290
Institute for Creative Technology (ICT), 360, 363
Inter Press Service (IPS), 42-43, 58, 322, 327, 330-336, 406
Inter-Services Intelligence (ISI), Pakistan, 204, 227-228
Interhemispheric Resource Center, 106
Internal Revenue Service (IRS), 213, 285
International Chamber of Commerce (ICC), 292
International Committee for the Red Cross, 43
International Federation of Journalists (IFJ), 64, 67-68, 314, 316-318
International Military and Educational Training (IMET), 59, 118
International Monetary Fund (IMF), 134, 374, 378, 388, 390, 394
International Republican Institute, 127
International Rescue Committee (IRC), 106, 119
International Studies in Higher Education Act, 166
IPS, *see* Inter Press Service
Iran, 37, 71-75, 220, 313, 371, 384, 398
Iran-Contra scandal, 12, 398
Iranian Hostage Crisis, 366
Iraq, 16, 23, 33, 36-37, 41-47, 53, 57, 61-75, 82-84, 86, 95, 97, 123, 129, 132-

133, 155-157, 168, 171, 190, 195, 197, 199-200, 217, 230, 232-233, 243, 270, 276, 281, 286, 288, 296, 302, 313, 319, 321-325, 327, 330, 333-334, 336, 355-356, 361, 364-373, 377, 384, 409
Iraq Survey Group, 286
Iraqi National Guardsmen (ING), 13, 257, 332-333, 349, 395
Iraqi Red Crescent, 43, 47, 331, 333
IRC, *see* International Rescue Committee
Irish Times, 58, 406
IRS, *see* Internal Revenue Service
ISI, *see* Inter-Services Intelligence
Islam, 287, 314, 317, 324
Islam Online, 324
Islamic Movement of Uzbekistan (IMU), 209
Israel, 114-115, 206-207, 219-221, 314, 394
ITAA, *see* Information Technology Association of America
Italy, 18, 68, 206, 208, 260, 278, 314
Jackson, Barry, 289
Jackson, Janet, 308
Jackson, Jesse, 48, 51
Jackson, Michael, 241, 244
Jakarta Post, 291
Jamail, Dahr, 18, 41, 64-65, 321-322, 324, 327-328, 330, 332-333, 335
Jane's Foreign Report, 58
Jane's Intelligence Digest, 219
Japan, 59, 72, 85, 135, 259, 261-262, 314
Jayasekera, Rohan, 16, 18, 307, 319
al-Jazeera, 47, 65, 314, 316-317, 333-334, 377
Jean-Louis, Leslie, 145
JECOR, *see* Saudi Arabian Joint Economic Commission
Jennings, Peter, 55
Jensen, Carl, 17, 19, 22, 237
Jerusalem Post, 220
JetBlue, 297
Johanstan, Christian, 146
Jolie, Angelina, 240
Jones, Meirion, 52, 71
Jordan, Eason, 66
Jordanian intelligence (GID), 209
Joseph, Josy, 60

Journal of Commerce, 220
Journal of the American Medical Association, 81
Judeo-Christian, 308
Juiced, 238
Junk Science, 151
Justice, Glen, 289
Kagan, Daryn, 46
Kagan, Donald, 369
Karlin, Mark, 274-275
Katuah Earth First (KEF!), 75-76
Kelley, Kitty, 302
Kelly, Petra, 279
Kennard, William, 245
Kennedy, Edward, 107, 109
Kennedy, John F., 248, 253, 393
Kerry, John, 48, 50-51, 181, 185, 242
Ketchum, 25, 282-285
KFPA Radio, 65-66, 137-138, 147
Khomeini (Ayatollah), 398
kidnappings, 324-325, 393
Killian, Jerry, 400
Kilpatrick, Michael, 156
Kimberly-Clark, 245, 250, 252
Kimmit, Mark, 327
King Jr., Martin Luther, 364
Kirkpatrick & Lockhart, 397
Kirkuk, 324
Kissinger, Henry, 119
Kivinen, Olli, 375
Klein, Naomi, 265, 270
KNFT, 297
Knight-Ridder, 246-247, 250
Koran, 229, 287
Kosovo, 373, 378-379
Kraft, 245, 250
Krongard, Buzzy, 223
KSTP-TV, 298
KTVO-TV, 297
Kucinich, Dennis, 231
Kutcher, Ashton, 240
Lakoff, George, 264, 267, 270
Lancet, 44-45, 407
Landsberger, Sheldon, 304
Landstuhl Regional Medical Center, 129
Langley Air Force Base, 215
Las Vegas Review Journal, 154

Latin America Working Group Education Fund, 97
Latin American and Caribbean Committee for the Defense of Women's Rights, 124
Latortue, Gerald, 142, 144
Latvia, 279
Lawyers Committee for Civil Rights, 183
Lay, Ken, 213
League of Women Voters, 183
Leahy, Patrick, 41
Lebanon, 314
Lee, Barbara, 230-231
Left Turn, 112, 407
Leno, Jay, 289
Levis, Nicholas, 228
Lewin, Daniel, 220
Lewin Group, 283
Lewis, Doug, 181
libertarian, 158, 173, 278
libraries, 56, 381-385, 391
Library of Congress, 285, 382, 393
Limbaugh, Rush, 297
LiP Magazine, 53, 55, 57, 407
Livermore Lab, 153
Lloyd, Terry, 65
Lobe, Jim, 58-60, 85, 149
London Telegraph, 223, 229
Los Angeles Times, 45, 120, 154, 206, 209, 219, 275, 286, 300, 304
Lott, Trent, 306
Loux, Bob, 153
Luntz, Frank, 288
mad cow disease, 282-283
Madison Dearborn, 176
Malaysia, 59, 260, 315, 383
al-Manar TV, 314
Mandela, Winnie, 314
Manta (Ecuador), 93-96
Mapes, Mary, 398
Marbeck, Sarah, 315
Mariani, Ellen, 160
Marmoulak (The Lizard), 313
Marrs, Jim, 205, 210
Martin, Kevin, 341, 351
Martin, Paul, 92
Mason Dixon Poll, 194
mass media, 32, 67, 239, 267, 337, 351-352, 368-369, 412

Matkal, Sayeret, 221
MATRIX, *see* Multistate Anti-Terrorism Information Exchange
Matrix, The, 360
Maxwell, Kay J., 183
McAndrews, Colleen, 184
McAuliffe, Terry, 230-231
McCain, John, 107, 109
McCarthy, Larry, 288
McCarthy Group, 176
McChesney, Robert W., 264, 338, 351
McClellan, Scott, 287
McCollum, Betty, 54
McCool, Gary, 384, 386, 391
McCullough, Noah, 289
McDonald's, 250, 304
McDowell, Rick, 41-42
McGovern, George, 195
McGwire, Mark, 239
McIntosh, David, 157
McKinney, Cynthia, 22, 205, 226-227
McLaughlin, John, 208
McManus, Michael, 283
McNally, Terrence, 318
Media Alliance, 270
Media Fund, 288
media outlets, 32, 97, 296, 301, 344-346
Media Relations, Inc., 295
media workers, 64, 295
Mediachannel.org, 280, 324
Mediaweek, 309
Meese, Edwin, 12, 157
Meigs, Jim, 216
Meinrath, Sascha, 271
MEJA, *see* Military Extraterritorial Jurisdiction Act
Merrill Lynch, 222
Messner, Andy, 268
Mexico, 91, 93, 106-108, 173, 198, 252, 297, 302-303, 315, 392
MI6, 333
Miami-Dade County (Fla.), 176, 192
migrants, 96, 106, 146
Military Extraterritorial Jurisdiction Act (MEJA), 83-84
Military Police Company, 141, 156
milk, 128
Miller, David, 323

Miller, Judith, 270
Milosevic, Milan, 373, 378
Milosevic, Slobodan, 375
Minority Rights Group International, 146
MINUSTAH, *see* United Nations Stabilization Mission in Haiti
Miranda, Anna, 55
Mission Rehearsal Exercise, 360
Mitchell, Pat, 247, 306
Monde, Le, 219
Moody-Stuart, Mark, 179
Mooney, Fred, 76
Moore, Demi, 238, 240
Moore, Dennis, 54
Moore, Michael, 90, 342
Moore, Stephan, 289
Moonves, Leslie, 399
Morgan Stanley, 222
Morie, Jacquelyn, 360
Morocco, 206, 229, 315
Morris, Dick, 189, 198
Mortgage Bankers Association, 289
Mortham, Sandra, 176
Mossad, 207, 218-219, 221, 223
Mother Jones, 21, 82-83, 96, 122-123, 127, 135, 408
Mothers of Tiananmen, 312
Mountain Justice Summer, 77
Mountaintop Removal (MTR), 36, 75-77
moveon.org, 230-231, 276
Mowrer, Frederick W., 212
Moyers, Bill, 264, 267, 270-271, 305-306
Mr. and Mrs. Smith, 240
Mreza Plus, 377
MSNBC, 192, 199-200, 208, 342, 364
Mubarak, Hosni, 313
Mugica, Antonio, 177
al-Muhannadi, Asma Khamis, 336
Multinational Monitor, 147
Multistate Anti-Terrorism Information Exchange (MATRIX), 54-57, 235, 360
Mumper, Larry, 90
Murray, Craig, 318
Muttawakil, Wakil Ahmed, 209
Meyers, Richard B., 225-227, 229-231
NAACP, *see* National Association for the Advancement of Colored People
NACLA, 93, 95, 408

al-Nami, Ahmed, 228
NASA, 133
Nation, The, 21, 52, 88, 119-120, 130, 151, 270, 408
National Advertising Division (NAD), 290
National Association for the Advancement of Colored People (NAACP), 51
National Association of Chain Drug Stores, 107
National Association of Latino Elected and Appointed Officials, 183
National Association of Manufacturers, 289
National Association of State Election Directors, 175
National Coalition for Haitian Rights (NCHR), 139, 143
National Conference for Media Reform, 263-265, 272, 365
National Data Archive Project, 182
National Defense Authorization Act, 131, 171
National Economics Council, 289
National Election Pool, 187, 199
National Exit Poll (NEP), 181, 190, 198
National Geographic, 119, 254
National Guard, 171, 242, 335-336, 398
National Highway Traffic Safety Administration, 128
National ID Card, 127
National Institute for Occupational Safety and Health (NIOSH), 112
National Institute of Allergy and Infectious Diseases, 101
National Journal, 291
National Lawyers Guild, 43
National Opinion Research Center, 189
National Public Opinion Survey, 277
National Public Radio (NPR), 122, 148, 151, 277, 404, 408
National Reconnaissance Office (NRO), 225
National Retail Federation, 107, 289
National Security Agency (NSA), 39, 208
NATO, *see* North Atlantic Treaty Organization
Natsios, Andrew, 133
Navajo, 103-104
Nazi, 322

NBC, 98, 193, 252, 300-303, 352, 360, 364, 369
Dateline, 98
Nightly News, 301
NCHR, *see* National Coalition for Haitian Rights
NEADS, *see* Northeast Air Defense Sector
Nepal, 314
Neptune, Yvon, 141
Netherlands, 133, 278, 309, 314
network programming, 346-347
Nevada Agency for Nuclear Projects, 153
New Freedom Commission, 78-79, 81
New Hampshire Public Service Commission, 385, 395
New Haven Register, 296
New Internationalist, 127
New Mexico, 173, 198, 297, 302-303, 392
New Progressive Institute, 126
New Standard, 328-329
New York Times, 21, 45, 51-52, 54, 96, 103, 117, 121, 154, 161, 190-193, 196, 206, 209, 212, 214, 223, 241, 245-246, 248, 270, 274-275, 282, 289-290, 302, 311, 315, 360, 363, 365, 383, 400, 402
New Zealand, 317
Newlyweds, 238-239
News Corp., 247, 251, 256
News From Indian Country, 103, 409
Newsday, 29, 31, 300
Newsnight, 50, 52, 70
NGO Watch, 158
Niger Delta, 150, 293
Niger Documents, 232
Nigeria, 121, 151, 293, 315
Ninth Circuit Court of Appeals, 150
NIOSH, *see* National Institute for Occupational Safety and Health
Nixon, Richard, 231
No Child Left Behind, 171, 282-284
non-depleted uranium, 155
NORAD, *see* North American Aerospace Defense Command
Noriega, Manuel, 384, 389
Norms on Business and Human Rights, 292
North, Oliver, 398
North American Aerospace Defense Command (NORAD), 91-92, 215, 225-226

North Atlantic Treaty Organization (NATO), 92, 121, 373-379
North Bay Progressive, 431
North District Court of Appeals, 159
North Korea, 134-135
North Korea Human Rights Act, 135
NORTHCOM, 36, 91-92
Northeast Air Defense Sector (NEADS), 215, 226
Northrup Grumman, 172, 178-180
Norvir, 304
NOVA TV, 377
NPR, *see* National Public Radio
Nuclear Energy, 161-162, 290
Nuclear Energy Institute (NEI), 290
Nuclear Information and Resource Service (NIRS), 161, 387
Nuclear Monitor, 161
Nuclear Plants, 162-163, 290, 386-387
Nuclear Power 2010 Program, 162
Nuclear Regulatory Commission, 153, 163
Nunn, Sam, 245, 247
Nuremberg Tribunal, 322
O.C., The, 377
O'Dell, Walden, 187
O'Dwyer's PR Services, 284
O'Harrow, Peter, 55
O'Neal, Shaquille, 238
O'Reilly, Bill, 297
Observer, the, 52
Ofcom, 313
Office of Management and Budget, 153
Office of National Drug Control Policy (ONDCP), 286
Office of Surface Mining, 76
Ohio, 48-50, 54, 159, 162, 168, 173, 182, 186-190, 192, 196-198, 254, 288
Oil for Food Program, 61-63
Okinawa, 233
Oklahoma City, 53, 206, 257
Olbermann, Keith, 192
Olsen, Ashley, 240
Olsen, Mary Kate, 240
Olson, Theodore, 157
Olympic Games, 301
Online Computer Library Center (OCLC), 391
Onses-Cardona, Damian, 141

OPEC, *see* Organization of Petroleum Exporting Countries
Operation Iraqi Liberation, 70
Operation Iron Grip, 327
Operation Joint Endeavor, 374
Order 65, 333
Organic Consumer Association, 164, 166
Organization of Petroleum Exporting Countries (OPEC), 71-72, 75
Orwell, George, 321, 336, 402
Otis, Lee Liberman, 157
Ottawa Citizen, 219
Owen, Ursula, 310
Owens, Bill, 178
Oxfam, 85, 409
Pacifica Radio, 22, 138, 147, 270
Pack, Michael, 306
Paige, Rod, 283
Pakistan, 204, 227, 315
Pakistani Inter-Services Intelligence, *see* Inter-Services Intelligence, Pakistan
Palast, Greg, 48, 50, 68, 70, 244, 397, 402
Palestine, 64-65, 67-68, 115, 315, 327
Pallotta, Ernesto, 323
Palm Beach Post, 101, 219-220, 409
Panama, 383-384, 389, 393-394
paper trail, 185, 187, 194
Papua, 313
Parenti, Michael, 23, 376-377, 379
Parents Television Council, 309
Parry, Robert, 192, 195, 398
Patriot Act, 40, 52, 54, 56
Paul, Ron, 54, 78, 80
PBS, *see* Public Broadcasting System
Peace Corps, 95
Peacework, 41
Pelosi, Nancy, 231
Penn, J. B., 283
Pentagon, 30, 32, 54, 64, 66-67, 82-84, 90, 92, 94-95, 118, 129, 133, 156, 169-171, 178-179, 203-204, 206, 210, 212, 214-217, 227, 286-287, 302, 323, 334
People for the American Way, 282
People's Weekly World Newspaper Online, 128
Perdue, Sonny, 194
Perkins, Bill, 305

Perkins, John, 8, 381-384, 387, 389-390
Persian Gulf, 22, 74, 156, 225
Peru, 315
Peterson, Laci, 241
petrodollars, 72, 387
Pew Research Center for the People and the Press, 347
Philip Morris, 292
Philippines, 58, 316
Phillips, Peter, 19, 266, 280, 323, 430
PhRMA, 304
Pickard, Tom, 208
Pilger, John, 366, 372
Pincus, Walter, 286
Pingree, Chellie, 183
Pitt, Brad, 238
Pixar, 358
Plame, Valerie, 232
Plant Variety Protection (PVP), 69
PNAC, see Project for a New American Century
Podhoretz, Norman, 369
Poindexter, John, 54, 398
Poland, 316, 377
Popular Mechanics, 214, 216
pornography, 308
Portugal, 278
Postlethwait, Robert N., 78
Powell, Colin, 59, 366, 369
Powell, Michael, 277, 341, 351
PR Watch, 16, 281-282, 285, 290, 293
President's New Freedom Commission on Mental Health, 78
Presidential Advisory Committee on Gulf War Veterans' Illnesses, 156
Presidential Records Act, 39
Priest, Dana, 96
privatization, 84, 128-129, 172, 174, 233, 289, 373
Progress for America (PFA), 288-289
Progressive, the, 21, 270, 297, 339, 410-411
Progressive NewsWire, 274
Project for a New American Century (PNAC), 218, 366, 368-371
Prometheus Radio Project, 271
prostitution, 326-327

PRSA , see Public Relations Society of America
PSNH, see Public Service Company of New Hampshire
Public Broadcasting System (PBS), 277, 305-306, 351, 365
Public Citizen News, 125
Public Employees for Environmental Responsibility, 152
Public Relations Society of America (PRSA), 285-286
Public Service Company of New Hampshire (PSNH), 386
Publisher's Weekly, 391
Punk'd, 240
Putin, Vladimir, 209
al-Qa'eda, 206-209, 219, 224, 228, 316
Qatar, 316, 333
Qualcomm, 304
Quayle, Dan, 369
Al-Quds al Arabi, 228
racial minorities, 148
Racketeering, Influences, and Corrupt Organization (RICO) Act, 137, 160-161, 233
Radio Act of 1927, 338, 349
Radio Free Europe, 318
Radio Television Serbia, 375
radioactive, 132, 153, 155-156, 178, 290, 387
raid, 142, 312, 332-333, 335-336
rape, 83, 116-117, 121, 139-146, 314, 324, 326-327
Rape of Nanking, 314
Rather, Dan, 8, 16, 241, 243, 397-399, 402
Ratigan, Dylan, 223
Rauh, Michael, 141
Raytheon, 181
Reactor Watchdog Project, 387
Reagan, Ronald, 12, 39, 120, 390
reality TV, 15, 238-240
recruitment, military, 169, 171
Refugees International, 119
Reid, Michael, 309
Renzulli, Virgil, 299
Reporters Without Borders, 65, 67, 376
Republican National Convention, 288, 302

Restore Open Government Act of 2004, 41
Reuters, 67, 209, 313
Rice, Condeleezza, 207
Rich, Frank, 191
Richardson, Bill, 302
RICO Act, *see* Racketeering, Influences, and Corrupt Organization Act
Ridge, Tom, 92
Rising-Moore, Carl, 129
Ritter, Scott, 61
Roberts, Les, 44
Rodriguez, Olga, 65, 68
Rodriquez, Ciro, 231
Roe v. Unocal, 150
Roker, Al, 101
Roldós, Jaime, 384
Roosevelt, Franklin, 340
Roper Committee, 340
Rose, James, 399
Rother, Larry, 311
Rove, Karl, 289, 397
Royal Dutch/Shell, 133, 151, 179-180, 292
RQ-1 Predators, 120
RTVS, *see* Serbian Radio and Television
Rubino, Frank, 389
Rumsfeld, Donald, 70, 91, 170, 226, 287, 369
Ruppert, Michael, 205, 216-217, 225, 227, 234
Russia, 72-73, 133, 149, 206, 278, 308, 316
Ryan, Karen, 281-282
SAF, *see* Students for Academic Freedom
SAIC, *see* Scientific Applications Information Corporation
Said Thalib, Munir, 313
Saintil, Napela, 145
Salim, Abdel Hamid, 43, 331
Salomon, Rick, 240
Salon, 169, 219-220, 283
San Antonio Express-News, 98, 410
San Diego Union-Tribune, 223
San Francisco Chronicle, 52, 154, 222
Santoro, Michele, 322
Sarokin, Lee, 158
Saudi Arabia, 178, 228-229, 316, 383, 387-388
Saudi Arabian Airlines, 229

Saudi Arabian Joint Economic Commission (JECOR), 388
Savage, Michael, 297
Saving, Thomas R., 289
Saving Private Ryan, 308
Schechter. Danny, 268, 270-271, 280, 324
Schippers, David, 204
Schmidt, Linda, 356
Schrecker, Ellen, 166
Schwarzenegger, Arnold, 302
Scientific Applications Information Corporation (SAIC), 172, 177-180
Scott, Peter Dale, 232
Scripps Howard News Service, 173
Sea Lanes of Communication, 60
Seabrook case, 385
Seattle Post-Intelligencer, 48, 52, 410
Secure Electronic Registration and Voting Experiment (SERVE), 17, 22, 129, 170, 180, 203, 295-296, 338, 342, 346
Securities and Exchange Commission (SEC), 98, 100, 134, 213, 223-224, 262, 352, 410
Seelye, Katharine Q., 190, 196
Selective Service System (SSS), 169-170
Senate Armed Services Committee, 230
Sensenbrenner, James, 308
September 11, 40-41, 53, 71, 203, 210-211, 213-214, 218-220, 222, 224, 227-228, 230, 291, 314, 401. *See also* 9/11
Sequoia Voting Systems, 172, 176
Serbia, 316, 373, 375, 377-379
Serbia & Montenegro, 316
Serbian Radio and Television (RTVS), 373
SERVE, *see* Secure Electronic Registration and Voting Experiment
Service Employees International Union, 108
sex discrimination, 293
Sgrena, Guiliana, 66
Shapiro, Neal, 300, 302
Shea, Colin, 196
al-Shehri, Waleed, 228
Sheikh, Ahmad Uhmar, 227
Shell, 133, 151, 179-180, 292-293
Shepherd, Cybill, 238
Schiavo, Terri, 241-242
Sicor Inc, 118

Silver Anvil Award, 286
Simon, Doug, 284
Simpson, Jessica, 238
Skull Valley Goshute Indian Reservation,
    153
Slaughter, Louise, 231
Slovenia, 373, 376-377
Smart Border Declaration, 92, 169
Smartmatic Corporation, 176-177
Smith, Lamar, 41
Smith, Nick, 303
snipers, 47, 329-331, 335-336
Social Security, 57, 275-276, 285, 288-289
Social Security Administration, 285, 289
Society of Professional Journalists, 283
Solomon, Norman, 18, 23, 29, 33, 265, 270,
    355, 364-365
Somalia, 120, 316
South Africa, 82-83, 147, 150, 401
South Carolina Educational Television, 305
South Korea, 317
Soyinka, Wole, 315
Space Program, 133
Spacecom, 376
Spain, 209, 259-260, 262, 278, 405
Spears, Britney, 238-239
Springer, Jerry, 309
Sprizzo, John, 150
Sri Lanka, 59, 317
SSS, see Selective Service System
Stanford University, 182, 184, 243
Star magazine, 240
Star Trek, 360
Star Wars program, 91
Stars and Stripes, 129
steroids, 238-239
Stewart, Martha, 238
stock options, 222, 224
Stockgate, 98-101, 410
Student Bill of Rights, 89-90
Students for Academic Freedom (SAF), 89-
    90, 168
Suarez, Fernando, 323
Suarez, Jesus, 323
Sudan, 117, 119-121, 317
suicide, 113, 129, 152, 170, 206, 209, 219,
    316
Sundance Film Festival, 399

Supreme Court, 88, 150, 157-159, 189,
    317, 319, 344, 352, 386, 395
Survivor's Rights International, 116, 121
Sweden, 278, 296, 318
Sydney Morning Herald, 210
Taliban, 67, 209, 228, 310, 377
Talk of the Nation, 151, 431
Tanzania, 85-86, 317
Taricani, Jim, 318
Tarpley, Webster, 205
Taurel, Sidney, 79
Telecommunications Act, 340, 345, 347,
    349
Tell Me Lies: Propaganda and Media Dis-
    tortion in the Attack on Iraq (Miller),
    323
Tenet, George, 207
Terrance Group, 277
Terror Timeline, 205, 210, 218, 221
Terrorism, 54, 56, 73, 118, 122, 150, 160,
    197, 199, 207-208, 220, 225, 228, 234,
    290-291, 366, 371, 398, 412
Texas A&M, 69
Texas Medication Algorithm Project
    (TMAP), 79
Thailand, 58, 317
Thaksin Shinawatra, 317
Thinkprogress.com, 275
Third World Forum, 322
Thompson, Ginger, 96
Thompson, Paul, 205, 210, 218, 221, 233
Thompson, Tommy, 292
Thornburgh, Dick, 397
Thornburgh, Ron, 184
Three Mile Island, 162, 290
TIA, see Total Information Awareness
Tiananmen Square, 312
Times of India, 204, 227-228
TimeWarner, 302
Titan Corporation, 83
Today Show, 300-301
Tompaine.com, 50, 52, 68, 71, 410
Tonga, 317
Tonight Show, 289
Toronto Star, 133
Torres, Manuel, 389
Tort Reform, 6, 37, 86-87
Total Information Awareness (TIA), 54, 57

Total Information Office, 53
total information warfare, 119
Touchet, Tom, 301
Tribune Company, 29, 245, 247, 250, 341
Tricontinental Centre in Belgium, 322
Tridish, Pete, 271
Trotochaud, Mary, 41-42
Truman, Harry, 186
Trump, Donald, 300
Truth News, 78
Truthout, 64-66, 115, 200, 411
Tsunami, 37, 58, 60, 291
Tucker Carlson Unfiltered, 305
Tunisia, 229, 317
Turbay government, 394
Turkey, 63, 195, 243, 318
Turkmenistan, 318
TV Hayat, 377
Tyndall Report, 301
U.S. Air Force, 58, 92, 356
U.S. Navy, 58-59, 61
U.S. Agency for Internal Development (USAID), 95, 127, 143, 377
U.S. Coalition Provisional Authority, *see* Coalition Provisional Authority
U.S. Counts Votes, 181-182
U.S. Department of Agriculture (USDA), 282-283
U.S. Department of Defense, *see* Department of Defense
U.S. Department of Education, 284
U.S. Education Department, 282, 284
U.S. Election Assistance Commission, 183
U.S. Foreign Agents Registration Act, 291
U.S. Foreign Corrupt Practices Act, 180
U.S. Justice Department, 399
U.S. Marine Corps Modeling Simulation Management Office, 359
U.S. Marines, 58, 141
U.S. Northcom, *see NORTHCOM*
U.S. Troops, 46, 59, 66, 141, 155, 233, 326, 329-330, 336
Udall, Mark, 54
UK Advertising Standards Authority, 308
UK Observer, 101, 411
Unilect, 181
Union of Concerned Scientists, 152, 163
unions, 31, 77, 134, 140, 295

Unisys, 177, 181
United Airlines, 160, 203-204, 222-223
United Farm Workers (UFW), 108
United for Peace and Justice, 230
United Kingdom (UK), 254, 318, 411
United Nations (UN), 43, 60-63, 74, 114, 117, 139-142, 145, 147-148, 158, 195, 233, 292, 337, 366, 369, 375, 383, 390, 393-394, 410
United Nations Commission on Human Rights, 292
United Nations Environment Programme, 375
United Nations Stabilization Mission in Haiti (MINUSTAH), 139, 141
United Nations System of National Accounts, 337
Universal Films, 300
University of Southern California, 23, 252, 360
Unocal Corporation, 150
UPN, 257, 301
Uranium, 46, 137, 154-156, 375
Uranium Medical Research Center (UMRC), 154-155
Urban Moving System, 221
Uruguay, 278
USA Today, 197, 218, 244, 283, 288, 296
USAID, *see* U.S. Agency for Internal Development
USDA, *see* U.S. Department of Agriculture
Uzbekistan, 96, 209, 318
van Gogh, Theo, 309, 314
Vandenbroek, Kevin, 303
Vargas, Arturo, 183
Venezuela, 72, 93, 177-178
Vercic, Dejan, 290
VerifiedVoting.org, 184
Verne Gay, 300
Viacom, 245, 248, 253, 257, 299, 301-302, 350, 352, 401
video games, 259, 261, 357-360, 362-363
video news release (VNR), 281-282, 284
Vietnam, 58, 123, 195, 241, 318, 322, 364, 397, 399-400, 402
Vietnam War, 58, 123, 322
Vigilant Guardian, 225-226
Vigilant Warrior, 225

Vioxx, 87
Virginian-Pilot, 220
Virilio, Paul, 362-363
voluntary personal retirement accounts, 288
VoteHere, 178-179
Voter Confidence and Increase Accessibility Act, 182
Voter Fraud, 16, 52, 137, 177, 198
Voting Integrity and Verification Act, 183
Voting Reform Task Group, 181
Wal-Mart, 293, 297
Wall Street, 100, 123, 150, 305
Walsh, David, 41, 43
War games, 74, 92, 203, 224-227, 356-357, 361
Waring, Marilyn, 337, 352
Washington Free Press, 106, 411
Watergate, 11-12, 231-232
Waxman, Henry, 38, 133
Waziristan, 315
Weapons of Mass Destruction, 61, 72, 270, 286, 365-366, 369-370, 400, 403
Wellstone, Paul, 194
West German Greens, 279
Westin, David, 301
Wharton, 246, 250, 252
White & Case, 291
Whole Earth Catalog, 290
Wilder, L. Douglas, 178
Williams, Armstrong, 283-284
Wilson, Joseph, 232
Wilson, Steve, 164-165
Winkler, Matthew, 298
Winokur, Scott, 222
WIRED, 119, 175-176
within-precinct error, 49
WJAR TV, 318
WKZO, 303
WMD, 199, 366-368, 370
Wolfowitz, Paul, 59, 369
World Bank, 378, 388, 390, 394
World Socialist, 41, 378-379, 411
World Trade Center, 90, 160, 204, 209-214, 218, 220-222
World Tribunal on Iraq, 47, 322
World War 4 Report, 116, 121, 412
World War II, 356, 373, 383

Worldcom, 99
WPE, 49
WTI, 322-323
WTVT Fox, 165
Wynn, Will, 302
Yale Daily News, 166
Yang, Li Woan, 187, 198
Yang Enterprises, Inc., 186, 198
Yemen, 318, 326
Yildash, Tahir, 209
yuan, 73
Yucca Mountain, 153-154, 178, 305
Yugoslavia, 82, 365, 373-379
Yugoslavian National Army (YNA), 373
Z Magazine, 93-94, 116, 121, 412, 431
al-Zaman, 326
Zeb Mountain, 76
Zeller, Jr., Tom, 191
Zenawi, Meles, 116-117, 121
Zim-American Israeli Shipping Co., 220
Zimbabwe, 319
Zimmerman, Herman, 360
Zucker, Jeff, 300
Zundel, Ernst, 311
Zwicker, Barrie, 205, 234

About the Editor

Peter Phillips is a Professor of Sociology at Sonoma State University and Director of Project Censored. He teaches classes in Media Censorship, Sociology of Power, Political Sociology, and Sociology of Media. He has published nine editions of *Censored: Media Democracy in Acton* from Seven Stories Press. Also from Seven Stories Press is the *Project Censored Guide to Independent Media and Activism 2003*.

Phillips writes op-ed pieces for independent media nationwide having published in dozens of publications newspapers and websites including *Z magazine*, *Counterpunch*, *Common Dreams*, *Social Policy*, and *Briarpatch*. He frequently speaks on media censorship and various socio-political issues on radio and TV talks shows including *Talk of the Nation*, *Air America*, *Talk America*, *World Radio Network*, *Flashpoints*, and the *Jim Hightower Show*.

Phillips is the national and international news editor with the *North Bay Progressive* newspaper in Santa Rosa, California. The *North Bay Progressive* is a monthly regional publication (circulation 10,000) serving a five county area north of San Francisco.

Phillips earned a B.A. degree in Social Science in 1970 from Santa Clara University, and an M.A. degree in Social Science from California State University at Sacramento in 1974. He earned a second M.A. in Sociology in 1991 and a Ph.D. in Sociology in 1994. His doctoral dissertation was entitled *A Relative Advantage: Sociology of the San Francisco Bohemian Club* http://libweb.sonoma.edu/regional/faculty/Phillips/bohemianindex.htm

Phillips is a fifth generation Californian, who grew up on a family-owned farm west of the Central Valley town of Lodi. Phillips lives today in rural Sonoma County with his wife Mary Lia

How to Support Project Censored

NOMINATE A STORY

To nominate a *Censored* story send us a copy of the article and include the name of the source publication, the date that the article appeared, and page number. For internet published news stories of which we should be aware please forward the URL to censored@sonoma.edu. The final deadline period for nominating a Most Censored Stories of the year is March of each year.

CRITERIA FOR PROJECT CENSORED NEWS STORIES NOMINATIONS

1. A censored news story is one which contains information that the general United States population has a right and need to know, but to which it has had limited access.
2. The news story is timely, on-going, and has implications for a significant number of residents in the United States.
3. The story has clearly defined concepts and is backed up with solid, verifiable documentation.
4. The news story has been publicly published, either electronically or in print, in a circulated newspaper, journal, magazine, newsletter, or similar publication from either a foreign or domestic source.
5. The news story has direct connections to and implications for people in the United States, which can include activities that U.S. citizens are engaged in abroad.

SUPPORT PROJECT CENSORED BY MAKING A FINANCIAL GIFT

Project Censored is a self-supported 501(c)3 non profit organization. We depend on tax deductible donations and foundation grants to continue our work. To support our efforts for freedom of information send checks to the address below or call 707-664-2500. Visa and MasterCard accepted. Review our website at: www.projectcensored.org.

Project Censored
Sonoma State University
1801 East Cotati Avenue
Rohnert Park, CA 94928
E-mail: <censored@sonoma.edu>